TRANSITION AND BEYOND

Observations on Gender Identity

by

Reid Vanderburgh

1

ISBN 978-0-692-88909-1

Book design/typesetting and graphics: Reid Vanderburgh

Have patience with everything unresolved in your heart

and try to love the questions themselves...

Don't search for the answers,

which could not be given to you now,

because you would not be able to live them.

And the point is, to live everything.

Live the questions now.

Perhaps then, someday far in the future,

you will gradually,

without even noticing it,

live your way into the answer.

— Rainier Maria Rilke

(from *Letters to a Young Poet*, 1903)

ACKNOWLEDGMENTS

To my test readers, thank you for taking the time to read this book and provide me with invaluable feedback: Andrew Garland-Forshée, Kathy Lessa, Cristina Vanderburgh, and Elaine Lerner.

Thank you to the late Anna Ingre, for information about Dissociative Identity Disorder. Thank you, Bo O'Dell, for our conversation about cognitive behavioral therapy. Thank you to Drs. Suzanne Scopes and Sara Becker for medical information – any medical errors herein result from my not being a doctor, rather than from their feedback. I'm grateful to WPATH (World Professional Association for Transgender Health) for permission to include excerpts from the Standards of Care.

To my friends and colleagues, thank you for your moral support and encouragement during this process: Andrew Garland-Forshée; Rodney Garland-Forshée; Ari Lev; Dian Ulner; John Kellermeier; Kate Bornstein; Ann Hinds; Rhonda, Mike and Sander Laughlin; Deborah Mulein; Donna Gans; Amy Baibek; Vicki Bauer; Marion Sharp; lore dickey; Katy Koonce; Simone Neall; Annik Larsen; Heather Leffler; Wendy Blenning; Beth Richman; the late Anna Ingre; Charlotte Redway; Shad Alexander; Jordan Shin; Kit Rachlin; Shellie Cox; Lori Gershick; Louise Welter; Heather Aidala; Deb Samuels; James and Heidi Green; Christa-Margaret Nelson; Marc LeJeune; Zander Keig; Jerry Deckelbaum; Aaron Yeagle; Sam Sappington; Clark House; Don Hicks; Bo O'Dell; Jude Patton; Helen Boyd; Silas Crowfoot; Kathy Bobula; Pam Moro; Paul Iarrobino; Michele Pearce; Meg Jeske; Marcia Wood; Duffy Stephens; Max Fuhrman; Rosemary Wyman; Roey Thorpe; Patricia Keeney; Debora Landforce; Eric Overby and Lurissa Sponsler-Overby; my fellow board members of PFLAG Portland.

Thank you, Kim Hraca, for once asking me, "Reid, do you consider yourself a Writer?" Thanks, Kim – now I do.

And most especially, I thank my clients. Without you, I could only have written my autobiography. While valuable, that's just one story.

DEDICATION

DURING THE SUMMER OF 1987 I RODE MY ALL-TERRAIN BICYCLE over 5,300 miles, across the United States and halfway back, alone. My mother promised that if I wrote a book about that adventure she would learn to ride a bicycle. I never got around to writing that book but now, 30 years later, I have written about an even bigger adventure that I didn't anticipate in 1987. My mother never did learn to ride a bicycle, but she did live long enough to appreciate the magnitude of my transition journey. She died in January of 2004, at 86. Though somewhat sudden her death was not altogether unexpected, given her frail health.

My oldest sister Jan died of cancer nine months later, at 62. Unlike my mother's death, my sister's felt out of time to me and hit me harder as a result. Jan was a lifelong scientist, successful and well-respected within her profession. Though she accomplished much during her long career as a forensic scientist, she never got around to writing the book or two I know she had in mind. Her death has prompted me to assemble some of my own writings into book form, lest fate catch up with me before I've had a chance to share my knowledge with the world. As I publish this third edition – I have turned 62 myself.

I dedicate this book to Elizabeth Vanderburgh and Jan Bashinski, for their faith in me and general inspiration.

TABLE OF CONTENTS

Can we be like drops of water, falling on the stone

Splashing, breaking, dispersing in air

Weaker than the stone by far, but be aware

That as time goes by, the rock will wear away.

– from *The Rock Will Wear Away*
Lyrics: Holly Near • Music: Meg Christian
Recorded on *Face the Music* (©Olivia Records, 1979)
Quoted by permission

INTRODUCTION TO THE 3RD EDITION

IN 1995, I WAS 39 YEARS OLD AND LIVING AS A LESBIAN when I first realized I'd probably be happier living as a guy. I did not take kindly to this realization for several reasons. First, I had quite a life built up in the Portland (Oregon) lesbian community. I was a found-ing member of nine years' standing of the Portland Lesbian Choir, and leaving that group was not on my horizon.

Second, I had a family of choice with whom my bonds were stronger than those with my biological family. All were lesbians. Most were fellow Choir members or members of my mixed chorus Bridges Vocal Ensemble. Or members of both. Queer folks find fa-mily as we are able and often the bonds forged through living in a hostile society are stronger than the bonds of blood connection. I was scared of my realization: if I became a man, would I lose my family of choice?

Finally, I had a negative reaction to the idea of being trans be-cause I had absorbed the mainstream belief that being trans was weird, sick, and perverted. Whenever I did see someone obviously trans I felt uneasy and off-balance, as if I was in the presence of someone who was psychotic or not fully human. I had some vague equation of "transsexual" and "drag queen" as synonymous, which of course had made it impossible for me to recognize myself as trans earlier in my life. I'd loathed wearing feminine clothing for as long as I could remember – not the attitude of a drag queen!

I'd never had conscious fantasies about being male. I had just never felt completely at home in my skin as a female, causing a low-grade anxiety and depression that was growing steadily as I aged. I hated women's bathrooms. I did not like introducing myself to others, as my former name was highly feminine. I avoided descri-bing myself as a lesbian and felt vaguely uncomfortable referring to myself as a woman. I had never had a gynecological appointment or a mammogram in my life. I was full of contradictions and was an enigma to myself – not an easy life for a Virgo.

I might still be living in denial had my then-partner not come out to me in the spring of 1995, telling me one night, "I've always felt like a man inside." This effectively held a mirror to my soul. I could no longer ignore what I saw there, but was not prepared to face it. The effect was rather like an ill-timed substance abuse intervention.

Because of the negative attitudes I'd internalized about what it meant to be trans, I had a difficult time feeling okay about the concept of even considering transition. Then one day a cisgender[1] friend said to me enviously, "What a gift, to be able to live as both sexes in one lifetime." This one phrase reframed the experience for me, for the first time putting a positive spin on the concept of being trans. Nowhere else had I encountered a positive interpretation of what it might mean to be trans (even from other trans people). I moved forward with a great deal more confidence and excitement at the possibilities inherent in the unexpected opportunity life had presented me.

Once I began taking hormones and had enough surgery to feel complete, life became simpler as my former lesbian life faded away gradually. However, what I found is that I did not become more male in my outlook on life. I became fully male in appearance while retaining many of the values I'd learned in the lesbian community.

I did not feel much more comfortable calling myself a man than I had calling myself a woman or a lesbian, though I felt fine calling myself a guy and definitely felt more comfortable in my own skin. I did not lose my lesbian family of choice and found many of those friendships have retained their original intimacy. I don't see those particular friends as often as I used to but when I do, our connection is still deep. What I lost was not relationships but my place within the larger lesbian community. That's not my tribe any longer.

---

[1] In addition to defining "cisgender" in the *Terminology* appendix, I also explain this term more fully in the *Preface*.

I gradually came to realize that I had not transitioned from female to male. I had transitioned from female to not-female. In the ensuing years I have come to agree with Kate Bornstein, a trans wri-ter and performer, who stated, "I know I'm not a man – about that much I'm very clear, and I've come to the conclusion that I'm probably not a woman, either."

I wasn't raised to be a man. I didn't absorb male socialization, despite rebelling against female socialization. I had neither the pri-vileges nor responsibilities associated with manhood. I didn't expe-rience testosterone dominant in my body until I was 41 years old. I have never thought of women as other than my equal, and don't believe I can.

Now I'm a guy, much more comfortable with male pronouns than female, but not really feeling like "a man." I'm living la vida media – life in the middle. I have not crossed the bridge from female on one side, over an immeasurable chasm, to become male on the other side. I have *become* the bridge.

Over the past twenty years, I have often been asked to do class presentations, from the community college through graduate levels. I have taught Continuing Education classes for therapists on issues related to working with trans clients. I have been invited to do trans-related workshops and trainings for social service agencies, work-places, and various governmental departments responsible for ser-vice provision within their communities.

In addition to this educational work, I had the rare privilege of working as a therapist with several hundred people who were con-templating or actualizing the identity trans. About 95% of my cli-ents were trans in some way or other. I learned something new about what it means to be trans from every client as their experience differed from my own and from each other's. I observed, correlated similarities, looked for patterns of experience, and drew general conclusions from my observations. This wide variety of experience has given me a holistic perspective on trans issues that I draw from in my writing and educational work.

As the years went by I found private practice too isolating for me. When I published the first edition of this book in 2006 the thought occurred to me, "I became a therapist to write this book." Over the next few years that thought grew to the point that I decided to phase myself out of direct service provision and focus on writing and teaching, a decision I haven't regretted though I enjoyed the time I worked as a therapist, witnessing so many people blossom through transition. By the time I'd published my second book, the thought occurred to me, "I became a therapist to write my first book; I was born to write my second book." I have embraced the identity Writer as my primary focus ever since.

I published the second edition of this book in order to include the information I'd presented in the journal article "Appropriate Therapeutic Care for Families with Pre-Pubescent Transgender or Gender-Dissonant Children," published in the *Child and Adolescent Social Work Journal* in 2009. I updated some of the personal stories throughout the book and significantly expanded the chapter *How Young is Too Young?*

In deciding to produce a third edition, however, my goal was different. There have been so many significant cultural changes in the past few years, I realized that this book would become outdated if I didn't produce a new edition. This book has become a textbook in several graduate-level counseling programs offering courses focused on working with trans clients. As the culture changes, the work changes – slightly. Despite progress in the arena of trans civil rights, some things remain the same: people still need to tell their families (however they define family), come out in their daily lives, and achieve sufficient levels of self-esteem to be able to consider transition. My goal in producing this third edition is to keep up with the times, helping educate the next generation of therapists to continue to be useful to trans clients.

My mother was precise in her use of language and like her, I find myself irritated by the small, everyday grammatical errors that have crept into our language. One example is the use of the third-person plural pronoun in referring to an individual person: "The client... they." However throughout this book I use the third-person plural in referring to individuals; I am no longer comfortable with the limitations of bi-gendered English, or with making assumptions about pronouns. I use 'they' in referring to non-binary clients, as this is a common pronoun choice among those who don't claim a binary gender identity. I use gendered pronouns when referring to specific individuals. In those instances I use the pronoun preferred by the person in question at a given point in time, though I change their name to preserve anonymity. If the person is using a gender-neutral name I use a gender-neutral pseudonym; if their name is gender-specific, I chose a gender-specific pseudonym.

In cases where a person might be recognizable from a scenario I relate, I have not only asked permission but have also asked them if I am relating their story accurately. If you think you recognize yourself in a story I relate in this book, you're only right if I've asked your permission to include your story; otherwise the resemblance is coincidental. Trans people and their loved ones often have similar stories to tell when it comes to transition processes and life experiences.

Part One of this book is written with therapists in mind and those who have an interest in the therapy profession. People who aren't therapists may also benefit from reading this section. Many trans people are forced by circumstance to work with therapists who don't understand much about trans issues. It can be validating to read about other approaches to therapy than the medical model. *Parts Two* and *Three* can be read without reading *Part One,* if desired. I am hoping this book will prove useful to a wide variety of people, from practicing therapists to trans people to friends, allies, and family members seeking information.

Music has always been important to me, long before the formation of the Portland Lesbian Choir. Throughout this book I have included lyrics from some of my favorite songs from the women's music circuit of the 1970s and 80s, music that was central to my life at the time. For example:

> "Go and fight what's keeping you down,
> but keep your armor sound –
> I never want to meet a martyr again.
> I wish you well, my darling,
> though the road be scattered and torn..."
> – Meg Christian, from *I Wish You Well,*
> recorded on the album *Turning It Over*
> (°Olivia Records, 1981) Quoted by permission

Transition is one of the most difficult things any person can undertake of their own volition. Facing the decision to transition requires courage, regardless of the answer to the question, "How do I want to live my life?" I wish us all well along our journey. While we need to keep our armor sound, we also need to allow others to help us as needed. The journey is so much easier when shared.

Reid Vanderburgh
May, 2018

• PREFACE •

AN OVERVIEW OF TRANSITION

IF YOU ARE NEW TO THE CONCEPT 'TRANSGENDER,' I suggest putting a bookmark in the *Terminology* appendix. If you're not new to the concept, you might want to skim the *Terminology* section to get an idea of how I view the various identities and descriptive language of this diverse group of people. Those with any familiarity with trans people already know that there is no consensus on definitions.

Because I view it as a convenient umbrella term, I use *trans* rather than *transgender* or *transsexual*. Some use transgender as an umbrella term while there are some who identify as transsexual and would not describe themselves as transgender. Others feel they are only trans while in transition, and will use the traditional words man and woman when they consider themselves done with transition. Many find transsexual an offensively medical-model term. I find using trans as an umbrella term helps avoid some of these controversies.

Throughout this book I use FTM, MTF, transman, and transwoman in referring to those who undertake transition with the goal of being seen as men or women on the other side of the process. This is controversial, as there are nearly as many different nuances to identity labels as there are trans people. It would be impossible for me to be fully inclusive in this book without it being unreadable. I use these shortcut labels to be clear about the direction of transition, not to determine or definitively label identity.

As an example of what an attempt at full inclusivity might look like... In the 1990s I attended a trans conference whose organizers handed out a post-conference exit poll to determine who had been in attendance. The conference was primarily aimed at those who self-identified as being on the male side of the gender spectrum. The usual questions were asked about ethnicity, age, socioeconomic status, educational level, geographic location – and then came gender identity. There was a checkbox for every single term the conference organizers had ever heard expressed about this community: transman, trannyboy, tranzguy, MTM ("man" to "male"), boi, etc. There were over 30 labels available. And a line to write in your own option.

I suspect some of the conference organizers had a lesbian community background; the lesbian community value playing out in that exit poll is reflected in a line from a commissioned piece the Portland Lesbian Choir once sang, poking fun at a value that can be taken to extremes at times: "We will stay until we rot before we leave somebody out." While this is a useful value when it comes to tackling various thorny issues such as racism, disability access, etc. it can also tend to bog down discussions at times and in this case, could bog down this book.

Many cisgender people (see the next section for my definition of cisgender) ask questions about terminology and definitions, confused by the variety of opinions they hear. I used to think there was no more diverse group than the lesbian community; ask four lesbians a question and you'll get five answers, I would say. Trans people, however! – ask four trans people a question and you'll get SIX answers! Small wonder cisgender people are often confused when trying to learn respectful ways in which to refer to varying types of trans individuals. Many have felt they just weren't getting it when it seemed to them they would hear conflicting explanations from various trans people. In fact, they probably *were* hearing diametrically opposing viewpoints and definitions. The terminology cisgender people use matters less to me than the manner in which they speak about trans identity. I would far rather deal with respectful ignorance than contemptuous dismissal.

PARADIGM-SHIFTING TERMINOLOGY

I would like to highlight a few terms that represent a paradigm shift. Misgender, cisgender, male-affirmed, female-affirmed, male-assigned, female-assigned – are all terms that move us away from the 'normal' and 'not-normal' conceptualization of trans identity that results in an 'us and them' view.

To *misgender* a person is to use inappropriate gender des-criptors, for example: "The article misgendered her by using male pronouns." The creation of a word for this process indicates a shift toward taking trans identities more seriously than has historically been the case. Additions to the trans lexicon are becoming increasingly mainstream; I was invited to write a blog entry for the Oxford Dictionaries, on the subject of adding *misgender* to the dictionary.[2]

Cis and *trans* are Latin prefixes, opposites of each other. *Trans* means to move across, and when coupled with the word *gender* means "to change gender."[3] *Cis* means "to stay in the same place." Putting the prefix *cis* in front of *gender* results in a word that describes the experience of the person who is comfortable living their life as the gender assigned them at birth, though there may be aspects of their gender role or body that don't suit them well. Cisgender is the companion term for transgender, each of them used to describe a variation of experience in the realm of gender identity. Ciswoman and cisman companion the terms transwoman and transman. It has become common to shorten the word to merely cis, as in, "He's cis."

Male-affirmed refers to a person assigned female at birth, but who identifies as male. *Female-affirmed* refers to a person assigned male at birth, but who identifies as female. These terms are appropriate for those who feel much more male than female, or vice versa, but they are not helpful for those whose gender is non-binary.

---

[2] Titled "The victory of 'misgender' – why it's not a bad word," the piece appeared in the Sept. 11, 2015 edition of the Oxford Dictionary blog.

[3] Many who transition physically state they have not changed their gender at all, but have changed their bodies to match the gender they have always been inside. This is one reason why some who transition physically don't use transgender as a self-descriptor.

These terms also seem to me more appropriate for those who achieve gender congruence young, who have never had to build up a life in their birth gender assignment. Children don't transition, in the traditional sense of the word; they don't have to undo a carefully-created social façade. Affirmation in their self-identified gender assures they don't need to build up a gender façade in the first place. They are living their true gender at an early age, prior to the need for hormones or surgery. (Andrews, 2014; Brill, 2008; Ehrensaft, 2011; Kuklin, 2015; Krieger, 2011)

Male-assigned and *female-assigned* are a means of stating what was put on a baby's birth certificate. It is a handy way of saying, "This is what my birth certificate says," without owning that gender assignment as an identity.

DEFINING TRANSITION

If you ask most trans people what *transition* means they will define the term to mean physical body modification via hormones and/or surgery. People undergo this process in order to live as a different gender than the one assigned them at birth, modifying their bodies to match their internal sense of gender identity.

I view transition a bit differently. As I define it, transition is a process that results in a paradigm shift in how a person experiences gender, regardless of whether they end up transitioning physically or not; they no longer fully identify with the gender assigned them at birth. The gender autopilot is permanently disabled for these folks. There aren't many things all trans people have in common, but a heightened consciousness of gender is one of them.

Because I view transition from this perspective, I use the phrase *full physical transition* to refer to those who would like to alter their bodies through hormones and/or surgery, with an intention of living full-time as a different gender than they were assigned at birth. Often people who undertake a full physical transition do so after a lifetime of doing everything they can to change their minds to match their bodies, unsuccessfully.

17

Not everyone undertakes full physical transition. Sometimes the barrier is money, sometimes people remain in their birth bodies and gender roles for social, work-related or family reasons, and sometimes they just don't feel sufficiently compelled to make physical changes. And sometimes they make some physical changes, but don't want all the changes associated with a full physical transition. For instance, a female-assigned person might choose to have chest reconstruction surgery with no intention of taking testosterone.

Defining transition in this manner makes room for partners, close family members and intimate friends – they transition as well, of necessity. No one who undertakes transition wants their loved ones to remain as they were, using the same pronouns and gender conceptualizations. It's everyone's transition, turning off the gender autopilot and coming to view gender not as fixed reality, but as a form of identity that doesn't always match the birth certificate. (Boenke, 1999; Pepper, 2012; Nult, 2015; Jennings, 2016)

DIFFERENTIATING GENDER AND SEXUALITY

Gender and sexuality are the core aspects of our identities that underpin everything else about us as unique human beings. Every human culture differentiates between people based on body, role, and sexuality. The numbers and types of roles available, what the boundaries are between them, what's okay and what isn't regarding sexuality – these are cultural differences. In the United States we recognize two genders, 'male' and 'female,' and consider them mutually exclusive. The mainstream American view is that gender matches genitalia, therefore one can determine a baby's gender by a cursory examination of their body at birth.

What confuses many Americans in considering the concept of trans identity is a melding of gender and sexual orientation in some kind of confused muddle that quickly breaks down when a trans person tries to explain who they are. For example many people are completely confused by the concept of a trans lesbian: someone who used to live as a man, transitioned to female, and is primarily or only attracted to women. The question sometimes asked when I present this scenario to students is, "But if she...he...she...is attracted to women, why didn't...she...remain a man?? It would have been a lot easier."[4]

Upon hearing the explanation, people usually say, "That makes so much sense, why didn't I understand that before?" *Gender* is an identity that addresses the question, "When I look in the mirror, I see a reflection that others will call a 'man' or 'woman' – does that reflect who I know myself to be?" *Sexual orientation* addresses questions such as, "What kind of people am I attracted to? What kind of people do I fall in love with? What kinds of relationships do I want to form?"

The question "Who am I attracted to?" is not the same question as "Am I content to live male (or female)?" A person who is attracted only to women may not be happy living female (or male), and may choose to transition in some way while remaining attracted to women. I will discuss this more fully later, as sexual orientation can shift during transition, but an initial understanding of the separation of gender and sexuality as different aspects of identity is key to being able to understand the issues involved in considering trans identities.

It is also key for the trans person to understand this separation, so they are not confused by their own identity emergence. Trans people growing up in this culture absorb the same mainstream beliefs about what transgender means as everyone around them. Trans people are not born understanding their identities and must piece together the answers based on their own feelings of difference as they grow up.

The difference becomes more apparent as the trans person ages, particularly as they experience the gender divide of adolescence, though some do understand their identities at young ages. One mother told me her child crawled into her lap at the age of 4 and stated matter-of-factly, "Mommy, I know you think I'm a tomboy, but I'm really a

---

[4] Note I didn't say that only cisgender people find this confusing. I once met a transwoman who identified as a lesbian; she told me another transwoman had wondered why she didn't remain male if she was attracted to women.

boy." That child is now 17 and living happily as an adolescent male, having started taking testosterone the day he turned 14. He began social transition when he entered kindergarten and has never looked back. What would he look back to? He never did identify as a girl. More about this process in the chapter *How Young is Too Young?*

Many of my adult trans clients told me they had similar feelings when they were young, but never said anything, feeling they would: (a) not be believed, (b) be laughed at, or (c) be punished. As children age the pressure to conform increases; any tolerance others may have had for 'cross-gender' behavior earlier in childhood tends to dissipate. Continued insistence on behaving as the 'wrong gender' is seen as more problematic in someone who is 16 than in someone who is 6. (Lev, 2004; Ehrensaft, 2011; Krieger, 2011; Teich, 2012; Andrews, 2014; Kuklin, 2015)

There are gender differences inherent in this experience. In mainstream U.S. culture it's not okay for a boy of any age to 'act like a girl,' and the punishment for expressing such desires is often swift and harsh. Occasionally the punishment is more insidious, taking the form of teasing or heroically ignoring the behavior, rather than any physical intervention. Regardless of the form of punish-ment, male-assigned children who are so treated often grow up with deep feelings of shame and guilt, feelings I heard expressed by many of my transwomen clients. (Krieger, 2011; Ehrensaft, 2012; Vanderburgh, 2015)

Stephanie Brill (co-author of *The Transgender Child: A Hand-book for Families and Professionals*) related the following anecdote in a workshop. A Montessori school had a dress-up day periodically; children were free to put on anything available in a costume closet. One male-assigned child was running around the classroom wearing a Superman cape and a tiara. No one made fun of them; no one said anything that might make them feel they'd done something wrong. No one knows who that child will be when they grow up – gay, female-affirmed, cisgender, straight, butch, whatever. No one in that classroom setting said to them, "Tiaras are for girls," so how would they know? They may have seen it as a crown, not a tiara at all.

My guess is, as an adult they won't even remember that incident. However, were they made to feel ashamed or bad in some way for putting on a tiara, they probably *would* remember the incident and the associated negative feelings. My transwomen clients often told me of times in their childhood when other people reacted in such a way that they felt shame and guilt for behaving in a similar fashion. This kind of experience is not limited to transwomen or to those who question their gender identity. During trainings and presentations, many cisgender men nod when asked if they experienced or witnessed school-age incidents that reinforced feelings of shame or guilt for not doing male right.

By contrast, female-assigned children rarely receive negative messages of any kind for wanting to wear pants, participate in sports, or play with the boys, though some adults may look askance at such gender expression after the inception of puberty. 'Tomboy' is rarely a shame-based label, while 'sissy' always is. This difference highlights the misogyny of our culture: it's not okay for a boy to behave in any way that appears 'female' to those around him. This difference also illustrates the effect of feminism on our culture; there was a time, well within my living memory, when a girl wear-ing pants to public school drew just as much negative attention as a boy wearing a dress would today.

There are contextual nuances to the gender expression of those assigned female at birth. A female-assigned child who refuses to wear a dress to a wedding may be punished. However, such behavior is more likely to be viewed as naughty rather than sick, shameful or perverted, as is the more typical reaction to a male-assigned child wanting to behave or dress in a manner that is seen as female. Thus the young male-assigned child who feels like a girl inside is more likely to grow up with deep-seated issues of shame and guilt than the young female-assigned child who feels like a boy. (Lev, 2004; Zamboni, 2006; Vanderburgh, 2009; Ehrensaft, 2011; Krieger, 2011; Kuklin, 2015; Vanderburgh, 2017)

IT'S ALL ABOUT PROCESS

The process of transition begins with the inner work of confronting the cultural paradigm of gender matching genitalia. This paradigm results in the view that people who challenge the paradigm are suffering from a mental illness or a delusion of some sort. Within conservative settings, 'immoral' or 'evil' may be a substitute for 'mental illness.' Coming to understand gender as an innate identity is the first step in facing the questions, "Now that I've realized I'm not content with my birth gender role or bodily sex, can I find a way to make it work anyway? Can I expand my gender role to suit me? Do I need to transition in some way?"

Those who were assigned male at birth often try crossdressing (wearing women's clothes) to see if this is enough. Does crossdressing permit enough female expression to allow them to be comfortable with their lives and social roles? If it does, wonderful – they are saved a great deal of money and possibly some psychic pain.[5] They have transitioned out of the male role they were raised to, into a combination of roles they define for themselves, male at times and female at other times. Their transition is completed by the expansion of their birth gender role and the sense they now feel of being in control of their own lives. Sometimes crossdressing isn't enough. One client tried 'dressing' for years and told me, "I realized I needed to transition when I came home one afternoon after a walk as Jeana and cried, it felt so bad to put on 'Bruce' again before my wife got home from work." *(Client session, 2004)*

There are few limitations placed on female gender expression. It's not easy in U.S. culture for a female to dress sufficiently male that people will see her as transgressing the female gender role. More women wear pants than dresses these days, except perhaps in formal

---

[5] I say 'possibly' because while many cross-dressers are selective about who they tell, others disclose to many people in their lives and then face the consequences, sometimes unpleasant!

situations. This fluidity of gender expression goes a long way toward helping most young transmen grow up fairly comfortable with their gender *role* and gender *expression*, though it can also lead to difficulty recognizing their discomfort with their gender *identity*. The male gender role is so narrow, it's sometimes easier for those assigned male to recognize when it's not a good fit for them. With few restrictions on the gender expression of those who are female-assigned, how are they to realize their gender is an issue?

However, if their gender identity is indeed the issue, their discomfort living in a female body will not lessen as they grow older. The discomfort will probably increase as they experience breast growth, menstruation, and estrogen as their dominant hormone. (Lev, 2004; Brill, 2008; Herman, 2009; Teich, 2012)

The first step in transitioning, physically or otherwise, is overcoming culturally-induced shame and stigmatization to attain self-acceptance. The next step is searching within for the answer to the question, "What do I need to do in order to be fulfilled in my gender identity?"

Both these steps can take years and are complicated by the various relationships people build up over the course of their lives, along with the need to make a living and get along in the world. This question would be easier for hermits to answer. But then, a true hermit, who never has interactions with others if they can help it, would not have much consciousness of gender at all. The sex of their body, yes, but gender is relational. Trying to have a gender relationship with oneself is like trying to clap with one hand. Gender is all about social boundaries – men don't have the same boundaries with each other as they do with women, or women with women, or women with men. (Lev, 2004; Ehrensaft, 2011; Vanderburgh, 2017)

Every step of the way, trans people need to check in with themselves, "Is this enough?" The path of transition is not linear, nor is it a cookie cutter one-size-fits-all process, though there are some commonalities. The steps outlined so far are shared by all who consider transition as adults: overcome denial, shame, and possibly guilt to be able to look at one's gender identity seriously; from that point, make decisions about what form of transition will answer the question, "How do I want to live my life?" The answers to that question lead to possibilities of experience that vary widely. The touchstone questions are, "How do I want to live my life?" and "Have I gone far enough with my transition to be content with how I am living gender?" Revisiting these questions with trans clients is the primary focus of the work.

What does it mean to be professionally competent in the area of gender identity therapy? What approaches and models work well with trans clients? This is the focus of the first section of this book.

In the second section, I'll discuss the individual's experience of transition, including issues such as disclosure (both at home and in the workplace) and resocialization. I've included two chapters specific to common complicating factors, addiction and religion.

The final section of this book covers relational issues. Everyone in the trans person's life undergoes their own transition, of necessity, with varying degrees of loss and grief. Family members and other loved ones must let go of the old before they can be expected to embrace the new. Family members are grieving what the trans person is moving away from with alacrity (albeit with some justified anxiety and fear as well). Support for family processes can help smooth the path for all concerned. (Boenke, 1999; Herman, 2009; Krieger, 2011; Ehrensaft, 2011; Pepper, 2012)

• PART ONE •

THERAPIST, PREPARE THYSELF!

I've been thinking all my life, trying to get it right.

But the goal was not in sight

So I think I'll try a new way

And I feel like singing

And I don't know what's beginning

But it feels so deep and true

And it's time to make a new start, from the heart.

— Meg Christian, from the song *From the Heart*,
recorded on the album *Turning it Over* ©Olivia Records, 1981)
Quoted by permission

• Chapter 1 •

A THERAPIST'S MANIFESTO

FEW THERAPISTS ARE IN A POSITION TO WATCH ANOTHER THERAPIST AT WORK. Generally we only have that experience when we are clients. My experiences as a client gave me valuable early insight into what doesn't work as well as what does work in helping clients navigate that first stage of questioning gender as fixed reality.

EARLY THERAPY EXPERIENCES

In the mid-1990s I saw three therapists in my process of coming to realize my lifelong social discomfort was related to gender issues. The first two therapists worked at an agency and were out of their depth in trying to work with trans clients. In hindsight, I realize they were not receiving adequate clinical supervision to help them rea-lize it. I can't fault the agency they worked for; 'adequate clinical supervision' for working with trans clients was nearly impossible to obtain at that time. The agency was trying to help clients who were now on their radar, but didn't have a handle on the process as yet. I had sought out a lesbian and gay counseling agency; at that time, ensconced in lesbian community, it never occurred to me to go anywhere else.

My third therapist understood pre-transition issues much better than the other two. She had been working with trans clients for about a dozen years at the time I saw her. Though my third therapist was licensed and working in private practice, it was her experience and knowledge of trans issues that benefitted me, not her licensure. The requisite knowledge is acquired on the job, through peer consultation, peer support, and post-graduate continuing education.

When I saw my first therapist, I was aware of being in the midst of an existential life crisis of monumental proportions. My then-partner had come out to me, saying, "I need to transition to male." This revelation propelled me into an identity crisis. I initially felt my identity crisis was related to being a lesbian involved with someone who was going to become a man: what did this mean about my lesbian identity and our relationship? I did not imme-diately realize my crisis involved *my* gender. After I'd seen my first therapist twice I had an epiphany between sessions, realizing I also was trans and not the lesbian I'd thought I was.

Recognizing this as the core of my life crisis, it was the first thing I brought up in my next therapy session. My therapist asked how long I'd been conscious of feeling this way. Because I could not say I'd had a *lifelong* conscious awareness of discomfort with my birth gender assignment, she discounted my conclusion and told me that she thought I needed some work to bolster my self-esteem as a lesbian. She did not spend much time exploring the conclusion I'd come to, that perhaps I wasn't a lesbian at all.

Ironically the cognitive-behavioral work I'd done with her had led directly to my epiphany. Had she explored my epiphany with me, our work together would have been valuable to me and I would now be writing about this therapeutic experience as a positive one. At the time I felt no certainty about my identity and was vulnerable to her feedback. My therapist's interpretation of my identity caused me to doubt my own intuition and process. I now recognize this as a fundamental error on my therapist's part, but all I was aware of at the time is that far from helping me with my self-doubt, her inter-vention increased it.

When any client's presenting issue is identity confusion, their therapist has to be careful to avoid making pronouncements about the client's identity (even when asked by the client, as in "What do you think? Do you think I'm trans?"). Such judgments can derail the client's own process of self-discovery. Without a sense of self as a bedrock from which to explore, the client will feel insecure about any conclusions they are drawing about their own identity. They may find themselves second- and third- and fourth-guessing their own conclusions. In this situation, it's important for the therapist to keep their eye on the ball: this is all about process, don't get bogged down in content! The content (what their identity is) is the client's job to disentangle; the therapist's job is to facilitate the process.

Therapy is the art of timing an intervention as much as anything else. My therapist might have waited until we'd established a good rapport and a trusting bond. She might then have said, "It's possible that your partner's revelation to you has rocked your identity as a lesbian. Before deciding transition is the right path, let's explore that possibility. Why transition if you don't really need to?" Had she put it that way, at the right time, I would have been more recep-tive to the idea.

I had never been in therapy before and didn't realize that my therapist wasn't very experienced or that she was counterproductive to my process. I probably would have stayed with her, to my detriment, had she not violated confidentiality. I had little trust in my intuition at that point so I wasn't sure whether my feelings of betrayal were valid. I told a friend of the incident and her angry reaction helped me feel justified in switching therapists.

My second therapist (at the same agency) tried to play devil's advocate, challenging my conclusions about my identity. She, too, was suspicious of my self-understanding, again because I had not had conscious knowledge of my 'transness' until I was nearly 40 years old[6]. She saw her role as one of trying to pick holes in my conclusion, testing it as if it were a scientific hypothesis. She occa-sionally got angry with me when I stuck to my guns, a reaction I now realize is inappropriate in a therapeutic setting. I left when I realized I wasn't getting anything out of our sessions. Since my friend had validated my feelings about my first therapist, I had more trust in my intuition and left the second therapist on my own.

---

[6] It may seem odd that both therapists focused on *when* I had conscious knowledge of my trans identity. The accepted clinical view of trans identity at that time is that a trans person had always known they were 'in the wrong body,' not that someone could repress this kind of knowledge until they were long-adult.

At that time there were few resources available to trans people seeking information or connection; nothing reflected my identity back to me. No one ever told me it's not uncommon for transmen (especially in my age range) to grow up without realizing *why* it is they feel different. The range of gender expression available to those raised female, especially living within lesbian community, affords a degree of comfort around gender expression that can obscure trans identity. I was free to express gender in a male kind of way, which allowed me to live in denial that I actually felt male in-side. My lack of conscious understanding of my identity is an experience I subsequently encountered in many clients.

Not only did my first two therapists distrust my conclusions, but I found no validation for my epiphany of self-understanding beyond a feeling of 'rightness' and the support I received from my third therapist. She helped me find out what normal meant to me.

Her normalization of the process of self-discovery helped me overcome the low self-esteem that had prevented me from coming to terms with my identity in my work with the previous two thera-pists. The matter-of-fact way in which this therapist approached my process helped me understand that what I was considering was neither weird nor bizarre, just right for me. After just three sessions I felt able to approach the social aspects of transition on my own, and came back to her two years later when I was ready for a hormone referral letter.

IDENTIFYING THE DIFFERENCES

The crucial difference between the first two therapists I saw and the third therapist is this: the first two saw their role as one of determining whether I was right in my interpretation of my gender identity, basing their conclusions on the DSM[7] symptoms of Gender Identity Disorder, while the third therapist saw her role as one of guiding me in a process of self-knowledge. (The DSM is the Diagnostic and Statistical Manual of Mental Disorders, used by psychologists, psychiatrists, and some therapists in order to categorize clients' mental health issues.) I was not served well by my first two therapists because they saw my gender identity as an issue for them to diagnose. My third therapist saw my gender identity as an issue that needed clarification, so I could then decide how to live my life. The following guidelines can help a therapist better understand how to work with a client whose presenting issue is gender identity:

❖ GENDER IS AN ISSUE OF CORE IDENTITY, not an issue of psychological pathology. The client is the only one who can make decisions about their core identity. It is not up to a therapist to determine whether or not a client is trans, any more than it is up to a therapist to determine a client's sexual orientation;

❖ THE PURPOSE OF THE THERAPY is not to change the client's mind, play devil's advocate, or provide some sort of cure, but to help the client understand and perhaps modify the natural defenses they developed over the years to cope with living in a narrow-minded, unsupportive culture. Such defenses, necessary while the client was growing up, are probably affecting current relationships in ways that don't serve the client well, including their relationship with themselves. These defenses may inhibit the client's ability to interpret (or even feel) their own emotions;

❖ THE GOAL OF THERAPY is to give the client a deeper understanding of themselves – their current relationship to their gender and sexuality; how their behavior patterns affect their

---

[7] In 1995, DSM III was the version in use. DSM IV was released a few years later. DSM V was released in 2013. This newer edition of the DSM contained a crucial change: Gender Identity Disorder is now Gender Dysphoria.

relationships; how gender has affected their lives; what they hope for the future; etc. This goal is much more easily achieved if the client has become aware of their own emotional process (see bullet point #2);

❖ IN LIGHT OF THIS SELF-KNOWLEDGE, the client can then make informed decisions about what 'transition' means to them. Is crossdressing enough? Hormones, or not? Surgery, or not? Which surgical procedures? Clients will be revisiting issues such as these throughout their transition; self-knowledge is always the key to the client's ability to answer these kinds of crossroads questions. *Informed* means not only informed about the effects of hormones, surgical options, etc., but more importantly, informed about who they are;

❖ THOUGH IT IS NOT THE THERAPIST'S JOB TO DETERMINE IDENTITY, it is the therapist's job to determine levels of ego strength and social support, both of which help facilitate a smooth transition in an unsupportive culture. Assuming the client made good decisions about how far to take transition, I believe the greatest predictor of post-transition suicide is lack of social support and isolation. Motivation, good self-knowledge, and extreme unhappiness with their birth gender assignment are not enough; the client must also be stable emotionally, able to handle negative reactions and bureaucratic issues *(e.g.* documentation changes, navigating healthcare systems, etc.) without being completely derailed when they encounter hostility or ignorance. Social support can help clients maintain perspective and a sense of self-worth during their resocialization process. This can be a tricky balance for clients who live in rural or small-town environments, far from the support available in most big cities, especially if they have little or no family support. The thera-pist's job in such cases is made more difficult by the knowledge that transition might help the client enormously, but the process may still feel overwhelmingly isolating (and possibly physically dangerous, in some areas) due to lack of social support. Support via the internet can be a godsend to such clients;

Because it is not the therapist's job to determine whether or not a client is trans, this task obviously falls to the client. Deep self-knowledge is the key to the client's ability to make the best decisions for their future happiness and fulfillment. The first two therapists I saw believed their job was to determine to their satisfaction if I was really trans or not. What a burden it would be, if that was indeed their task! Making that kind of determination for another person is not a job I would want. The third therapist I saw was much more at ease with me, and more relaxed. Of course she was; she saw the task of determining my gender to be mine alone. She helped me acquire self-knowledge and when she saw I had that, sent me on my journey.

PSYCHOEMOTIONALLY-FRAGILE CLIENTS

For more-fragile clients, establishing a strong therapeutic alliance may be enough for them to proceed with physical transition, if this is the decision they arrive at in answering the question, "How do I want to live my life?" At this point the therapist will be a pivotal source of support as the client cautiously moves forward into unexplored territory.

This is a chicken-and-egg situation, as the emotional fragility of such clients is probably linked to their socialization along an inappropriate gender vector. Another factor is their hormone balance; living with the wrong hormone balance contributes to feelings of being un-centered, anxious, depressed, etc. Gaining ego strength and greater emotional stability may be dependent on moving forward with physical transition.

In most cases it is not clinically appropriate to wait for the trans client to gain ego strength before proceeding with physical transition: the ego strength will develop more fully if the client is living as their true selves rather than continuing to hide within a persona that is not who they really are. It takes great strength for any trans person to survive, cope, and adapt to the wrong gender role or body type; this strength can then be utilized to weather the stresses of transition.

Some of my older clients lived far too long in their birth gender and made the decision to transition physically in order to save their lives. They had little resilience left, as they had drained their emotional reserves through years of being deeply unhappy with their bodies and social gender role. Some such clients were very fragile emotionally and I wished their path did not include physical transition, but I also realized the process itself was what might save them from suicide. And it's possible some may have committed suicide anyway. It's never going to be an easy path for such clients, whether they transition or not.

In cases where pre-transition clients were isolated in their experience of gender, I offered to connect them with others further along the path than they, to help begin their process of making connection with others. I did what I could on my end to prevent isolation. I had permission from several clients who were willing to be contacted by those who needed trans mentors.

BE WARY OF JUDGMENT

Ellen is a friend of mine who describes herself as bigendered. If she were of a younger generation, she might call herself gender-queer or non-binary. In the late 1980's, Ellen explored whether full physical transition might not be the right path for her. (I use female pronouns for her because she is most often present in my life in her female persona, though I've also spent time with her as Robert) Ellen's gender self-concept does not conform to any of the available categories. She describes her experience of gender:

"The 'Ellen' part of my life is much more open and social, and more integrated with my male life, than is true of most crossdressers

I know. It's like I'm a guy part of the time and a TS [transsexual] the rest of the time. I have pushed the envelope just about as far as it can be pushed without transitioning physically. Describing me as a crossdresser is a bit too casual. Is a TS crossdressed? They are my clothes. Am I 'passing' as a woman? Or for that matter, am I hiding my 'real' identity when I am in male garb? The real identity seems to be both. The bigendered thing is complex and even others in the transgender community have a hard time understanding it, but it works for me." *(E-mail correspondence, 2006)*

During the mid-to-late 1980s, Ellen had an interesting time of it as she came to terms with her identity. The internet was rudi-mentary and sparsely available at that time, and the world wide web didn't exist at all. There were few resources Ellen could turn to for accurate information, or to reflect her identity back to her in a way that might have shown her who she was.

As Ellen points out above, however, she might still have that difficulty today, as her gender does not conform to either mainstream American male or female, but also does not conform to the various categories most often described among trans people: "transgender," "transsexual," "crossdresser." Neither female-affirmed or male-affirmed work for Ellen, as she would adopt one or the other depending on whether she was Ellen or Robert in a particular situation.

Ellen's therapy experiences were varied. She first saw a cis-gender male psychiatrist, who was quick to assure her "lots of men crossdress, don't worry about it." While reassuring, this attitude did not help Ellen break through the internalized shame she had felt for years, which was her goal in therapy. She discontinued therapy after two sessions.

Her next foray into therapy came a few years later, as she worked with what she describes as a 'New Age-type' psychologist who encouraged her to integrate her male and female personas. This seemed like a reasonable idea. However, Ellen found the therapist's approach too mystic for her personality. In addition, she wanted to be able to express her female self out in the world, rather than integrate the female into the male; 'Ellen' is an extrovert, more so than 'Robert.' Ellen says of this therapeutic experience:

"Although he did not disapprove of my experimentation with crossdressing, he wasn't entirely comfortable with it either. Looking back on it, his objective was to get past the transgender issue – to put it back in the closet by getting me to integrate my masculine and feminine sides. I was not opposed to the idea. I tried to feel and express some sort of integration. Crossdressing whenever my wife was out of town didn't seem like any kind of long-term solution, and I yearned for a way to express all my facets as normal men and women do, without dressing up. But my 'integration' did not feel like a genuine change, but rather something I felt forced upon me, to please him." *(E-mail correspondence, 2006)*

Ironically Ellen's most helpful therapist knew nothing about trans issues. She learned as she went along and was quite helpful to Ellen in sorting out whether or not transition was the right path for her. This therapist helped Ellen clarify her feelings about the various aspects of gender: expression, role, and identity.

During her quest for self-knowledge Ellen saw two other therapists, both experienced in working with trans clients. One told her she was a 'classic crossdresser.' This felt too much like a pigeonhole diagnosis for Ellen's comfort. The other therapist felt Ellen was a transsexual, and encouraged her to try hormones to see how they made her feel. The permission this therapist gave to try hormones caused Ellen to realistically evaluate the potential losses and gains if she pursued physical transition. This helpful process allowed her to finally realize physical transition wasn't her path, because there were losses involved that she didn't want to incur.

Ellen has gone on to carve out two lives, one as Ellen and the other as Robert. She moves effortlessly between them, unashamed and no longer hiding from anyone. She met her partner Linda ten years ago; though Linda is around Robert more than Ellen, she has no problem interacting with either.

The lesson here is to not steer the client toward any path, either for or against transition, but to facilitate the client's journey of self-discovery. Viewing gender as an identity is a good first step. It is equally helpful for the therapist to be clear, as much as possible, which of their own reactions and interpretations are culturally-based assumptions, which are based in their preconceived notions of transition, and which are based in what they are actually observing in the client.

GID – OR DID?

If I found myself hesitant about a client's interpretation of themselves as trans, the question I asked myself was not, "Is this client really trans?" Rather, I asked myself, "Is this client trying to be more fully who they are, or are they trying to become someone else?" The latter is a client fleeing their past in a manner reminiscent of someone who has DID (Dissociative Identity Disorder).

One of the hallmarks of undiagnosed or untreated DID is that not all alters[8] are equally aware of each other's presence within the individual. Hence people with DID often have experiences of lost time, periods of time when one alter was in charge and when another surfaced, time will have gone by that can't be accounted for. Often people with DID only learn they have it when others in their lives confront them with 'uncharacteristic' behavior, or seeming irresponsibility because they have not been somewhere they were supposed to be. (Kluft, 1996; Bray Haddock, 2001)

There are points of similarity between gender dissonance and DID. Those who are trans often dissociate from their bodies at a young age, as do those who later develop DID. The difference is the motivation for the dissociation. DID is often the result of ongoing extreme childhood abuse, usually sexual in nature and often

---

[8] *Alter* is the term used for the various personalities in discussing someone with DID.

involving incest. A person with DID learned very young to dissociate from their bodies during the abuse, to save their psyche from destruction. Older conceptualizations of DID used terms such as multiple personalities, which is misleading. Often, there are young alters who are different ages from each other, each holding pieces of memory to prevent the full memories from being accessed all at once, overwhelming the psyche with pain. Some alters are not fully formed personalities at all. (Kluft, 1996; Bray Haddock, 2001)

Some of the clients I saw had been misdiagnosed with DID at earlier times in their lives. A therapist had heard, "I have always felt like a girl (or boy) inside" and rather than explore the gender issue, had concluded too quickly, "This person has DID." Dissociation due to gender dissonance, however, is the result of being born in a body that does not match the person's gender identity; this dissociation is a form of not owning the body because it is not a good match for the psyche. Unlike DID this form of dissociation doesn't result in loss of time, or shifts in behavior. Gender dis-sociation dissipates as the person transitions into a new congruence. This congruence can be the result of introducing a new hormone balance into the body, or can result from allowing a fuller expres-sion of gender, as in Ellen's case.

Most clients presenting with some degree of gender dissonance are going to be exactly what they seem and not suffering from DID – trans, perhaps unsure whether to transition physically or not, and seeking guidance. Such clients have developed a great deal of inner strength over the years, coping with their inappropriate birth gender assignment. By the time they seek therapy with a goal of transitioning, they may be fairly certain of who they are and in need of support in taking the necessary steps. They tend to feel a certain jubilation or relief, along with justified existential trepidation about the vastness of change in front of them.

Such is not the case for those who are trying to become someone else to escape a terrible past, who feel no jubilation at all. While some trans people need help sorting through their options and perhaps dismantling feelings of shame or guilt, they feel congruent in the room, which the client with DID often does not.

The idea of someone with DID transitioning raises the inevitable question, "If the client has different alters, who is it that is calling the shots on transition? Who is saying, 'This is the right path,' and does that alter have the right to make such a decision on behalf of all the others? Is there internal consensus that transition is right? Who is the real person?"

Kate began physical transition in 1990, at age 28. She has DID. Some fifteen years into her transition, I worked with her for two years and met six of her fourteen alters. Kate is the most prominent alter, called Mom by all the others. Kate is cognizant that she was created by the other alters to be the face presented to the world, and that she is a construct. The male alters (all young) were quite comfortable with the idea of Kate transitioning, wanting a 'mom' to take care of them.

Kate's transition therapist was unaware of Kate's DID, and that Kate was a construct the other alters were hiding behind. Highly intelligent, Kate had read all the professional literature available about transition; she knew precisely what to say to smooth her path. She cheerfully disclosed her DID status in her first session with me, as she felt long-since complete in her transition and wanted to be able to bring her whole self into therapy.

During the course of our work together, several of her young alters allowed Kate full access to the memories they were holding, essentially integrating themselves into Kate. Kate never regretted transition, nor did any of her male alters express a desire to actu-alize a male gender expression or role. Kate told me once, "I know that one of those male alters, probably the youngest of them, is the boy I would have been if all had been well in my childhood. I'm not sure at all that 'Kate' would exist if that had been the case. But it wasn't, so that alter is quite happy being held close to my heart. He doesn't care what should or could have been. He's safe now. I've never found out his name. He doesn't want to be known to that degree." *(Client session, 2009)*

• Chapter 2 •

THE THERAPIST'S OWN WORK

THERAPISTS-IN-TRAINING ARE OFTEN REQUIRED to spend a certain number of hours in therapy themselves while in graduate school, working on their own issues. One of the reasons for this requirement is that therapists understand their own issues well enough to recognize in the moment how much of their reaction to a client's story is based on their own history and how much has to do with the client. This self-knowledge is essential to the therapist being able to maintain appropriate boundaries during a session in which a client brings up issues that are close to home for the therapist.

'Do your own work' in this context means sorting through family of origin issues, relationship patterns, personal idiosyn-crasies, and comfort levels with socially-controversial matters. But what does 'do your own work' mean in the specific context of working with sexual or gender minority clients?

EXAMINING SEXUAL ORIENTATION

The Kinsey scale provides a snapshot of sexual orientation. On a scale of 0 (totally heterosexual) to 6 (totally homosexual) an individual rates their sexual orientation. (Levay, 2002) It's not a perfect assessment, as it does not account for fantasies that might be different from one's relational preferences, or the fact that sexuality can shift over time (particularly true for those who have repressed homosexual or bisexual feelings due to shame or guilt). Nevertheless the Kinsey model is a good first step for any therapist seeking self-knowledge.

The emergence of sexuality is one of the markers of adulthood in any culture. Prior to puberty children are curious about their bodies and how various bodies differ from each other, but sexuality is not a matter of urgent identity prior to adolescence. Most people can remember the emergence of their sexual identity: "This is what it means to be in love! Now I understand!" Regardless of the content of the memories, the important point in this discussion is that they are concrete, accessible, and 'languagable.'

Now consider what it means for a cisgender therapist to work with a cisgender client whose sexual orientation differs from their own. What it means for a therapist to have done their own work in this context is that they have reached a level of comfortable knowledge of their own sexual orientation. They have thought deep-ly about sexual orientations different from their own, have thought deeply about different ways people relate to each other, and have come to understand their comfort level and biases concerning different types of relationships.

If they intend to work with LGB clients, a straight therapist will also have done their homework to understand how the various communities work together and where there are still sources of tension. For instance they would understand that within the lesbian community, there is a general lack of respect for bisexual women. As another example such a therapist would understand the emo-tional impact the AIDS epidemic has had on gay male community and the generational differences in this experience. And so on. (Bieschke, 2006)

EXAMINING GENDER IDENTITY

Going a step further, what does it mean for the cisgender therapist (regardless of their sexual orientation) to have done their own work in the context of trans clients? Using a sexuality model such as the Kinsey scale is not sufficient work on the therapist's part, because it does not address gender identity. The question on the table now is: "Do you remember the first time you had conscious knowledge of realizing you were assigned male (or female) at birth, and how did you feel about that knowledge?"

There is a subtle distinction that must be made here. Most parents, consciously or otherwise, assume their child is going to grow up straight, get married to someone of the opposite sex, and have children. It comes as a shock, often unpleasant, if they later learn their child is gay, bisexual, or lesbian. (The exceptions to this are gay, lesbian, or bisexual parents, who probably don't make this assumption blindly, remembering their own experiences) When I ask, "Do you remember your emerging sexual identity?" I am not asking about the biases and assumptions people grew up with. Most people understand this, especially if they are gay, lesbian, or bisexual. They are well able to distinguish between cultural expectations and the reality of their sexuality.

We must make that same distinction in asking the question, "Do you remember the first time you had conscious knowledge of realizing you were assigned female (or male)?" This question is not about the gender socialization we were subjected to. Many people have concrete memories of being steered toward or away from various gender-specific clothing or toys. What most people don't remember is their first realization of their unique gender identity.

When I ask people to try to access these memories, most are unable to go further than memories of other people's gender expectations and their reactions to them. Memories of gendered socialization are memories of reaction to others' expectations; they do not address the question, "Where did the reaction come from?" The place inside a person that caused them to have the reaction they did to a gender expectation – that is a place of identity, of ownership of one's self in relation to gender.

There is a growing body of literature, written by people who identify as trans in some way, examining the concepts of gender and identity in existential terms. What does it all mean? Zoe Dolan addresses the issue in her essay *Transgender No More:* "Consider how 'when did you first know?' unfolds into pieces: the question presupposes that knowing anything about the self is possible, and that the words for apprehending and describing such knowledge can express the phenomenon beneath the surface." (Dolan, 2015) The quest for the existential meaning of life and identity is often undertaken by people seeking inner peace amid the maëlstrom of life. Trans people are forced into the realm of searching for meaning, often emerging the stronger for the journey inward.

THE EMERGENCE OF GENDER IDENTITY

Sexuality theory posits that sexual orientation is an innate identity people are born with and that this identity emerges fully during adolescence. (Levay, 2002; Lev, 2004; Bilodeau, 2005; Bieschke, 2006) Some people who end up a 0 or 6 on the Kinsey scale understood who they were attracted to at a very early age. A friend of mine who places herself at 5.5 on the Kinsey scale once told me, "I had my first crush on a girl when I was 7, but I didn't know that meant I was a lesbian until I was about 15."

Gender identity is also innate to the individual but it seems to emerge as a core identity so early it may not be measurable. (Dykstra, 2005; Brill, 2008; Vanderburgh, 2009; Ehrensaft, 2011; Krieger, 2011; Pepper, 2012; Teich, 2012) One can observe pre-verbal toddlers already playing with gender and various roles, figuring out what gender expression best fits their innate gender identity. One friend told me, "From the age of about 18 months we thought we were raising a gay male child; we could not keep Dana out of my closet and make-up." Dana is now a happy 26-year-old transwoman, ecstatic to have completed her gender-confirming surgery right out of high school and now three years into her first serious relationship.

If you ask a four-year-old child, "Are you a boy or a girl?" they know the answer, based on personal experience of identity; if they trust you enough they will answer honestly even if the answer isn't what you're expecting based on their birth gender assignment. (Brill, 2008; Vanderburgh, 2009; Ehrensaft, 2011; Krieger, 2011; Pepper, 2012)

In the 1980s singer-songwriter Fred Small wrote a song for a lesbian couple he knew; they wanted a lullaby to sing to their children. The song *Everything Possible* has been iconic in gay and lesbian community ever since:

> You can be anybody that you want to be,
> you can love whoever you will.
> You can travel any country where your heart leads
> and know that I will love you still.
> You can live by yourself,
> you can gather friends around,
> you can choose one special one.
> But the only measure of your words and your deeds
> is the love you leave behind when you're gone.

Gay and lesbian parents are raising their children with just such a message, wishing it had been given them when they were young. In the new millennium progressive heterosexual parents are also sending this message to their young children. In addition, there are far more mainstream representations of gay and lesbian identities as a normal part of the fabric of society. This is enabling young LGB children to recognize their identities.

I recently met two families in the Portland area whose cisgender girls have stated, "I'm a lesbian." One girl was seven and the other five. Five and seven may seem young to recognize a lesbian or gay identity. Consider that by the age of five, children are in school and interacting with large numbers of their peers. They are developing crushes on other children. One gay male friend of mine, now in his mid-forties, told me, "I was humping other boys on the playground from the time I was five. But I didn't know that meant I was gay until much later. I don't think I even heard the word until I was about 15, then I thought, 'Oh, *that's* what it is!' Then I understood that I was gay."

Contrast this with the experience of Dana, dressing in mom's clothes at the age of 18 months. Her gender identity was emerging far earlier than her attractions to other children. At 18 months, les-

44

bian or gay identity would not yet be on the radar for the children mentioned above.

This developmental difference in the timing of identity emergence makes it difficult for a person to analyze the question, "What's your first memory of knowing you were a boy or a girl?" because it's not a memory, it's a *feeling*. Memories depend on language. An identity that emerges during a pre-verbal developmental stage is not subject to analysis through verbal means. At 18 months, Dana had no capacity for verbalizing her feelings; her identity revealed itself through her behavior. By the age of four, she had the verbal ability to approach her parents and ask, "Am I a girl and you're just not telling me?"

Feelings, emotions, are a body process. This is why massage, acupressure, or acupuncture sometimes results in a flood of emotion that seems to come from nowhere. Unknowingly, the body worker has touched not just a portion of a client's body, but has touched an emotional storehouse as well and released its contents. Such modalities can therefore be an excellent way to bring deep-seated feelings to the surface, to then be dealt with in a more intellectual manner. (Kepner, 1999)

A note of caution: People who have PTSD (post-traumatic stress disorder) issues need to be careful about utilizing bodywork modalities, as they can be triggered or experience some kind of flashback. One friend with PTSD issues stemming from an assault said that she found acupressure was the only effective method that allowed her to bring the emotions about the assault to the surface so she could work through them. However, she sought out such methods deli-berately, knowing this might be the effect and so was prepared for (and desired) the resulting flood of emotion.

Because of the ethical constraints of the therapy profession, it's difficult for a psychotherapist to also do body work with clients. Unfortunately, for clarifying gender identity this is precisely the combination that might be most helpful, as our earliest memories of

45

gender identity emergence are going to be more emotionally-based then verbally-based.

It is possible to compromise by utilizing methodologies that by-pass the intellect and go directly into unconscious emotions. It is also possible for clients to access body work and then see their the-rapist, recording whatever emotions come up during the body work. Expressive arts and visualization can be helpful modalities, both for trans clients and for therapists wanting to work with gender identity issues.

While body work or expressive arts are a quicker method of accessing early emotional material, this may not be practical for a particular therapist, or resonate with their style of working through issues. If a therapist is open to change and allows themselves time to work with the issues in a consultation or therapy setting, they will find their own relationship to gender identity gradually emerges into consciousness for examination.

As an example of this, I know a cisgender therapist who fully understands that gender is a core identity issue. I asked her once how it was that she had such a visceral understanding of trans issues when she was not trans herself. She said she became interested in the issues intellectually about ten years previously, and then began attending a gender identity consultation group. She attended meetings for four years before seeing her first trans client. She got to know individual trans people and regularly attended trans conferences and other events. She processed through whatever came up for her as a result of this work, but she did it on her own time before she started working with trans clients. This is a therapist who understood her responsibility was to be clear about her relationship to her own gender before she could consider herself qualified to sit with a trans client.

Because there is no real separation between mind and body, if one allows the connection space to exist, an emotional body process can eventually be accessed through the mind. I used expressive arts with some of my clients, as this is a quicker route to the same end. Some clients don't resonate with this methodology, in which case I used more traditional psychodynamic techniques to access the client's deepest feelings around gender identity. While not as quick, this is more effective than trying to use expressive arts if the client is not open to such methodologies.

"SEEING" GENDER

Adrienne, 26, remarked in session, "I see trans people," parodying the line from the movie *The Sixth Sense*, "I see dead people." At the time Adrienne said this to me she had just accepted the fact that she needed to transition physically. Upon reaching this new level of self-acceptance she came into session laughing at herself; she had started seeing 'transness' in every person she encountered, though cognitively she knew the impossibility that every person in the city of Portland is trans!

What happened to Adrienne is one of the few things trans people have in common with each other, the development of a heightened consciousness of gender. Therapists desiring to work with trans clients would do well to enhance their own awareness of gender, perhaps not to the point of seeing trans people everywhere, but certainly to the point of turning off their gender autopilot. Thera-pists who reach this point in their process should notice that they no longer assign gender automatically, and that they are acutely aware when they or other people slip on pronouns.

SERVING ONE'S OWN

In recent years I have been contacted by increasing numbers of trans people entering the therapy profession. Each had reached a crossroads in their trainnig: "Do I come out professionally, knowing that if I do so, I risk being forever a 'trans therapist' rather than 'a therapist who happens to be trans?'" The reason such a high per-centage of my practice consisted of trans clients is because I was pigeonholed 'trans therapist' early in my career. I didn't regret this development as it dovetailed with another professsional goal of mine, to write and teach about trans issues.

I have had e-mail correspondence with various trans people who wanted to serve while simultaneously wanting to live their lives privately. I have helped them face that crossroads and determine their comfort level with privacy, whether to disclose their trans status to clients, how to work with clients whose transition journey differs from their own, or hits too close to home, etc.

I also have an interest in helping people determine, "Have I entered this profession for the right reasons?" A colleague once quipped her take on the therapy profession: "When the going gets weird, the weird turn pro." If a therapist has entered this profession in order to work out their own 'stuff,' whether knowingly or not, this is not going to serve their clients well. Nor is it helpful for a trans person to become a therapist in order to be an activist, with the primary intention of changing the therapy profession. This is a sociological-level goal and has little to do with the goal of wanting to help individual clients. The last thing any trans client needs is to find they are working with a trans therapist whose own transition issues leak into their work with clients, or a therapist whose focus is sociological and not on the client's individual issues.

COGNITIVE BEHAVIORAL THERAPY

Because of its popularity and prevalence in the therapy profession, it's worth discussing how a cognitive behavioral therapist would approach helping a client who is exploring transition. Some clients latch onto the word 'behavioral' and assume (incorrectly) that c.b. therapists try to change a client's behavior so they would not be trans any longer. While this is the paradigm underlying repa-rative or conversion 'therapy' (see the chapter *When Worlds Collide* for a fuller discussion), this is not how c.b. therapy works.

The philosophy underlying c.b. therapy is that thoughts, emotions, and behaviors are linked. If someone wishes to change a behavior pattern, changing the thoughts they have about the behavior can help form a new habit (or break an old one) as well as changing their emotional responses over time. Giving them a new thought to challenge the old one is also helpful, as it can help re-program the 'old tapes' many people have (often a critical parent's voice) lurk-ing in the background of their conscious mind. (Leahy, 2003)

A friend of mine was trained as a c.b. therapist. I'll call him Dave. Some years ago Dave decided he wanted to lose some weight. He knew himself well enough to know that he would feel deprived and oppressed if he approached his weight loss by con-ceptualizing it as a diet. Instead he said, "I'm not on a diet. I'm changing my lifestyle." Reframing his goal helped him develop positive thoughts and beliefs about his weight loss program; over time he lost the amount of weight he had in mind and has main-tained his new weight in the years since.

I had a conversation with Dave about how the c.b. approach plays out with trans clients. He told me that homework is a key ele-ment in the c.b. approach; the purpose of the homework is to help the client shift the thought processes that happen automatically in the back of their mind, keeping them stuck in certain belief patterns that may be holding them back or are causing them distress. Home-work can also help a client keep on track, giving them concrete goals to work on between therapy sessions.

Dave said that when a transwoman seems to have an unrealistic view of what it means to dress like a woman, the homework he might have her do is go sit in a mall for half an hour and write down the kinds of clothing she sees on the women around her. He also challenges thoughts that seem automatic to him, and possibly inac-curate. As an example, he told me of a transwoman client who believed all women are perfectly made-up each day. Dave had seen his client's partner, a cisgender woman who dressed very casually, always in pants. He suspected the partner didn't wear make-up, so he asked his client, "Does your partner use any make-up?" The client had to think about this and finally said, "I'm not sure. She helps me with mine." Dave said, "Well, that's being a supportive girlfriend. But does she use any herself?" This was the homework for that session: "Find out if your girlfriend wears make-up."

The interventions and homework of cognitive behavioral therapy aren't designed to make a client feel bad about the thoughts and beliefs they've held in the past, but to plant seeds of change, knowing these will bear fruit in their own time as the client is ready to change. (Leahy, 2003)

WHEN IS AN ISSUE NOT AN ISSUE?

It can be a temptation when working with a post-transition[9] client to view all their issues as stemming from their gender identity or transition process. Competency in working with trans clients includes understanding that once the client feels finished addressing the question, "How do I want to live my life?" transition often ceases to be their most prominent therapeutic concern. Exploring how gender and sexual identities affect various therapeutic issues is a key component of the work, with any client. Viewed from this perspective transition becomes part of the 'gender backdrop' of a post-transition person's life and not the automatic focal point any longer.

On an individual basis a therapist may reserve judgment and bookmark the thought that perhaps transition is more of an issue than a post-transition client realizes. I worked with a number of clients who had considered themselves done, when in fact they were facing post-transition issues common to many trans people (I will focus on such issues later in this book). These clients had not recog-nized the connection between their transition and their current is-sues. Many were relieved to find they had entered a new stage of transition, as they had been wondering what was wrong with them.

Despite the fact that transition may still be a primary issue for the post-transition client, if the therapist's going-in position is that transition is the main issue for *every* such client, the therapy rela-

---

[9] Post-transition is client-defined.

tionship may end up being short-lived. Most who self-describe as 'done' are clients who have reached a point where they themselves view transition as a backdrop of their life; it is a historically-rele-vant process they once undertook and not a current process that is subsuming all else in their lives.

• Chapter 3 •

QUESTIONS OF A SKEPTIC

THERAPISTS (EVEN RETIRED THERAPISTS) HAVE A PECULIAR VIEW OF THE WORLD. We notice people within the context of relationship and interconnection, a result of our training and spending our professional hours helping clients resolve personal and interpersonal difficulties. Keeping this in mind, forgive me when I say I was excited to be given the opportunity to meet with a family at odds over an impending transition.

In the spring of 2006, Mark was an 18-year-old client living with his parents in a suburb near Portland, about to go off to college and anxious to begin taking hormones so he could be seen as male by the time he left home in late summer. His mother (Dianne) was fully supportive of her son, recognizing how gender had played out throughout his life and that this was a core identity. Mark's father Kenneth, however, was convinced his 'daughter' was suffering from a mental illness.

The family came to an agreement: Kenneth would come to a family session with me if Dianne and Mark would go to a family session with a therapist of his (Kenneth's) choosing. Kenneth is a scientist and distrusted emotion to such a degree that he believed emotionality should play no part in major life decisions. "Just the facts," was his attitude. He believed Mark (whom he called by the birth name Ellen) had been deluded by various websites he'd read (including mine), and that "she is self-diagnosing a mental illness."

Kenneth brought into the session a series of skeptical questions: "Since Gender Identity Disorder is listed in the DSM, it must be a mental illness. Therefore, what scientific evidence is there that anyone should undergo a sex change? People with mental illnesses are inherently incompetent to 'self-diagnose' themselves, therefore objective tests are necessary. If such tests are not available, how can one then prescribe a sex change?"

Kenneth asked that I write answers to his questions during the family session, which I declined to do because I find it difficult to focus if I divide my attention between writing and talking. I offered to send Kenneth an e-mail later that day, answering every question fully. Later in this book I will provide my responses, but right now I want to focus on the questions themselves.

I was excited to receive these questions for two reasons. First, I rarely had the opportunity to meet resistant parents. Though many of my clients encountered resistance from family members, it was unusual for (a) a client to be willing to bring a resistant parent into session, or (b) a resistant parent to be willing to attend. The questions Kenneth provided reflected the general attitudes of most resistant parents, though some also opposed transition for religious reasons, not a factor in Kenneth's case. Having the opportunity to engage directly with the family was an unusual gift.

Second, the basis for the questions is excellent, though Kenneth's questions are worded in a judgmental way that pre-supposes trans identity to be pathological. Nevertheless, every trans person should be approaching their own transition with a similar skepticism and objectivity. To paraphrase Kenneth in a non-pathologizing way: "How do you know with certainty that transition is necessary, that there isn't some issue that therapy might help you resolve?" *Every person considering some form of transition should ask themselves precisely that.*

WHERE KENNETH AND I DISAGREE

Kenneth and I part company in our views of where the answers should come from. Kenneth looks to science for answers, trusting no other source of knowledge, including that which arises from within the person. His attitude is similar to parents who are resistant for religious reasons, looking only to a holy book for answers to existential questions: science is Kenneth's 'religion.'

However, identity can't be proved scientifically. Science is not the correct methodology to employ in answering questions about identity. If a person says, "I'm heterosexual" how can they possibly prove that identity using science? I helped clients learn to tune into and trust their own intuitive process, as this is the source of self-knowledge. Through this knowledge of Self, clients are in a better position to answer objective questions to their own satisfaction.

Occasionally a client hoped I would provide external validation for their identity, either on their own behalf (distrusting their own emotional process and interpretation) or on behalf of skeptical family members. I helped my clients realize that their identity is what it is and that they don't need to justify themselves to others.

There is no answer (yet) to the question, "Why are some people trans and some people cisgender?" Many of my clients had deep-seated shame and guilt about being trans, and would have loved a blood test they could point to, to be able to say to their loved ones, "See, this is proof." I helped them realize that the answers lie within them and that no answer is right or wrong, just right or wrong for them.

Intellectual processing is necessary when considering the sci-ence behind physical transition – how do hormones change the body, how quickly, what dosages are generally recommended, what are common side effects and risk factors, etc. However, only emotional processing and a good understanding of one's emotional responses can answer questions about identity. While necessary as part of decision-making, especially in cases where there might be medical reasons to hold off on physical transition, learning about the physical process doesn't take the place of self-knowledge.

Despite my trust in the power and inherent truth of intuition and deep connection to one's emotional process, I also believe it is necessary to step out of oneself when considering physical transition. Transition takes place in a relational context even if the person in question is not in a romantic relationship. People have friends, co-workers, family. Most who transition physically don't live (or want to live) a hermit existence. They do wish to interact with other people, but they want to do so within the context of a different gender role and (possibly) hormone balance. This is a boundary issue: how to involve others in the transition without allowing them control over what emerges during the process of self-knowledge.

OBJECTIVE QUESTIONS ABOUT TRANSITION

The combination of intellectual and emotional processing helps anyone contemplating transition to develop a well-rounded view of transition as a deeply personal and at the same time a deeply interpersonal process. I would encourage anyone considering transition to ask themselves non-judgmental questions:

1. Looking back over the course of your life, what leads you to conclude that transition would make your life better than it is now?
2. What have you already tried to help alleviate the gender dissonance you feel? Have you tried anything that did help, to some degree? If so, why is that insufficient now?
3. Why are you seeking transition at this particular point in your life? Why now, why not at an earlier time (relevant if you're well beyond adolescence)?
4. Have you met or had online conversations with other trans people? If so, how have their stories affected you? What are some of the similarities and differences between your experience of gender and theirs?
5. If you have not attempted to meet (in person or via social media) any other trans people, why is this the case?

In working with trans clients, I didn't give out this list of questions as a homework assignment. Rather, I listened for the answers as clients told me their story. My clients had been living with the questions much of their lives and had already done their own soul-searching toward the answers before calling me for their first appointment. My office was not the first stop on their journey!

If I didn't hear answers to the above questions when I listened to a client's story, I asked questions overtly, always making clear the questions were necessary in helping clients answer for themselves, "How do I want to live my life?" Again, the art of timing – such questions have to come at the right time, one at a time, not in an overwhelming fashion. Each question can provide fodder for several sessions, if thoroughly unpacked.

Transition is a holistic process, encompassing all relationships, from oneself to the most superficial of daily interactions. Any non-judgmental process that requires one to question transition from the most objective to the deepest personal perspective is worthwhile and will prove helpful as the client charts the most appropriate course of action.

THE IMPORTANCE OF HOLDING OUT HOPE

In early 2011 Mark's mother Dianne sent me an e-mail thanking me for helping their family five years before. Mark was about to graduate from college, and was engaged to a young woman named Audrey. His father Kenneth couldn't be happier with the course his son's life had taken. He proactively offered to tell Audrey's father John about Mark's transition, remembering how difficult it was for him to accept the process.

In 2013 I talked with Mark directly. He was in graduate school, studying sociology with an intention of becoming a teacher. He and Audrey had been married about a year. Mark laughed as he told me, "Remember my dad would only come to that session with you if we saw this psychiatrist he picked out? He figured a psychiatrist was a real doctor so it would all be scientific. We saw that psychiatrist one time, and he agreed with you! He said that this seemed to be my identity, so transition was probably the right thing for me."

Though freely admitting he still doesn't understand trans identity, Kenneth also recognizes in his logical, scientific way how much happier Mark is on the other side of transition. Kenneth is now a staunch ally to his son.

• Chapter 4 •

MODELS OF GENDER IDENTITY

THE CURRENT AMERICAN MAINSTREAM VIEW LIMITS GENDER to just two flavors, male and female. Often, this assignment is made prior to birth, on the basis of an ultrasound. Whether the assignment is pre-birth or not, gender is assumed to match genitalia. Graphically the mainstream gender conceptualization looks something like this:

Figure 1

●

male

intersexed

(the gray area)

female

●

This is how many Americans, trans people included, conceptualize gender, with mutually-exclusive categories for male and female. If asked to draw the mainstream model of gender, many would not think to include the gray area, having never considered intersexed people.[10] The widespread acceptance of this model keeps trans people off the radar of mainstream America, because there is no place in this model for any identity other than male or female, and the two are viewed as mutually exclusive. While many who transition physically do claim male or female with alacrity, their gender journey through life does not resemble that of cisgender males or females. Their socialization and childhood experiences, the lengths to which they must go to live

---

[10] Intersexed, now known as disorders of sex differentiation or divergence of sex development, is popularly defined as "indeterminate genitalia and/or chromosomal abnormalities." The dilemma itself is an indication of the depth of the cultural imperative to 'gender' people as soon as possible. Other questions that arise include: "What is determinate about genitalia? What are normal chromosomes?"

as self-actualized adults, are beyond the wildest imaginings of their cisgender friends, partners, and relatives.

Further, those who undergo physical transition can only approximate a cisgender male or female body. Should they place them-selves in that middle portion of the model, with those who have a sex differentiation disorder, or at whichever endpoint feels more comfortable psychologically? Is the model based on the observable body, or on self-determined gender? If it is based on the body, does that mean the body as it appears prior to transition-related surgery or after? Where does that leave the trans person who greatly desires surgery but can never afford it? Where does it leave the person who feels neither male or female? Now let's consider the following conceptualization of a gender continuum:

Figure 2

NORMAL	MANY PEOPLE	TRANS
100% **comfortable** with birth gender assignment	ARE IN BETWEEN	100% **UNcomfortable** with birth gender assignment

This model more closely resembles the reality of the situation. For instance, my brother (a cisgender male) and I would have no choice but to put ourselves in the same place in the Figure 1 model, however in Figure 2, the difference between us is much more apparent – he is much closer to 100% comfortable with his birth gender assignment, while I was far on the side of uncomfortable.

This model also reflects a cultural assumption, more insidious and subtle than the first model, making clear how important it is to use terms such as cisgender. The assumption under the model in Figure 2 is that being comfortable with one's birth gender assign-ment is somehow inherently better than being trans in some way. Prior to the coining of the term cisgender, there was no word for those who are content with their birth gender. They inherited the words man, woman, male, female – and normal. This highlights the importance of words like cisgender, providing the opportunity for the development of a level playing field. Those who claim to be not-man, not-woman, not-female, or not-male, to whatever degree, were historically given separate words which continue to carry a cultural stigma with them: transgender and transsexual. Abnormal. Disordered. Marginalized and invisible. The cultural bias is that being not-trans is better than being trans. How can the playing field ever be level with such a conceptualization? Now consider the following continuum:

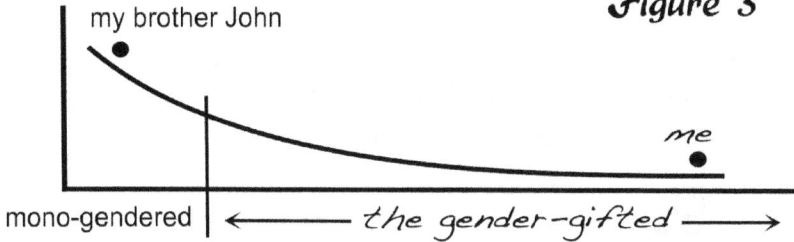

Figure 3

my brother John

me

mono-gendered | ←———— *the gender-gifted* ——→

Under this model, those few who are trans are considered 'gender gifted,' with a broader worldview available to them than those who are cisgender. Various cultures throughout history have adopted this attitude toward trans people, though it is a foreign concept in this country to imagine a culture where having a trans child confers honor and status on an entire family. (Cromwell, 1999) It is difficult for American trans people to shift their accul-turated beliefs sufficiently to view their trans identities so posi-tively, but it is well worth the effort to try as it may help them em-brace all they have to offer the world. Rather than asking people to accept and honor them *despite* their trans identity, why not ask peo-ple to accept and honor them *because* of their trans identity?

The difficulty with this model is that it perpetuates a hierarchy of gender. Rather than putting cisgender people at the top of the hierarchy, this model substitutes trans people as being the epitome of gender correctness. I introduce it to shake up the status quo, to put forth a model so out of step with mainstream American views that it stalls the autopilot for a bit. In my lesbian community days, one of the more popular sentiments was 'question authority.' Let's extend this further: don't just question authority, question reality.

My hope is that someday there will be no hierarchy of gender at all; gender will be recognized as an aspect of a person's core identity. What that day would mean is that no child would grow up feeling uncomfortable with an assigned birth gender, because gender would not be assigned but would be recognized as an aspect of identity which will eventually emerge. This would not be a genderless or gender-neutral society, as I think we are hardwired to differentiate gender, but would be a society freer of gender stereo-types and rigid gender roles. The gender continuum would then become something like this, with each individual finding their place as part of their normal maturation and individuation process:

Figure 4

masculine   gender   *feminine*

neutral

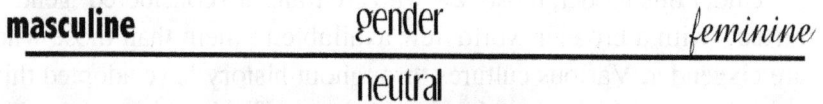

Note that this continuum does not address the sex of a person's body or their sexual orientation. It can be used in the context of gender identity, gender roles, and gender expression, in various life contexts. Nor does it place a value judgment on any one point in the continuum or use a scale that allows for determining percentages of people who identify a certain way. The need to determine how many people resonate with a particular identity has too often been used in American culture as a means of determining the level of acceptability of that identity. (This is known as the tyranny of the majority)

It shouldn't matter whether 1% or 10% or 50% of the population claim any particular identity or place themselves in one spot on any continuum. Truly honoring diversity means honoring the concept that any given identity label plays out very differently in each of our individual lives. Percentages lose their meaning as the meaning of any identity label is determined on an individual level. Just as maps lessen the time it takes us to find our way, labels are merely short-cuts that give us a little information about a person. What we tend to lose sight of in the U.S. is that the label is not the person any more than the map is the territory.

THE DSM MODEL

Changing the paradigm of a continuum of gender also changes the nature of the therapist-client relationship, and the therapist's treatment plan. Over the past twenty years, those who have transitioned have done so under the medical model outlined in DSM IV and more recently DSM V.

In reading the DSM IV definition of Gender Identity Disorder (GID), I am struck by how 'ill' trans clients were perceived to be, and by language stating that the desire to transition is a simulation of a different gender than that assigned at birth. Among the criteria for an adult diagnosis were the following:

"....In adolescents and adults, the disturbance is manifested by symptoms such as a stated desire to be treated as the other sex, frequent passing as the other sex, desire to live or be treated like the other sex, or the conviction that he or she has the typical feelings and reactions of the other sex. Persistent discomfort with his or her sex or sense of inappropriateness of the gender role of that sex.... In adolescents and adults, the disturbance is manifested by symptoms such as preoccupation with getting rid of primary and secondary sex characteristics (e.g. request for hormones, surgery, or other procedures to alter sexual characteristics to simulate the other sex) or belief that he or she was born the wrong sex....The disturbance causes clinically significant distress or impairment in social, occupational, or other important areas of functioning." *(American Psychiatric Association, 1994)*

The medical model language of the DSM IV, with its focus on diagnosis and symptomotology, helps explain why so many trans people continue to believe that the therapy profession will not be helpful to them during their transition process. Preceding iterations of the DSM were no less pathologizing.

DSM V was released in 2014. This latest edition changed the diagnostic language from Gender Identity Disorder to Gender Dysphoria, and gives credence to gender identities beyond a binary model. Nevertheless many trans people are offended at the presence of anything to do with gender identity in a volume outlining forms of mental disorders and illness, regardless of the wording. Further, the older paradigm of pathologization has created a long-standing distrust of the mental health profession that will be slow to change.

Most trans people are unaware that therapists don't necessarily consider the DSM a particularly useful tool, but a diagnostic language they must learn in order to bill insurance companies and converse with each other about client issues. The DSM provides a means of categorizing various observed clusters of behavior, giving mental health professionals a common language. It contains no information to help a therapist or psychologist understand how to help the client who receives the diagnosis. Hence the importance of good clinical supervision and consultation opportunities for therapists desiring to work with trans clients.

Trans people have a 'history' as a people, handed down pri-marily via oral tradition and more recently the Internet, that rein-forces an 'us vs. them' mentality when considering interactions with mental health or medical professionals. There was a time when the idea of a trans therapist was unheard of; how can one of 'us' be one of 'them?' In 2002, I attended a trans conference. I went to a work-shop aimed at couples who were remaining together through transi-tion. The workshop facilitator had each of us state why we were there, what we hoped to get from the workshop, etc. Intending to be respectful, I said I wasn't currently in a relationship but was a thera-pist wanting to learn more. After the workshop, a transman approached me and said, respectfully but with some distance, "I hope this was useful to you when you work with trans clients." I was taken aback as it belatedly occurred to me that he hadn't recog-nized me as a transman. Because I was a therapist, he had assumed I was cisgender.

Prior to DSM V, many who transitioned physically only vaguely recognized themselves in the DSM description of Gender Identity Disorder. The definition was more depressed than many felt their lives had been. The longer ago a person transitioned physically, the more closely they seem to fit earlier DSM definitions. The only people allowed to transition in previous generations were those who exhibited many of the DSM symptoms, or who were savvy enough to lie about it. Often, transition took place within a gender clinic setting, reinforcing a model of being 'set apart' from others.

The current transition process retains some of this gatekeeper flavor, but the timing of various procedures (hormones, surgery, etc.), the eventual goals of transition, and the length of time sug-gested for therapy is much looser. The current Standards of Care no longer absolutely require therapy prior to beginning hormones or having surgery. (World Professional Association for Transgender Health, 2011) The therapist's treatment plan is more dependent on the individual client's situation and life goals than was the case when physical transition took place within gender clinics. This change is largely due to the involvement of trans people in determining best practices in the area of transition.

In addition, the therapy profession as a whole has evolved in the direction of being more client-centered, more of a collaborative effort (often called a therapeutic alliance) than used to be the case. The result has been a gradual paradigm shift in treatment planning, away from diagnosis and pathology, and toward identity formation and self-knowledge. These factors have led to the availability of transition to many people who would have been denied access to the process in earlier times.

NON-OUTLIERS TRANSITIONING PHYSICALLY

Looking again at Figure 2 (pg. 57), the original paradigm of physical transition allowed only the outliers to proceed, those who were far to the right of the continuum and who could state categorically that they were 100% uncomfortable with the gender assigned them at birth and always had been. Involvement of trans people in defining transition processes has allowed those closer to the center of the model to also consider physical transition, those who are not necessarily 100% uncomfortable with their birth gender assignment, but who are uncomfortable enough to say with confidence, "This is not how I want to live my life."

People whose life experience has been less extremely depressing than the DSM's definition, who have been better able to adapt to living their birth gender, are freer now to re-examine that gender role and consider other decisions about how to live their lives. Because people closer to the middle of the spectrum of Figure 2 are questioning their gender identity, this has led to the emergence of more nuanced forms of trans identities: genderqueer or non-binary; identifying as transsexual but choosing to not transition physically; requesting non-binary pronouns with no intention of body modification; a male-bodied person seeking an orchiectomy and hormones, but with no intention of living a female role all the time; a female-bodied person desiring chest surgery but no hormones or lower surgery, or hormones and no surgery at all; a person who does not identify as male or female seeking hormones or some form of surgery; a male-assigned person requesting hormones to induce breast growth but with no desire for other body modifications or a full-time change to a female gender role.

In recent years I have seen all the above scenarios play out in clients and friends. All consider themselves trans in some way. A few consider themselves transsexual, though they would not fit the traditional definition of the term. They are not among the outliers and in previous years would have been screened out had they sought any form of physical transition.

Yet all these people have done considerable soul-searching, parsing out how far they needed to go with physical transition in order to find a comfortable gender role. Their conclusion resulted in a gender identity that transcends a gender binary system. They also see themselves as works in progress, recognizing that living an identity so far outside the available roles is uncharted territory, requiring all the more vigilant navigation to remain sure of the right direction for them.

Most therapists still work from a gender binary model, and would structure their treatment plan accordingly for non-binary cli-ents. Such a therapist might state something like this in conceptual-lizing their treatment plan: "I'm trying to help this client sort out whether they wish to live as a male or female, which gender role fits them best." The very language used in the previous sentence reflects a bias: "which gender role" and "male or female," as if those were the only choices. While many of the client's issues undoubtedly do stem from living in the mid-spectrum region, it is an assumption on the part of the therapist that the gender binary system does in fact reflect all gender identities rather than reflecting a cultural construct.

The issues such clients face often have more to do with cultural hostility and the weight of constantly having to assert their identity, rather than difficulty with the identity itself. Most of my non-binary clients were under 30 and many were in college. As graduation approached they became more acutely aware of the difficulties that lay ahead if they desired to maintain a gender-fluid identity while in the job market. Many felt pressured to conform to gender norms as they began the job interview process. Some veered toward the non-profit or entrepreneurial job sectors in an attempt to avoid gender conformity. Being able to remain true to a non-binary gender iden-tity is a form of privilege, many came to realize, as they faced the need to pay the bills and repay student loans.

My belief is a client's gender identity is what it is, and there is a fluid spectrum of identity. Working from this model the client's non-binary identity is not automatically the issue. The issues are: how well does the client cope living with a mid-spectrum identity in a culture that believes the binary gender model is reality and not a model at all? What defenses has the client developed to protect their gender identity from a hostile culture? Do these defenses hinder relationship development, or the client's ability to accept intimacy? Is there anything underlying the client's interpretation of their gender that might be problematic (childhood sexual abuse, for example) in considering physical transition as an option that will lead to increased comfort with life? These issues (plus those specific to individual circumstances) defined the treatment plan I developed for any given client.

Whether living a middle-ground or a binary identity, my clients paid out of pocket for their transition processes. Insurance coverage was rare for transition processes. Though more insurance plans cover transition than in previous times, this may not benefit the non-binary client. It is likely that insurance will cover binary transitions, and may look askance at the non-binary transition process.

A MORE DIFFICULT DECISION

People closer to the middle of the spectrum have a tougher decision-making process ahead of them than the outlier clients. For the outliers, physical transition is usually the option that makes most sense for them, though actualizing their identities is still difficult and may come at the cost of various relationships. Those in the middle of the spectrum have a wider range of options to consider, as full physical transition may not be the option that fits them best. It is this wider range of options that makes their decision-making difficult. The primary focus of therapy with such clients is self-knowledge and helping them cope with the ramifications of knowing that having only testosterone and estrogen available does not facilitate expressing more than one gender through one's body.

My female-assigned non-outlier clients often (though not always) took refuge in the lesbian community, whether their strongest attractions were to women or not. Some adapted reason-ably well over the years, primarily because they were able to have full masculine gender expression within the lesbian community. Nevertheless, they never felt completely at home in the lesbian community because 'female' did not fit them well.

For those who were not particularly attracted to women, the lesbian community was a place of refuge because it allowed for comfortable gender expression, despite a lack of fulfillment in sexual relationships. For those who were attracted to women, their own discomfort with their female bodies often prevented them from fully enjoying the benefits of their sexual relationships. Many would make love to their partners, but could not allow their partners to reciprocate, feeling too self-conscious about being perceived female. While the non-outliers resonated to some degree with female identity, they felt they were turning their backs on a core part of themselves if they accepted the label 'female' as an exclusive identity.

A number of my female-assigned non-outlier clients were primarily attracted to men and were frustrated because they were seen as lesbians upon entering a gay bar. It was difficult for them to hold the attention of the men they were attracted to and even more difficult for them to form lasting relationships. This became the focus of therapy for more than one of my clients who had no intention of fully transitioning physically, as they were not outliers on the Figure 2 spectrum. They disliked being seen as heterosexual women, and thus pursued relationships with gay, queer, or bisexual cisgender men. They were then frustrated because those men usually didn't see them as male. Few of my clients were able to find cisgender men who truly saw them as they saw themselves. Many of my non-outlier gay-identified clients ended up in relationships with other non-binary people, finding it refreshing to be involved with people who have moved beyond the gender binary.

Kevin (23) said, in describing the end of one romantic relationship with a cisgender man he'd met a month before, "He kept insisting on calling my genitals my 'pussy.' When I called him on it, he said they were female body parts, so that's why he used that term.

67

I said if they were on my body, they weren't female body parts because I'm not a woman."

Kevin started taking testosterone in early 2003 and never regretted his decision. At the time he had no intention of having surgery, though he later decided to have chest reconstruction surgery. He remained uninterested in lower surgery, though he did have a hysterectomy to lower his risk for various forms of cancer. He enjoyed penetrative vaginal sex (his terminology), and this did not change as a result of his transition. His relationship to his breasts did change; he found them less appealing once he was being seen not-female in all situations. As he put it, "I used to take a lot of pleasure in my breasts, but when I had more testosterone in my system, they felt less like part of me."

It was a difficult decision for many of my non-outlier clients to take hormones, as they couldn't be certain they wouldn't change their minds at a later point. Some of my non-binary clients were fairly certain they didn't want to take hormones, feeling, "I'm not particularly comfortable with either binary gender male or female, so what's the point of taking hormones?"

THE THERAPEUTIC RELATIONSHIP

To work effectively with non-outlier clients requires the therapist to give up the notion of the gender binary. The trans client these days may request an entirely new pronoun (hir or ze, for example, or the plural pronoun they), or may say they are not sure what pronoun they prefer. Or a client may say, as some of mine did, "I'm not planning on transitioning physically because it just doesn't seem right to me, but I prefer male pronouns over female regardless of how my body looks." Or vice versa. Several of my clients were attempting to live genderfree, as one put it.

Charles (22) has a neurological problem, incurable but not life-threatening. Because so little research has been done on the inter-active effects of hormones with other medications he takes, he was not inclined to take testosterone. Because Charles is not an outlier on the Figure 2 continuum, he was able to live female, though he felt he would be happier were he able to take testosterone. He was clear that he would like chest surgery, but was resigned to having to wait for years to save the money. Were Charles an outlier on the Figure 2 continuum, he would probably feel psychologically compelled to take hormones despite the lack of medical research. His feelings of gender dissonance would probably outweigh his fear of adverse consequences.

His primary reason for seeking me out? Charles needed someone to talk to who would not pathologize him for not participating in the gender binary. He had family of origin issues he wanted to work through, and was not interested in working with a therapist who had to do mental gymnastics to get beyond his female gender present- ation. He had tried that before, and that particular therapist's own issues with mid-spectrum clients got in Charles' way of working on his family issues. The therapist didn't seem able to work with Charles effectively because they could not assign Charles to a clear female or male category in their own mind.

In fairness to therapists – family systems training is not only ex- clusively heteronormative, but also completely gender binary, with a great deal of focus on the traditional roles and relationships: mo-ther, father, brother, sister. It is hard for a therapist to re-vision their family systems training using expanded notions of what 'family' means. In order to work with non-binary clients, the therapist's own work includes coming to understand how it would affect a non-binary client to continually have gendered family relationships foisted on them. The last thing such a client needs is to have such relationships foisted on them by their therapist.

GENERATIONAL DIFFERENCES

My younger clients were generally more open to exploring the fluidity of identity. Some described their experience of gender in binary language but most seemed to understand non-binary identities in a way that seems difficult for many of my older clients. One young female-affirmed friend of mine has known she was a girl since before she could talk, yet fully respects that some of her high school friends are non-binary; she has no problem using whatever pronoun her friends request at any given time.

My older clients were usually more attached to the gender binary system. These clients had difficulty with fluid identities beyond the familiar male and female, and were sometimes quite judgmental of those who live a middle-ground identity. Trying to figure out a 'gender box' for all people is a cultural artifact for Americans. I find it exciting that the up-and-coming generation of trans and non-binary people is challenging the gender binary system in a way that seems unprecedented to me; I look forward to seeing what happens as they age and influence subsequent generations.

Some of my older clients didn't feel clearly male or female, either. They also lived a middle-ground identity, but were of a generation that finds it difficult to give credence to such lived experience. One 60-something friend of mine had identified as a crossdresser for many years at the time we met in 2007. She re-marked to me, "If I was 40 years younger, I'd probably be calling myself genderqueer."

I found it useful to encourage cross-generational discussion among my non-outlier clients. After talking with younger non-binary people, some of my older clients found themselves energized by new ideas and conceptualizations that matched their lived experience. Many of my older non-outlier clients had attempted to find support in peer groups based on age and often felt their ex-perience wasn't validated by those whose life path included physical transition. It had not occurred to them that perhaps age and birth gender assignment weren't guarantees of finding peer support.

One younger non-binary friend remarked, "I had an epiphany that really helped me make sense of my identity. I used to think, 'Why wasn't I born with an identity that was at one of the poles, male or female? It would have been a lot easier.' But then I realized that no one really IS at the poles – all of us are in the middle. When you think about it like that, there is no actual identity that is 'male' or 'female,' we're all unique in how we do gender. So, we're all in the middle. And that's why we have all this trouble around gender – we're most of us trying to fit into categories that are so artificial, they don't come close to reflecting who we could be if we weren't culturally wedded to these poles as if they were opposites and mutually exclusive." *(Personal conversation, 2017)*

One focus for the non-outlier trans client is that of existential search for identity and the meaning of life. Some, especially my younger clients, were hostile toward the larger culture for its lack of acceptance. Some despaired of ever finding where they fit in. While this is a common issue among adolescents, for my non-outlier clients the dilemma was an ongoing social problem, not a life stage they will grow out of. Upon realizing that we are all in the middle, my young friend has become more relaxed and accepting of their identity; they have a new box to fit into, a framework for understanding their identity, a box we all could share if our culture permitted it.

• Chapter 5 •

STAGES OF TRANSITION

PSYCHOLOGIST ERIK ERIKSON expanded on the concept of Freud's stages of psychosexual development, changing the focus from a narrow sex-based view to a more relational perspective and adding further stages throughout the life span, in recognition of the fact that humans never stop developing. (Erikson, 1980) His model of human development is useful in considering transition as a developmental process of identity emergence.

Erikson was a spiritual man, interested in the "timeless" aspects of human nature. Erikson once said: "...soul is the seat for experiencing God as Divine Other and for mystically transcending a single-gendered adult who had been held captive in one time, space and single-sex body." (Hoare, 2002) I believe Erikson would have seen the need to transition as a spiritual path, along the lines of the two-spirit view of Native American tradition.

There are two layers to the conceptualization of transition as a developmental process. First, as with chronological maturation, there are stages based on how long a person has been in transition. For instance, someone who begins taking hormones is in a stage that resembles adolescence regardless of their chronological age.

And second, the issues that are faced by someone in transition recur in various stages with a different focus. A person who has been repressing their gender for a lifetime asks the question, "Who am I?" from a point of confusion, in the earliest stages of transition. A person who has been taking hormones for awhile also asks, "Who am I?" but the question is asked from the perspective of someone who is resocializing themselves in a different gender role. The difference is similar to that of a toddler asking, "Who am I?" and a young adult asking the same question.

For simplicity's sake I use the term *transsexual* for those who undertake some form of physical body modification via hormones and/or surgery, and the word *transgender* for those who do not. I don't want my sentences to become unwieldy or confusing as I describe the stages of transition, so have sacrificed any attempt at precise definition of identity. (Which isn't possible anyway!) I also alternate between male and female, as the process is very similar regardless of birth gender assignment.

The following staged model is intended to describe the client who realizes they are indeed trans in some way, not to imply that everyone who comes into a therapist's office in a state of identity confusion will end up identifying as trans. As this book is focused on trans experiences, I focus on those people whose confusion re-solves itself as a realization of trans identity and a need to transition in some way.

DEVELOPMENTAL STAGES OF TRANSITION

❖ *Denial or Unconsciousness:* The client may come into session with the intention of sorting through what they perceive as sexual identity confusion. They are unaware that their issues stem from gender identity, not sexuality. They may be coming to therapy because of partner insistence. They have no knowledge of trans issues as applied to themselves. They may have a fundamental misunderstanding of what it means to be trans, paralleling that of the mainstream culture, making it impossible to have recognized their trans identity. People around them may have assumed they are gay, whether they have lived as a gay man or not.

Pivotal questions: "Why am I so anxious? Why do I feel so uncomfortable acting like a man? For those with attractions to men: Am I gay? For those with attractions to women: I don't think I'm gay because I'm attracted to women, but there's still something wrong. What's wrong with me?"

❖ *Confusion:* The client gradually realizes sexual orientation doesn't explain what's going on, though they are still unsure where the problem lies. They are feeling raw and vulnerable at this point, and unsure of any identity: reality-testing is a hot button. They may feel they have no identity anchors any longer, making it difficult for them to evaluate their own experience.

Pivotal questions: "What does it mean to be a woman? Why do I feel uncomfortable going into women's bathrooms? I *have* to be a woman – what other choice do I have?"

❖ **Pre-decision:** The client is beginning to connect their confusion with gender identity, but doesn't want it to be true. They don't want to consider transition – scary, overwhelming, shame-filled topic – but they can no longer deny gender is the key issue.

Pivotal questions: "I have to be a man – what other choice do I *have?"* (Note slightly different emphasis from the same question in the *Confusion* stage.)

❖ **Epiphany:** The client's internal process reaches a point where they have an epiphany realization, seemingly suddenly, that being transgender or transsexual is not out of the realm of possibility to consider. At this point the client is better able to face the issue of physical transition as a possibility, without the issues of shame and disgust holding them back from entertaining the possibility. The shame and disgust are not completely dismantled, but softened to the point the client can face their gender honestly. Regardless of whether or not the client actually undergoes a physical transition, reaching the stage of being able to consider it is the key. I consider this stage the calm before the storm; confusion has lifted and some clarity has emerged, but the processes are still internal and private. The social processes have yet to begin.

Pivotal questions: "What have I been so afraid of? Other people have done this – why shouldn't I at least consider it? What form of transition would suit me best? Should I change my name? But if I decide to do that – I have tell everyone!!!! Am I ready to tell *anyone????"*

❖ *Early transition:* Some consider the permanent changes wrought by hormones or surgery to be the point of irreversibility of transition. Realistically, the point of irreversibility is the first time a client tells someone who isn't bound by confidentiality. This stage of transition can be marked in a variety of ways: the client begins hormones, or begins telling others about their transition, or begins shifting their life to accommodate a change in gender role, embracing some form of non-binary identity. Whether or not there is a physical transformation, there is a transition into a new level of self-acceptance and a different path in life. For those who take hormones, this is the beginning of a paradoxical push-pull stage: "I've waited this long, I want to just become a woman and get on with life," while simultaneously feeling, "I have a lot of life to change and this is overwhelming." The client will probably feel increasingly gender congruent before attaining the ability to be seen as a woman – a frustrating time period.

Pivotal questions: "Why did I wait so long? Why can't this process go faster! Why can't this process go slower! Who am I these days??? How do I tell everyone in my life who I am? Will I be accepted, at work or at home or within my various families (biological family, family of choice, family by marriage, or committed relationship)?"

❖ *Learning the boundaries:* How does the client learn the boundaries of his new gender role? Deconstructing gender roles becomes a key therapeutic issue. Whether in full physical transition, or learning how he actualizes 'transgender,' the *Pivotal Questions* are similar:

"What is socialization, what is hormonal? What is okay for a man to do, what isn't? How do I act in all-male settings? What are the rules!!! How do these rules fit with my self-concept and world-view? Do I want to play by all these rules, or am I willing to accept whatever consequences if I just be myself, even if it means I'm 'breaking the rules?' How do I feel now about men, about women, and what kinds of relationships do I want? What gender expression suits me best?"

❖ *The point of invisibility:* For those who don't choose physical transition, this stage is the point at which they can be seen as their intended gender, whatever that gender is at a particular point in time. If they are not perceived by others as their intended gender, usually due to physical attributes, this point is achieved when they have sufficient self-esteem that they don't care. Those who transition via hormones or surgery are generally seeking to achieve invisibility permanently. The person in this position is seen as female in all situations now. She has learned what gender expres-sion suits her best and how to achieve it. She's disclosed to the important people in her life. Relationships are settling in; she is be-ginning to re-emerge from self-involvement back into a position of responsibility to others in relationship. She may experience feelings of isolation, while at the same time feeling perfectly fine with her new gender role; she may be confused by these seemingly contradictory feelings.

Pivotal questions: "How do I disclose to new people who never knew me before? How do I come out, and when? How much privacy do I desire? If I want to be private about my identity, what is my reasoning, my motivation? Am I ashamed of who I was or who I am now? If I don't want to be an activist, everyone's education about everything trans, is that okay? Who is my tribe?"

❖ *Done?:* Several years into his new role now. For those who did not choose physical transition, the question may arise from time to time, "Is this doing it for me? Do I feel any need to transition fully, to live full-time as other than my birth gender?" For those who have undertaken physical transition, no one slips on names or pronouns at this point, unless it's deliberate. New friends have no idea he was ever female, unless he tells them. If he's not able to be seen as male in all situations, he has come to terms with this and it doesn't bother him: "It's other people's problem if they have a problem with who I am." He has reached a point where he has some long-term friends who never knew him as female. He may have more people in his life who never knew him as female than who experienced transition with him.

Pivotal questions: "How does he know when he's done? What does 'done' mean? Existential questions arise about how much physical intervention is necessary now that the social gender role is achieved to his satisfaction (or at least tolerance, if he can't always be seen male). What do I do now that I've achieved this lifelong goal? What other issues would I like to work on in therapy? How do I set new goals now that I've achieved the one goal that took so much of my energy for so long?"

❖ *Now what?:* The issues at this stage are similar for all who transition, whether physically or not. She is many years into transition now and her previous life is a vague memory, rarely revisited.

Pivotal questions: "What do I do with the heightened awareness and unique knowledge I possess? Do I mentor? What do I have to offer others, either trans or cisgender, because of my unique life journey? Is it okay if I choose to be private and not make myself available to others? If I do want to give something back to others coming along behind me, can I do that and maintain my privacy?"

TRANSITIONAL STAGES AND THERAPEUTIC ISSUES

One thing to note about the above stages is the number of pivotal questions associated with each stage. I have found that the more questions associated with a given stage, the more stressful that stage seems to be for clients to navigate as they proceed on their journey; this is particularly true when the pivotal questions are social in nature and not solely matters of private contemplation.

For those who transition physically, *Learning the boundaries* is often the rockiest time in terms of intrapsychic processes. In terms of social processes, *Early transition* is often one of the most difficult. The notion of a binary gender system is deeply ingrained in U.S.

culture; many people get very testy when they can't pigeonhole someone's gender. It's nearly impossible for most people from the United States to get beyond gender if they can't assign someone 'male' or 'female' without question. As a result the first few months on hormones are often very stressful for those in transition if they are not treated well by people they interact with, or if they are unsure how they are being seen by others.

This early transition difficulty can be exacerbated for some clients if they have partners or other close family who aren't supportive of the process. Denise, for instance, wanted to explore living full-time as a woman. However, her wife stated, "It disgusts me to think of you as a woman. I'm not ready to see it." Denise was already uncertain whether she would be accepted by strangers and was set back in her process of self-acceptance by the lack of support she encountered at home. Though she was prepared to take her tran-sition at a slow pace, to allow her wife time to catch up to her, it was difficult for her to hold onto acceptance of her own identity in the face of her wife's blunt statement.

Most of my clients made their first appointment with me having already moved through the first few stages on their own, or with other therapists. Their work with me began after they had reached the **Epiphany** stage; often, fear or anxiety induced by the epiphany propelled them into therapy. Some had begun their physical transition without seeing a therapist, later realizing it was more difficult than they'd expected. Such clients began working with me at the **Early Transition** stage.

A few clients saw me during the **Confusion** or **Pre-Decision** stage, though this was less common in my practice than it would be for other therapists. I was well-known in my community as a trans therapist. A client who had yet to recognize their issues were related to gender would not have sought me out. If their denial was working effectively, they would find all kinds of reasons *not* to see a trans therapist!

A number of my clients were at the ***Point of invisibility*** or ***Done?*** stages by the time they made their first appointment with me and were cycling back into therapy to work on issues of invisibility, reintegrating into their families, or developing new relationships. Most had worked with other therapists at earlier stages of their transition and had either relocated since beginning transition, or did not feel their previous therapist would be as beneficial to them for what they thought of as post-transition issues.

Some had tried to access their pre-transition therapist, only to find the therapist continued to try to address their transition, when the client was viewing it as history and no longer the front-and-center issue it had once been in their lives. Several clients called me after having worked with other therapists early in their transition. To the clients' consternation, their *therapist* considered them done once they achieved a gender expression that made them invisible, not recognizing the invisibility itself as a therapeutic issue. Ann told me in our first session, "I made an appointment to see my transition therapist, and when I got there she congratulated me on how good I looked. I hadn't seen her in a few months, and it seemed clear to me she thought this was a wrapping up and goodbye and good luck session. How could I then tell her I was afraid to leave the house? I felt like I'd be disappointing her." *(Client session, 2010)*

Many clients cycled back into therapy at the point where they were on the cusp of entering a new stage in their transition process, and were feeling some anxiety. For example, Joanne's transition was going so smoothly she was suspicious. "I should be encoun-tering more resistance, or something, this seems too easy!" she told me. She had told all her friends and family, and received support. She was pleased with her appearance and voice. She had a new nametag at work and no difficulty with co-workers adjusting. She was at peace and stopped coming in for regular sessions.

A few months later she changed jobs and found herself at a new stage of her transition. She had reached a place of invisibility and was having difficulty coming to terms with the paradox of choice: "Yes,

I love living female and at the same time, I'm not completely comfortable allowing people to assume I've had a fully female life like cisgender women." *(Client session, 2008)* She cycled back into therapy for a time, to process through her motivations and the various choices available to her.

THE PARADOX OF LONG-AGO TRANSITION

I worked with a handful of clients who transitioned in the 1960s or 70s. Interestingly, their therapeutic issues were identical: learning how to come out late in life. They had no practice coming out to others. These are people who transitioned at a time when transition meant: take hormones and have surgery, move elsewhere if pos-sible, perhaps acquire a new profession, and never tell anyone. Ne-ver look back, never seek out other trans people. Become 'just a man' or 'just a woman.' End of story.

For many years they were content. They were outliers on the gender-comfort spectrum, had always known they needed to transition, and had done so in their late teens. For their generation, late teens was the earliest possible opportunity. Had they been born in the late 1990s or after the turn of the century, they would have desired to transition socially in kindergarten and physically at the inception of puberty.

These are people who never felt they were part of queer community. They had no idea of the emergence of trans identity, trans resources, support groups, etc. What propelled them into therapy was seeing some mainstream reference to trans identity – an Oprah episode, or something on the Discovery channel – and reali-zing, "Oh my God, these are my people." After this experience they had undergone a gradual shift from feeling fine with their level of privacy to feeling they were stifled in the closet.

Joseph had established himself in a social service professsion. He was well-respected in his community, having always been civic-minded and involved in local issues. He had been married for over 25 years, and had adopted his wife Denise's two children (John and

Valerie) by a previous marriage when the children were 2 and 5 years old. The children knew Joseph wasn't their biological father, but had no idea he had once transitioned.

Joseph began his physical transition in 1970, at age 18. At that time, transition processes were often covered by insurance companies; Joseph had chest surgery and phalloplasty (with a completely successful outcome) as a matter of course, fully covered by insurance.[11] This was the expected path of transition in 1970 and Joseph followed it without a second thought or any regrets.

For many years Joseph was quite happy and rarely thought of his transition. In 2006 he saw a television show about a trans individual and was taken aback to hear about transition in a mainstream forum. He started doing some Internet research and quickly found that transition had become easier in some ways: defining one's own identity, finding resources for mental health and medical issues, good support on the Internet, etc.

But he also found that some things were more difficult: little or no insurance coverage, and a more conservative social climate than that of the early 1970s. Joseph transitioned during a time of social acceptance of sexuality and self-exploration. While he feels many older people of that era were conservative in their conceptualization of sex and gender, Joseph also remembers the 1970s as a time in which younger people were open-minded and supportive.

Joseph found himself thinking about his transition more than he had in years. Being in social services, he couldn't help but question his remaining private about his identity, as it went against the grain for him to not help out. His privacy began to feel stunting and he felt oppressed. He began drinking more than was good for him (his words), as did his wife Denise. Their glass of wine with dinner turned into more than one as they processed through what they were feeling.

---

[11] It is beyond the scope of this book to discuss when and how insurance companies joined ranks to deny coverage of transition processes. Suffice to say, the process began in the early 1980s as the country swung to the right socially during the Reagan administration. Trans people had no voice in the public discourse to counter the denial of coverage.

Joseph eventually concluded he needed to come out, to give something back, in keeping with his generous civic-minded nature. However, he also realized he had a host of issues akin to those faced by the pre-transition individual, from a very different perspective. As the pre-transition person questions, "How will my workplace respond to my transition," Joseph had to ask, "How will my workplace and my clients respond knowing I was once female and that they are just now finding this out?" As the pre-transition parent has to ask, "How will my children respond to my transition," Joseph had to ask, "How do I tell my adult children I was raised female?"

Behind each of Joseph's questions was the underlying thought, "People are going to feel I've betrayed them by my previous silence." Yet Joseph felt compelled to come out, now that he had become aware he could make a difference. The reason he entered his profession – to spend his life in service to others – meant he could not turn his back when he learned he could be of service to his own people.

Joseph took his time with this coming out process, first coming out to those above him professionally, seeking their advice. He had no experience with coming out, no experience of having friends who know of his transition. His family had been completely supportive of his transition, having recognized how male he was from the time he was a toddler. Over 40 years into transition, his early years were a distant memory for all concerned.

Within his family, he first came out to John and Valerie, now 27 and 30. They were stunned at first, but came to understand his previous silence. The revelation had less impact on them than his disclosure during their childhood that he was not their biological father. Had he not told them that earlier in their lives, it is likely the fact of their adoption would be more relevant to them than Joseph having been assigned female at birth.

It is also likely that were John or Valerie very conservative, they would have had difficulty with his revelation. Joseph and Denise raised their children to believe in a progressive value system. The values of accepting people for who they are and respecting various forms of identity sustained the family relationships as Valerie and John processed through what Joseph's transition meant to them.

Denise was supportive of Joseph's process, though she recognized his coming out had meaning for her as well and that there would be questions asked of her: "Does this mean you're some kind of lesbian? Did you know when you married him?" Her most difficult process was with her conservative parents, who had never known of Joseph's transition. She had a strained relationship with them at the best of times and often felt at odds with them, given her progressive worldview. She knew from various conversations about world events that they had no respect for trans identity, holding the view that birth gender assignment trumps all. Unfortunately she was right in her prediction that this revelation would spell the end of her relationship with her parents. They felt blindsided and betrayed (her mother's words) by the news, having known Joseph for over 25 years.

Joseph lost his job over his announcement of his trans identity and eventually switched careers. He and Denise moved to another city, not to maintain privacy but because Joseph had a job offer. They are open about their identities now and bless the day they made the decision to come out. Joseph feels a new level of peace.

Not everyone who transitioned long ago will reach the same conclusion about coming out that Joseph and Denise did. For some it will be enough to make anonymous donations to various trans organizations. Others are binary in their views of gender; they will not support or understand non-binary identities, or organizations that recognize such identities as legitimate. Regardless of their personal conclusions, as trans identity is increasingly in the lime-light in U.S. culture, those who transitioned long ago will find themselves facing the same crossroads Joseph and Denise have.

I ran into Joseph and Denise socially in 2017. Interestingly, Joseph's process has paralleled that of many who transition now. He feels rather 'done' with his activist stage of coming out and being of service and now, like many in mid-transition, would like to be more private again about his identity.

WORKING WITH THE UNMOTIVATED

It was interesting to note the differences in clients who felt good about the therapeutic care they received early in their process as opposed to those who did not have good therapeutic experiences, or had been transitioning without a therapist at all. Those who did not have good experiences with therapists early in their transition process were often more wary, sometimes even hostile, toward me in their first session. Most were only coming in because a partner had given them an ultimatum: "Seek therapy or I will end this relationship." A few came to see me after some years on hormones (obtained via the Internet) because they had saved the money for surgery and were seeking a referral letter to give their surgeon.

What I observed is that such clients had the same level of motivation to see me as someone coming in for a court-mandated reason: none at all. They tended to come in expecting me to diag-nose them, or to have a kind of professional distance that put them in the position of being disordered or sick in some way. Their early experiences were with therapists using a medical-model approach to transition, or an approach that invalidated trans identity and pur-ported to 'cure' them.

Sometimes I felt in the position of doing triage with clients who had been more wounded by previous therapists than if they'd avoided the therapy profession altogether.[12] Clients who had bad experiences with previous therapists usually came to see me only because they knew I'm trans, though often they still didn't fully trust me until we met. Some had developed a negative, narrow belief about what 'therapy' means and it took time for them to shift this belief.

Differing personality styles and patterns of behavior also play out. The client who wants to be completely independent and not rely on

---

[12] If a person has to choose between this kind of therapeutic experience or going through transition with the support of a few friends and no therapy at all – go with the friends.

anyone for anything is also the type to want to do transition alone. Therapy with such a client involves first 'unpacking' their need to do everything alone. It was my experience that clients who sought help with their decision-making process early in transition generally had somewhat easier access to their own emotional process and were not as guarded about sharing that process with me. They had no intention of going it alone, recognizing through their confusion that they were experiencing an existential upheaval that has few parallels in human experience.

Uninvited here comes pain, creeping around again.

But I know it's a passing thing, I have paid my misery dues.

And the news I have to offer is that we don't have to suffer.

We were born to rise and shine.

(And this message to you has been brought by the heart.)

Worlds of wisdom come and flown, leaving me all alone.

But the wings that will take me home

are those that have brushed the heart.

—Meg Christian, from the song *From the Heart,*
recorded on the album *Turning it Over* (©Olivia Records, 1981)
Quoted by permission

• Part Two •

Transformation
and Resocialization

I'm afraid of my freedom,
but my running days are done.
So I start to sit still in my moments,
sitting through changes, sitting through pain.
Look in the mirror and finding a friend.

—Meg Christian, from the song *Turning it Over,*
recorded on the album *Turning it Over*
(©Olivia Records, 1981)
Quoted by permission

• Chapter 6 •

PRE-PHYSICAL-TRANSITION PROCESSES

THOUGHTS ON THE STANDARDS OF CARE

I JOINED WPATH (World Professional Association for Transgender Healthcare) in 2001, shortly after receiving my master's degree. I had mixed feelings about any professional organization focused on trans identity. Having written my master's thesis on the transition process, I had done enough research into the history of transition in this country to have a profound respect for those professionals who took a public stand (often unpopular) on behalf of helping people transition physically. However as someone who has undergone physical transition I had also come to realize how poorly the medical model fits the process, the model that has historically been the paradigm underlying the Standards of Care (SOC), which are produced by WPATH.

The SOC were developed to help shepherd trans people safely through this profoundly life-transforming process, as well as to protect doctors and surgeons. The Standards provide recommendations about therapeutic processes, as well as guidelines for sur-geons and other medical practitioners. Previous iterations of the SOC presented a more linear path of transition than the current (2011) version. There is more recognition now of various forms of trans identity and that the path of transition is unique to every individual. Gone, too, is the necessity for a diagnosis of gender identity disorder in hormone and/or surgery referral letters. The most recent DSM version has replaced Gender Identity Disorder with Gender Dysphoria; the WPATH SOC updates preceded this change, bringing the two closer in alignment.

Previous versions of the SOC required two referral letters to obtain trans-related surgery below the belt; one letter had to be from a doctoral-level practitioner (psychologist or psychiatrist). Though the current SOC still require two letters, the requirement now is that both be written by qualified mental health professionals. Neither has to have a doctoral level degree; the level of education is not as important as knowledge of trans issues. (World Professional Association for Transgender Health 2011)

AN SOC FOR RAISING CHILDREN

In 1996 I wrote an article for a local queer newspaper in which I said that I thought transition was the most difficult, life-changing process a person could undertake willingly in life. A friend of mine read this article, and commented that she thought the decision to become a parent rivaled transition as a difficult, life-changing event. (She has two daughters, both now young adults)

I can't disagree because I'm not a parent.[13] On the other hand my friend has never desired to transition. We agree that neither of us can claim to know which is the more difficult or life-changing process as neither of us has undergone both. We each said that if the wording were changed to read: "the most difficult, life-changing process I've undergone," we would absolutely agree.

The reason for my misgivings about earlier versions of the SOC became clear to me after this conversation with my friend. To continue the analogy between having a child and transition, con-sider what it would mean to have a 'Standard of Care' for the pro-cess of having children. It's easy to imagine what the steps might look like:

❖ *The pre-decision phase,* in which the prospective parent(s) are required to undergo therapy to learn more about themselves, what residual childhood issues they may need to resolve in order to short-

---

[13] My apologies to my 25-year-old stepdaughter! However, she came into my life at the age of 15, a scenario quite different from the process of bearing a child biologically or raising an adopted child from infancy.

circuit some of the more destructive family patterns they learned from their own parents. In addition, prospective parents might be required to take classes in human development, to learn how babies and children develop into functioning adults. There might be some requirement that prospective parents volunteer at local daycare centers, to interact with babies so they might learn whether they have the patience, desire, and temperament to raise a child.

❖ *The action phase,* in which the prospective parent(s) have decided to adopt or become pregnant, and now begin the process. Adoption papers are filled out, or pregnancy ensues. At this point, the therapy would shift to support around existential fears of having made the right decision. If pregnancy is the mechanism, the person carrying the child might need counseling because of hormone fluctuations they will experience. (Because there have been a number of transmen who have carried babies to term after beginning physical transition, it's wise not to gender the pregnancy process) Group therapy might be the most logical setting at this point, to allow parents-to-be to compare their experiences and find they are not alone.

❖ *Welcoming the child* would be the next phase. The parent(s) would come home from the hospital or adoption agency with this new life in their arms. And then – all they have to do is raise the child to adulthood.

Is it logical to assume that this would mark the end of a 'stan-dard of care' for the process of having a child? That the parent(s) would be told, "Okay, you've received all the support you need. Now you have your child, everything is grand, have a great life"? Yet this is precisely how the SOC used to work around transition from one sex to another. The current SOC still pay far less attention to those issues that arise after surgery decisions have been made. If considered from a developmental perspective, this seems illogical. If one undergoes a life-transforming process, how can that process ever have an "end" as long as the person is still alive?

Further, surgical techniques (particularly for those assigned female at birth) do not allow the person more than an approximation of their intended gender when it comes to bodily sex. Even a transwoman who attains perfect surgical results and the ability to be seen as female in all situations may be obliged to tell partners why it is she never experiences a menstrual cycle, why it is she can never become pregnant, etc. The need to disclose to partners (and medical practitioners) keeps the individual's trans status on the radar for years after they would like to be able to consider themselves done.

Previous versions of the SOC contained two sentences addressing post-transition therapy, suggesting it might be a good idea to check in once in awhile. It may be a good long while before the paradigm shift underlying the 2011 version of the SOC takes hold, allowing for greater understanding of the need for continued support throughout the various stages of transition (see Chapter 5, *Stages of Transition,* for a further discussion of transition stages). The former medical-model focus of previous versions of the SOC makes all the more striking how WPATH presented this newest version:

"'The latest 2011 revisions [the seventh revision since its original 1979 publication] to the SOC realize that transgender, transsexual, and gender nonconforming people have unique health care needs to promote their overall health and well-being, and that those needs extend beyond hormonal treatment and surgical intervention,' said SOC Committee Chair, Eli Coleman, PhD, Professor and Director at Program in Human Sexuality, University of Minnesota.

"'The previous versions of the SOC were always perceived to be about the things that a trans person must do to satisfy clinicians, this version is much more clearly about every aspect of what clinicians ought to do in order to properly serve their clients. That is a truly radical reversal . . . one that serves both parties very well,' said Christine Burns, SOC International Advisory Committee Member.

"More than any other version, the 2011 SOC also recognize that gender nonconformity in and of itself is not a disorder and that many people live comfortable lives without having to seek therapy or medical interventions for gender confusion or unhappiness. This version provides more detailed clinical guidelines to address the health care needs of children, adolescents, and adults with gender dysphoria who need assistance with psychological, hormonal, or surgical care.

"In addition to clearly articulating the collaborative relationship needed between transsexual, transgender, and gender noncon-forming individuals and health care providers, the current SOC provide for new ways of thinking about cultural relativity and culture competence. The document includes a call to advocacy for professionals to promote public policies and legal reforms that promote tolerance and equity for gender and sexual diversity. This document recognizes that well-being is not obtained through quality health care alone but a social climate that eliminates of prejudice, discrimination, and stigma and promotes a positive and tolerant society that embraces sexual and gender diversity." *(WPATH press release, 2011)*

THERAPY DURING PHYSICAL TRANSITION

In considering physical transition as a long-term process, I am reminded of one of the most fundamental differences between Freud's stages of development and those of Erikson. Freud's stages stopped at the end of adolescence, as if adults don't develop once they are done with puberty. Erikson recognized that people never stop developing and that there are different stages of adulthood as there are different stages of childhood. (Erikson, 1980)

By focusing more on the social nature of transition than used to be the case, the current SOC imply (though don't spell out) that therapy can continue to be useful to trans people throughout their lives, though the issues change over time: coming out to people who never found out, boundaries around disclosure, dealing with people's varying reactions over time, dealing with frustrations and disappointments, sexuality, dealing with living a new gender role, dealing with feelings of 'now what?' The list goes on and on.

None of these issues can be dealt with completely prior to beginning physical transition, just as a child cannot deal with the life stage issues that adults face. Though disclosure can (and often does) begin prior to starting physical transition, most of my clients found that family and friends go through yet another process of acceptance once the physical realities of transition are apparent.

Ralph, 24 at the time he began taking hormones, was irritated with his immediate family: "You'd think I'd never told them any-thing at all! I put together this great packet of information, told them six months in advance, and they had already gone through that 'Ohmygod' stage, and then they went through it all over again when I visited and they heard my man voice." *(Client session, 2009)*

I helped him see that his family had to go through their own transition; all they could picture before his visit was Ralph as they had always known him, with a new name and a different pronoun. The fact of facial hair and a deep voice made them feel all the more keenly that they were losing 'Roberta,' rekindling their grief and loss process.

However Ralph was my client, not his family. My primary goal in his therapy at that point was to help normalize his family's process, to help him understand they had their own transition process to go through and that it wasn't his responsibility to go through it with (or for) them. I gave him PFLAG[14] (Parents, Families and Friends of Lesbians and Gays) information to pass along to his parents. He told me later that PFLAG helped his parents a great deal and they now

---

[14] PFLAG used to stand for Parents, Families and Friends of Lesbians and Gays. In 2015, the national organization changed the name to PFLAG, no longer an acronym but the actual name of the organization. This change reflects the fact that PFLAG serves friends and family members of a long and now-unwieldy acronym: LGBTQQIAA. Rather than trying to find a fully inclusive name, the acronym has *become* the name. As a nearly-40-year-old organization, there are few within the acronym who haven't heard of PFLAG, whether they could accurately state what the acronym stood for or not. But they could accurately state, "PFLAG is where my family and I can find support."

fully accepted his transition; some months later, they made him a birthday cake to celebrate the anniversary of his beginning hormones.

Though not stated in the SOC, it has been my experience that the post-hormones individual may be in greater need of the therapist ally/witness than the pre-hormones individual. In addition to the interpersonal stresses of early transition, these are people who have to get to know themselves all over again as they navigate a stage 'this is your brain on hormones.'

I worked with a number of clients who began their transition without benefit of therapy at all. Some were buying hormones from friends, while others were finding their hormones via the Internet. Eventually they realized issues were arising they needed help with (all related to either the workplace or intimate/family relationships) and they sought therapy. None had felt in any particular need of a therapist prior to beginning hormones. None of these clients had changed their mind about whether or not physical transition was the right decision. Rather, they were finding it a more overwhelming journey than they'd imagined.

A useful mantra to share with clients is, "Expect change, but don't expect to know in advance what the changes will be or where they'll come from or where they'll lead." Without hearing this stated overtly, some clients feel they're doing it wrong or that they made the wrong decision, solely because they find it's a difficult, challenging process emotionally. Just because a particular path is right for a person doesn't make it easy to navigate.

Another reservation I have about the SOC has less to do with their existence than with their scope, which seems to focus on the issues that come up for a client before physical transition rather than recognizing that issues are going to come up at various stages of life both pre- and post-transition. In part, it is this focus on pre-transition issues that may lead clients to wonder if they're doing something wrong if they're still overwhelmed well into physical transition.

Regardless of these reservations, the shift from a medical model to a holistic, less-pathologizing view of trans identity is a welcome change in this seventh version of the SOC.

THE PENDULUM SWING

The current SOC have done away with specific suggestions (they never were requirements with force of law) of how long a person needs to be in therapy prior to starting hormones, or how long to live with hormones before making a surgery decision. Initially I was gratified by this change; no more cookie-cutter ap-proach. A few months after the new SOC were released, a col-league took me out for coffee and said bluntly, "I feel hung out to dry by these new standards. I've only worked with half a dozen trans clients and that's not enough to feel I can trust my clinical judgment about what's a red flag and what's a variation of normal. I know the old approach wasn't quite right, but I feel unsupported by these new standards. They're not giving me enough professional guidance!"

Over lunch recently another colleague told me, "I've been wri-ting quite a few assessments for insurance companies so they'll cover surgery. It's great this is starting to happen. But I've also received calls from people I've never met, saying, 'The new stan-dards say therapy isn't required to get surgery, but the surgeon I contacted still requires a letter. I don't need therapy. So write me a letter and mail it to me. I'll pay you.'

"I replied, 'I won't write such a letter for someone I've never even met.' This offended them, as if I was saying sight-unseen that they needed therapy. They would then demand a referral to some-one who would write a letter on that basis. And I told them, 'I don't think it's ethical to write a letter on demand like that, without even meeting the person, so if I knew of a therapist who would do that, I wouldn't refer anyone to them anyway.' Then they hung up on me. This has happened half a dozen times."

The legacy of decades of gatekeeping and medical-model ap-proach is keeping some trans people from making good use of the therapy profession. Some are reading the latest SOC and inter-preting them to mean, "See, we knew it all along, we don't need therapy in order to become our true selves!"

The most-recent SOC are moving in the direction of informed consent, as it should be. To reiterate: informed means not only "I know what hormones will and won't do for me" and "I know what this particular surgery will and won't do for me" – informed means, even more importantly, "I know as best I can who I am and what's best for me in moving forward with this life-changing process."

The value of therapy isn't in the realm of information about the physical processes; that information is readily available online. The value of therapy is in the realm of facilitating self-knowledge and providing a sounding board and touchstone of calm in the face of a possible storm of social and familial upheaval. A good therapist facilitates a process of self-knowledge that will allow the client to know as certainly as possible in advance of the experience which form of transition is the right path.

The new Standards are part of a pendulum swing among trans people, toward taking control over their own processes. My hope is that eventually the pendulum will swing back a bit, allowing knowledgeable therapists to be of service to those considering some form of transition.

BEYOND THE DSM

At some point it is likely that gender identity issues will not be addressed in the DSM. If trans identity is a reflection of assigned gender not feeling true to one's self, then it has no place in a book whose purpose is to describe psychological problems. I hope that a future removal of gender identity from the DSM will soften the resistance many trans people feel toward seeking out therapy when their transition process throws them a curveball.

At that point, it would be less likely that newly-trained therapists would try to make trans identity an automatic pathology. The removal of homosexuality from the DSM[15] resulted in precisely this sort of shift, away from pathologizing sexual orientation and toward a model of helping people accept themselves, deal with homophobic attitudes within their families, etc. While there are still therapists who attempt to cure homosexuality, this is not the mainstream stan-dard within the profession nor is it considered ethical treatment. Within the mental health profession sexual orientation is now viewed as a fixed identity, not as an issue of behavior. I believe that over time, the same will be true when discussing gender identity.

Gender identity is a trickier issue to sort out than sexual orientation because there are questions on the table that involve irrever-sible medical procedures. Whether or not to pursue physical body modification is always a question that comes up in the early stages of questioning gender identity. This difference will keep trans identities tied to the medical profession, necessitating a balance between the medical model doctors subscribe to and the identity emergence model I (and many knowledgeable colleagues) use in our conceptualization of trans identities.

It is my hope that future generations of therapists will be more beneficial to trans clients than has historically been the case. This type of professional shift happened with the emergence of LGB identities from the closet, and I see no reason to believe the same will not happen as T identities emerge further into the light of day.

HORMONE REFERRAL LETTERS

Most of my clients came into my office certain that hormones were the next logical step in their journey; I usually agreed with them. Doctors familiar with transition processes are also familiar with the SOC and most will not write a hormone prescription without such a referral letter from an experienced therapist. Before writing a referral letter (see *Appendices* for a sample), I looked for several things:

---

[15] A 1973 revision of the DSM shifted the category to *ego dystonic homosexuality,* meaning "it's only a problem if the client is having difficulty adjusting to being gay." A 1987 revision removed homosexuality altogether.

❖ Had the client done their homework about the effects of hormones (both desired and undesired effects)?

❖ How much consideration had they given to trying other ways of alleviating their gender dissonance, such as crossdressing? (This question is more applicable to MTF than FTM clients, who have usually been dressing as they pleased for quite awhile)

❖ Were their expectations of the physical results realistic?

❖ Had they had some form of communication with people who are taking the type of hormone they desire? If not, why not? If so, had these conversations focused only on the desired effects or had the discussions included undesired effects, emotional changes, coming out to others, etc?

❖ Did the person believe life would be perfect post-transition?

❖ Did the person believe they could transition in the closet?

❖ If the person had difficulties with various kinds of relationships, did they believe transition was going to solve these problems automatically?

I encouraged clients to tell me their story, rather than using the above as a checklist and asking overtly. Generally, these questions were answered as the client talked and I was able to get a picture of how gender played out as a backdrop of their lives. I took this approach because I wanted to dismantle the medical model para-digm of the intake, the medical history, so often utilized by doctors and some mental health care practitioners. Given my identity development approach, avoiding the medical model from the outset helped me form a solid therapeutic alliance during the first session.

I believe clients should ask themselves questions along the lines of those I outlined in the chapter *Questions of a Skeptic*. Most had done this sort of soul-searching before they made their first therapy appointment, though some made their first appointment because they were too scared and confused to ask the questions, much less answer them, on their own.

Among my client base, those who started hormones described feelings of relief, peace, lifting of depression and/or anxiety. One person said, "I feel normal for the first time." No one ever said, "My life is perfect now" or "My body is exactly the way I've al-ways dreamed it could be." A person who believes life will be perfect, that hormones will solve all their problems, is not being realistic about the effect hormones will have on their lives. Begin-ning hormone therapy makes life *harder* in the short term, as the person is then faced with the task of disclosing to those who don't already know what's going on while simultaneously getting to know themselves all over again with this new hormone balance.

Those who transition physically to male have no choice about disclosure; it does not take long (a month or two, on a full dose of hormones) before the physical changes will be apparent even to the most obtuse. People will only ask, "Do you have a cold?" for so long before they realize the voice is continuing to drop below the deepest bronchitis. Hormones transform male bodies to female more slowly and subtly, allowing male-assigned people the luxury of telling others in their own time. Female-assigned people sometimes feel hijacked by their own process, testosterone acts with such speed on their bodies. Their process can be less overwhelming if they disclose to significant people in their lives before starting to take hormones.

Even if they never see other family members and friends face-to-face, keeping physical transition a permanent secret is not an option, in most cases. Unless the client is willing to risk the people in their lives finding out through a third party, they have to undertake the task of telling relatives and close friends.

There are cases in which a person has made a conscious decision to withhold the information, for example, in the case of an elderly relative or a family member with a terminal illness. However, this kind of deliberate decision-making process is quite different from believing that transition can be done in the closet. Rather than hold this over the client as a threat ("You have to tell people, it's not an option!"), I framed it as an opportunity for empowerment: "It's your transition, you have control over the language you use, the format you choose, in telling people who you really are." I helped clients realize that if they didn't take advantage of this opportunity, other people would find out eventually through the grapevine and it was likely the language used wouldn't match what the client would say.

Knowledgeable doctors in the Portland area now prescribe lower doses of hormones at the inception of physical transition, increasing the dosage gradually over a period of a few months. This slows the pace of change, allowing the client more time to disclose. While appreciating this aspect of the slowed process, many of my female-assigned clients find themselves frustrated by the lack of physical change they experience, since they know full well the testosterone will have a speedy effect on their bodies once they are on the full dose. Those assigned male at birth don't expect speedy results, so are less inclined to chafe at the initial lower doses.

Regardless of the direction of transition, hormones will have an impact on emotional and intellectual processes, causing the person to be in a state of some internal vulnerability and self-consciousness as they get to know themselves all over again, while simultaneously having to deal with other people's reactions to the news.

In the long term hormones are beneficial for those who are taking this step for the right reasons – their birth gender role is an intolerable place to live because it does not match their internal gender identity – but that does not make it easy. Emotional stability, a willingness to seek out support from others, working knowledge of the effects of hormones, and realistic expectations are key components to making the process easier and smoother than it might be otherwise. These are the kinds of things I looked for in writing a hormone referral letter.

'RUBBER-STAMPED' CLIENTS

I worked with a few clients who were 'rubber-stamped' through their transition processes by other therapists; these clients were fragile emotionally and had difficulty navigating interpersonal relationships on the most superficial levels. Danielle (22) regretted in hindsight that she had begun hormones as quickly as she did, with no preparation for the psychoemotional ramifications. Her former therapist had focused on gender expression and was con-fident of Danielle's outcome because she was beautiful as a woman.

Danielle moved to Portland three years after she had begun taking hormones and called me for an appointment shortly after her move. It was clear she had significant issues related to a difficult family of origin, issues best addressed prior to beginning such a stressful process as transition. Throughout her childhood her father had been extremely judgmental and critical of Danielle for 'not doing male right.' She never told him she was trans until she was well along in the process of physical transformation and living over 2,000 miles away. To this day he continues to call her by her birth name and male pronouns. He completely dominates the rest of Danielle's family, and they are afraid to support Danielle by using her new name and female pronouns.

At the time she came to see me, Danielle was still far too emo-tionally tied to her family of origin; her father's reaction dominated her psyche. She had not let go of her need for her father's approval sufficiently to be able to have a happy outcome from transition: I would have focused on this prior to her transition, had she been my client at the time.

She had believed her emotional problems would be solved by taking hormones, that they would magically make her able to feel whole and sufficient unto herself, without needing her father's ap-proval any longer. When this didn't happen, she continued on the path, certain that every subsequent surgical procedure would make the difference. It didn't work out that way. Once Danielle reached the end of the list of surgeries available (she was well-paid within the high-tech sector, thus could afford what she needed), she finally realized she'd been approaching the whole issue in the wrong way. She came close to suicide at that point, but instead chose to call me.

Danielle had no doubts about her gender. She loved living fe-male and enjoyed the various effects of her new hormone balance.

Nevertheless she found the process of renegotiating boundaries nearly intolerable. Where she had rigid boundaries before, now she had impermeable walls and wasn't happy at all in her transition process. Danielle used the term 'rubber-stamped' to describe her own early transition process, feeling she had been given the green light because, paraphrasing her words:

❖ She knew what to say to convince her therapist that she was trans based on the DSM IV description of GID, which she had read prior to her first appointment;

❖ Her therapist placed undue emphasis on the fact that Danielle could be seen female easily as the main criteria for transition;

❖ Her therapist had not done work around Danielle's emotional fragility because Danielle had lied to her, telling her she had support from her family of origin. Danielle rationalized this by telling herself it was true, she does have the support of her siblings, and a lukewarm kind of support from her mother. What she hid from her therapist is that the reaction that always had the most impact on her psychoemotional self was that of her father, who was hostile toward her transition. No one else's acceptance mattered to her.

I worked with Danielle to help her further the process of differentiating from her family of origin (therapist's terminology for growing up and becoming one's own person in the world). Any trans person will be hurt if their family can't accept them, but most are not held back in their own process by such lack of support. They move on. Danielle was still so emotionally entwined with her birth family, she felt unable to be a whole person, complete in herself, without her father's support and approval.

These kinds of issues should be addressed prior to beginning transition or the process has little chance of significantly helping the client in life and can make them feel worse. This is not a judgment based on gender identity, but on ego strength and the psychological ability to weather transition. Some family issues can get in the way of transition and make it more difficult. Framing the issue in this way empowers the client to take control of their transition, making it clear that consciously determining the order of events (family issues first, or transition?) is in their best interest.

Danielle had lied to her former therapist, so how could that therapist know she had such issues? Part of the problem here is her first therapist's emphasis on Danielle's physical appearance – how well would she be able to physically express 'woman'?

Rather than putting the focus on gender expression, I helped clients open up about their family of origin, to determine how much influence the family structure had on the client's ego strength and ability to withstand the pressures of transition. I was forming a genogram in the back of my mind as I heard their stories. (See *Appendices* for a sample genogram) Genograms are family trees, diagrams with added information about family patterns: which family members form automatic alliances, which people are es-tranged from each other, which relationships are enmeshed (un-healthily close, with poor personal boundaries), etc. (McGoldrick, 2008)

If I heard elements of enmeshment, estrangement, conflict – various terms used in the structure of a genogram – I might have the client create a genogram in session, to make overt the patterns of their family of origin. Making such patterns overt is one way to help clients come to see their parents as human beings, and to see that relationship patterns carry over through generations.

This process helps clients see that difficult family patterns (a) aren't their fault, and (b) can be changed as they move forward with future relationships. Most importantly, making the patterns overt can help begin the process of changing the client's relationship with themselves and who they can be to others, which can only help facilitate transition.

My work with Danielle included helping her create a genogram. Seeing her father's complete dominance of her family on paper helped her externalize the power dynamics and absolve herself from blame for his disappointment in her. She was also able to see how he might have developed that way, based on his own family of ori-gin and place in his family system as he was growing up.

Had she been my client prior to her transition, we would have done this level of work before she began taking hormones. I worked with several clients who desired to begin taking hormones imme-diately when they first came to see me, but then postponed that step when it became clear to them that they needed to work through various family of origin issues first. I always told them, "I'll write you a hormone letter when you feel ready for one. This isn't about withholding your letter. This is a collaboration." In putting it that way, I let them know my clinical judgment was about their readi-ness to undertake such a stressful process, not about their gender identity at all. Again, it's all about process – the content is the cli-ent's to determine.

It may seem odd that someone as intelligent as Danielle wouldn't see the power dynamics at play all along and be able to transcend them on her own. However, the dynamics of our family of origin aren't dynamics to us as we're growing up – they are normal. Our first example of relationship is within our own family. If we grow up with loving parents who love each other, we internalize the belief that this is normal. If we grow up with a fractured family with no trust in each other, we learn this is normal. Our early experiences of 'normal' color our future relationships; if we want to change how we experience relationship, the first step is to lay out our original family dynamics for examination in a dispassionate manner.

During our last session Danielle said, "Eventually I'm going to reach out to him and try to establish a relationship. But not yet. I can see the day will come when I will do it. And if he tries to box me back into that straitjacket, I'll tell him, 'If we're going to have a relationship, it's not going to be that. Your choice. The ball's in your court, you have my email address and phone number.' And I'll turn my back if need be."

I saw Danielle for a few sessions a year later when things came to a head in her family. She did cut ties with her father, and though sad about the outcome she was also moving on with her life, happy in a new relationship and at peace with herself. One of her sisters had been emboldened by Danielle's example of self-empowerment. She had also broken free of the family dynamic and re-established contact with Danielle. They now have a close relationship.

Our society is structured such that parents have complete control over their children's lives. The power imbalance in the nuclear family is so extreme, it is virtually impossible for children to grow up without some degree of resentment for their childhood experi-ences. Most people are (eventually) able to look back on their child-hood with some empathy for their parents, especially if they become parents themselves. At this point they can understand their parents are human, and were (hopefully) doing the best they could with the information available to them at the time. Or they are able to recognize that their parents' flaws had nothing to do with their children.

These kinds of processes are part of growing up. When clients are not far enough along in this maturation process, this should be the therapeutic focus, prior to beginning transition. Outcomes like Danielle's are far too likely otherwise.

HORMONE DECISIONS

The most major decision faced by those who question their gender identity is, "Should I take hormones or not?" This is an unfair question, as the only way to know the answer with certainty is to try it. I worked with a few clients who had reached a point of spinning their wheels, therapy having taken them as far in their self-exploration as they can go. They had weighed (and reweighed several times) their decision, considering all the ramifications and options, and still weren't entirely sure. They had reached a point of obsession, unable to focus on anything else in life until they came to some resolution.

I encouraged such clients to do controlled experimentation with hormones, with the caveat that they do so when they had sufficient space in their lives to be able to check in with their own emotional process. The point of the experiment was to provide more data in the attempt to answer the question, "Are hormones right for me?"

As part of the experiment, I encouraged journaling, making art, talking with friends, talking with me, talking with other trans people, finding mentors. Journey inward, through the journaling and artwork, and journey outward, through interactions with others. The journey inward helps the person center into their emotions while un-der the influence of a different hormone balance: 'This is your brain on testosterone' (or estrogen, as the case may be). The journey out-ward helps the person center into how it feels to interact with others while experiencing a new hormone balance.

Partners, close friends and family members often feel that peo-ple in early transition become self-centered. Self-centeredness is a necessary attitude, as the transitioning individual tracks their reac-tions to the hormones. I encouraged my clients to view this time as one of experimentation, not as an irreversible step. Hormones are not a flip of the switch process, causing immediate changes. Most have been certain hormones are right for them before they make their first appointment with me and this experimentation does no-thing to change their minds. Others have never been sure. They never will be, unless they give it a try.

Some people distrust the early weeks on hormones, believing this leads to feelings of gender euphoria that might not be real over the long term. While the gender euphoria stage is quite real, it does pass. Those who have realistic expectations of transition are not surprised when the euphoria passes and they are still faced with the need to get up every morning and go about their day.

I tried to help my clients distinguish between the euphoria of finally taking a step toward self-actualization and their actual feel-ings with a new hormone balance. I asked people not to look at the big events in their lives, but at the small, everyday interactions they have with others as they move through the world. Our lives are comprised of very few big events, but many small ones. I encouraged my clients to be especially self-aware and present in each moment as they conduct the business of life.

Trans people describe their experience of hormones in various ways: "I feel normal now." "I feel peaceful in myself." "I feel less angry and irritable." Those who take estrogen often attribute their lower anger levels to the fact that they are also blocking testos-terone. However I feel there is more to it than that. Many of my clients who transitioned to male use similar language to describe their experience of testosterone, feeling less anger and frustration with life in general. In this instance perhaps testosterone is getting a bad rap. The experience of the right hormone balance after a life-time of feeling 'not right' seems to lead to less anger and frustration and increased feelings of centeredness, regardless of which hor-mone is now dominant.

BACKING OFF TRANSITION

I normalized for my clients the life-transformative nature of transition. Several tried hormones and then stopped for a time, realizing that they were not ready to disclose to others their journey. Since physical transition can't be done secretly, these particular clients were holding off until they worked through the issues that were keeping them from disclosing their trans status or until they could order their lives in such a way that transition would be easier.

Joel first came to see me in 2006, a 27-year-old transman who had no doubt about his male identity. His mother suffered from a chronic illness and Joel was her primary caregiver. His mother was a conservative Christian and Joel was certain she would reject his transition. His sister was a lesbian and their mother would not have anything to do with her, to the point of returning cards and letters unopened, marked, "Return to Sender."

Joel began taking hormones in 2006, but stopped after a few weeks when his voice began dropping slightly. Though he felt centered and sure of his decision with his new hormone balance, he had a panic attack at the thought of disclosing his intentions to his mother. He grappled with questions: "Can I transition and remain her caregiver? If she won't allow me to remain her caregiver through transition, how can I reconcile this to myself, knowing she can't afford to hire someone really good to check in with her every few hours? Will I end up feeling forever guilty, as if I've abandoned my mother? If I don't transition, will I forever resent my mother for having held me back when she had no say in my decision-making process? She has a chronic illness, but she's only 55; she's going to live a long time still." *(Client session, 2006)*

I metaphorically held Joel's hand as he grappled with his priorities and conflicting feelings. There is no right or wrong answer in a case such as Joel's. It isn't even as easy as saying there is a right or wrong answer for Joel. *Any* decision he made would involve change, compromise and potential loss.

Joel finally told his mother in early 2007, about six months after we started working together. He first told his mother's sister Ruth, as he knew she would be supportive. His aunt was by his side when he told his mother and Ruth helped her sister understand that Joel had always been a boy, bringing forth years of memories of the two sisters discussing Joel's defiance when forced into any feminine role or clothing. "Remember when…" dominated the conversation.

Though Joel's mother went through a grief process, she also acknowledged over time that she could see how much happier Joel was with his life after he began taking testosterone. Though not how he viewed his own identity, Joel recognized his mother was happier viewing his need to transition as a birth defect that was rectified by a medical intervention. He felt guilty over this, as she still could not accept her daughter's lesbian identity.

As an example of reordering one's life: Kathy (47) got cold feet when another transwoman, three years on hormones, described feeling the hormones ran away with her and "hijacked her thought process," Kathy quoted.

Kathy decided to wait awhile. She was not ready to come out in all facets of her life. Her living situation was not amenable to a peaceful transition. It's difficult enough dealing with the world during transition; the last thing anyone needs is to come home to another difficult situation. In the case of relationship, the trade-off (potentially holding onto a good relationship) may feel worth the risk of initial discomfort at home. In the case of roommates who are unsupportive, which was Kathy's situation, there is no trade-off to make this worth the emotional stress.

Kathy spent several months looking for a living situation that met her criteria, then moved in with two older lesbians (partners, both cisgender), who lived in the country and had a small cabin for rent. Though it gave her a longer commute than she'd had before, the peace and privacy were more than enough compensation for Kathy. The women who owned the cabin were supportive of Kathy's transition, which she disclosed to them during the interview process. With her own private living space to come home to at the end of the day, Kathy felt comfortable moving forward with transition and began taking hormones shortly after her move.

Kathy lived in her cabin for the first three years of her physical transition. At that point she began to feel isolated in her country existence and craved a return to a more urban environment. She moved back into Portland and now lives in an 'artsy' neighborhood in the middle of the city, with two cisgender roommates who fully accept her. Kathy believes that because these new friends didn't go through transition with her, they didn't have to change their view of her after they met, making their acceptance of her easier.

SMOOTHING THE WAY

I encouraged clients to view physical transition as a continuation of self-exploration. Some believe the exploration is done when they feel ready to begin taking hormones: "Now I can be who I really am!" In reality, physical transition is just the beginning of another set of stages on the journey.

I view early physical transition as being similar to a vision quest, in which an individual goes off alone in order to seek spiritual enlightenment and attunement with nature. In the case of transition, the person seeks enlightenment and attunement with themselves. Vision quests are undertaken alone, ideally in nature, away from the distraction of cities and technology. Transition is made more difficult because it is undertaken while maintaining the various responsibilities of life. I sometimes used Kathy's situation as an example for other clients. She slowed down her own process until she could order her life in a way that would help make her transition smoother.

While living alone can be a wonderful way to reduce stress, it can also be helpful to have supportive roommates or a partner to come home to at the end of the day. However the person in tran-sition should be mindful that the transition is not something others will want to talk about exclusively. The transitioning person needs to focus on themselves, but others may grow tired of never talking about anything else! Finding support on via social media sites can be helpful, especially in situations where there are no face-to-face support groups available. The more sources of support a person has, the better.

Animal companions can also be extremely important at this time. Coming home to unconditional love from a creature that doesn't care about gender can be one of the greatest stress-relievers available to any trans person.

• Chapter 7 •

MEDICAL INFORMATION

PRIOR TO SEEKING ME OUT, MOST OF MY CLIENTS conducted a great deal of Internet research about the physical effects of hormones. I stressed to these clients, because most available information does not, that the psychoemotional effects are also powerful. Image-based as our culture is, most people (trans and cisgender alike) focus primarily on the effects of hormones on the physical body, which can certainly be dramatic. But more unsettling to most trans people is the effect hormones can have on intellectual and emotional processing. The following is written based on effects my clients and I noticed in undergoing this transformation.

INSURANCE COVERAGE

Until recently, most insurance plans did not cover transition procedures. On the one hand this perpetuated gender dissonance as a fact of life for many trans people. Hormones are relatively inexpensive and accessible to many trans people, though the steps to obtain a prescription (therapy, doctor visits) are financially problematic for many, and it may be difficult if not impossible to find supportive professionals locally. Surgery may feel like an impossible financial goal.

On the other hand... in 1999 I met two transmen from Belgium, who had had phalloplasty surgery provided by their national health insurance. My initial reaction was, "How wonderful! When will our country finally have national health coverage?" But upon hearing their stories I modified my opinion, realizing no system is perfect and that government or insurance company involvement has its potential drawbacks.

111

According to these two transmen, Belgian trans people were put through a rigorous screening process. One could be screened out for deviating from a narrowly-defined notion of what constitutes a transsexual. For example, a gay transman might not have been allowed to transition as quickly as a heterosexual transman – his attraction to men might be seen as residual femininity, not as a genuine sexual orientation separate from his gender identity.

The Belgians I met advised any gay American transmen considering going to Europe for surgery to take along an obliging female friend who would pretend to be their partner. They stated they'd known several gay Belgian transmen who did precisely that when applying for their own phalloplasty.

While U.S. insurance companies have usually excluded transition from coverage, this didn't affect the non-outlier trans person; if transition were a covered benefit, they might still be denied coverage for transition because they aren't participating in the gender binary. Many of my clients who fit this description were already taking hormones, and saving slowly toward whatever surgeries would make them more comfortable with their bodies. Or they wanted various forms of surgery without taking hormones at all. Paradoxically, the exclusion of transition procedures from insurance coverage has led to the availability of physical transition to those who are not outliers on the gender comfort spectrum.

In recent years, insurance companies are starting to cover transition processes. Predictably this has led backward to a medical mo-del many knowledgeable therapists had moved away from, prefer-ring an identity emergence model. A medical model approach lends itself better to the diagnostic codes that are the key to insurance reimbursement.

The bureaucracy of prior authorization is also problematic. One colleague told me, "I had a run-around with an insurance company not long ago. They wanted me to call and get authorization for every single session with trans clients. Philosophically I agree with that – it's not a cookie cutter process, and some clients need fewer sessions than others. But I'm in private practice and don't have staff who can call and sit on hold waiting for authorization. The insur-ance companies are used to dealing with clinics and hospitals, who have staff for dealing with insurance billing and such. Now I'm trying to get them to agree to authorize a minimum number of ses-sions, if this is a client who is completely new to me. It's an uphill battle." *(Private conversation, 2017)*

In Oregon our public health plan is now covering transition pro-cessses. However not all doctors participate in the Oregon Health Plan, and not all those who do know anything about transition. Nor are all doctors willing to facilitate transition in the first place. As a result there is great confusion on the part of many who access bene-fits through the Oregon Health Plan; they don't know how to access a benefit that has been granted them. Such issues will arise as other public health plans begin covering transition processes.

Despite my reservations about involving insurance companies in the process, many people would be helped immeasurably if their transition was paid for. When Joseph *(The Paradox of Long-Ago Transition)* learned that insurance companies had been excluding transition processes for decades, he told me, "I'm not sure I would have survived if insurance hadn't picked up the tab. I actually felt quite supported by the fact that this bureaucratic institution paid the bills." *(Client session, 2006)* Joseph came from a working class background and does not believe he could have transitioned physically, even to the point of chest surgery, without insurance coverage.

DOCTORS – DO NO HARM!

The need for adequate medical supervision of hormones is well illustrated by the experience of Joan, who lives in a small town far from Portland. She had a hysterectomy in the late 1990s. In 2004 a gynecologist prescribed testosterone for her rather than estrogen as a menopausal hormone replacement. While small doses of testosterone are often prescribed for cisgender women going through menopause, the dosage prescribed for Joan was two-thirds the full dose of a transman seeking physical transition.

A few months later Joan was essentially transitioned physically. She had developed a male-sounding voice and a fair amount of facial hair. Joan made an appointment to see me to talk about how to handle being perceived as a man when she never had any desire for such a change.

Joan's doctor had advised her to take estrogen initially, but she found the emotional mood swings intolerable and felt easier in her own mind using testosterone for hormone replacement. However the social result of being perceived as a man, and the toll the process has taken on her marriage, have left her bitter and angry with her doctors. She sued her original doctor; the case was settled out of court.

At this point Joan and her husband are estranged from each other, though neither has sought a divorce. At first her husband relished the increase in Joan's sex drive and the lessening of her "female emotions," as he put it. She reacted "more like a guy," as he described it, which he enjoyed very much.

Over time, however, her masculinization increased to the point that she was no longer physically attractive to him. He also experienced some social discrimination and taunting in public, as they were perceived as a gay male couple. He is a stoic man, not given to talking about his feelings with anyone, resulting in virtual silence between them. For her part, Joan has enjoyed some of the psychoemotional effects of taking testosterone as a hormone replacement, but is bitter toward her doctor, given how the results impacted her marriage.

In 1996 I met a transman (Luke) at an FTM conference in Boston. He had transitioned in the mid-1980s in small-town Indiana. He did so by finding a sympathetic doctor who wrote him a hormone prescription after hearing Luke's story. Though well-intentioned, the doctor did not do his homework to determine the proper hormone dosage to prescribe; he had Luke injecting a full dose of hormones every three days, rather than every other week.

Luke told me, "It was three years before I learned my doctor had prescribed a massive overdose of hormones. And before I learned that excess testosterone is converted to estrogen by the body. No wonder I never stopped having periods!"

This sort of error is much less likely to happen in the Internet age. My clients came into my office knowing all about hormone dosages, desired effects, possible side effects, etc. Nevertheless it should not be incumbent on the client to tell their doctor the proper hormone dosage. Some also told me stories of doctors who were well-meaning but didn't know how to find out what their role should be in facilitating transition. It might seem stories such as Joan's and Luke's belong to a pre-Internet era and would never happen today, but the information is still not as widely available as it should be.

It may be the case that insurance involvement will facilitate a push toward further education on the part of doctors. It is in the best interest of insurance companies that they be reimbursing people who know what they're doing. Otherwise they may find themselves a party in a malpractice suit such as Joan's.

EFFECTS OF HORMONES

There is no blueprint involved in changing the hormone balance of one's mind and body. It would be nice to be able to say to clients, "This is precisely what will happen to your body and brain, and when, if you switch from being testosterone-based to being estrogen-based (or vice versa)." What I've described below are the most common effects my clients reported, but there is so much individual variation, some may find their process differs particularly in the psychoemotional realm. All the reactions I describe are based on taking a full dose of hormones and will be slower if the dose is lower.

Because I was a therapist and not a doctor, I focus on the psychoemotional effects of hormones and don't go into medical detail about how and why such changes occur. Please consult a knowledgeable doctor (or doctor's website) if you'd like that level of explanation.

FTM RESPONSES TO INJECTIBLE TESTOSTERONE

❖ *A sense of well-being and self-confidence is common,* and can often be felt after the first shot or two. Some of this can be attributed to an expectancy effect and may wane over time, but test-osterone seems to facilitate a less emotional, more 'que sera, sera' world view. 'What, me worry?' is how I think of it. Coupled with the giddy sense of well-being from having begun such a major life transformation, this translates to the 'cocky teenage boy' phase of early physical transition. This can be a difficult time for those close to the person in transition; it may help to realize this is a phase.

❖ *Increased sex drive,* usually within a few weeks of beginning hormones. This may or may not be connected with attractions to specific people. It may appear as a general constant feeling of being horny, with no particular context or cause. It may feel as if sex is the only drive in existence. Over time, while the drive remains heightened, it becomes part of the package and less intrusive in everyday life. One advantage FTMs have over cisgender men is control over hormone levels. One client five years into physical transition cut his dose in half (what he calls a maintenance dose), so tired was he of being distracted by his sex drive. However this client also consulted his doctor prior to taking this step. He had had a hysterectomy, so knew there was no danger his body would revert even slightly to being estrogen-dominated. He would never get a period, for example. He said in session, "I looked on it as an experiment. If I'd started feeling irritable and anxious again, like I did before I started transition, I would have upped the dose. I found the dose that was right for me to maintain my feeling of well-being while at the same time cutting down the sex drive."

❖ *Changes in emotionality are common.* I don't say less emo-tionality, as that is not always the case. Some FTMs have reported a new inability to cry, while others find it easier to cry. While testosterone does not appear to facilitate emotionality as estrogen does, the experience of centering into oneself can facilitate access to one's true feelings. For others, overriding estrogen seems to also override their ability to physically feel their own emotions. Emotional processing will be different in some way; it is important for the person in transition to track this aspect of transition, as these changes will affect all levels of relationship and communication.

❖ *Deeper voice,* usually within 1-2 months. There is tremendous individual variation in this process; one client's voice was notice-ably deeper within a week of his first injection, while other people still have a midrange voice after six months. On average an FTM can expect his voice to reach an adult male register in about 3 months, if he's taking a full dose of hormones. Generally people will start asking, "Do you have a cold?" after about a month and the voice will continue dropping steadily thereafter until it settles.

If a client is a singer, I advised singing along with his favorite male singers once his voice has settled, in order to retrain his singing ear. Prior to beginning hormone therapy, I had been a first alto singing in mixed formation in an auditioned ensemble. To my embarrassment I could not reliably match pitch for a month or so after my voice settled into a baritone range, but a few weeks of singing along with Billy Joel helped tremendously. Some clients worry they will not be able to sing post-transition. However, if a person has a good ear for pitch and harmony before transition, that's not going to change. They will need to invest the time in retraining their ear to hear their voice as their own. While there is no guarantee a person will retain a soloist-quality voice, they will retain the knowledge they had about vocal production. If singing is central to their lives they might want to invest in voice lessons, to learn how to control their male voice, where the breaks are, and how to smooth over them. I now sing baritone in an auditioned men's chorus.

❖ ***Cessation of menstrual cycle*** is usually complete after 1-2 months. This will depend on where a person is in their cycle when they begin taking hormones. In general, a transman who begins taking hormones at the full dose can expect to have one full period and possibly another spotty period after starting hormones. Beyond that, periods cease altogether as long as the person continues on a full dose of hormones. If they are pre-menopausal and do not have a hysterectomy, periods will resume if they stop taking hormones, though over time the estrogen-producing organs will atrophy and become non-functional. It may be counterintuitive that a transman could become pregnant as a result of unprotected sex with a cisgender male, but it has happened. Unless such a pregnancy is desired, transmen having sex with cisgender men need to take such possibilities into account, especially if they are not taking testosterone regularly, are not on a full dose, etc. Condoms are useful beyond preventing STDs (sexually-transmitted diseases).

❖ ***Body and facial hair growth*** depend a great deal on genetics and ethnicity. I advised clients to look to the cisgender men they are biologically related to for a clue about how much hair they can expect to grow (or lose). Characteristics such as male pattern baldness are sex-influenced, meaning they are genetic traits that are triggered by testosterone levels. A number of my clients lost their hair post-transition, because baldness runs in their families. They were not bald while they were still female, as they did not have sufficient testosterone in their systems to switch on the necessary gene. In general, body and facial hair growth will begin to be noticeable after a few months, and will continue to spread and grow thicker over the course of one's lifetime. (Note: This is true of cisgender men as well)

❖ ***Clitoral growth*** also varies widely. An FTM can expect to attain an average size of about 2 inches when erect. Clitoral growth makes much more apparent the relationship between penis and clitoris; they are the same type of tissue, both capable of erection and tremendous orgasmic sensation. Several clients have told me that once they had a metoidioplasty procedure (see *Available Surgeries* for details about the procedure) they were capable of in-tercourse that was pleasurable to their partners as well as them-selves. These clients were partnered with cisgender women. I have not heard feedback from anyone attempting anal sex (as the partner doing the penetration) after a metoidioplasty.

❖ *Muscle development and masculinization* are ongoing processes, as is the case for cisgender men throughout the course of their lives. Testosterone facilitates muscle development, and my clients generally found the nature of their workouts changed to focus more on strength-building as their capacity is greatly increased in this area. One common effect of taking testosterone is a heightened sense of well-being after a workout, beyond what the same person experienced prior to transition. While workouts can help boost anyone's endorphin levels, it would seem there is something in testosterone that heightens the sense of well-being achieved by physical activity.

❖ *Skin thickening and toughening* is a gradual response many FTMs notice when giving themselves their hormone injection. Over time it becomes more difficult (though not necessarily more painful) to penetrate the skin with the needle. Some FTMs switch to a thinner needle, which penetrates the skin more easily. However it takes longer for the testosterone to pass through the thinner needle into the body, thus the injection takes longer. For those who have difficulty giving themselves an injection, this trade-off may not be optimal. Some eventually decide injections have become too difficult and switch to a sublingual tablet form of testosterone, placed under the tongue every day and allowed to dissolve gradually. While this form of testosterone may be covered by insurance, it costs more than the injectible version; the out-of-pocket cost will probably be higher than for the injectible.

❖ **Fat redistribution** causes body fat to migrate from the hips/thighs to the gut. While the FTM may be able to wear the same clothes, he will notice his pants fit differently, with more room in the seat and less around the middle.

❖ **Facial masculinization** is a very gradual process. Some clients are disappointed because they can't see any day-to-day changes. Those who take regular photos (every month or so) are amazed to look back at a series of pictures taken over time, realizing how much their appearance has changed. Those who wear glasses notice the changes, whether they take photos or not, as they will find their glasses may not fit right over time. They will probably need a wider frame to fit their face, as they will notice their old glasses are indenting the skin at their temples.

The above effects are desirable to most FTMs. However there are also potential adverse reactions, some of which can be serious. Unfortunately, some FTMs are not in a position to access good medical care and may transition on their own due to life circumstances. There are a number of websites with accurate medical information and advice about how to help prevent adverse reactions before they occur. There are also regional and local websites that can aid in finding a knowledgeable doctor. It may also be possible to find a doctor who would like to be of service; an excellent resource for the doctor is *Medical Therapy and Health Maintenance for Transgender Men: A Guide For Health Care Providers* (R. Nick Gorton MD, Jamie Buth MD, and Dean Spade Esq). Potential adverse reactions to FTM hormone replacement therapy are:

Breast cancer	Diabetes
High cholesterol	Liver disease
Cancer of endometrium	Hypothyroidism
Hypertension	

MTF RESPONSES TO TESTOSTERONE-BLOCKERS
AND ESTROGEN

❖ *A sense of well-being and emotional rightness* with the world is a common response, often noticeable within the first few days. Some of my clients reported such feelings within hours of their first dose. I didn't attribute this to an expectancy effect as it surprised my clients considerably to feel any effect at all so quickly.

❖ *Gradual decrease in libido* is common. Many MTF clients welcomed the cessation of the constant reminder of being male. Some clients did not experience a decrease in libido as much as a shift to a more whole-body (rather than penis-centered) experience of orgasm. The decrease in sex drive is often, though not always, accompanied by erectile difficulties. However, some of my clients had been on hormones for several years and were still capable of sustaining erections, though most have also said their sex drive was lessened to a degree.

❖ *Heightened emotionality,* across all situations, usually within a few weeks. One client described a new ability to feel more than one emotion at a time; she called it emotional multi-tasking. While on the bus home from work she was able to (simultaneously) feel (a) residual anger over a work situation; (b) excitement at an upcoming visit from her sister; and (c) frustration over a roommate situation. It is important for clients to track their emotional changes, as this particular hormonal shift can have dramatic effects on their various relationships. The decrease in libido and heightened emotionality generally coincide; both depend on the gradual lowering of testosterone levels in the system, as well as on the increased levels of estrogen that are appropriate for an adult female.

❖ ***Skin softening*** is a gradual response to lowered testosterone levels, with a byproduct of being more easily injured (cuts, bruises) than when testosterone is the dominant hormone. Some of my MTF clients were in various building trades prior to their transitions; those who chose to remain in their professions told me they bruise more easily than they did prior to beginning hormones.

❖ ***Loss of muscle mass*** is a double-edged sword; while most of my MTF clients welcomed the rounded shoulders and lack of biceps they associated with womanhood, many also lamented the accompanying loss of physical strength, especially those in occupa-tions that require some physical strength. Clients employed in vari-ous physical trades have told me they had to learn new ways of lifting and carrying, to avoid hurting themselves.

❖ ***Facial and body hair grow more slowly*** and become finer in texture. If the individual has been experiencing male pattern balding, this process is slowed though not reversed completely. Only laser treatments or electrolysis will completely eliminate facial and body hair (though laser is less certain to result in permanent hair removal), though several clients told me their body hair (particularly on their back) fell out and didn't grow back.

❖ ***Fat redistribution*** causes a migration of body fat from the gut to the hips and thighs. Along with lost muscle mass my clients noticed an increase in percentage of body fat and a tendency toward water retention.

❖ ***Feminization varies tremendously.*** Most of my clients experienced some degree of breast growth (accompanied by some pain as the breasts develop). Some may still feel the need for breast implants at some point, while others are content with the amount of growth provided by the hormones. In addition to breast growth, estrogen often softens the square masculinity that may have been present prior to beginning hormone therapy. However, taking hormones will not reverse the innate skeletal structure, height or hand/foot size. There are various surgeries MTFs can undergo to reshape their facial structure, though these are quite expensive.

❖ **The genitalia shrink gradually,** though only to a degree (just as the clitoris will only enlarge to a degree when transitioning to male). Several clients have told me that after a few years, their penis had shrunk sufficiently that they were able to view it as an over-grown clitoris. One client who mentioned this had undergone an orchiectomy procedure, removing her testicles. Lack of testicles and the smaller size of the penis created a visual effect that allowed them to switch their mental perception. This particular client did not feel any need for further genital surgeries.

The above effects are desired by most MTFs. However there are also potential adverse reactions. For this reason it is not a good idea for anyone to transition physically without medical supervision. Unfortunately, some MTFs are not in a position to access good medical care and may transition on their own due to life circumstances. For people in this position, I advise doing whatever they can to change the circumstances that prevent their receiving the care they need and deserve. If this is impossible, there are a number of websites with accurate medical information and advice about how to help prevent adverse reactions before they occur. Potential adverse reactions to MTF hormone replacement therapy are:

Benign pituitary tumors	Increased sensitivity to stress
Gallbladder disease	Liver disease
Hypertension	Hypothyroidism
Weight gain	Migraine headache
Tendency for blood to clot, causing related conditions: • Aneurysm • Pulmonary embolism	Worsening of depression (if already present, and if depresssion

• Deep vein thrombosis	is unrelated to the need to transition)

Whether FTM or MTF, many of my clients told me prior to beginning hormones that the physical changes are their heart's desire, only to find after the fact that the emotional changes were equally important. Initially they viewed hormones as a means to an end – altering their bodies. Once they began taking hormones they realized that the resulting emotional centeredness was as crucial to their well-being as the physical changes they had craved.

AVAILABLE SURGERIES

Early in a client's transition process, taking hormones, being seen as their intended gender, and disclosure to others were the issues most consistently brought into session by my clients. Most of my clients did not bring up surgery options until much further into their transition, when earlier social issues are largely over and done with. That said, most FTMs are clear from the outset that chest surgery is very important to them; chest reconstruction is one of the few surgeries that affects the social presentation of gender. Once trans people have been taking hormones awhile body issues emerge once again as clients begin grappling with the fact that hormones have only taken them so far on their journey toward mind-body congruence.

Many of my clients felt the need for some form of surgery to feel complete in their transition. Most surgeries require a therapist referral letter. Surgery referral letters make less sense to me than hormone referral letters. By the time my clients reached the point of surgery, they had a great deal of experience living their new gender role. They were in an excellent position to say from personal experience, "I know transition is working for me, this is just another step."

Lower-surgery status is the only aspect of transition that is private, giving trans people the luxury of making such decisions in their own time. There is no social pressure to hurry lower surgery, as it does not affect others' perceptions of gender. Without insurance coverage, most people had to save money for years prior to seeking surgery. An inadvertent and beneficial byproduct of having to wait was an absolute certain knowledge that surgery was the right next step.

If insurance is covering transition processes, it is likely the mandated process will include a waiting period between beginning hormones and being eligible to seek surgery. It is equally likely that some trans people won't use that time to seek self-knowledge and a deep understanding of their goals and motivations. They will instead circle the date on their calendar, accessing their surgery benefit at the earliest possible moment. With therapists positioned as the gatekeepers to surgery, many clients may spend the minimum time in therapy and not make full use of its potential support.

Despite this potential scenario, living with hormones for a time does provide visceral evidence to the trans person, "This is right for me." On the other hand, people who are seeking hormones can't say with certainty, "I know this is right" because they have no experience living with the desired hormone balance and usually little experience being seen as adults in their intended gender. While surgery seems the bigger step to most cisgender people, I view beginning hormones as the bigger leap of faith.

For transmen, chest reconstruction is in a different category than any other available FTM surgery as this surgical option can dramatically affect gender presentation and expression, and may make all the difference between a client being accepted as male or not. Thus this surgical option might be as vital an issue as hormones for a client, if their chest is particularly large.

In general, however, most of my FTM clients were seen as male upon taking testosterone – the voice change is the hallmark of adult male status. The presence of a female chest often constricted such clients from expressing gender exactly as they wish. Wearing tight-fitting T-shirts or a tank top was not a psychologically-comfortable option for most of my pre-chest-surgery FTM clients. Many also felt too self-conscious to work out, knowing they may be seen as female and not feeling comfortable using any locker room. One client told me, "I loved the endorphins I got from a good workout and went to the gym pretty much every day. But I just couldn't use either locker room. I used to sneak into a tanning booth to change." *(Client session, 2004)*

Facial feminization surgery (FFS) can feel just as important to some transwomen as chest surgery does to a transman.[16] Several of my MTF clients wished they could afford FFS when beginning their transitions, as they felt it would be easier for them to be seen as women if they could alter the fine bone structure of their faces. Some felt so strongly about the subject, they hesitated to pursue transition at all, feeling there was no chance they would be seen as women without having FFS. These clients were saving their money for FFS procedures before beginning the process of telling others or taking hormones.

Clients who couldn't afford surgery rarely brought the subject up in session, preferring not to consider the various options at all rather than process through that which they considered unob-tainable. It is likely they didn't want to give serious consideration to surgical options for fear of realizing they do desire such procedures, leading to greater depression and frustration at not being able to achieve their heart's desire immediately.

Unfortunately the depression and frustration is still present for such clients, though often not on the surface. In this case I tended to take the view of a wise mentor who once told me, "Don't tamper with a client's defenses if you don't have anything to replace them with." Since I couldn't provide the means for surgery, I didn't bring the issue up with clients until they were ready to bring it into session for themselves. Unlike psychoemotional issues, those stem-ming from desire for surgery are not treatable through psycho-therapy; no

---

[16] Ironically FFS can be obtained with no therapist referral letter at all. Though obtained by transwomen for the sake of transition, the medical establishment views FFS as a form of cosmetic surgery, no different from a ciswoman deciding to have a face lift. Other forms of feminizing surgeries, such as breast implants, also require no therapist letter.

amount of talking through the desire can replace surgery as an alleviation for mind-body dissonance.

MALE-TO-FEMALE SURGERIES

Note: This section is intended as an overview. The following website is a springboard for exploring the various options available:

http://www.susans.org/Sex_Reassignment_Surgery/MTF_Surgeons/

ORCHIECTOMY

When my MTF clients talked of surgery, many were considering an orchiectomy (removal of the testes). The most common reasons my clients desired this procedure were: (a) They wouldn't have to continue taking testosterone-blockers if their primary source of testosterone was removed; (b) They would be able to wear tighter-fitting pants without worrying about having a crotch bulge; and (c) They could more easily come up with the money for this procedure than for the full gender-confirming surgery.

Many of my MTF clients had no objection to wearing pants. What they found, however, is that women's pants are not designed to accommodate a male 'package' and that they felt self-conscious wearing them in public prior to having an orchiectomy, unless they learned how to tuck (taping the penis and testicles up under the buttocks), which is uncomfortable and not good for the tissue on a long-term basis. Once my clients began taking hormones, the self-consciousness they felt about that 'package' often increased and they felt more inclined to do what they could to reduce its size. The client was feeling more female psychologically and emotionally, and found a crotch bulge all the more distasteful as a result.

There are two potential downsides to having an orchiectomy far in advance of vaginoplasty. First, some doctors opine the shrinkage of the penis will be all the more pronounced and quicker with nearly all testosterone removed from the system. Since parts of the penis are used to create the vagina, the shorter the penis, the less depth available for the eventual vagina. Physicians who hold this belief will only recommend orchiectomy in cases where it is medically problematic for the patient to take the medications that block testosterone uptake.

Second, vaginoplasty utilizes all available skin to create labia; removing skin via an orchiectomy may jeopardize the potential for a good surgery result if vaginoplasty is a future goal.

The medical advantage to having an orchiectomy is that the testosterone-blockers (spironolactone is the most commonly-prescribed medication) are challenging for the liver to process. All medications are filtered through the liver. The fewer medications a person has to take, the better for their liver function. Another advantage is related to an annoying side effect of the spiro-nolactone. The primary function of spironolactone is to help people with kidney stones. My MTF clients often complained, sometimes with more humor than at other times, of having to go the bathroom constantly.

VAGINOPLASTY

Vaginoplasty is what most cisgender people think of when they consider 'the surgery' for an MTF. This procedure involves inverting the penis and using some of the tissue to create a vagina. When done properly, and if the patient follows their after-surgery instructions, the results can be so cosmetically-perfect that only a doctor can tell the difference between a post-surgery MTF's and a cisfemale's vagina. Even then, it will take a close examination if the surgical results are optimal.

The initial after-surgery care is quite painful. The patient must dilate several times a day, inserting a tube into the new vaginal opening to keep it from closing as a wound might. If she does not do this, she may lose the entire opening. Throughout her life she will have to periodically dilate to prevent losing depth, but during the healing stages she must dilate often in order to prevent losing her new vagina entirely.

Many of my MTF clients talk of vaginoplasty as much from the perspective of social safety as from the perspective of furthering their transition. They cite cases in which an MTF has been arrested for a misdemeanor offense and put in the men's cell block because she had not had vaginoplasty, which puts her at great risk for rape or even murder. In some cities (and a few states), trans people have the legal right to be housed separately from other inmates, or according to the gender they choose. However this is not always respected even when the laws apply, and in far too many places such laws aren't on the books.

Interestingly, the clients who mentioned this in session were not at much risk for arrest, yet still the first sigh of relief they expressed to me post-surgery is how much safer they felt out in the world now that they no longer had male genitalia. As May wryly put it, "I don't worry so much about not passing all the time. I'm not afraid anymore of being murdered if someone figures out I'm trans. I used to be afraid if anyone saw I still had a penis, they'd run screaming, 'Man in a dress!' Now they might still look at me like I'm from Mars if they see I'm a transgal, but they won't see me as a threat to rape them or something." *(Client session, 2009)*

One interesting point about this comment is that very few people will ever see what is under May's clothing. Her gender expression and general appearance are the same as they were prior to her surgery. Nevertheless she felt more confident and relaxed in social situations than she did prior to her surgery.

FEMINIZING SURGERIES

Some MTFs don't attain as much breast growth from hormones as they would like and seek breast implants. Most of my clients didn't consider this procedure, for financial reasons. This may be just as well; I have noted a tendency among many early-transition MTFs to go a bit overboard in their attempts to actualize femininity. If they were in a position to obtain breast implants during this early phase of transition, they might end up with breasts so large they would draw an unwanted level of attention.

There are various facial feminization surgeries available to MTFs, as well as a procedure to reduce the size of the Adam's apple. A few of my clients have opted for a rhinoplasty (reducing the size of the nose), but most have not been able to afford to consider these procedures, though many wished they could undo the facial masculinization of having lived in a testosterone-based body.

Several of my clients opted for facial feminization surgery early in their process, before living as women full-time. These clients were among the fortunate few who had full choice over the pace and order of their transition, as they had the money to afford what they need. As Kelly put it, "Because I'm older now (56), I know it will be much harder for me to be seen as a woman if I don't have FFS. I might as well not transition at all until I've had FFS, because no one will ever see me as a woman. I can't even experiment with what it's like to be treated like a woman. I'll always be seen as a man in a dress." *(E-mail correspondence, 2007)*

While some of my clients had unrealistic views of their appearance, Kelly was probably right in her self-assessment; 56 years living in a testosterone-based body had not been kind to her facial features, given that she felt female rather than male inside. After she obtained FFS she moved forward readily with her transition and hasn't looked back. She had little difficulty being seen female, and is quite happy to be living as a woman full time.

FEMALE-TO-MALE SURGERIES

Note: This section is intended as an overview. For a more-comprehensive description of available procedures and links to surgeons' websites, Hudson's site http://www.ftmguide.org/ is an excellent resource. Dean Kotula's book *The Phallus Palace* offers photographs of some procedures. Surgeons experienced with trans procedures often post some surgical-results photographs on their websites, though these represent optimal outcomes.

Those who are able to attend an FTM conference will have an opportunity to view outcomes in person, as such conferences include workshops in which a few transmen will show their surgical results (Note: Such workshops are often FTM-only, though there is no restriction about stage of transition). If an FTM finds it im-possible to attend a conference, an alternative is to subscribe to a social media site and pose questions about surgery results.

CHEST SURGERY OPTIONS

The two chest surgery options are *bilateral mastectomy* and a *keyhole procedure* (also known as a *periareolar* or *subcutaneous mastectomy*), which utilizes liposuction to reduce chest size. Chest size is the primary consideration in deciding which procedure is appropriate for any given client. Consultation with an experienced surgeon is critical before making the decision about which type of surgery is most appropriate for any individual.

The keyhole procedure, available to those with smaller chests, involves making a small incision and 'sucking out' the fatty tissue, hence the resemblance to liposuction. The advantages to this procedure are (a) lack of lateral incision scarring, (b) it's a bit cheaper, and (c) nipple sensation is retained. However the nipples may not end up in the most optimal location on the chest and may be larger than is typical for a male.

The bilateral mastectomy procedure involves surgically removing the breast tissue, preserving and resizing the nipples, then grafting them back into place in a more 'male' location on the chest. (Some surgeons are now performing this procedure without removing the nipples, though this may not result in optimal nipple size or placement on the chest) While technically resulting in a double mastectomy, this procedure is more accurately referred to as chest reconstruction surgery. This procedure will leave scars across the chest, though the surgeon will attempt to follow the line of the pectoral muscle as much as possible. With sufficient chest hair growth, the scars may eventually fade to obscurity, hardly noticeable without close examination, though there is no way to predict in any situation exactly how visible the scars will be. Scarring is usually more pronounced with African-American FTMs; the tendency to keloid (develop thick scarring) is often more pro-nounced for people of this racial background. There are over-the-counter products available to help minimize scar tissue.

A potential downside to this procedure is that nipple sensation may be lost during the removal/grafting process, though it is rare that the graft itself is lost, resulting in no nipple at all. Surgeons typically use microsurgery procedures to help increase the chance of retaining nipple sensation.

LOWER SURGERY OPTIONS

Metoidioplasty involves freeing the clitoris from the folds of the labia, closing the vaginal opening, and using the skin of the labia to form testicles with saline or silicone implants. When erect the resulting penis may be capable of intercourse, depending on how much clitoral growth is attained from the introduction of testosterone into the body.

As an optional procedure the urethra can be re-routed through the penis, resulting in the ability to urinate standing up, without the need for any prosthetic device or an STP ('stand to pee'). Some FTMs do not opt for the urethral procedure as it is more prone to complications and infections. If standing to urinate is not a personal goal, the urethra can remain where it is, necessitating sitting down to urinate or the use of an STP.

Metoidioplasty was the most commonly-sought lower-surgery procedure among my FTM client base, if they chose any lower surgery at all. The idea of having a penis that is entirely their own sensate, orgasmic flesh appealed to them, as well as the relative affordability when compared with phalloplasty.

Phalloplasty techniques have advanced considerably with the development of microsurgical procedures, but the basic idea is the same: take flesh from another part of the body (the forearm or abdomen are the most common sites), shape this flesh into something resembling a penis, and graft it onto the body in the appropriate place. Surgeons make every attempt (often successfully) to preserve full sexual sensation, incorporating the orgasmic, sensate tissue of the clitoris into the new penis.

The resulting penis is not capable of natural erection as a cis-man's penis is. There are various techniques to get around this difference. In Belgium, for instance, surgeons insert a small air pump into the penis; the control for this pump is a small button implanted just under the skin near the base of the penis. Pressing this button a few times inflates the penis, causing an erection. I have seen several Belgian phalloplasty results in person during workshop presentations; they are impressive cosmetically. The recipients were quite pleased with their sexual functioning as well, though their penis was not stiff enough when erect to perform anal penetration.

Most of my clients did not consider a phalloplasty, partly because of money, but in some cases because (in the client's opi-nion) it did not resemble a cisman's penis closely enough to be worth either the money or pain involved. More than the cosmetic issues, the lack of natural erectile ability was the key factor for most of my clients, if they had the money to even consider lower surgery.

HYSTERECTOMY

Doctors' opinions differ when asked about the medical necessity of a hysterectomy for a physically-transitioning FTM, though they agree there is no reason not to undergo the procedure. The comments I've heard most frequently from doctors who recommend a hysterectomy are:

❖ Having a hysterectomy reduces the risk for some cancers (*e.g.* ovarian or cervical), because the at-risk tissue is removed;

❖ Removing the estrogen-producing organs early-on allows the testosterone free rein, resulting in a quicker physical transition.

The majority of my FTM clients have not had hysterectomies. Though my clients didn't agree on everything, prioritizing chest surgery over a hysterectomy was a point of general consensus, despite the possible cancer risk. The attitude I heard expressed most often is, "It's always something, cancer's everywhere. My quality of life will be so much better with chest surgery, I'd rather do that now and save money for a hysterectomy later."

NON-OP VS. PRE-OP

Some of my clients talked of surgery at their first appointment, long in advance of taking hormones or disclosing their intentions to others. In the case of FFS or chest reconstruction surgery this is understandable, as discussed previously.

I didn't challenge pre-hormones clients if they brought up lower surgery as a goal in their first few sessions, but I did point out that they didn't have to make such decisions immediately. I said to them, "Take the hormones awhile and then revisit the question, 'Do I feel the need for any form of surgery in order to feel complete?' It may feel like enough to live with the right hormone balance and a different gender role."

Those who still felt the need for surgery after taking hormones for awhile and living their new gender used terminology such as *pre-op* to describe themselves. Surgery was still on their list of transition goals. Those who felt complete in their transition without having any form of surgery referred to themselves as *non-op*. This is a crucial difference in terminology, though to some it seems as though the two terms are interchangeable because they are similar.

The person who identifies as pre-op is making an identity statement along the lines of: "I need surgery to feel complete in my transition and won't feel done with transition until I achieve this goal."

The person who identifies as non-op is making an identity statement along the lines of: "The hormones and switch in gender role are enough for me. The exact configuration of my body doesn't matter so much to me." This is not necessarily a permanent statement; some do revisit surgery as a possible goal and may change their minds later in their lives.

As with any other aspect of transition self-knowledge is key. However, in the case of surgery the self-knowledge can be difficult to acquire. Those who do still desire surgery and feel they will never be able to afford it may do all they can to convince themselves they are non-op when in fact their deepest feelings may be pre-op. Supporting such clients as they try to make peace with their bodies may be become the therapeutic focus for many.

THE SCOPE OF INSURANCE COVERAGE

The mainstream American perception is that gender equals genitalia. The scope of insurance coverage reflects this belief. Lower surgery is covered, while facial feminization surgery (FFS) is still considered cosmetic and therefore usually excluded from coverage[17]. The basis for this exclusion is: 'We are defining tran-sition to mean that you are altering your body to match your gender. Since we are equating your gender with your genitalia, we will cover your lower surgery. And a transman's chest surgery, because breasts are defined as being exclusively female. But we will not cover your facial feminization surgery because that doesn't fit our parameters of gender equaling genitalia.'

Viewing physical transition as a holistic process of life adjust-ment, such a narrow view of the process is unrealistic. From a holistic perspective, it becomes clear that different people will choose different options from the range of possibilities. As she explored transition options with me, Katrina (52) said to me, "If I can't have facial feminization surgery, I might as well stop here and go on being Alvin. I'll never be able to be seen as a woman if I don't have FFS, so what would be the point? I'm not one of those in-between people; I've always known I'm not a boy. I want to look like a girl, not like a girl who had to grow up as a boy!" *(Client session, 2009)*

---

[17] Keep abreast of expansion of insurance coverage – this may very well change in the future.

I worked with so many transwomen through their transition process, I became accustomed to being able to tell if someone would be able to be seen as their intended gender on the other side of transition. Often, those transwomen who had yet to start the process held the belief they would always be seen as a man in a dress. Many times I was able to reassure them, "I don't think you'll have any trouble being seen as a woman over the long term, if that's your goal." But in Katrina's case, she was right; she would have had difficulty being seen as a woman if she weren't able to have FFS.

I introduced Katrina to several transwomen further along in their process than she was. One told her, "I'm right there with you, I need FFS too and I'm going to do that before any other surgery. But I haven't let that hold me back from living as my true self. I've told all my family now and they're slowly adjusting to the idea of me as 'Sandra' instead of 'Stanley.' I figure that once I save enough for FFS, I'll have everything else already done – family told, job told, documentation changed. Doing it all at once would just be too much! I've gotten used to being stared at. It's not so bad, just stay safe. It's a lot better, for me anyway, than living as a man!"

Katrina had not looked at her situation in quite this way before, and this conversation emboldened her to ask me for a hormone letter. The experience of centeredness she achieved with the right hormone balance showed her that Sandra had been right; FFS was the icing on the cake that would allow her to live fully as Katrina and not be seen as trans. But the cake itself – the cake was being Katrina regardless of what her reflection looked like in the mirror. Katrina had to save for seven years before she had the money for FFS; she underwent FFS surgery in 2016, paying $65,000 for the processes she needed. In 2017, I contacted her when her insurance company began covering transition-related procedures.

Katrina said, "Hearing that my insurer will now pay for my hormones but not for FFS makes me SO MAD!!!! I don't pay much for hormones at all. But how about those years I endured the stares, being afraid to go anywhere outside our known territory? What about all the scrimping and saving, living in that crappy little apart-ment that we picked because it was near where I worked and then we could sell our car? When I think of all the transwomen coming of age now, who are going to have their hormones and new vagina paid for but will have to go through three or five or ten years of hell because this is considered *cosmetic????!!!!* When are those insurance companies finally going to get it?" *(Email correspon-dence, 2017)*

• Chapter 8 •

EARLY-TRANSITION THERAPY

PART OF MY VALUE TO CLIENTS WENT BEYOND MY KNOWLEDGE OF TRANSITION PROCESSES. I also had a resource table with lots of business cards: doctors (both allopathic and naturopathic), massage therapists, a vocal coach, chiropractors, other therapists, etc. Being able to offer resources to clients is an essential part of the job, particularly for those in early transition (whether physical or not). Often my job more closely resembled case management than traditional therapy as I helped clients by doing presentations in workplace or school settings, to facilitate a smooth transition.

Those therapists who live in smaller or more conservative communities may have more difficulty finding resources, but putting forth the effort comes with the territory of being an effective therapist for clients in transition. Since transition is a whole-life process, having cards to hand clients becomes part of the job. Being able to say, "This is someone you can see for electrolysis" or "This doctor has experience working with hormone management" be-comes a powerful intervention in and of itself, regardless of the nature of the referral. Having a good reference library of books to recommend to clients is a powerful intervention, visible to the client every time they enter your office.

LOSS AND GRIEF COMES WITH THE TERRITORY

Often there is a substantial element of loss and grief involved in early stages of physical transition, as well as excitement and relief at developing congruence between mind and body. The older the client at the time of transition, the more life that person has to change and the more potential for feelings of loss and grief.

The therapy profession does not always adequately address the loss and grief component of transition. This is not necessarily due to professional myopia on the part of therapists; some of my trans clients told me they were afraid to tell previous therapists any feelings they were having of loss or grief. Their worry was, "If I tell my therapist I'm feeling grief or loss, they will think I'm having second thoughts, or that maybe transition isn't right for me, and will block or question my process. So I'll pretend I'm 100% excited about this and not having any negative feelings at all."

Not only were these clients afraid to tell their therapists of their feelings, they did not often tell other trans people either. Not knowing others might feel similarly, each seemed to fear that their feelings were abnormal or wrong in some way, that they were not 'supposed' to feel this way. Some wondered whether having such feelings did indeed mean they should not transition.

Therapists have long understood that supposedly-happy events, such as the birth of a long-anticipated child, or a marriage between two people who love each other, always carry with them a component of stress simply because the change is so big. (Holmes and Rahe, 1967) Any change involves letting go of what was, to make way for what will be. Making room for the new spouse or life-partner involves giving up the ability to be spontaneous and care-free, answerable only to oneself. Making room for a child entails taking on full responsibility, 24/7, for the development of another human being. Joyous, yes, but also a huge change from the life of the child-free individual.

What does the trans person give up in transitioning? The list is complex and touches on every area of life. Loss of familiarity, the ability to live on autopilot, is one common feeling among trans people. While trans people don't feel at home in their own bodies, nevertheless, there is a certain comfort in knowing the expectations of one's birth gender role. The trans person may have chafed at that role, but giving it up is a venture into the unknown and is scary!

The most major loss involves relationships. A trans person may lose all, a few, or no friends and family members because of transition. However every relationship transitions, changing profoundly from what it was before. For instance, the lifelong friendship between two men, best friends from kindergarten, won't remain the same if one transitions. The trans person must let go of every previous relationship and allow it to morph into what it will become in the future.

There may be elements of the trans person's old life that will not be present in their new gender role and must be let go of entirely. I sang in a lesbian chorus that was the center of my life. I had to let go of the chorus in order to transition. This was very difficult, as I had no way of knowing beforehand whether I would have as good a bass or tenor voice as I had as an alto. And regardless of vocal quality or range, the lesbian chorus would no longer be the place for me as a singer. I lost the chorus, though not the individual friend-ships I'd developed among its members.

This loss was traumatic as I had no way of knowing whether I would ever have a chorus home again. Choral singing is a fundamental part of my spiritual self-care; balancing what I might gain against what I knew I would lose made my decision-making process emotionally painful and difficult. Though I have a new chorus home now, I could not have known 20 years ago that this would be the case. Part of the fear of losing what is familiar is the fear of not knowing in advance what might take its place – and fearing nothing will.

As a therapist, part of my work with trans clients involved helping them understand that feelings of loss and grief are not just common among trans people, but are part of the transition process. Identifying the feelings, talking them through, bringing that process into the therapeutic setting, are key elements in transition. Repressing the grief process merely prolongs it, making it difficult for trans people to truly let go of the past in order to fully embrace the future.

Sarah transitioned out of a fundamentalist Christian background. She lost her entire family, including her wife of 20 years, in the process. The loss of that many relationships was so overwhelming for Sarah, it was difficult for her to allow the feelings of grief to surface. She was mired in a state of depression for nearly a year. She couldn't allow herself to feel the full impact of her losses. As I didn't have anything to replace her repression with, I didn't tamper with this defense. I offered her support, metaphorically holding her hand as she slowly built a new life, forming new friendships and relationships. However, though people can develop family of choice over time, nothing can replace biological family relationships.

Eventually Sarah's grief surfaced to be worked through. In the meantime her need to move slowly kept her from moving forward as quickly as she might have otherwise. Had just one or two people in her family supported Sarah's emergence out of Steven, she might have been be able to face her grief, work through it, and move on with her life more quickly. All this said, Sarah never once expressed regret at having transitioned.

Sarah's depression remained with her for years, though she now has quite a few friends who never knew her as Steven. Dear though they are to her, she never found another religion that resonates with her as fundamentalism did and this has left a gap in her life that other relationships can't fill. She tried Metropolitan Community Church (MCC), a church founded in the 1960s as a spiritual haven for gay men and lesbians forced to leave their original churches. She did not find MCC conservative enough for her and did not feel comfortable joining. Lack of a spiritual home has been a difficult loss for Sarah, though she still does not regret leaving the façade of Steven behind.

Despite the overwhelming loss, the gain is greater yet. And this is the crux of the matter, so difficult for cisgender people to truly understand: gender dissonance is a powerful motivator that will not be denied, no matter what the cost in terms of relationship to others. Relationship to self is the only relationship that is lifelong and can't be let go of while the person yet lives.

If the sense of gain does not outweigh the sense of loss, that is the time to question, "Is transition the right decision?" This unfortunately becomes an early-transition decision; I have known people to back away from transition because the answer for them was, "No, the gains aren't outweighing the losses." In the pre-transition stages feelings of loss and grief weighed against the gains are hypothetical, as the trans person has yet to experience hormones and often has not yet begun disclosing the possibility to others. They have yet to have any experiential proof that they are making the right decision, or how much support they can expect from others as they move for-ward. Starting a process so intense and life-changing with no idea what the outcome will be is scary indeed, and I worry more about the client who says, "This isn't going to be hard" than about the client who is afraid and overwhelmed.

Transition is akin to driving down an unfamiliar dark highway at night, no other cars in sight. Your headlights only illuminate a few dozen yards ahead of you, yet you keep driving, trusting the road will unfold in front of you. While you have a general idea of your destination, you can have no idea what the entire road before you looks like as you navigate your way, or where the road will take you while you journey. You can drive a thousand miles down that road only ever seeing 50 feet in front of you. What a leap of faith, to start the journey at all.

EXPECT CHANGE!

Some of my clients started to disclose their intentions prior to physical transition and received supportive responses. However there is a difference between intellectual or hypothetical knowledge and the reality of physical transition. Friends and family members can't picture the end result. Even the most accepting will go through further stages of acceptance once they begin seeing the physical changes. Before I started taking hormones I mentioned chest surgery to my mother as a future goal. One of her questions was, "Will the scarring be extensive?" I replied, "Given our genetics, I expect chest hair to cover most of the scars." She looked extremely taken aback and then said, "Oh, yes, I guess that will come, won't it?"

I told physically transitioning clients, "Expect change. You can't know in advance what the changes will be, what direction your life may take, precisely how your relationships will change, but you can know in advance that nothing is automatically fixed." I also norm-alized for them the idea that change involves positive feelings as well as feelings of loss, hoping they would bring all their feelings into session and not just the ones they thought would be acceptable to me. Most of the feelings of loss and grief tend to arise during the early transition process. Before beginning the process of disclosure and physical transition, clients feared impending loss but were still dealing with hypotheticals, not reality.

The trend I noticed is that pre-transition therapy is often more what I consider decision-making counseling: going over various options, education about the effects of hormones, discussing coming out strategies and work situations, etc. Most of the clients I've seen had a clear sense of their gender identity before they ever walked through my door. They had done a lot of soul-searching. They already knew that 'this' (fill in the blank, depending on their birth gender assignment) didn't work for them. What they couldn't know with certainty is whether 'that' (being a different gender than they were assigned at birth) would work for them. No matter how they felt inside, most were not fully experiencing what it is to live that gender in the world because the larger culture was not treating them as their intended gender.

There are exceptions to this generalization. Several of my trans-women clients were able to be seen as female long before they started hormones; they did know with certainty the female gender role suited them better because they'd had the experience of social interaction as female. I've also met a few transmen who had a simi-lar certainty of 'rightness' because they were perceived male in all situations. However, only five of my transmen clients were per-ceived as adult males in all situations prior to beginning hormones; the others were seen as lesbians or as pre-adolescent boys, who are treated quite differently from adult males.

THE DIVIDING LINE: STARTING HORMONES

Even if the client was perceived as their intended gender in all situations, they had not experienced the brain alterations associated with changing the hormone balance of their bodies. Most people (trans and cisgender alike) focus a great deal on the visible physical changes wrought by hormones and don't focus on (or perhaps don't know about) the even more dramatic psychoemotional changes brought about by shifting one's hormone balance.

This invisible change is indescribable to those who have not undergone such transformation. It does not do justice to the depth of the experience to say, "It changes the way in which an individual's brain processes information and emotions," yet that is precisely the effect. There is a great deal of hormonal basis in the old stereotypes about women being more emotional than men, or men having a more linear, solution-focused processing style.

Rhoda (43) had a stressful job. As a man she was quite used to dealing with the various situations that would come her way during the course of a workday and wasn't particularly reactive to work-place stress. A month or so after starting hormones, she said in session, "I feel like crying at work all the time! How do women handle this???" *(Client session, 2008)*

Going the other direction, a transman may be perceived as male by others and still find his relationships changing as his estrogen is overridden by testosterone. This can be disconcerting to the people he relates to, as his appearance may not change much at all in the first few months of his physical transition.

Mitch (44) was in a relationship of 15 years when he began taking hormones. He and his partner Candace had been having communication difficulties for some time and had been in couples counseling for four months at the time Mitch began taking hormones. About two months into his physical transition, he told me his couples therapist felt he was shut down during sessions and that he wasn't sharing his feelings as much as he had been.

"Do you agree with her?" I asked him.

He replied, "I'm not sure. I'm not saying as much as I used to, but I'm also not feeling as much emotion. Mostly I'm just frustrated when she says I need to talk more, because I don't always have anything to say. But I know I used to." Mitch and I went on to discuss how testosterone was affecting his levels of emotionality. He felt he spent less time spinning his wheels (his words) and wanted to 'just do it,' whatever 'it' was.

I suggested he tell their therapist that his emotional process was changing due to testosterone and that he didn't yet know precisely who he was or how he felt with this new hormone balance. To her credit, their counselor (not someone who had worked with trans clients before) shifted her conceptualization of their relationship from 'similar hormone balance' to 'different hormone balance.' From seeing them as a lesbian couple, she now saw them as having some of the difficulties she'd encountered among male-female couples. As others in their lives had to transition their view of Mitch's and Candace's relationship, so did their therapist.

Whether perceived as their intended gender or not, most of my transitioning clients came to their first session with a certainty about their own transition because they already knew how uncomfortable their birth gender assignment was. They could answer the question, "How do I NOT want to live my life?" This gave them a sense of self-knowledge that the transition process dislodged into a feeling of uncertainty of identity that was foreign to them. Mitch had felt much more certainty about his feelings and behavior prior to start-ing hormones than he did two months into the process. He asked me to help him interpret himself to himself, after he began experiencing testosterone as his dominant hormone.

This was the dividing line between the types of therapy needed by my clients, and the line was marked by introducing hormones into the system. On the one hand is therapy with a client who has certain knowledge of who they are, and that their role in life is not what they want it to be. They may come in certain of who they are, they may come in seeking help figuring out who they are, but they nearly always come in with an unconscious certainty of how they make decisions, how their brain works, how they experience emotion, etc.

The dividing line is a process of uncertainty of self, self-consciousness and vulnerability in the face of 'this is your brain on hormones.' The boundaries of relationship are all different as the client shifts from being perceived female through an uncomfortable gender-limbo period of confusing others to a point of being perceived male all the time (or vice versa, though some transwomen have more difficulty being perceived female across all situations). Thus the client is trying to learn a new gender role as an adult, which is very difficult.

This situation was exacerbated for my transmen clients by the speed with which testosterone acts on the female body. By the time they have been on a full dose of hormones 2-3 months, most transmen can expect their voices to have deepened to an adult male register. From this point forward they will be treated as adult males when interacting with people who never knew them as female. This fairly abrupt shift brings with it a sense of having been thrown in the deep end of the pool without certain knowledge of being able to swim.

Most of the doctors I referred clients to start with a half-dose prescription, to allow the body to adjust, increasing to the full dose some months into the process. While some of my clients chafed at the delay, I pointed out the opportunity this gave them to get used to the hormone balance and to take more time coming out to people who may have a problematic reaction. Mitch did not experience such a dramatic change in his processing until he was on the full dose of hormones. While on the half dose, he did experience some increase in sex drive but did not notice other changes.

Once on a full dose of hormones, not only is the client having to learn what the expected social gender roles are in various situations, they are also having to get to know themselves all over again; this can lead to feelings of uncertainty, vulnerability and an inability to trust intuition. Many clients lived with similar feelings throughout their lives, having felt gender dissonant as small children and received no support for their feelings. What clients didn't expect was to find those feelings of uncertainty heightened after beginning hormone therapy!

These feelings crop up at a deep level, paralleling the gender socialization experience the client had as a small child learning the same types of things and learning at the same time that their innate gender was something they had to hide. Now they have to learn to disclose it, share it with others, while also getting to know themselves. This adds new levels of vulnerability, as the client realizes they need to dismantle the fortress in which they've hidden their true selves throughout their lives.

WHO *AM* I?

What I found is that the clients who were most certain physical transition was right for them often were equally certain that they would be the exceptions when I told them it's normal to experience some feelings of uncertainty, vulnerability and general sense of instability of identity early in the process. These clients fully believed they had been able to live their intended gender and that the hormones were icing on the cake. They believed they already had the cake. Thus they were more likely to be taken by surprise as they gradually realized they were feeling some degree of insecurity during transition.

What does this sort of uncertainty of self look like? It doesn't have to involve major issues or serious dilemmas; it often involves minor things, as people usually anticipate the more major issues that might arise (such as changes in sex drive). As an example:

I started taking testosterone in 1997, at the age of 41. No one told me any of what I've just written and I was unprepared to learn new things about my brain functioning. About three months after starting hormones, I was printing someone's name and thought, "That doesn't look right." I had to spell the name out, letter by letter, to realize I'd inverted two letters. This is not a problem I'd had before; I immediately connected the change to my increased testosterone levels. The introduction of testosterone into my system had switched on a gene that would otherwise have lain dormant. To this day I have to be more careful than I was before physical transi-tion when I write down phone numbers or names, repeating the in-formation as I write to prevent such inversions.

Knowing what was going on did not free me from feelings of disconcerting vulnerability as the thought occurred to me, "What else am I going to find out about myself????" Dyslexia is not some-thing one expects to suddenly crop up at 41 when it was never pre-sent before. I found myself wondering, "Am I going to find myself acting bizarrely in a social situation, being completely different than I've been in the past?"

The uncertainty of not knowing precisely what is going to change leads to varying degrees of social anxiety and self-con-sciousness. It takes some time before a new hormone balance feels normal, though the relief from the anxiety and depression associated with the previous hormone balance can be immediate. Many of my clients had been diagnosed with depression or anxiety in the past and prescribed medication, when in fact what their brain needed was a different hormone balance.

RELATIONAL ISSUES

I did my best to prepare my pre-transition clients for these kinds of processes and encouraged them to come in to talk about it. I didn't want my clients believing this type of difficulty meant (a) they made the wrong decision, (b) they weren't doing their transi-tion properly, or (c) there was something wrong with them. While they did need to be checking in with themselves to see if they felt a sense of 'rightness' about their new hormone balance, the expe-rience of shifting emotional and information processing is not an indicator of having made the wrong decision.

As an example of how these shifts in processing can play out in relationship... In 2003 I saw a couple named James and Karen; they had been involved for over ten years prior to James' transition to male

(I had not been James' gender identity therapist). Karen (a ciswoman) had always seen James as male and knew herself to be bisexual, so they did not anticipate problems with his transition.

About six months after James began hormones they sought out couples counseling (for the first time) with me as they were arguing quite a bit and were panicky that their relationship was going sour. Neither had connected the change to the effects of testosterone on James' psyche. His communication style and situational reactions had altered, but in subtle ways that had made them unable to correlate the changes with his increased testosterone levels.

For instance, James was quicker to react with anger if Karen forgot to get something for him at the store after agreeing to do so. Rather than seeing this as a shift due to hormone levels, both he and Karen were concerned that he was acting in a passive-aggressive manner. They wondered if there was something more major that he was upset about and not expressing, using the forgotten item as a means of expressing his anger. This is a common relationship problem and James had been in therapy some years before to work on exactly this issue. He thought he'd resolved the problem and had learned some communication tools that had helped him avoid passive-aggressive behavior in the years since.

In exploring the nature of the communication difficulties they were having, I asked if James' gender identity therapist had pointed out that shifting the hormone balance could alter both emotional and thought processing. I could see the light bulb go off for Karen, though James was a bit slower in making the connection. Karen, however, was in the observer position rather than the experiential position. She said, "Of course! It's the effect of the hormones!" We then had a discussion about how the gender stereotype of men being quicker to anger and aggression has some reality to it, based in higher testosterone levels.

While there is some basis in fact for the stereotype of men being aggressive, I feel the situation is more complex than that. I have noticed the rush of adrenaline in an emergency or anger-provoking situation is quicker and stronger than it was for me prior to beginning hormones, causing an impetus to action. I have heard similar reports from other transmen. However, this does not have to translate to aggression; the conscious mind can assess the situation and contribute logic in deciding the appropriate course of action.

I told the couple that while it was possible James had had some sort of relapse into a former behavior pattern, it was also possible that the changes they were observing were due to his new hormone levels, particularly as the incidents they had related were strikingly similar to experiences I'd heard from other FTM clients.

Paradoxically, the reason it took James and Karen so long to make this correlation is because they'd been together over ten years. They knew each other so well, the last thing they expected was to have to get to know each other again. I advised them to read some books about male-female communication, to talk things through when a similar situation arose again, and see what came up for each of them. I also pointed out to them that they were experiencing a shift from being two women in relationship (though James had never felt like one inside, nevertheless he'd had an estrogen-based system) to being a male and a female in relationship, with hormone balances that were now quite different from each other.

Two weeks later they came in for a follow-up session and were at peace. They had read (and found helpful) Deborah Tannen's *You Just Don't Understand,* which deconstructs men's and women's differing communication styles. James was better able to understand the male point of view than he could prior to beginning hormones, and Karen resonated with the fact that she was now involved with a man, not a woman. Though she had fully supported James' gender identity, she now realized he'd had the internal identity of male, but not the hormone balance that would cause him to react 'like a man.' I told them the door was always open for future sessions if other things arose that they could not figure out on their own, but I sus-pected I would not be seeing them again. (I didn't)

Why is it that James and Karen did not call James' gender identity therapist when these new issues cropped up? As James put it, "I just had a feeling she wasn't going to be able to help with this one. Karen came with me to one session at the beginning of my tran-sition and the therapist wasn't very good at working with us as a couple. She tended to focus on me and my transition. It's like Karen was there just to help me transition."

He had thought this new situation was a recurrence of the passive-aggressive communication problem he'd dealt with in therapy previously; when he tried to contact that therapist, he found she'd retired since he'd last seen her. They called me because they'd heard about me through friends and thought a trans therapist would be ideal; they did not want to have to educate someone new about trans issues and worried that a cisgender therapist might make James' transition the focal point. (Ironically his transition *was* at the root of their current problem, but neither knew that at the time.)

The question then arises, would a cisgender therapist have made the connection between James' transition and their communication difficulties? Probably, if the therapist had worked with many trans clients (particularly with couples). Had James been able to see the original therapist who helped him with his communication and relational patterns, however, she might not have made the connection; she had no experience with trans clients.

The same can be said for Mitch's and Candace's couples therapist; though she accepted what Mitch told her about his shifting sense of self, she did not realize on her own that this is what was happening. Rather, she interpreted Mitch as being shut down with-out realizing he was now experiencing his emotions through a testosterone rather than an estrogen filter. Mitch told me she laughed at herself in their last session, telling the couple that she had tried not to blame testosterone, not wanting to fall into the trap of automatically stereotyping Mitch as 'acting like a man' now. She later took a class I taught, in which we discussed as a class what might be hormonal in the various stereotypes about gender and emotional processing.

151

WHY NOT RESUME THERAPY?

One could make the argument that a post-transition person can pick up the phone and call the therapist they saw during their pre-transition stage, get back into therapy as issues arise. However if that were happening consistently, more therapists would have recognized these issues long ago. In 1998 I ran into my helpful pre-transition therapist at a social event and told her I was about to enter graduate school to become a therapist myself. She said, "I'm really glad to talk with you. Most of the time I never see my clients again after they start transition and I never learn what they are doing with the rest of their lives."

I experienced this same phenomenon with clients. I would see them for a period of time, they would move on after resolving whatever issue brought them into therapy in the first place (or quit coming if the therapy approached an issue they weren't ready to deal with), and I never heard the end of the story. If I were not trans myself, I don't know that I would have realized what kinds of issues crop up post-transition, or how much they differed from pre-transition issues.

Why is it, then, that trans clients often don't go back into the-rapy after starting hormones, or having surgery, if it truly is a life-long developmental process? To explain this I need to delve further into the developmental process of trans children.

Being born gender dissonant results in an early awareness of being 'different' from other children. I put the word 'different' in quotes because for many trans people that's the best description they have for how they felt. Many were not able to pin down the difference to understand its relationship to gender. Whether con-sciously aware of the nature of the difference or not, feeling gender dissonant colors the entire developmental process.

Those clients who knew the nature of the problem very young tended to report having had constant fantasies and dreams of sud-denly waking one morning to find a Pinocchio-like transformation has taken place and they are suddenly 'real boys' (or 'real girls'). Those who didn't know why they felt different often pinpoint distinct memories of discomfort around gendered situations (bathrooms, locker rooms, being forced into frilly dresses or suits and ties). These children grow up with a consciousness about gen-der as a social reality that is foreign to most cisgender children.

The trans child cannot help but absorb some gender social-ization, albeit reluctantly, for self-protection and to move through the world without attracting hostile attention. A boy who consis-tently acts out the female gender role is likely to receive hostile reactions from adults and children alike. There is more latitude given girls who act out a male gender role; they are labeled tomboys but rarely punished or discouraged from such behavior. Thus, a budding transman may suffer less psychological damage during pre-adolescent development than a budding transwoman. Nevertheless, if the child is gender-dissonant and not a girl at all, 'tomboy' is a re-fuge and not reflective of actual identity. Whether male- or female-assigned, gender-dissonant children grow up with a degree of self-consciousness and unhappiness around gender identity that is fo-reign to the cisgender experience.

At varying points in their lives such folks reach a decision point, "I just can't live like this any longer." At that point they begin the process of figuring out how to rectify the situation. Whether through research on the Internet, talking with other trans people, or at their local library, the trans person bumps up against the requirement of seeing a therapist in order to obtain hormones. The implication (as the trans person sees it) is, "I know better than you do who you are because I'm a professional mental health care expert." Thus the trans client often walks through the door viewing the therapist as a gatekeeper and not an ally, regardless of how the therapist views their role.

This scenario will change over time, as the tone of the 2011 SOC is not as paternalistic as has been the case in the past. Further, many doctors and clinics who provide hormone prescriptions are moving toward an informed consent model, only recommending therapy for those clients who seem to need it. For now, however, the therapist is often put in the position of having to dismantle the gatekeeper image their client probably has of them. If the therapist does not address this issue from the beginning of therapy, it may be difficult to establish a therapeutic alliance. The client is likely to have the feeling, "I know a lot more about this condition and about myself than this therapist ever will, so I'm paying my therapist in order to educate them. I'm not getting anything out of this." Which may become a self-fulfilling prophecy.

Given this situation, where's the incentive for the client to return to therapy post-transition when they probably feel in need of it but don't believe their former therapist can help them? They never allowed their transition therapist 'in' to form a true alliance, so never received the full benefit of therapy the first time around. I've met many trans people who saw their transition therapist for the minimum amount of time possible, got their hormone referral letter, and never went back again.

Is it possible a trans person may come to a point of never need-ing gender identity therapy again? Certainly. This would be particu-larly true if the person meets a partner and establishes a healthy, intimate relationship. However... in 2002 I was contacted by a transman (Wayne) who needed advice. His presenting issue? He had met a woman who "really mattered," as he put it, and he was scared to disclose the fact that he was a transsexual (his termino-logy) because he felt he had so much more at stake with this woman than ever before. He'd had four long-term relationships, all with ciswomen, prior to contacting me. None had had any problem with his being a transman but he was still very worried about disclosing to this new woman in his life.

What struck me most is that Wayne was *32 years into his tran-sition* at the time he sought me out. When this man began transition the Vietnam War was far from over and Richard Nixon had just been re-elected to his second term as president. I heard from Wayne again several months after he came to see me. The disclosure had gone well and they were engaged to be married.

I didn't see Wayne again, though I know he felt well-supported by me and would have called had other issues arisen for him. What can therapists do to ensure their clients understand it's normal to feel the need to come back once in awhile? Changing one's view of trans identity and physical transition from psychological pathology to developmental process is not rocket science, but it does require some inner work on the part of the therapist.

From personal experience, the client will be able to resonate with the concept of transition as a developmental process, but they may not be familiar with the idea that models of human develop-ment exist that offer parallels to transition. Sharing this model with them can be a comforting thought to the trans person, putting their experience in the context of human development rather than the context of the DSM. And showing that their therapist also is view-ing transition from a developmental rather than medical model perspective. The client will then be much more inclined to view their therapist as an ally to call upon in times of stress, at any point of transition.

• Chapter 9 •

WHO IS MY TRIBE?

I TRANSITIONED OUT OF LESBIAN COMMUNITY and tried for some years to pin down why I never felt like part of a trans community. Though I no longer felt a sense of belonging, I recognized the pow-er and constancy of the lesbian community I had tried to fit into. Paradoxically while I own the label 'trans' with no trouble at all, I doubt the existence of a trans community.

I used to explain this paradox by saying the degree of diversity among trans individuals is such that it's impossible to form community. This is a population that has nothing in common beyond some degree of not resonating with the gender assigned each of us at birth. No other characteristic – race, religion, ethnicity, class, educational level, nationality, size, age, sexual orientation, political affiliation, and of course gender itself – is common to us all.

However this explanation never seemed to fully explain the difference I felt between the concepts 'lesbian community' and 'trans community.' Lesbians don't share demographic categories, either. I remember endless processing discussions about whether a woman who occasionally sleeps with men can claim lesbian as an identity, for example. Some of the processing I hear among trans individuals about ownership of identity feels very familiar to me. Yet I still felt a difference in the sense of community.

BARRIERS TO FORMING TRANS COMMUNITY

I see two fundamental differences that are barriers to the formation of a stable sense of community based on trans identity.

The first is based in the physical transformation many trans individuals undertake, morphing their bodies to allow themselves fuller access to a gender role that better fits their sense of identity. Trying to form some sense of community among people who are changing so deeply feels like trying to map a territory whose boundaries are constantly shifting.

The second difference is subtler. When one moves from heterosexual to an L, G or Q identity, one is forever removed from the mainstream and has no access to heterosexual privilege again while living in authenticity with one's true self. The person who lives in authenticity with their LGQ identity automatically gives up heterosexual privilege in order to live a self-actualized life. Those who deliberately remain closeted are still living a marginalized existence, never free to acknowledge their partners or lovers, perhaps never free to have a partner or lover who matches their ideal. They may have perceived access to heterosexual privilege, but as they are not heterosexual theirs is a somewhat hollow existence.

Bisexual individuals are in a different position, one of invisibility, as they constantly have to assert their identities to counter the assumption that they are gay, lesbian, or heterosexual, depending on the perceived gender identity of their partners. If they are holding hands with their partner, their sexual orientation will be misidentified by strangers, as is not the case for two lesbians or two gay men or a heterosexual couple holding hands.

Regardless of the exact nature of their sexual orientation, when the gay, lesbian, queer, or bisexual person comes out, their identities automatically place them in a marginalized position, and it is this automatic loss of privilege that creates the underlying basis for community. Would there be a lesbian community if there was no loss of privilege in two women falling in love with each other? Would there even be differentiating labels if it was the norm that people grow up and fall in love, without any regard to the gender identity of their partners? The only reason for the differentiating labels is because there is a culturally-based hierarchy of acceptance that dictates one form of identity (heterosexual) as superior over gay/lesbian/bisexual/queer identities.[18]

The binary nature of our culture has resulted in binary communities, gay and lesbian; as a result, bisexuals have no identity-based community of their own. As younger people embrace queer identities, the result has been the emergence of queer community, a move away from a binary view of identity. Younger trans and bisexual people are embracing queer community as their own, leading to the possibility of lifelong community.

In recent years, more people have been transitioning into a trans identity; male-assigned to transwoman, female-assigned to transman. The exact terminology used has individual variation, but it is becoming increasingly common to own a trans identity after a physical transformation. This is not universal; in many parts of this country, transition is still male-to-female or vice versa. Viewing transition this way, it becomes a process of trading one mainstream binary label for another – male rather than female or vice versa. Unless the person in question has difficulty being seen as their intended gender, or deliberately comes out as trans, they are not coming out of a mainstream identity into a marginalized one, rather they are trading one mainstream identity for another. While male and female identities don't carry equal status in U.S. culture, these two categories constitute the mainstream of gender. Gay, lesbian, queer, and bisexual are never considered mainstream identities, while male and female always are.

What I have observed is that many trans people form or attend peer-support groups (some more social, some more therapeutic in nature) when they are early in their process of self-acceptance, or early in their resocialization process. As time passes many stop attending support groups regularly, fading off the scene gradually to a point of just living their lives. What passes for trans community are

---

[18] Note that I'm not saying the relationship dynamics are the same; gender socialization and hormone balances create very different relational experiences between male/male, female/female, or female/male relationships.

those who are in support groups still, and those who are participating in activist efforts on behalf of trans civil rights. Those who participate within queer community are still not participating in a trans-specific community, focusing specifically on trans issues.

This lack of ongoing social community seems particularly problematic for those who took refuge in gay or lesbian community prior to their transition. If the gay or lesbian community no longer feels like home to the post-transition individual, what replaces it? As one formerly-lesbian client put it, "There's no such thing as going to the trans bar every Saturday night to go dancing and hang out with the gang!" *(Client session, 2006)* It's hard to form community if your people aren't lining up behind you.

FINDING COMMUNITY AMONG THE GLB TRIBES

There is little among trans people to equal the consistency of various social organizations within gay or lesbian community. For instance, the Portland Gay Men's Chorus, with whom I now sing, is a vibrant community organization over 150 singers strong and entering its 38th season in 2017. There are founding members of that group singing still, while many members hadn't been born when the chorus was founded. It's hard for me to imagine that kind of consistency of community among trans people.

Some trans people join an LGBT organization and then find the T isn't as well understood or supported as they would have liked. Jim and Darcy transitioned from being a lesbian couple to being seen as straight. With their two adopted children they had moved to a new community, post-transition. They attended a meeting of an organization dedicated to supporting LGBT families raising children only to find that many of the group members didn't under-stand why this ostensibly straight couple was accessing their sup-port, even after learning Jim had transitioned from female. Others seemed intrigued and supportive. Jim and Darcy didn't want to be poster children for trans experience, nor did they want to be the group's education around trans issues. They wanted support as queer parents and didn't feel they were going to get it. They stopped attending meetings and felt more isolated than ever within their community. Like many before them, they realized that an orga-nization using the term 'LGBT' doesn't mean there will be under-standing or full acceptance of the T component.

Politically, G, L, B, Q, and T can form natural alliances; the same people who have so resisted marriage equality are also unlike-ly to support trans civil rights. However, G, L, B, Q, and T often don't fit well together when it comes to forming social or support organizations. (Vanderburgh, 2017)

DIVERGENT PATHS: TRANS AND CISGENDER SOCIALIZATION

The nature of transition and the subsequent resocialization process results in a person very different from the cisman or ciswoman a trans person would have been had they been born in a body that matched their gender. My birth gender socialization and subsequent transition journey have made me a far different person than I would have been had I received male socialization from the cradle and not had to rebel against female socialization.

Pre-school acculturation involves learning those cultural values and norms that allow people to function in society with others: so-cial politeness, acceptable public behavior, limitations on language, etc. Subcultural and geographic differences are crucial in this process, resulting in different communication and behavioral styles as adults, but the goal is the same: civilizing children so they can function in their culture as they mature. As children enter the school setting, gender roles begin to assert themselves and children are set firmly on the path toward growing up to be a man or woman. (Andrews, 2014; Dykstra, 2005; Brill, 2008; Vanderburgh, 2009, 2015; Ehrensaft, 2011; Krieger, 2011; Kuklin, 2015)

This process of gendering starts at home but learning proper public behavior (e.g. "Use your inside voice!") generally takes pre-cedence in earlier years, until the child enters the 'real world,' usually

160

the time when they are taken to daycare, nursery school, or kindergarten. At this point much of their social behavior is learned from peers, who also take over the primary role of enforcer of what is proper. The child (trans or not) who deviates significantly from their expected gender role is often teased and possibly ostracized, especially if they are expected to live up to the label 'boy.'

For boys, the path toward 'man' becomes narrower and more rigidly defined as they age; the consequences of not doing male right are harsher. For girls, the path toward 'woman' is much less rigidly defined, with more permissiveness to explore gender expres-sion and few (if any) negative consequences. In most areas of this country, it's hard to not do female right. The male equivalent of 'tomboy' is 'sissy.' While 'tomboy' is often viewed as a neutral or positive role, 'sissy' is always viewed negatively. (Dykstra, 2005; Brill, 2008; Vanderburgh, 2009, 2015; Ehrensaft, 2011; Krieger, 2011; Kuklin, 2015)

The cisgender person generally moves along a particular gender vector toward the label assigned them at birth – boy or girl, man or woman – without giving much thought to their gender. The excep-tion to this is the cismale who 'doesn't do male right,' for whatever reason. Particularly during adolescence, such people are likely to be harassed and bullied. One gay cismale friend, now in his mid-40's, described having his head stuffed into the toilet in the boy's bath-room, being peed on, etc. during his high school years. He has never taken gender for granted, though he has no desire to live as a woman; he has visceral memories of gender oppression, giving him empathy for trans people.

In transitioning, the trans person moves along a vector from an inappropriate gender assignment to one that feels more comfortable, through a process of adult resocialization. While the trans person may end up with a new label – male instead of female, or vice versa – the journey is such that they may feel isolated within their new gender role while at the same time feeling much more at home and centered in their identity.

161

This paradox is unsettling for many, leaving them wondering, "Now what? Why do I feel so different from others, so new and yet so centered at the same time?" It is this feeling that can leave the post-transition individual with a sense of conflict: "I am now just a woman, but I still feel different from other women." Some despair, thinking this is not how they are supposed to feel, and wonder if they will ever settle into a feeling of belonging. Many feel intense loneliness.

What I have observed is that this sense of loneliness and isolation is a mid-transition issue that does fade over time. I worked with a number of long-post-transition individuals who felt similarly at earlier points in their transition, yet now felt they had fully reintegrated into family, subcultures and society at large.

When one considers the nature of long-term friendship, it becomes more clear why such feelings might dissipate over time. If a child's family moves to a new town, at first the child feels alone and isolated, wondering "Will I ever belong here?" It takes quite awhile for new friendships to develop the patina of long-term relationship, and it is the shared experience of long-term mutual memory that helps create the feeling of belonging. Just so, the trans per-son needs a length of time living their new gender role, being accepted and valued as a member of a community, in order to create long-term relationships in their new gender role.

Some such relationships may be with people who knew them before transition. Nevertheless, the relationship post-transition is a new relationship if both parties involved allow the transition to shift gender conceptualization. This is difficult for both, as the closeness of the relationship is at risk of shifting. Some relationships end up closer; others end up less close, or end altogether. It's a hard risk to take with a close friendship.

SHIFTING PRIORITIES

Many of the trans people I've worked with had been trans activists early in their transitions (particularly my younger clients). As they settle into their new gender role, many gradually move away from activism and reach a point of picking and choosing where or when they come out, if at all. Those who identify as heterosexual may feel they are now part of mainstream society. Those who are gay, lesbian, bisexual or queer in some way find varying degrees of support within those communities and may choose to blend in with the marginalized group rather than feel further marginalized by coming out as trans. Ironic though it may seem, it is often not easy for gay, lesbian, bisexual or queer trans folks to find acceptance for their trans identity within those communities; often age is a factor, with younger cisgender people being more accepting. At the least, it may be controversial and discussion-provoking when an individual tries to be openly-trans within this context. (Vanderburgh, 2017)

A heterosexual transperson has the option (unless they can't be seen as their intended gender) of living a mainstream life, the price being public acknowledgement of their life journey. The GLB trans person may feel forced to choose between acceptance within GLB communities and acknowledgement of their life journey. The permutations of choice, the range of sexual orientations, the degree of comfort and safety inherent in living privately, the shifting nature of peoples' goals during transition – these factors make impossible the formation of a trans community to compare with the stability of lesbian or gay community. Or the emerging queer community.

The point of intersection for those who transition is during the early transition process itself, regardless of the direction of their transition, creating a sense of community similar to that available to gay men and lesbians. However as transition proceeds, the different gender roles, physical changes, and life goals cause such divergence that the sense of community fades. As the trans person moves further from their birth gender assignment, they often move further from a sense of community with other trans people.

PRIVATE VS. THE CLOSET

Despite the Supreme Court decision regarding marriage equal-ity, the cisgender GLB individual's innate sexuality is still not fully accepted by mainstream society as legitimate, leading some to remain closeted for reasons of social acceptance, safety, and job security.

One gay cisman described his experience of living in integrity with his identity, "I get to know a lot of different kinds of people as an insurance agent. I have long-term, ongoing relationships with my clients and co-workers. If they're straight, they always assume I'm straight, too. If I reach a certain point of closeness with them, like we're talking about our families and home life to some degree, I want to tell them I'm a gay man; at that point I have something at stake emotionally in whether they accept me or not, but I have to tell them if I'm going to be true to myself and to my life partner. Even if I lose out financially, or don't get a business relationship off the ground, what I gain is my integrity." *(Private conversation, 2013)*

In the realm of gender, however, 'male' and 'female' *are* the mainstream. For those trans people who comfortably own 'male' or 'female,' transition does not mean loss of access to the mainstream (if the person in question is able to be seen as their intended gender); transition has allowed them *greater* access to the mainstream by giving them more comfort in their own skins and social identity.

I dislike the word stealth in the context of transition, implying as it does some degree of hiding and secrecy, when in fact many trans people are just trying to be private. Transition forces the trans person to live a 'fish bowl' existence for a time, undertaking a private, personal process in a very public way. It is natural for many to desire privacy, if the option becomes available to them during their transition process. This is particularly true for those who are introverted by nature; privacy comes naturally to the introvert.

'Private' or 'low disclosure' means not talking about the pre-transition identity, which the trans person never fully owned to begin with. A transman who says, "I'm a man" and does not disclose that he was raised female is living in authenticity with his male identity

164

and choosing not to disclose how he got there. Every use of the right pronoun is an affirmation of his identity, bolstering his self-esteem and sense of well-being. On the other hand, the closeted GLB cisperson is encouraging others to assume they are heterosexual; their true identity is negated in the process.

That said, the enormity of transition and the life journey involved in self-actualization are such that I don't believe desiring 100% privacy for a lifetime is the healthiest option for every trans person. This decision has so many factors innate to individual circumstances that there is no right answer, but every trans person owes it to themselves to evaluate their lives honestly and forthrightly. As with the initial decision to transition, the key question is, "How do I want to live my life?" One must weigh safety, job security, desire for privacy, family circumstance; a whole host of factors should go into this decision-making process. An additional question that comes up for post-transition individuals is, "Can I find my tribe if I never disclose my life journey?"

Unfortunately too many trans people assume complete privacy is the way to go and never seriously question whether this is the right path for them. This can lead to unhealthy levels of isolation and loneliness, which can lead to contemplation of post-transition suicide. Motivation is the key component here: why is the trans person choosing a completely private existence?

One former client (Dave) now lives in another state. He is one of the facilitators of an ongoing peer support group in a nearby city, and is a role model for those considering transition. He identifies as a straight man and is married to a ciswoman who also identifies as straight. They are raising two children from his wife's previous marriage. Dave and his wife have a rich, full life; they belong to a mainstream progressive church, a hiking club, and have made many friends among their cisgender neighbors.

Dave made a conscious choice in this situation. His volunteer work with early-transition transmen is enough for Dave; he wants the rest of his life to be separate from trans issues. He's quite content to be private among his cisgender friends and neighbors. As Dave put it, "I got tired of educating people, answering the same questions I answered ten years ago! I just want to live my life and maybe help out a few other guys." *(E-mail correspondence, 2004)* Dave views his support group work as his contribution to those who are coming along behind him, not as something he needs in his own journey as a transman. As far as Dave is concerned, his transition journey was finished a long time ago.

I conceptualize 'private vs. open' as a mid-transition issue, with clients coming in feeling somewhat isolated and confused. They are at a crossroads in their transition. They are beyond the point of needing to go to trans conferences on their own behalf (though they may go to reconnect with friends). They no longer have questions about hormones, surgeries, or the intricacies of name changes. Either they have already completed the procedures they desire or they have sufficient information to do so and are counting their pennies until they can afford it. They often find trans support groups somewhat boring, as they hear the same questions they asked and answered years before. If they continue going to support groups, it is often sporadically and with a deliberate intent of helping others, not because they get much support out of it themselves.

While some (like Dave) make themselves available as mentors or teachers to those coming along behind them, these folks also have their own issues to deal with. It is at this point in transition that trans people need mentors once again, but not in the same way as early-transition folks do. Most have not conceptualized it this way, but they have resonated with the information when I suggest to them that they are beyond needing trans mentors or peer support groups. They have already realized the lack of trans community to help them at this point in their process, and feel isolated as a result.

In general I consider someone to have reached this stage when there are more people in their lives who never knew them before transition than those who did. Another possible benchmark is whether there are people now considered 'old friends' who never knew the person pre-transition. (There are exceptions to these benchmarks, for instance those who transition in small communities and will be interacting with the same circle of friends and family for the rest of their lives.) The choice becomes, "How or when or do I tell these new folks that I was raised to be a boy/girl?"

One client (Ken) put the dilemma well, "I feel guilty, because I used to be a lesbian and now I'm seen as a straight white man. And there's a part of me that's really comfortable with that because my life is so much better now as a guy, not because of male privilege, but because I'm so much happier in my own skin. I was meant to be a guy! And I can't help being white, or straight, anymore than I can help being happier living as a man. But there's another part of me that feels like I'm selling out if I don't wear a sign around my neck that says, "Hey, I'm a transguy."" *(Client session, 2003)*

Ken is now happily married to a woman he met six months after starting hormones. He's an intelligent, compassionate, articulate man, on hormones since 2002 and contentedly relaxed living as a man. He completed his phalloplasty in 2006 (fortunately covered by insurance, or he would never have been able to afford the surgery) and is quite happy with the results. Though happy living life as the man he's become, Ken is also keenly aware of social injustices he no longer experiences. Yet even if he wanted to he can't work for social justice from within the lesbian community any longer. The lesbian community is not his tribe.

In 2005 Ken scheduled an appointment with me after a three-year hiatus. He had just attended an FTM conference and it brought up issues for him about living privately. When I mentioned the con-cept of cismale mentors to Ken, he grew very excited, seeing at once the potential this idea held for him. We brainstormed possible venues for meeting men he could come out to, to help him solidify his own masculinity, give him a tribe, and at the same time allow him to feel he was participating in the grassroots effort of changing hearts and minds.

I do many educational presentations in a wide variety of settings, far more than most trans people, because it's part of my job. In addition to my writing, this is my contribution to helping educate the larger culture about trans issues. For Ken, the idea of coming out to a small handful of cismen and cultivating them as his allies made him feel he would be doing his part as well. No one in his current life knew his history of living female for 28 years and this had led the gregarious and extroverted Ken to feel uncharac-teristically cut-off and isolated from others.

In addition to feeling isolated, he felt the need to talk to other men (cismen) about various existential questions: how do I feel about growing older, what do I do with this sex drive of mine as I remain married to the same woman for years, how do I show my feelings as a man, etc. Remaining private and never telling anyone at all didn't feel right to him, though he had been confused about what the alternatives might be.

In 2010 I contacted Ken for an update to his story, eight years into his physical transition. In 2006 he had moved to another part of the country, following his wife as she was promoted and sent to another office. He has found his boundaries around post-transition disclosure. His general rule of thumb is, once he knows someone well enough that they begin telling family stories, sharing their backgrounds on a regular basis, he tells them he wasn't a son in his family, but a daughter. He has found that while people have initial questions, he's so far along in his physical transition, the topic rarely comes up once he's addressed their general questions.

Ken told me, "This one guy, I told him pretty early on after we moved to this town, because we really clicked and I could tell we were going to be best buds. That was four years ago. He had questions at first, of course, but then we gradually moved on to other things and now it never comes up. A couple of months ago I said something about my cousin not accepting me and my friend looked confused. He forgot for the moment that I once transitioned! That was the most validating thing that's ever happened around my transition." *(E-mail correspondence, 2010)*

GENERATIONAL DIFFERENCES IN TRANSITION

Another factor influencing how people approach transition and post-transition disclosure is their generation. My adult clients ranged in age from 18 to 71. Most were seeking physical transition, though clients in their late 50s or 60s often told me surgery was not an ultimate goal; they felt that achieving a correct gender role would be quite sufficient to help them feel happy in their remaining time. My oldest client (a 71-year-old transwoman) was ecstatic to take hormones and never did shift social gender roles, for fear of losing social support and possibly her living situation in a retirement facility.

A number of 60-something crossdressers worked with me over the years. Some felt, 'I know if I were 30 years younger, I'd probably transition, with things being so much more open and accessible than they used to be. But do I really want to take that step now?' Many decided that no, they didn't want to change all that life, upsetting everyone in their lives, when crossdressing had been sufficient to allow them to live fairly happy lives.

A few wondered, "Am I really a crossdresser, or do I have a deep-seated need to transition?" They had come in to explore the issue, for two reasons. First, transition was more readily available now, leaving them wondering, "Was I keeping this under wraps just because it would have been such a difficult process?" More commonly, they were meeting others who had transitioned out of a crossdressing identity, leading them to wonder, "Is that me, too?" My work with such clients involved helping them clarify their identity; many happily remained crosdressers, while some realized they did indeed desire to transition physically.

What I've observed is that older clients (over 40 or so) tended to have a more binary view of gender and took a less activist approach to their transition. They had more life built up, more people would be affected by their transition, they had careers to consider. They tended to feel that their own transition processes were quite overwhelming enough without taking on activism on others' behalf.

Among my clients, the exceptions to this generalization have been people who lost everything, from lifelong relationship to career. As they started over, they felt they had less to lose and had a backlog of injustice fueling their activism. Two 50-something cli-ents were outgoing people and had excellent family support; they embraced an activist stance, living as their true selves and openly working for social justice on behalf of trans people. But in my experience, this wasn't the norm for the older client.

My teen and 20-something clients tended to put more energy into activist efforts, especially those who transitioned in college. This time of life is more activist in general; much of the social change in the world is driven by younger people taking a stand.

The generational differences in how my clients viewed transition also reflect the degree to which feminist values have changed U.S. culture. My younger clients' mothers tended to be more influenced by feminist values. In 2007, one 19-year-old client told me, "My mother always told me not to let others limit me, to stand up for myself, and be who I really am. When I told her I was transitioning and how much it meant to me that she'd always said that, she said, 'Damn, I wish I'd never told you that!'" While my client's mother was mostly joking, her own feelings of losing a daughter did make her feel her overtly-feminist message was coming back to bite her.

Some younger clients had difficulty understanding the attitudes of older trans people; I suggested my younger clients have a conversation with their grandparents about transition, gender roles, etc. Their grandparents are the same age as my older clients' pa-rents. It is the grandparent generation that formed the worldview of my older clients. I found that this perspective helped bridge the generation gap I experienced between younger and older trans people. This topic also comes up in the context of accessing support groups, as the goals and needs of the participants is based not only in the direction of their transition but also in their age and life circumstances.

LONELINESS AND ISOLATION POST-TRANSITION

Humans are social creatures, born with what social psycho-logists call the need for affiliation. (Kassin, 2010) This is a fancy way of saying, we need each other. Some prefer a small circle of close friends while others like to have a wide variety of acquaintances. Some need a lot of time alone, while others prefer the company of people most of the time. Whether introvert or extrovert, people do not tend to prefer living their lives in complete isolation from their own kind. The difficulty for transpeople arises when transition forces a shifting of tribe from one group to another. As there is no stable trans community for those long into transition, such folks may feel isolated even when surrounded by others.

This issue was particularly troubling for my Euro-American transmen clients whose attractions were to women, moving from the more social tribe of women to the quieter tribe of heterosexual Euro-American men, who do form connection with each other but in a less outspoken, more subtle way than ciswomen do. It can be difficult for transmen to join this quiet tribe; the rules are esta-blished on the grade school playground and they were not privy to the lessons.

Rather than trying to make the rules explicit for my clients, I encouraged them to develop their own cisgender support system. These rules are best learned in the real world, not as lessons imparted by a therapist. In the real world context not only did the client discover the reality of the available support, but also had the opportunity to discover that coming out to close friends did not lose them any status in the eyes of their friends if they have chosen their friends wisely.

Transwomen bump up almost immediately against the breadth of possibility inherent in female gender expression. How to dress, when to wear what, how to accessorize, how to make connection – these questions terrified some of my transwomen clients, yet often they were equally afraid of trying to find out the answers. Patsy, 55 when she started her physical transition, said, "I'm intimidated by women! I'm so afraid to approach them for advice, because it would just crush me if they rejected me. I want so badly to be accepted as one of them." *(Client session, 2009)*

Transmen have an advantage over transwomen in that they are rarely altering their gender expression much during the course of their transition. Most of my transmen clients have worn men's clothes exclusively all their adult lives; transwoman have not been permitted the luxury of being able to wear women's clothes all their adult lives prior to transition. On the other hand, there are trade-offs: transmen are perceived as adult males very quickly if they are taking a full dose of hormones and are then expected to know 'the rules' of social interaction as well as any cisgender man.

MENTORS AND FINDING A TRIBE

Regardless of when it comes up during the transition process, there is a link between finding cisgender mentors and the question, "Who is my tribe?" While I don't believe trans community exists in the same form as gay or lesbian community, that doesn't mean trans people have no tribe at all. The tribe isn't among other trans people, but will be based on shared interests, shared worldview, some form of common ground, rather than on trans status. If there are other trans people in any individual's tribe their presence will be based on their shared worldview and common interests, rather than shared trans status. And this is the crux of the difference between the post-transition life and the GLB life – there is no such thing as a post-GLB life. Being part of a gay or lesbian community is for life. Having transitioned is for life as well but the sense of community, the tribe, will not stay the same over the lifespan.

It is seductive, the ability to blend in and be part of a cisgender tribe, a new circle of friends and family, to live forever private. Historically the paradigm of transition has been such that the goal was just that: be able to gradually leave your old life behind, get a new job (perhaps even a new career), form new friendships, and don't tell anyone if you don't have to.

Many of my clients were fortunate enough to be transitioning in a time and place where this goal is open to question. They looked around and ask, "What is my motivation if I don't disclose to some of the people around me? It might help effect social change if I come out now and then, to challenge the mainstream cultural belief that a transsexual is a drag queen who went one step further." Some are not in a position to disclose their life journey once they have transitioned. They feel too much risk for their physical safety, for their job, or for their family. But these days it is not a foregone conclusion that this is always the case.

Thus society slowly changes as trans people join the main-stream, find their personal tribes, and then change that tribe forever by expanding what it means to be part of the mainstream, through disclosure of their personal journey. Friends and mentors become allies. GLB identities are far less marginalized than was the case 40 years ago, largely because GLB people began less coming out to friends and family in the decades after the 1969 Stonewall uprising. The degree to which T identities become less marginalized is directly linked to the numbers of post-transition people who come out to others, putting a face to the identity 'trans,' and exposing the fallacy of the current cultural beliefs about what 'transsexual' looks like. (Vanderburgh, 2017)

NON-BINARY MID-TRANSITION

It might seem counterintuitive to think of a non-binary person as having transitioned. No one, however, is assigned non-binary at birth. The non-binary person's transition is a process of realizing their birth gender assignment doesn't reflect who they are and that their identity isn't as binary as male or female. This transition may or may not involve a physical component of accessing hormones or surgery but does involve an internal readjustment of identity and a social component of coming out to others.

Non-binary people grapple with issues of invisibility and being consistently misgendered. Those trans people who claim male or female as their gender are often quite happy to be invisible and not be seen as trans. But the non-binary person's invisibility can lead to a weary feeling of making no headway. Constantly correcting others about pronouns gets old quickly. One common mid transition issue for those who are non-binary is a jaded feeling of cynical frustration at the larger culture's tenacious subconscious tendency to enforce the gender binary.

At times some non-binary people may take out this frustration on their trans siblings who do identify as male or female, accusing them of 'woodworking' (blending into the woodwork) and taking full advantage of the gender binary system. It can help to remind the non-binary client that identity does exist on a spectrum of possibility; if a person has always felt female or male inside and not in the middle, then they *are* living true to their identity by transi-tioning. It isn't their fault that their identity happens to fit into the gender binary system.

On occasion, some who transition fully to male or female may voice doubts that non-binary identities are legitimate. This can leave the non-binary person feeling, "NO ONE supports me, either cisgender or trans people, my only support will come from other non-binary people." This kind of global judgment is often based in the pain of rejection and anger at being misunderstood by those they feel *should* understand; such feelings may hold a client back from fully participating in their world.

Some years ago, a non-binary person (I'll call them Chris) appeared on a panel for a human sexuality class at a local college. A friend of mine taught the class and told me of the experience later. "This was an evening class and like most such classes, the students were a bit older than the day students. They were mostly working adults who were going back to school. Some identified as gay or lesbian and a few were trans but not visible; I only knew they were trans because they had come out to me in papers they'd written. Chris

174

had taken my class the year before, so I invited them to be on the panel. I was appalled at what Chris said to the class: 'I hang out with non-binary folks as much as possible. No offense, but you [meaning cisgender people] are kinda boring.'

"One of the other trans people on the panel came up to me after the class and said, 'I was horrified when Chris said that! I tried to help the students feel it was still okay to ask questions after that. I don't think you should have Chris on the panel anymore.' And I haven't. How can Chris sit on a panel trying to educate a class so non-binary identity will be respected, and then turn around and disrespect the class? I told Chris it wasn't appropriate to talk like that, and they got offended."

TRIBES ARE SO BINARY

Mainstream U.S.culture is binary in nature. Not only are we limited to two genders and two sexual orientations (gay/lesbian or straight), our entire society is also structured to recognize romantic relationships as being between two people. Those in polyamorous relationships receive about as much cultural respect as those who are non-binary or bisexual. All challenge our binary system.

Gay and lesbian identities don't challenge these binary structures; gay men and lesbians often don't recognize the legitimacy of bisexual identities and have just as little idea what to do with non-binary identities as does the mainstream culture. Polyamory may or may not be accepted within lesbian or gay community, particularly in light of marriage equality. Will lesbian and gay marriages eventually parallel those of their straight counterparts, only recognizing couple relationships as legitimate?

Finding a tribe is difficult for those who exist outside the binary system, whether because of sexuality, gender, or relational affiliation. It is tempting to take Chris' route: "I only hang out with other non-binary people." But society only truly changes when those who are marginalized participate fully. It is difficult for the pioneers, the first to openly participate in an arena in which they have been unwelcome or invisible in the past. Those who do so with an open heart, expecting to be met halfway, are more likely to be successful than those who approach the situation with anger at past injustices and an expectation of more of same.

Those who are expanding a tribe to include non-binary identities will probably find their efforts successful – over time. Allowing others time and space to expand beyond the binary is an essential component, requiring patience and a willingness to remain open while witnessing others expand their worldview. It can help to re-mind clients with non-binary identities that they once experienced the same challenge to their worldview; their self-acceptance didn't come automatically, raised as all of us were in this very binary cul-ture. This may allow them to have patience with others in their life, giving them an opportunity to eventually have a tribe with more than non-binary people in it.

• Chapter 10 •

TRANSITION AS A
DEVELOPMENTAL PROCESS

THIS QUESTION IS DECEPTIVELY EASY: Why is physical transition so hard? It would be simple to say, 'because mainstream U.S. culture is hostile and intolerant toward those who don't fit gender norms.' However transition is still stressful even for those who don't experience much overt hostility or rejection.

Though a few of my clients lost their entire family, most re-ceived a midrange level of support from within their family ('family' includes spouse/partner/children, family of origin, and family of choice). Some distress and unhappiness is to be expected as family members grapple with their own loss and grief process, letting go of their old gender perception in order to accept the new.

I took great care to stress to my pre-transition clients that their families would go through some loss and grief process and to be prepared for this eventuality. Most of my clients were well able to allow their families this process, recognizing that it was not their responsibility to own that process on behalf of their families, though some still felt a degree of guilt over causing upheaval.

Yet no matter how supportive the partner, or family, or work situation, transition is still difficult. Why is this the case even for those who experience a relatively smooth process? Because, as the chart on the next page shows, it's an *overwhelming* process. At some point or another, every question on this chart will be visited and revisited by (or upon) the transitioning individual. Particularly toward the beginning of transition it can feel as if all these issues are coming up at the same time, calling into question every aspect of the client's life.

THE MANY LEVELS OF TRANSITION

INTRAPSYCHIC
The individual, alone

INTERPERSONAL
The individual one-on-one with another person

INTIMATE GROUP
The individual as part of a family (family of origin, or of choice)

COMMUNITY
The individual as part of a subculture (e.g., lesbian, Latino, etc.)

SOCIETAL
The individual as part of a larger culture (e.g., the U.S.)

	INTRAPSYCHIC	INTERPERSONAL	INTIMATE GROUP	COMMUNITY	SOCIETAL
INTRAPSYCHIC Internal processing, Self acceptance, Abstract concepts	Perception of body, without considering relationships with others	Questioning sexual orientation, but in the abstract	Figuring out new role in family of origin (e.g. brother v. sister), or in family of choice	Figuring out new role in communities of choice (e.g., male in lesbian community?)	Effect of gender role on world view and political stances
INTERPERSONAL Relationships, Processing with individuals	Effect of transition on intimate relationships, is sexuality shifting?	How is partner reacting? How are potential partners reacting differently?	How are family members reacting? How are they behaving differently?	How are friends reacting? Losing any? Finding new allies?	How is it to be with partner out in the world?
INTIMATE GROUP Group processing, family acceptance, Redefining roles	Maintaining self-center despite group pressure and adverse reactions	How is relationship being perceived by family of origin or of choice?	Is transition creating conflict between family members?	How is subculture viewing the family? Suspicion, curiosity? Coming out issues. Conflict, confusion.	How is mainstream society viewing the family? Suspicion? Curiosity? Coming out issues. Confusion.
COMMUNITY Identity/label issues, Community loss or acceptance	Feelings of isolation and not fitting in. Still part of this community?	Shifting sexuality perceptions can affect how partnership fits in.	Shifting sexuality perceptions can affect how partnership fits in.	Individual community members challenged re gender issues. May resist processing.	Community may distance itself from transition, an attempt to maintain homeostasis
SOCIETAL Politics and culture, Living trans in a narrow-minded society	What does new gender role mean culturally? How does it affect world view?	Shifting sexual orientation affects how partnership is viewed by society	Family of origin may reject transition as having negative social impact on the family	Family of choice may reject transition as negatively affecting societal view of the subculture	Fluid gender increases societal discomfort with trans issues. Potential violence, backlash.

178

INTRAPSYCHIC AND INTERPERSONAL LEVELS

Traditionally therapists work with clients from a combination of two levels, the *intrapsychic* and the *interpersonal.*

Intrapsychic refers to the client's relationship with themselves. At this level the trans client explores issues of core identity and self-acceptance. Self-conceptualization and self-knowledge are the foci of the therapeutic process at this level, and it is at this level that therapists feel most at home. A legacy of Freudian psychology, therapy in this culture has traditionally been viewed as an individual endeavor. Family systems theory has expanded this to recognize that family structures exert a powerful influence on the individual; nevertheless, most therapy is still at the individual level.

Interpersonal refers to the individual's one-on-one relationships with others. At the interpersonal level the therapy focuses more on the client's romantic and family relationships (both family of origin and family of choice). At this level trans client issues are centered around sexual orientation, physical experiences of sex, body image, boundaries, and intimacy.

Being raised in what feels like an inappropriate gender role often leads gender-dissonant individuals to hide their true selves in order to survive childhood. Dropping these defenses can be very difficult. Paradoxically, the more the trans person cares for someone, the harder it is to allow them 'in.' Being intimate means allowing the other person the opportunity to share the trans person's world. This is a scary proposition for someone who learned young that it wasn't safe to share their true identity with anyone who felt like 'family.'

Generally speaking clients first work at the intrapsychic level. In order to work on relationships with others, a person must first center into who they are as individuals, which is intrapsychic work. With a firm basis in identity to work from the client is then able to explore what it means to be in relationship with others – interpersonal work.

Post-transition issues often arise at levels beyond the intrapsychic and interpersonal, as the client reintegrates into society in a new gender role, learning new boundaries and an unfamiliar set of rules and expectations. This is not to say that intrapsychic and interpersonal work end as transition begins. Viewing transition as a developmental process, the intrapsychic and interpersonal level work will be revisited over time. As the transitioning client broad-ens the scope of transition to bring in extended family, co-workers and neighbors, the therapeutic work continually cycles back around to the intrapsychic and interpersonal, from different perspectives.

As transition proceeds, existential questions of identity in rela-tion to the world continually resurface for examination. A two-year-old may ask, "Who am I?" but the context is very different from the adolescent question, "Who am I?" Yet it is just as necessary for the two-year-old's development to ask that question and come to some answer as it is for the adolescent.

As a trans client 'matures' in their transition process, the issues they face at all the different levels will also mature in nature, be-coming less self-focused (the seeming-narcissism of early transi-tion) and more self-in-relation focused. Thus the person who has been taking hormones for three years and has come out to everyone in their life may still be revisiting some of the same issues in this chart, but not from the same level of 'maturation' as the person who is just beginning to face their intention to transition.

INTIMATE GROUP LEVEL

The *intimate group* is the client's immediate and extended fa-mily, both family of choice and of origin. How are various family members handling the client's potential transition? How are they treating the client? Is the client's family rigid, such that family members are taking sides about the transition, creating a schism in the family structure? Is the family structure more fluid, such that members are freer to have their own opinions without fracturing the family bonds? How has the client's family of choice reacted? Have they lost many individual friends? Genograms can be useful here; if the client has a particularly strong family of choice, the genogram concept can be extended to create a genogram specific to that family structure.

If the therapist has had training in family therapy, family ses-sions may be helpful, particularly with those family members who are willing and able to assume an ally role during transition. Such sessions can help family members express their own feelings about the transition, helping further their own process of adjustment.

After transition has begun (before and after are client-defined), the family's homeostasis will continue to be in flux as all the family members adjust to the client's new gender role and presentation. Homeostasis is a family therapy term referring to the balance of alli-ances and roles within a family that keep the structure stable. (Note that 'stable' doesn't always mean 'healthy.') Another way to view the stability of a family structure is that it is resistant to change. (Hoffman, 1981) The more rigid a family system, the more likely it is that a major event like transition will shatter the structure. A flex-ible system will weather the stress of a major process or event by bending rather than breaking.

Major events like transition will naturally disrupt the homeosta-sis of any family structure, as all the roles and alliances are turned upside down while family members adjust to the transition in one way or another. Homeostasis is only fully re-established when all family members have come to some resolution about the transition.

This does not mean all have come to *accept* the transition; some may come to the resolution that they can never accept the client's transition. This may affect the homeostasis by causing new factions within the family that did not exist prior to transition. In some family structures, the transition places the client in the scapegoat role; the transition is used as a wedge, allowing various family members to break off relations with others in the family by using the transition as the excuse.

Rhoda (27) believed her transition had caused her parents to divorce after nearly 30 years of marriage. With much bitterness, her mother told her this was the case and it had not occurred to Rhoda to question this interpretation. Rhoda's father was blaming her mo-ther for allowing their only son to help her around the house too much, play with dolls, etc. He felt this had caused gender role con-fusion that led Rhoda to believe herself to be female.

Rhoda remembered her childhood as one of distress at school, ameliorated by her mother's acceptance of her choice of toys, games, and activities at home. Her mother had accepted Rhoda's fe-minine nature early on, while her father still uses male pronouns and the name Ronald four years into physical transition.

With the aid of a genogram, I helped Rhoda deconstruct her fa-mily's patterns of communication; gradually she came to see that her parents had had a distant and sometimes hostile marriage for years. Rhoda eventually realized that she was being blamed for her parents' divorce so they would not have to look at themselves as culpable parties in their own dysfunctional cycle.

Though Rhoda's mother accepted her new daughter, she was still complicit in attaching blame for the divorce to Rhoda's tran-sition. Through our work together, Rhoda realized that children are not responsible for the feelings their parents have for each other. She was then able to set appropriate boundaries with her parents: not seeing her father if he continued to misgender her, and dis-agreeing with her mother when she blamed Rhoda for the divorce.

SOCIAL GROUP LEVEL

Beyond the intimate group is the *social group,* and a client will be a member of more than one. The social group is a demographic category; within mainstream U.S. culture the distinctions are most often drawn along the lines of race, class, gender, ethnicity, religion, and sexual orientation. For instance, if the client is currently living as an African-American lesbian, there are going to be questions about acceptance among their African-American friends of all sexu-al orientations and genders, friends of any gender or race, and les-bian friends of any race.

Clients may want to do research on the Internet to learn more about experiences others may have had within a specific culture. The concept of physical transition has only existed since the late 1940s. This can make it difficult for clients to predict what kind of acceptance they may receive, depending on their ethnic and cultural background.

In addition, reaching out to others with whom they share various identities or characteristics can help the client strengthen their base of social support as they proceed with transition. This support can be among trans and cisgender people alike and will serve not only to prevent isolation, but to continually remind the client that many cisgender people can be allies during their transition process.

The bonds of various cultural backgrounds are strong and clients may be fearful of losing their place. Maureen (24) was born into a somewhat conservative religious sect and spent her childhood co-cooned within an enclave, home schooled and somewhat isolated geographically. From an early age she knew she needed to tran-sition, but was deeply afraid. Her background was such that her intimate, social, and interpersonal connections were all the same people; she didn't know what she would do if they rejected her. All were her family, whether related by blood or not.

I encouraged her to view the members of her family one by one and choose the person she felt most comfortable with as her first venture in disclosure. Maureen chose to disclose to a sister close to her in age and found her sister was not surprised or put off by the idea of Maureen's transition from Mark. With the help of her new ally Maureen strategized further disclosures without needing as much support or input from me.

This is a tricky area therapeutically as it involves cross-cultural work, and the therapist's understanding of some cultures will be necessarily limited. The following mantra is particularly applicable with work at this level: "Don't just do something, sit there." It can be easy for a therapist to feel inadequate when listening to clients talk about cultures that are literally foreign to them. Another useful mantra is: "I am enough."

Lei is a 35-year-old transman originally from rural Taiwan. He has taken his father's first name, though his name change isn't legal as he has no plans to transition physically or socially for some time to come. His intention is to wait until his parents have died (they are in their mid-sixties and in good health).

Lei is well-paid within the high-tech sector and sends half his earnings back to his family; he is the only family member to have left Taiwan and earns more by himself than the rest of his family combined. Lei finds himself at sea when he visits Taiwan as his journey of self-knowledge has taken him far from his role as Jun (his birth name). He has lived in the United States for over ten years and now feels between cultures. His American trans friends don't understand why he doesn't take hormones and his family doesn't understand why his hair is so short.

It would be easy for a western therapist to question Lei's commitment to his trans identity, given that Lei isn't planning to take hormones for many years. It would be easy to see Lei as non-binary, when in fact he identifies as male and would love to switch to being testosterone-based. However his cultural values include support for the family at the expense of individualism; a person who puts themselves first and ignores the needs of their family is considered selfish in the extreme. It is a Euro-American value to prioritize self-actualization, and to see people as co-dependent if they put other people's needs first.

Lei believes that if he transitioned physically it would create a schism within his family, with the younger generation largely supporting him and the older generation believing him to be insane. The resulting battle would disrupt the harmony of the family for years, a scenario Lei finds intolerable. He has made his peace with his situation by identifying as a transman among his friends and requesting male pronouns, while allowing his family to continue to address him as Jun and 'she.'

My role in working with Lei was to help him clarify his options and be his witness as he sorted through the conflicts inherent in his situation. I gave him information about transition and helped him write a letter to his parents, coming out as a transman. Though he doesn't intend to send the letter, he wanted the practice finding language to explain transition to them in case he changes his mind at some point in the future. For now the satisfaction he feels as a contributing family member trumps his need to transition.

Writing a coming-out letter was empowering to Lei, giving voice to his identity and reinforcing for him that he was *choosing* his path of not transitioning. I also told him overtly, "If you reach a point of wanting to begin taking hormones, I will write you a refer-ral letter." Taking this worry off the table allowed Lei to focus on his here-and-now experience.

SOCIETAL LEVEL

At the *societal level* issues of mainstream acceptance and safety emerge. At this level of consideration, issues may include coming out within a community, feeling guilty or ashamed if they decide not to come out, and safety in an unfamiliar gender role. At this level the therapist may also be an ally and advocate, facilitating a workplace presentation, for example.

Many of my clients didn't want to be out as trans in all arenas of life. Therapeutically the issue is one of motivation and its impact on self-esteem, self-efficacy, levels of anxiety and depression, and self-consciousness. Clients who wish to begin transition and then cut themselves off from their past, living completely privately, are also cutting themselves off from the opportunity to develop cisgender mentors who can help them navigate the resocialization process, and learn the rules of monogendered situations more quickly.

The client who wants to live privately may never learn that it is possible to have cisgender allies who are honored to support trans people during their transformative process. It may be that once decades have past post-transition, disclosure is not necessary to develop true intimacy with others, but this is not the case in the first few years after beginning transition.

Further, the days of being able to be private about transition, with total control over identity information, are long gone. The power of the Internet, coupled with name change and docu-mentation requirements put in place post-9/11, have made it impossible for trans people to be certain they can completely di-vorce themselves from their previous legal identity.

As we have moved into the new millennium, trans identity is becoming a mainstream civil rights issue. Some trans people are embracing this move, feeling jubilant as we see announcements every day of some form of recognition of the legitimacy of trans identities. Other trans people still wish to live privately and resent the limelight. Many now fear the limelight. One colleague remarked to me, "Even 9/11 didn't make my trans clients as anxious as Trump's election; none of my clients felt at risk from Osama bin Laden the way they do with Trump as president." *(Personal con-versation, 2017)*

Therapy at this level involves helping clients find their privacy boundaries and navigate their feelings of being in the spotlight more than they would wish. Some find they are put in the position of educating others more than they would like. A few years ago I had a conversation with Kim, a 38-year-old transwoman friend of mine who had come out at work as needing to transition physically. She works for a small high tech company; her cisgender boss has enthusiastically embraced her process. She said to me, "I just want to get on with my life as a woman! I'm not an activist at heart, but I feel like my boss is putting me in the position of becoming one. He's all gung-ho about getting our insurance company on board with covering transition. I'm all for that, but I don't want to be the one to go in and educate them! I want someone like you to do that, not me!" *(Personal conversation, 2015)*

Work with clients in this situation shifts back and forth between the various levels of interaction, as self-esteem is intrapsychic work, while discussions of disclosure can shift from sociological discussions (societal level) to talk about co-workers (intimate or social group) to fears about partners (interpersonal level).

TRANSITION AS A DEVELOPMENTAL PROCESS

As with child development processes, first comes the development of identity; building on that foundation the child explores who they are in relation to others. However while identity issues are a crucial foundation, establishing identity first doesn't mean this issue is never revisited. Humans are constantly revisiting the concept of who they are, as they progress through further levels of maturation. The person in transition asks, "Who am I?" first from the intra-psychic level, as the toddler would. Then from the interpersonal level, as a pre-pubescent child would. Then from the social group level, which is where adolescents tend to live. Then from more adult levels of subculture(s) and society as a whole.

An individual who faces gender identity issues grapples first with the question, "Who am I?" in the context of deciding whether or not to pursue physical transition, based in knowledge of their own identity. If the client decides to transition physically, the question "Who am I?" will surface again in a different context. If the client becomes female after a lifetime of being treated male, the context becomes "Who am I as a woman? How do I relate to people now, and how do they relate to me?" For those who transition to male, questions arise about male privilege, forming connection among those who have been taught not to show emotional process, how to form romantic relationships, etc.

The individual is grappling with the same kinds of developmental questions any child goes through in the course of maturation. At birth, a doctor assumes gender and tells the parents, "It's a boy," or "It's a girl." From that point on the child's development is shaped along one of two vectors (male or female), into fairly rigid roles based entirely on perceived gender identity. It is becoming increas-ingly common for parents to 'gender' their child prior to birth, via ultrasound technology. This might give a head start to the process of gender socialization; who knows what effect the mother's gendered thoughts have on the developing fetus?

And what of the situation where the interpretation of the ultrasound is incorrect? Two friends of mine, a cisgender male-female couple, had an interesting experience while pregnant. The ultrasound results seemed to indicate a male fetus. For the next five months, both parents developed an increasingly-gendered conceptualization of their child. When the child was born, the doctors proclaimed, "It's a girl!"

It took several weeks for the baby's father to 'unlearn' the gender assumption he'd internalized after the ultrasound; he found it difficult to bond with his daughter during the first few days of her life outside the womb. He had preferred to have a daughter anyway (the couple had two sons already), so this was not a case of a man being disappointed in not having a son.

Interestingly the mother did not have a similar problem, possibly because of the complex of hormones released in a mother's system that cause her to bond with her baby, what we in this culture have often termed the maternal instinct. As one mother put it to me, only half-jokingly, "If it weren't for that bond created by hormones, many of us would be inclined at times to want to get rid of our children when they are being especially trying."

A person who transitions as an adult is returning to ground zero (birth) and redeveloping along different lines. Unlike child development, this intrapsychic developmental process takes place in an individual whose brain structures are fully developed. This is not a person whose infant brain is doubling in size between birth and age five. This is not a person whose brain soaks up new information like a sponge, indiscriminately and unconsciously. This is a fully functional, mature adult whose development was steered along an inappropriate gender vector from the time of birth.

How do various issues play out when considered through the developmental lens of transition? Let's assume a client is currently living as a lesbian, but is now questioning gender identity and considering transition to male.

At the *intrapsychic level*, the client may believe this will mean that post-transition, they will still be attracted to women.

At the *interpersonal level,* they would assume this would mean they would become a heterosexual man.

At the *intimate group level,* the client might believe their family of origin will see this as proof that all lesbians secretly want to be men, if the family accepts the transition in the first place. The client may experience a great deal of ambivalence, wanting to be seen as a man yet not wanting their former lesbian identity denigrated. Among family of choice, probably primarily lesbian, the client might fear losing their place as family.

At the *social group level*, transition would mean severing ties with the lesbian community or at the least drastically changing the nature of the client's role within that community, though hopefully retaining their individual lesbian friends (part of the intimate group).

At the *societal level,* the client may see being a straight man as more socially acceptable than being perceived as a lesbian, though they may have guilty feelings of ambivalence about accepting both male and heterosexual privilege, as well as uncertainty what that privilege might look like.

If the client is a person of color, or part of a non-mainstream religious community, there will be further issues of acceptance within their various communities. Will they be marginalized within a marginalized community that has always relied on support from each other?

As if all this existential processing were not enough, the client may find their sexual orientation emerging more fully post-transition and that they are attracted to more different kinds of people than they realized. Their experience of sexuality may shift, necessitating revisiting all the various levels of acceptance yet again! (I discuss shifting sexuality more fully in the chapter *For Partners Only.)*

This is just one example of how transition can have a profound effect on a client's sense of self and identity. The role of the therapist is to witness and normalize the process. When I gave clients the *Ramifications of Transition* handout, I told them, "I don't give you this to try to scare you away from transition, but to make concrete why it is you will probably feel overwhelmed as you go through this process. At some point every question listed here will come up for you, and possibly others specific to your life situation." The specific questions and feelings that came up for each client then became the focus of therapy as the client proceeded on their journey.

• Chapter 11 •

THE RAMIFICATIONS OF WORKPLACE
DISCLOSURE

ONE OF THE MOST SIGNIFICANT DIFFERENCES between coming out trans and coming out as gay, lesbian, queer or bisexual is that physical transition can't be hidden. A gay man can pick and choose who he tells about his sexual orientation, though he may feel unhappily closeted if he's forced to keep silent at work. If he desires privacy, there may be whole groups of people in his life who never find out he's gay. A person who transitions physically loses control over their own information. Transition is the biggest gossip most people ever encounter, and many can't resist spreading the word.

The client has to decide who needs to hear the news directly from them and make sure these disclosures happen within a short time period. One small-town client said, "Because of the way my family all talk to each other, all the time, I knew I was going to have about an hour. I was really methodical about it. I went from one house to another, telling them all, and by the time I got to the last person they had just had a phone call from my aunt." *(Client session, 2005)*

Most families are less tight-knit than this particular client's; nevertheless, it is important that the client consider how close friends and family will feel if they find out something of this magnitude via a third party. It is common for close friends to feel betrayed and hurt ("Why didn't you tell me yourself? Didn't you trust me?") if they don't find out this news directly from the client. It often helps close friends and family members to hear, "It's not that your reaction didn't matter; it's that it mattered so much. That's why it was so hard to tell you."

191

One interesting paradox concerning the public nature of transition is that it seems to give license to others to feel they can ask very personal questions. I mentioned this in a class I taught and a ciswoman raised her hand, saying, "That's exactly the experience I had when I was pregnant. Total strangers would come up to me and ask if they could 'feel' the baby, then reach out to put their hand on my stomach!"

As with pregnancy, the process of physical transition is so visible that others seem to lose sight of the fact that it is also one of the most private processes a person can undertake. Clients reported to me that they were asked the most breathtakingly personal questions without a second thought, such as: "Are you going to have 'the surgery'?" or "So, how do you and your partner make love?"

Again using sexual orientation as an analogy, imagine asking an acquaintance who's just told you he's gay: "So, do you like to take it up the ass?" If this sounds crude beyond belief, personal questions about their body and surgical status can affect the trans person similarly. I encouraged my clients to do some self-examination on this score. Many clients told me, "I don't mind answering any question." However, when we explored further their motivation, some began to realize that they were not completely comfortable talking about their heart-deep dreams with everyone under the sun.

A few of my extroverted clients enjoyed the opportunity to educate and answer questions, but most realized they wanted more privacy. Many of my clients chose to come out to important people in their lives via letter or e-mail, feeling overwhelmed by the sheer numbers of people they had to tell and not wanting to bare their soul over and over.

Many developed a printed FAQ (Frequently-Asked Questions), answering in writing some of the questions they were most often asked. Others crafted tactful replies that let the inquirer know they were asking too personal a question. Carol, for instance, had a standard reply when people asked her whether she'd had 'the surgery.' She replied, "I've had all the surgery I need to feel complete." Most of my clients came to some form of compromise, sharing some aspects with people they felt close to but not wanting to share their process with strangers.

Often my clients came to realize that their first reaction ("I don't mind answering any question") was rooted in a desire to explain themselves to others in an attempt to justify their transition or to gain others' validation. Their motivation had been one of feeling unconsciously that they had some obligation to justify their transition by explaining it to people who were just one step removed from the stranger category. Low self-esteem and lack of self-worth are insidious, and so common among the gender-dissonant. Many of my clients had not felt they had the right to establish boundaries when discussing their transition process. How can it be otherwise, when most had negative childhood experiences around gender identity and/or gender expression?

THE PERSONAL BECOMES PUBLIC

I helped my clients determine their boundaries and preferred means of communication as they contemplated how to come out at work. For those who worked outside the home, disclosure in the workplace was more unnerving for most than telling their extended families.

Workplace relationships are professional in nature and often co-workers don't socialize outside the work environment beyond an occasional lunch together. Yet these are people who spend 40+ hours a week with each other. For many people, workplace relation-ships account for more social interaction than any other area of life except immediate family. Yet such relationships are not based in emotional connection or shared interest (beyond the desire for a paycheck). This most personal and private of transformations be-comes public knowledge, often the biggest gossip ever to hit the workplace, and the transitioning individual loses control over their own information.

Carl (28 at the time he began physical transition) worked in the Human Resources department of a company with about 500 employees. Because of the nature of his job he routinely interacted with people from every department in the company. He was not the first person at his company to transition; the company had policies and procedures in place, smoothing Carl's process considerably.

A year later Carl realized he had a problem he could not easily control. Several of his co-workers had asked him early on, "Can I tell other people for you so you don't have to?" Carl gratefully agreed; he was overwhelmed and tired of explaining. He carefully told his co-workers what to say and sent them an e-mail that they could forward to others.

Carl didn't consider that over time his transition would become history and his birth gender invisible to others. In good faith, not realizing Carl's position on disclosure might change over time, his co-workers took it upon themselves to automatically tell new employees about Carl's transition. They thought they were sparing him the ordeal of continuing to come out.

Transition is such an overwhelming process when considered as a whole, it is not only common but advisable to take it a step at a time, not thinking too much about what might happen four steps down the line. Trans people can't know with certainty how they are going to feel a year, two years, or more, into their process. How will they feel about disclosure once they are no longer 'in transition'? This is not a question someone new to hormones can answer about themselves a year or more in advance.

Carl took his situation with good humor. He realized that a year into his transition his former female identity was so far behind him that new employees just shrugged and said, "I never would have known," and that was that. Though Carl could have gone to his co-workers and told them not to continue outing him, he no longer knew precisely who was taking on this task and who was not. He chose to put his energy elsewhere and not worry about it.

Carl went to work for another company four years into his transition. He was surprised how comfortable (and relieved) he felt to be private at work, not disclosing his trans identity. Though unashamed of his trans status, and continuing his activism on behalf of trans civil rights, Carl is now in the position of being able to go to work each day and know he's not the poster child for trans people. At times he feels a little guilty about not being as out as he was at his old job, but he also realizes he didn't come out before – his transition outed him.

SURPRISING LEVELS OF SUPPORT

One client's workplace experience took her breath away, so unexpected was her boss' response. Upon finding out that Trina (34) was planning to transition, the owner of the company called her into his office. He began by telling her that he would have a zero-tolerance policy for harassment and that anyone who gave her grief about her transition would be called to task by him personally. He then asked her a few questions about transition and she told him that money was one reason she was taking her process so slowly. Trina outlined for her boss the various expenses she faced, finishing by telling him she expected to spend several thousand dollars over the course of the next year on electrolysis alone.

Her boss then said, "You bring the electrolysis bills in and put them here on my desk and I'll make sure they're taken care of." He also told her she could take off days from work (with full pay) for anything related to her transition, from doctor's visits to recuperating from any surgery she might eventually undergo. His reasoning for offering this level of support? He saw his support as an investment in his company. He had offered the same type of support to an employee who has an autoimmune disorder, paying for certain medications she could not afford on her own and that were only partially covered by insurance. His investment in Trina's transition was minimal, balanced by the good work she did for his company.[19]

---

[19] It was on this basis that a number of major corporations began covering transition processes for employees, regardless of their insurers' exclusions.

So unprepared was Trina for this level of support, she had no idea how she felt about it. Trina's next appointment with me was after work that same day and she came in saying, "This is going to amaze you!" (And she was right!) Throughout the subsequent few sessions she kept returning to this experience, saying out of the blue, "Wasn't that an amazing reaction?"

Ironically one of Trina's biggest fears had been transitioning in the workplace. She had told everyone else in her life and had reached a 'gender limboland' point physically; she was not being seen as a gay man any longer, a common experience among my transwomen clients, but was confusing strangers about her gender identity. She had hesitated to take the plunge, living female full-time, primarily because of her fears of losing her job or being ostracized by co-workers. Upon disclosure Trina did experience one co-worker's discomfort, but the other 50 or so employees had no problem with her transition. By the time she finally disclosed offi-cially what was going on, her appearance had changed so much that no one was surprised by the news.

This level of workplace support exceeds any other I have heard about. Trina knows full well how lucky she is; her fears of work-place disclosure had been based in hearing others' stories. Most of my clients had experiences somewhere between outright firing and Trina's.

Trina left her job a year after coming out. Though her boss was supportive, her immediate supervisor made her work-life difficult. Trina believes the woman didn't approve of transition and used her supervisory position to make it hard for Trina to do her job effect-ively. Trina never could decide how conscious her supervisor was of her actions, as nothing was ever quite egregious enough for Trina to feel she could complain to HR.

Trina was eventually hired as a webinar trainer, a job she once would have thought impossible for a transwoman. After half a dozen sessions with a vocal coach, however, Trina was never again misgendered when she spoke. She now considers her voice one of her best assets professionally.

Supportive employers who are able to think outside the box can come up with creative solutions to circumvent potential problems before they crop up. One employer solved the issue of healthcare benefits: she dropped the pre-transition employee as if he had left the company and added the post-transition employee as if she was a new hire. The new name and different gender allowed the transition to slip under the insurance company's radar. This allowed the em-ployee to avoid the possibility of having problems with the insur-ance company because of the transition issue.

The employee was not trying to get any part of her transition covered by the insurance company, which had transition-related ex-clusions in place at that time. She wanted to retain her health benefits for the same reason any employee would: routine doctor visits, prescription medications, the possibility of catastrophic injury or illness, and coverage for her spouse and children. The employee was concerned she might lose basic medical coverage or be dis-criminated against in some way were the insurance company to find out she was transitioning.

THE BATHROOM ISSUE

The biggest challenge for many who transition on the job has been working with their employers to figure out, "What bathroom should I use?" There are few public settings in U.S. society that are monogendered; bathrooms and locker rooms are the most common.

These are difficult situations for any trans person to navigate. Pre-transition, many use the restroom and locker room that might not feel comfortable, but that calls the least attention to them-selves.[20] In the

---

[20] This can leave pre-transition transmen in a quandary, as they are often seen as teenage boys prior to transition. Some work up the nerve to begin using male restrooms prior to beginning hormones, as they will probably not be challenged in the men's restroom and know from experience that they will be questioned if they tried to use the women's restroom. However, in the workplace, using male restrooms in advance of taking hormones may not be an option.

workplace the pre-transition employee usually con-tinues to use the restroom associated with their birth gender assign-ment, despite their self-consciousness and discomfort, not wanting to call attention to their transition and risk being fired, make co-workers uncomfortable, etc.

Those trans people most uncomfortable with bathrooms and locker rooms are early in transition, forced to choose a bathroom at work when everyone knows what's going on or having been told by their employer which bathroom they are expected to use, regardless of whether it is the one they would choose. It is precisely this kind of situation that makes most trans people wish they could just go about their transition in a private way and avoid interacting with others about their process. Some workplaces focus on the dis-comfort of their cisgender employees and customers, not con-sidering that the discomfort and self-consciousness of the trans employee is usually greater. (Weiss, 2007)

The city council of one Oregon town held public meetings during 2005-6, with the debate waxing furious on both sides of the issue of trans people using public bathrooms.[21] Trans activists and cisgender allies argued for inclusivity and civil rights. Conservative people countered with the scenario of male predators putting on dresses and going into the women's bathroom or locker room. The argument that trans people are inherently predatory is ludicrous yet often invoked in such situations. After several hours of heated debate an older transwoman who had not spoken up raised her hand and said wearily, "You know, sometimes I just have to pee."

All too often in these debates the talk turns academic, moral or philosophical, losing sight of the very human reality that at some point during the day everyone has to go to the bathroom. Employers can address the fears of those who know nothing of trans issues by

---

[21] Since that time, the state of Oregon has put in place laws protecting individuals based on gender identity and sexual orientation. This issue is no longer up for debate in Oregon. Though it is not legal to deny a transperson access to the bathroom of their choice in Oregon, not everyone knows about (or respects) this legal status, and challenges may still happen.

offering employee education and not leaving it to the trans em-ployee to take on this burden alone.

Addressing such fears does not mean pandering to them. One university had the issue arise when an employee transitioned to female. One co-worker raised an objection to the transwoman employee using the women's restroom. The university's solution: designating a specific bathroom not for the transwoman but for the one cisfemale who raised an objection.

The HRC (Human Rights Campaign) website has useful information available on transitioning in the workplace. Jillian Weiss' excellent book *Transgender Workplace Diversity* is also helpful as HR departments develop policies and procedures to help facilitate transition. It can be helpful to employers to realize that many people have successfully transitioned on the job at other companies.

It is helpful to the trans employee if the employer offers a training of some kind. Reading about the transition process does not provide a forum for fellow employees to get their own questions answered. Transition can be made smoother by providing such a forum. Many cities have knowledgeable people who can conduct trainings for management and co-workers, helping smooth the path for the transitioning individual. I have often conducted such trainings. Sometimes the trainings were proactive and not scheduled because a particular employee was transitioning. When the training was because of a transitioning employee, that person usually chose not to attend the training. Not only did they not want to be in the spotlight if the opportunity arose to hold back, they also wanted co-workers to feel freer to ask whatever was on their mind.

As with families, co-workers need their own process of transition. Unlike families, however, most co-workers don't have a long-standing emotional investment in the transperson's previous gender. The word "co-worker" has no gender attached to it, unlike words describing family relationships ("father," "sister," etc.) Thus the emotional process should be easier for fellow employees than it is for immediate family.

The difficulty in the workplace is that people are supposed to leave personal issues at the door and not bring them into the work environment. The person undertaking physical transition can't help but bring the process to work; unfortunately their fellow employees are expected to leave their personal reactions behind when they get to work, an unrealistic expectation. Allowing co-workers to express their feelings in a more overt, deliberate setting may help them process through their reactions more quickly, so all can get on with their work and move forward.

When the issue of bathrooms arises, I ask the cisgender employees to consider the relationship they already have with the person in question. I try to keep the focus on this one individual's transition, to move the discussion away from the vague 'boogey man' fears many have, residual to childhood socialization of the ta-boo of setting foot in the wrong bathroom or fears of a predator in the women's bathroom.

I ask them to consider the fact that bathrooms have stalls, and that they have no idea what goes on in the stall next to theirs. And, I emphasize, *that's as it should be*. If anyone does know what's going on in the stall next to theirs, a line has been crossed that shouldn't be, a value of privacy has been compromised; it does not matter why that line has been crossed, or who did the crossing, this is unac-ceptable behavior.

WORKPLACE RELATIONSHIPS

Clients often face challenges with interpersonal workplace relationships brought on by circumstances beyond their control. Michael (29) had a difficult time becoming accustomed to his new gender role, though he did not encounter any strong resistance from co-workers or management. Michael is an engineer and came into session saying, "I've had weird things come up at work. I go to meetings with customers who don't know I was ever female and I find these guys (usually men, but not always) are looking to me for answers when the lead engineer is a woman. They automatically look to me and that makes me really uncomfortable. I'm not used to having the lead engineer ignored so they can talk to me, and I don't know how to handle it. I finally said to one guy, 'You should be talking to M. because she's the lead on this project.' So he did, for a little while, but gradually he was focusing on me again. I felt like I was in *Alice Through the Looking Glass* where everything Alice wants to accomplish, she has to go backward to do it."

Michael found, to his surprise and consternation, that female customers often played out the same scenario in meetings. He found that women can reinforce this type of white male privilege to the same degree as men.

Michael was experiencing conflicting feelings in these situations, which are common in his profession. He was elated to be seen as a man. He felt guilty at benefiting from male privilege. He had no idea how to 'turn off' the privilege or even if he could do so without offending the customer. He did not know what to say to his female co-worker M., who was usually lead engineer on projects because she had more experience and seniority than Michael. He found his feminist beliefs conflicted directly with how he was treated by others in the workplace.

Michael felt better after having a frank conversation with his co-worker M. about the situation, as it reassured her that he was aware of the dynamic and didn't know any better than she how to change it, other than by doing what he'd been doing. Both felt better after talking about it honestly, rather than ignoring it simply because they couldn't change it. Institutionalized sexism is beyond the individual's power to change. All one can do is acknowledge it and try through assertive communication to make a difference in each particular situation.

Most of my clients experienced a gradual workplace acceptance of their new identity, as they moved through the 'limboland' period of early transition into a more comfortable place of actualizing their new gender role. Very few experienced prolonged difficulties, particularly if their co-workers were given training and an open period of adjustment.

If the transitioning person has been overly defensive or touchy, their co-workers may have reacted accordingly; co-workers may feel they have to walk on eggshells and aren't free to ask any ques-tions at all, even if their intentions are respectful and stem from a desire to learn more and become allies. This can lead to resentment and anger on the part of co-workers and may cause tension that has less to do with gender and more to do with communication and process. There is a fine line here between getting tired of educating people and being so defensive that people are afraid to ask any-thing at all.

I tried to (gently) remind such clients that their cisgender co-workers can't know what it feels like, that there is an inevitable period of adjustment, that their co-workers will probably slip on names and pronouns for awhile, etc. Such clients usually have similar difficulties in other arenas – family of origin, close friends – and find disclosure challenging, regardless of the level of support offered.

TRANSITION—OR WAIT UNTIL RETIREMENT?

A number of my clients were making transition decisions later in life. Many grappled with the question of whether they could wait until they retire to transition to a full-time life in their proper gender. Some developed convoluted paths as a result.

Jill (58), for instance, moonlights as a parachute trainer (I have changed the moonlighting profession for Jill; her actual moon-lighting job is such a niche market she would be too easily iden-tified were I to name it accurately). Her income came primarily from her day job as an architect, but she considered parachute training her avocation and her passion in life. Her reputation as a parachutist was stellar and her trainings were in high demand. This is a strenuous, male-dominated arena and Jill felt that she would never be accepted as a transwoman (or as a woman, for that matter, among those who might not know she was trans).

However Jill had been living as a woman full-time in all areas of her personal life. She disclosed her transition to all her friends and family and had good social support. She would be willing to transition at her day job, but she was adamant about not transitioning within the parachuting community.

Jill sought gender-confirming surgery but didn't want to take hormones. She did not want to risk breast growth, changes to her facial structure, skin softening, etc. (all of which are unpredictable) for fear of losing her place as a trainer. She felt strongly enough about her female identity, she wanted to do all she could to actualize it, including surgery, but was willing to wait 5-7 years to begin hormones. Given her age she believed that was as long as she could continue doing the trainings she loved so much.

Jill's situation was not unique among my older transwomen clients. Many had built up careers spanning decades and were unwilling to risk financial security in order to transition fully prior to retirement. Their fears were legitimate, given that many had cho-sen male-dominated professions earlier in their lives.

In addition they had internalized the male role of breadwinner and focused a great deal on the financial aspects of their lives. Those who were divorced, with grown children who were now self-sufficient financially, still focused on the realities of the situation as they perceived it: their life savings would go toward completing the transition, at which point they would be "unemployable trannies" (Jill's words, in talking of her fears for her own future) and where would it all end?

Further, most had a great deal of emotional investment in the façade they had built up. Their thought process went something like this: "Because I haven't been able to be true to myself, I've put my family first. I can't take pride in who I am so I'll take pride in what I've been able to provide. I can't afford to jeopardize my role as a provider - what else do I have to be proud of?"

People in this situation put a great deal of thought into how far they can take transition, given their individual circumstances, and come up with creative paths that allow them to move as far and fast as possible. These paths often don't follow the rather cookie-cutter approach outlined in previous iterations of the Standards of Care. Jill had difficulty finding two professionals who would write her surgery referral letters, given that the SOC clearly stated a person should not have lower surgery prior to starting hormones or if they have not lived their intended gender for at least a year, full-time.

The SOC were worded this way to prevent someone from taking the irreversible step of obtaining surgery only to realize later that physical transition is not the answer for them after all. Jill falls into the category of people who knew from the age of about four, "I should have been born a girl." She has never wavered in her self-concept as a girl; she never felt until fairly recently that she had the wherewithal to make such drastic changes in her life. She was born poor and has supported a family (either family of origin, or by marriage) since she was 16.

I worked with Jill in 2010. In 2012, she learned that there were new Standards of Care that might support her path. Heartened by this new information, she once again sought out letters for surgery. In 2014, she underwent the surgery she had long desired. She still has not taken hormones, and has decided 2019 will be her last year as a parachute trainer. She said to me, "That's going to be my 65th birthday present to myself – my last parachute jump and my first dose of hormones!" *(Email correspondence, 2015)*

MALE PRIVILEGE AND TRANSMEN

I am sometimes asked how male privilege has played out for me professionally. The quick answer is, therapy is a female-dominated profession and it is not necessarily an advantage to be perceived as a man in a profession where most therapists and clients are women, though my niche role as a trans therapist gave me a built-in client base from the time I established my practice. However I have experienced male privilege in some aspects of my professional life.

When I moved back to Portland after receiving my master's degree in the San Francisco Bay Area, I wasn't yet known as a trans therapist. I approached a local college about teaching a Continuing Education class on trans issues to other therapists, and as the day neared I put some thought into how to disclose my trans status. I wanted class participants to assume me to be a cisgender man, as a springboard for discussion about assumptions, how their percep-tions changed when they found out I had lived as a woman, what they had thought 'trans' looked like, etc.

After some thought I decided, "I'll wait until someone asks me, 'How do you know all this?'" Based on my history in lesbian com-munity I knew perfectly well that if I had stood up in front of a primarily-lesbian class before my transition and started talking about new ways of viewing lesbian identity, someone (or more likely several someones) would ask, "What are you basing all this on? Have you read so-and-so's work? Have you considered such-and-such?" I assumed the same would happen in teaching a class to my peers: as a therapist, speaking to other therapists, teaching them about a therapeutic topic new to them, someone would ask, "How do you know all this?"

Much to my astonishment I taught a daylong class, to 25 women and four men, and not once did anyone ask any variation of, "How do you know all this?" It had never occurred to me no one would question my knowledge and I had no contingency plan for coming out. So I never did. To this day I have no idea how many people in that first class actually figured out how I know all this. At that time I did not have a website and there would have been no simple way for people to find out I had transitioned if they didn't already know.

At the time I was puzzled by this experience. Still attempting to understand what had happened, I related the story to a friend who teaches Women's Studies at a community college. She laughed at me and said, "Of course they didn't question your knowledge – they saw you as a man. People always challenge me when I teach women's studies classes."

I was astonished, saying, "But you have a master's degree in women's studies, you're the chair of the department, why are they asking you how you know all this? Maybe it's my lesbian community background showing, but I find that ridiculous. Maybe if you were presenting something really new, but not at the intro level!" She laughed at me again, and said, "Yup, that's your lesbian community background alright." The fact that I was surprised not to be challenged told me she was right: I had been treated differently from the way I knew I would have been treated prior to my transition.

What intrigues me most about this experience is that the women in the class (I'd say about half were lesbians) didn't question my authority any more than the men did. They all gave me a degree of professional respect they might not have automatically accorded someone they perceived to be a woman. It would seem male privilege in a professional environment is more covert and uncon-scious than in previous generations. This can make it more insidious, harder to both perceive and counter.

All that said, I disagree with the blanket statement, "Transmen have male privilege." It is simplistic to view transition as meaning some switch has been flipped that confers privilege. There are conditions of secrecy surrounding a transman's experience of identity that are foreign to the cisgender man. His safety, livelihood, perhaps life itself, may be at risk if his trans status becomes public.

Whatever the individual scenario, simply applying the term 'male privilege' to a transman is a heteronormative, cisgender approach to identity that negates the complexity of his experience. Conditional privilege is a more accurate descriptor; as long as he isn't known to be trans, a transman will experience male privilege in the same way as others of his same race, class background, religion and age. (Schilt, 2011; Vanderburgh, 2017)

CHANGING JOBS

Several of my clients found their work suffering during their first year or so on hormones. For a few this was due to actual differences in their brain functioning with a different hormone balance, seemingly related to the different ways in which their brain processed information. Joel was a project manager who transitioned to male. As a female he had found multi-tasking easier than he did in a testosterone-based body. He developed a new work style that allowed him to function just as well on the job, but he did approach his work differently.

Trina found her work suffering in part because she came out at work long after coming out in every other arena of life. As she put it, "This was the last place where I had to let go of being Martin. I realize now that I had also let go of the job itself, to a greater degree than I'd realized." *(Client session, 2006)* She made uncharacteristic mistakes in her work a number of times in the weeks following her disclosure. A co-worker made the observation that Trina just didn't seem to be 'there' at times, at which point the light bulb went on for Trina and she thought, "You have no idea how right you are!"

There are so many factors involved in transition, it's not always easy to know how much transition is affecting one's job performance. Is it hormones, family stress, workload unrelated to transition, etc? The 'etceteras' are numerous and can make understanding the situation difficult.

As Carl did before her, when Trina switched jobs she found she enjoyed working in an environment in which she had never been known as male. Despite the level of acceptance many receive on the job, if they desire to live privately the thought will always be in the back of their mind, 'These people knew me by *OldName* and are well aware that I transitioned.' As it becomes easier to be seen as their intended gender, many also desire to work in a place where no one knows about their transition.

Transitioning at work is never easy. The balance between public and private is delicate, and the workplace is the most challenging milieu in my employed clients' attempts at maintaining privacy. Those who can transition while in school, working within queer community, or while between jobs often do so deliberately, recognizing the difficulties they would face otherwise.

During the economic crisis that began in 2008, I was unsure how the depression-like conditions would affect my practice; would people choose not to transition, hunkering down and hanging in there until times were better? Far from it. Many who were laid off called me, saying, 'This is my chance, before I have a job again.'

The clients who were most affected by the economy were those who had already started transition. Ed had saved nearly all he needed for chest surgery; the company he worked for went out of business shortly before his surgery date. He cancelled his surgery date, feeling insecure about when he might get a job again, whether it would pay well, would he have benefits, etc. In 2011, Ed felt secure enough in his new job to reschedule his surgery.

• Chapter 12 •

RENEGOTIATING BOUNDARIES

CHANGING GENDER ROLES IS A PROCESS OF RENEGOTIATING SOCIAL BOUNDARIES. Gender roles are established sets of relational boundaries: "How is a man 'supposed' to behave in this situation?" v. "How is a woman 'supposed' to behave in this situation?" Not knowing the answer, particularly in mono-gendered situations like public bathrooms where previous knowledge doesn't help, can have a somewhat-paralyzing effect on anyone relatively new to transi-tion. At the least it's unnerving and causes something akin to social anxiety. At its worst it causes a kind of social parlaysis, particularly if the person is worried about what others think. (If this sounds familiar, consider adolescence)

It's a scary thought to realize gradually that everything you learned about how to behave with others no longer applies. Or more accurately: the trans person no longer believes they automatically know how to behave in any given situation without standing out. An apt analogy is that of the spy behind enemy lines. In foreign territory, hoping to be seen as a native, the spy is constantly vigilant and self-monitoring. The spy knows that at any time it is entirely possible that someone will stop and say, "Wait a minute. You didn't do that right. You should have known better. You're not one of us. Who are you?"

Those who feel less fear than a spy may still have a feeling simi-lar to moving to a new country and being invisible as having done so. The expectation will be there on the part of the natives that the newcomer will know all the social nuances that are second nature to them, and will look sideways at those who 'break the rules' or don't follow various social norms.

To continue the analogy: if the natives know there is a new-comer in their midst who looks like a native but isn't, they are often more forgiving of social *faux pas* that they would find most odd amongst themselves. Just so, the trans person who comes out and says overtly, "How am I supposed to behave?" often receives sym-pathetic support from cisgender people.

That said, given the history of violence and discrimination against trans people in U.S. culture, it is not paranoia for trans people to fear being seen as trans and to desire to be seen as their intended gender as quickly as possible. While some in more progresssive communities are daring to live their lives as openly-trans people, this is a recent phenomenon and not a safe option in most areas of this country. Paranoia is an irrational fear that has no basis in reality, which cannot be said of the fear many trans people experience, particularly in light of the sociopolitical climate of 2017.

ONE TRANSWOMAN'S EXPERIENCE

More than once I encountered a paradox in my work with trans-women: they did not believe they were being seen female, though in my opinion they would have to work at it to ever be seen as male. Karen had been taking hormones for just over three months when she first came to see me in 2005. She was 25 years old and knew how to style her hair and apply make-up appropriately for her complexion. She had excellent fashion sense and had already determined how she enjoyed expressing her female gender. [22]

I knew many of my other transwomen clients would envy Karen her ability to be seen female so completely, so quickly, and would not understand why Karen herself couldn't see it when she looked in the mirror. Karen had only been taking hormones for three months; they had not yet had much effect on her body. She still had the musculature, no breast growth, and coarse body hair of a male. When she took off the clothes and make-up, she saw Kevin in the mirror.

---

[22] Karen fell into the category of client who was told by a previous therapist that she was done with transition because she was seen female in all situations.

Further, Karen had not had time to absorb the fact that she was being seen female and still reacted as if people were seeing her either as a gay man or as a man in a dress. When men would whistle at her admiringly or cat-call out car windows, she would cringe and tense up, poised for flight. She used to be chased and beaten up by such men when they perceived her as male.

Given Karen's gender presentation I knew there was no way these men were seeing her as anything other than an attractive young woman. Because of my own female history I recognized the treatment Karen was receiving: everyday garden-variety sexual harassment that young women are often subjected to.

I did some psychoeducational work with Karen, talking about sexual harassment and pointing out that this type of behavior is common in our culture. She reacted with outrage when it sank in that the harassment she was experiencing had nothing to do with her being perceived as trans or a man in a dress, and everything to do with her being perceived as an attractive young woman. I had to laugh when she said, in an affronted tone, "But that's just not right!" Of course she was right – and had just verbalized the entire basis of the modern feminist movement.

Karen was able to recognize the harassment because she'd experienced similar treatment when perceived as a gay man. She did not recognize it as a response to her being female. She had been living female for so little time, she had yet to learn how to recognize what it felt like to be treated like a woman.

I asked her, "How are women treating you in public bath-rooms?" She was quite happy in such situations, saying, "Oh, every-one is so nice in the bathroom! It's so different from the men's room; women talk all the time! They're not afraid of interacting with each other; they like it."

Again based on my female history, I said, "Since you haven't been in women's bathrooms until recently, you may not know how women behave when they perceive a man in what they think of as their bathroom. They will stop, look, ask questions, maybe say something like 'I think you're in the wrong bathroom.' If they are chatting with you, then they are seeing you as one of them, not as a man at all."

I pointed out to Karen that when one is very early in transition, it can be difficult to know exactly what others are seeing. Karen needed to understand that if she was being treated in ways that felt unfamiliar, different, or odd – it was because she *was* being treated like a woman, not like any kind of man, and this was treatment she wasn't familiar with. I would not have put it this way had it seemed to me that others might be perceiving Karen as trans or as a man in a dress, but given her appearance I knew this was not the case.

Karen had not looked at her situation in quite this way before. I advised her to confide in some of the supportive people she'd mentioned in session – a sympathetic aunt, and a cisfemale friend from school. She needed mentors, ciswomen who could talk to her about how they felt in similar situations, who could explain the 'rules' of all-women settings to her. She also came to understand that coming out to friends made it less likely that they would set her up with dates in situations that might prove dangerous for a transwoman.

I suggested Karen talk with her friend from school about how it felt to have men whistle and cat-call sexist remarks. To date Karen had felt isolated in her experience. She'd never received sympathy for such treatment when she'd been living male and it had not occurred to her that she might have a different experience talking to women about it once she was living female. Women commiserate with each other all the time about their experiences with men.

Karen had been staying home far too much, feeling the social paralysis to such an extent that it had become difficult for her to leave the house. Being able to go out with someone she knew was the key to helping her begin reintegrating into society. A few months later, Karen had no difficulty going out in any social situation.

For awhile it was still difficult for her to deal with the ubiquitous cat-calling she experienced from men, but she gradually came to believe she was not being seen as trans or as a man in a dress, but had joined the ranks of women. The sense of anger and fear she still felt no longer held her back, as she had come to realize sexism comes with the territory and that other young women face the same treatment (and also feel fear and anger).

This confidence translated to a willingness to be more open about her trans identity, if it would help educate the general public about what it means to live trans. Karen began participating on educational panels for classes. One reason so many people equate 'transsexual' with 'drag queen who goes one step further' is because the most visible post-physical-transition trans people are those MTF's who can't always be seen as women, or drag queens for whom 'female' is theater and who are flamboyant with their gender expression.

During educational presentations I point out that one of the differences between MTF and FTM physical transition is that virtually all transmen are only known to be trans if they come out, while this is not always true for transwomen. I've tracked this with my own clients, and estimate that about 60% of my transwomen clients have (or will have) no difficulty being seen female all the time. About 30% will have to work harder at it, but will be able to be seen female most of the time, with some effort. Only 10% or so will have difficulty ever being seen female.

Among the 10% are several clients who identify as 'transdykes' and enjoy expressing gender as a butch lesbian might. As with butch lesbians, this means these clients are often called 'sir.' They were surprised when I told them that it is a common experience for butch lesbians to be mistaken for men, especially in women's bathrooms. They found it gratifying to realize their experience was not unique to them as transwomen, as it gave them a point of connection to cisfemale butch lesbians.

To have someone like Karen stand before a class and proclaim herself trans is a powerful experience for students. My standing before them shows the invisibility of transmen who have been on hormones for awhile; Karen standing before them shows the same is possible for transwomen.

ONE TRANSMAN'S EXPERIENCE

Because of the wide latitude of gender expression permitted wo-men, a number of my pre-transition transmen clients said, "I don't think I'll have any problem adjusting to the male gender role because I've been observing men, acting like a man, dressing like a man, for years."

What they couldn't fully realize before transitioning is how dif-ferently other people would treat them if they're being perceived as an adult male. I tried to prepare them for the difficulties that lay ahead but I had the feeling some believed they were going to be the exception and that their transition would be a piece of cake. If a client believed he would be the exception, it was all the rougher for him when he realized transition is an unnerving experience with a steep learning curve after all.

A number of my transmen clients limited their dating pool to the trans or queer community, having found it psychologically difficult to venture forth into the straight world. Raymond (age 26) had been taking hormones for about five years when he first came to see me. He and his genderqueer partner were having relationship difficulties and eventually did separate, at Raymond's instigation.

About six months after their breakup Raymond began dating a self-identified heterosexual ciswoman, his first attempt at forming intimate relationship outside the queer community. Raymond had rarely experienced any particular insecurity or self-consciousness dating trans people, or cisgender people who identified as queer.

To his surprise, he found himself almost paralyzed with social anxiety at the prospect of dating a ciswoman who was not part of queer community, though he knew full well she had no problem with his being trans. Not only did she know about Raymond's trans status before their first date, she had had a long-term relationship with a transman at an earlier time in her life. Though her previous relationship had ended, its demise wasn't related to her partner being trans.

214

Raymond never had the sense that she was fetishizing him, in order to "add trannyboy to her sexual résumé," as he put it. Nevertheless, one of the first things he said in session after meeting Laura was, "I don't know how to act or what she's expecting of me. I'm afraid I'll disappoint her by not being enough like a bioboy."

Raymond was not talking about sex; he hadn't gotten that far yet. He was finding it difficult to navigate issues such as, "Is she expecting me to hold the door for her? Am I supposed to pay for her coffee automatically if we stop in somewhere for a latte? What am I supposed to do or say if we're out dancing and some guy comes on to her?" He had no confidence that he knew the rules any longer, and worried she would view him as less than a man if he didn't 'do male right.' Not knowing what 'right' was in any given situation made him feel awkward and at sea.

Raymond found his anxiety lessening as he realized that the mushiness of boundaries he was experiencing is not unique to him, or to transmen, but is a cultural phenomenon inherent in male-female relationships. He felt comfortable negotiating social boundaries within queer community, but much less so navigating the boundaries of what he considered mainstream society. He'd never felt part of mainstream society before his transition and experienced an alienation from his own culture of origin that unnerved him at first.

As Raymond discovered, some women felt offended if he held the door for them while others were offended if he did not. Some expected to share the bill for a meal, others expected they would take turns. None felt it was Raymond's obligation to pay for everything. He had an "Aha!" moment at one point and said to me, "I've decided if I just treat everyone with respect, then I'm okay. If I do something they didn't expect or completely want, like holding the door, that's okay with me because I did it out of respect and courtesy, not out of disrespect."

GENDER ROLES ARE NOT MONOLITHIC

In the course of my work with people in transition I discerned certain patterns of behavior that many of my clients shared, particularly if they received similar types of socialization. I incorporated a new exercise in my work with some of my clients who desired to transition. I asked them to write down the various messages they internalized as part of their gender socialization. I then asked them to rate their feelings about these various messages as positive, negative, or neutral. (I didn't have a particular scale I used, clients were free to use other language than positive, negative, etc. if they chose.)

The purpose of this exercise is two-fold. First, it helped the client make explicit the childhood teachings they received around gender roles and expression. This helped make the resocialization process less overwhelming. And second, it gave the client a base to work from in making decisions about which aspects of their original socialization they might want to work toward changing and which they considered positive and helpful.

Religion, birth gender assignment, class, race, ethnicity, cultural background, educational level of family members, family structure and composition – all these factors affect the specific socialization a person receives. The broad demographic categories we use in characterizing people are shaped by the specific circumstances of their lives.

Harriet is 61 years old and was raised in an agnostic household. She is Euro-American; her family has been in this country since the mid-1800s. She was raised middle-class in a small town in rural Oregon. She was the only male-assigned child, the oldest of four. Harriet's mother was seriously sexually abused as a child (by her father) and never had an opportunity to deal with the resulting trauma to her emotional self; she became an alcoholic.

When Harriet was 14 her mother committed suicide. Never particularly demonstrative, her father retreated ever further into his work. Though Harriet finished college, it took her quite a few years to obtain her degree; she is the only member of her generation to do so. Her mother attended one year of college before dropping out to marry and become a housewife. Her father had graduated with a degree in engineering. He was a factory foreman.

Contrast this with the experience of Pauline, who is 56. Also Euro-American, her working-class family has been in this country for well over 100 years. The family has lived in the same small town in rural Oregon for three generations. Pauline was raised in a mainstream Christian religion and her family attended services regularly. Both her parents had attended a local community college, though her mother had dropped out when she realized she was pregnant. Her father left college when her mother became pregnant, needing to work full-time to support his growing family; he never obtained his degree, though he was able to find work readily and was never unemployed.

Pauline was an only child. Neither parent had ever experienced any abuse, nor did they perpetrate abuse of any kind on Pauline. There was no alcoholism or other form of addiction in this family, other than an uncle Pauline described as the black sheep of her father's family. She seldom saw him, as he rarely came back to Oregon. Pauline describes her family history in idyllic terms, though her gender dissonance cast a pall over her memories of childhood.

Though both these clients used to fit the demographic category 'straight white man,' their family socialization processes were markedly different, and they absorbed radically different views of what it means to be male, what family means, how to be in relationship with others, etc.

However because of their similarity in age and their geo-graphical proximity while growing up (rural Pacific Northwest), these clients did experience similar peer socialization processes; it is important to help clients distinguish between the effects of their home life and their school life, as these two processes combine to shape the maturing individual. Though much about these two people is similar – age, race, ethnicity – their home lives were different enough that their memories of childhood socialization bear little resemblance to each other. Harriet has memories of fighting (sometimes physical), shouting, and chaos, of feeling she had to protect her younger siblings from the rage that surrounded them. Pauline remembers a fairly placid home life, always stable and loving.

Harriet had great difficulty trusting anyone as she proceeded with transition. Though lonely and wanting connection with others, her family background had instilled in her that others aren't to be trusted with one's deepest feelings. She attended trans support groups, but didn't share much of her own difficulties. To hear her tell the tale, all was rosy and smooth sailing. She worked as a research chemist, and was happiest when immersed in a research project on her own.

Pauline, by contrast, blossomed through transition and immediately became a popular attendee when she came to trans group meetings. She made friends easily and told me, "I knew I'd be happier after I transitioned, but I had no idea how MUCH happier!" As was true for Harriet, the hormones gave Pauline a sense of inner peace. But unlike Harriet, Pauline found it much easier to both give and receive support.

VESTIGES OF MALE SOCIALIZATION

I have observed the following general trends in my Euro-American early-transition transwomen clients, especially those born before the 1980s (including both Pauline and Harriet). Not all of my clients exhibited every tendency to the same degree, nevertheless, this is what I observed:

❖ Difficulty asking others for help, though several of my transwomen clients who were in AA didn't have this problem; they had learned through their recovery process the value and necessity of admitting they can't shoulder the weight of the world;

❖ Difficulty recognizing and/or accepting connection when conferred by ciswomen;

❖ Difficulty identifying their feelings, or seeing them as valid;

❖ A tendency to isolate after an emotionally-difficult encounter;

❖ A tendency to pontificate at times, without listening to or giving credence to others' viewpoints and experience;

❖ A tendency to have a hierarchical view of transition, probably stemming from male competitiveness. One 20-year-old MTF client said, "I want to be the youngest-ever to access facial feminization surgery." This can lead to 'more trans than thou' attitudes, *e.g.* physical transition is superior to crossdressing, post-surgery is superior to pre-surgery, etc;

❖ A tendency to want to fix things for others, and to feel guilty if they can't. 'Fixing things' in this instance means the action-oriented behavior that ciswomen often criticize in men: "I just wanted him to listen, I didn't mean he had to DO anything about it!" is a common lament;

❖ Difficulty forgiving themselves and having self-compassion, if they feel they have not 'done female right,' resulting from a tendency toward perfectionism;

❖ Difficulty looking women in the eye and smiling;

❖ Difficulty feeling entitled to pursue transition, as if everyone else's emotional process and needs trump their own.[23]

I discerned elements of many of the above male socialization tendencies in both Harriet and Pauline. However in Harriet's case her family history of abuse and alcoholism added layers of defenses that made it more difficult for her to access her own emotional process. Pauline found it easier to step back from her male socialization and begin deconstructing how the above patterns had played out in her life, because she found it easier to feel her own feelings. Harriet had

---

[23] Many of my female-socialized clients also have difficulty taking themselves seriously enough to consider transition. Male socialization emphasizes taking care of others' physical/monetary needs, while female socialization emphasizes taking care of others' emotional/relational needs. Both socialization paths emphasize that others' needs come first.

the added steps of dealing with patterns common to adult children of alcoholics. (See the chapter *Parallel Processes*) Their very different childhood situations meant they did not do 'straight white man' similarly and thus their transitions have played out differently as well. The danger of demographic categories such as 'straight white man' is the tendency to view them as monolithic, without sufficient consideration for individual differences.

Though I didn't have my clients draw out a genogram of their families as part of an intake process, I tried to gather enough information about their families in the first session or two that I could draw my own informal genogram of their biological families. If it seemed that it might be helpful to the client, I had them do a genogram either as homework or in session. Particularly for those from alcoholic or abusive families, externalizing the source of some of their more-problematic patterns was helpful in bolstering their self-esteem and sense of self-efficacy.

The above patterns were less prevalent among my younger MTF clients. I believe this difference is due to the degree to which the modern feminist movement influenced my younger clients' mothers in how they raised their male offspring and the example they set of what it means to act female.

What do the above patterns have in common? They are all part of mainstream U.S. white male socialization, and a result of not having experienced female socialization. My MTF clients were often unaware that the above traits were affecting their transition, trained as they had been from earliest childhood to repress their feelings. Difficulty accessing their own emotional process made it hard for such clients to begin looking at their own particular male socialization and how it played out during their transition.

What such clients experience is that women don't accept from other women behavior based in the above male socialization tendencies. Ciswomen might not like the ways in which men are socialized, but they easily recognize behavior that is based in male socialization;

they are not very forgiving when they encounter such behavior in another woman, especially if they don't realize she is a transwoman.

VESTIGES OF FEMALE SOCIALIZATION

What my Euro-American FTM clients noticed is how constricted the male role seems compared to the role they are leaving behind. FTMs have an easier time, as a general rule, discerning how they are 'supposed' to behave, in part because their original socialization gave them more permission to be observant of others' experience of the world. In addition, my FTM clients had usually been expressing gender as they liked and had no learning curve about dressing male.

Further, my FTM clients found that guys simply don't care; they don't observe much about other guys. Women, on the other hand, are constantly checking each other out. One MTF colleague jokingly referred to the process as one of being graded. She knew she'd made a passing grade (pun intended!) if she was ignored, as that meant she had dressed appropriately for the occasion and was being seen female. Nonetheless there are some aspects of female socialization that caused difficulties for many of my transmen clients, especially if they were trying to live a private existence:

- ❖ A tendency to give in to others too readily, not expressing one's true desires;
- ❖ Difficulty stepping forward and automatically taking the lead in emergency situations;
- ❖ A tendency to step into the care-taking role a bit more than is expected of men;
- ❖ Difficulty flirting with cisgender people of any gender, parsing out the rules of engagement;
- ❖ Difficulty figuring out the rules of male support and bonding;
- ❖ Difficulty seeing men as their equal and tending to react with an obsequiousness or defensive reactivity instilled by female socialization.

What my transmen clients found is that others often assumed they were gay men, regardless of their actual sexual orientation. What others were observing is residual female socialization, which looks like 'not doing male right.' Most cisgender people then unconsciously assume, "Oh, must be gay." The logic boils down to: 'Doesn't act quite like a man, I don't see gay men as fully male, therefore this dude must be a gay man.' This is not only a misinterpretation of the transman's identity, it is also insulting to gay men to believe that they are not 'real men' on par with their straight counterparts.

Some of my transmen clients found that their female partners were disconcerted to be involved with a man who treated them as an equal and with a visceral understanding of what it is to live female. They were not used to this kind of treatment from a man. Some transmen have dated women from more-traditional cultures and found their expectations of how men and women behave were mutually-exclusive.

Daniel became involved with a woman (Dara) whose parents had emigrated from the Middle East a few years after she was born. Daniel and Dara married two years after they met. Though fully Americanized in many respects, Dara's view of the woman's role at home clashed with the egalitarian feminist model Daniel saw as a form of fixed reality.

Dara saw it as a referendum on her cooking if Daniel wanted to fix a meal. For his part, Daniel was uncomfortable with Dara's insistence on doing all the housework. He said, "She just wanted to shoo me away from anything to do with cooking or cleaning and was offended if I suggested sharing tasks. She assumed I was criticizing her, like she wasn't doing it right. It took me a long time to really get it that the feminist model isn't the only one and that a woman wouldn't automatically want an egalitarian feminist relationship if given the option." *(Client session, 2008)*

He and Dara processed through their very different upbringings and both relaxed their expectations. The most important skill they have acquired is that of respectful listening, as they explain their points of view to each other in a non-judgmental way. Now, four years into their marriage, their relationship is more traditionally-gendered than Daniel would ever have imagined he could be comfortable with – and Dara is quite happy if Daniel occasionally cooks dinner or helps out with the laundry.

PEOPLE OF COLOR

Given the demographics of the Pacific Northwest, most of my clients were Euro-American, as I am myself. Beyond demographics, the client-therapist relationship is based in Euro-American values; many other cultures view the biological family or circle of close friends as the place to turn for help with life crises. These value systems clash with the SOC suggestion of therapy to obtain hormones and/or surgery.

I worked with a few clients of Asian descent whose parents were either from Asia or were first-generation; I noted a tendency toward politeness that comes across as difficulty sharing painful emotions. It can be hard to disentangle this from the cultural tendency to not share personal processes with people outside the family, which caused more than one Asian client difficulty talking to me about transition. They were only seeing me because they could not get hormones legally otherwise; they would far rather have talked things through with sympathetic family members or friends of their own generation, foregoing therapy altogether.

This tendency to avoid therapy was more common among my MTF Asian clients than those who transitioned FTM, who had no qualms about seeking out my support through their transition. Ray, an FTM client of Asian descent, had a difficult time being taken seriously by his father, who told him, "Whatever makes you happy. You're still our daughter." Ray was unsure whether his father was deliberately ignoring his transition or if there was a language barrier preventing his father from understanding what transition means. Ray does not speak his parents' language well enough to convey the concept 'transgender' to them and they don't speak English well enough to understand Ray when he speaks beyond a basic level. His parents' native language contains no equivalent for the word 'transgender.'

Four of my clients were Mexican. Nita (22) is strikingly beau-tiful as a woman and had no difficulty gaining her family's accept-ance. She said, "It would be different for me if I was a gay man or if I couldn't pass as a woman. It's such a macho culture that as long as I look good as a woman and not like any kind of man, I'll be fine. I won't have the same power men have, but as long as I'm clearly a woman, it'll be okay." *(Client session, 2003)*

For my non-Euro-American trans clients considering transition, there was the additional burden of the question, 'If I am rejected by my ethnic or racial community, who do I turn to for support in this culture where my race puts me in a one-down position and I might not have other community?'

Jocelyn was 28 when she first came to see me seeking transition. She had hesitated for years to investigate the process because her fa-ther was a minister of a black church (not in Portland). She said to me, "The black church is family; it's not just church, we're not just a congregation. When I was growing up it was a long time before I even found out that 'aunt' didn't mean the same to white people that it did to me. Pretty much every adult in our church was like an aunt or uncle to me. All family. And that scared me, to risk all that." *(Client session, 2009)*

At the same time, Jocelyn knew who she was meant to be. Even-tually she was emboldened by the online support she received from other African-American transwomen. She told her mother first and found a lack of surprise that surprised her. "Honey, I've always known there was something special about you," was her mother's reaction. Followed by, "But I don't know how to tell your father." Finally they decided the best way was for Jocelyn to show her father some photos of herself at her most beautiful, and sit down with him alongside her mother.

She told me some years later, "He took it a bit better than I thought he might, but he worried about my eternal soul. I think he felt better when I told him I had no intention of giving up church, but would go to another church. I didn't want folks staring at me instead of listening to him preach. So I joined a congregation that has quite a few trans members. And the congregation is about a quarter black. But I still go over to the house most Sundays after church, and now it's fine. Just took some time, like it does for every family. I think it would actually be harder if I'd been gay. At least everyone in my family identifies as either a man or a woman, so I still fit in. But no one in my immediate family is gay or lesbian, that would set them apart." *(Email correspondence, 2017)*

SPEAKING UP

My MTF clients often felt self-conscious about their voice, causing many to hold themselves back from social interaction. As Julia put it, "I do fine in person, because I've got the gender expression thing down and feel comfortable as a woman. Once people see me, even though my voice is deep, they just put it down to my being like Bea Arthur – a woman with a deep voice. But on the phone I get called 'sir' all the time. It's a constant struggle for me to remember, 'Bea Arthur probably had this happen to her all the time.' As long as I remember that, it's okay and I can laugh it off." *(Client session, 2005)*

I referred many MTF clients to a colleague whose profession is helping people retrain their voices. Her primary clientele are people whose voices have been damaged in some way, often through an industrial accident, but she also enjoys helping transwomen find their natural voice in a way that comes across as female rather than male. Those who are able to find their 'female voice' usually find themselves less inhibited in their ability to move through the world and interact with others.

SOCIALIZATION AFFECTING RESOCIALIZATION

Here's an example of how early socialization can affect the reso-cialization process. Allison moved to a tourist town in another state and started a small business a year or so into her transition. She was 59 at the time and was changing careers after finding it impossible to transition within her former job. I did a phone session with Allison a few months after she'd moved and she said she was lonely and feeling isolated. She is gregarious and extroverted by nature, so it surprised me to hear she wasn't being accepted.

As Allison is not someone who experiences difficulty being seen female, it seemed to me unlikely that her trans status was affecting her level of acceptance among the locals. I had a hunch her male socialization might be getting in her way, so I asked her to describe the interactions she'd experienced with some of the women who live in her town. She said that several had come into her shop and they'd had conversations, which had petered out quickly.

I asked her to describe an example, and what emerged is that Allison had been waiting for questions, such as "What did you do for a living before you moved to OurTown?" Instead she had been hearing general comments about the day's weather, or some such.

Speaking from my own female background, I said, "That's how many women make connection with each other. It's different from how men do it. A man will ask questions and then engage in conversation about that specific topic. And the topic has to be non-emotional, such as about jobs or cars. Women throw out remarks which are supposed to lead to other remarks, which can then go in a million different directions and become a three-hour conversation about life, the universe and everything. If these women were throw-ing out remarks, they were expecting you to respond in kind. This is how women connect and form friendship." Allison had been offered connection by these women, but she didn't recognize it. Her socialization had taught her the man's way of connecting and she had yet to learn that women do it differently. She had been depressed because of her isolation.

An example from the other direction... Tim (age 27) joked about an incident that took place at a local grocery store. While waiting in a particularly slow-moving line, he had seen a gardening magazine headline and had spoken to the young woman behind him in line, throwing out a remark about his garden. She had responded in kind, but had allowed the conversation to close rather than become a detailed comparison of their yards. Tim said good-humoredly, "I forgot for a minute that straight guys aren't supposed to do that!"

MALE V. FEMALE SOCIALIZATION

These two very different responses to similar incidents highlight one difference between male and female socialization, the effect of perfectionism. My MTF clients who don't feel they are 'doing female right' often engaged in harsher self-condemnation than my FTM clients. Allison was harsh in judging herself, while Tim was able to laugh off the incident in the grocery store. My FTM clients were usually better able to joke about their resocialization process than many of my MTF clients, whose response was more typically to berate themselves or feel it was hopeless to consider they would ever be able to live successfully as women.

Tim was also able to deconstruct the incident on his own and to realize why the encounter differed from what he might have experienced pre-transition. He came into session already knowing what had happened, and why. Allison needed to process through the incident with me in order to understand what was happening. I had gently warned her she might feel isolated once she moved to a small town, but it wasn't until this phone session that she said to me, "I didn't know what you meant, but now I understand."

Though women are not as highly valued in the larger culture, there are nuances to this devaluation; it may not play out the same way among women as it does among men. During a 2005 class I taught at a college in southern Oregon, I asked participants to do an exercise in which they were to pair off and conduct a five-minute conversation about a mutual acquaintance. After a few minutes I then asked them to switch pronouns for the person they were discussing (call a man 'she,' for instance).

In the discussion afterward, one woman raised her hand and said that she and the person next to her had not known each other prior to the class and didn't have any mutual acquaintances. They chose instead to use then-president George (W.) Bush as their topic of conversation.

I asked her whether it was difficult to switch pronouns for him and she said that while it had not been difficult, she had noticed that she was much angrier at the president when using female pronouns than she had been when using male pronouns. This had made her realize that she had lower expectations of men than of women. When she disagreed with him, she realized a voice in the back of her mind would whisper, "What do you expect – he's a man!" She had not been conscious of this attitude before and was not pleased to find it present in herself; she had thought of herself as someone who was able to judge others based strictly on their behavior. Finding that she also had a gender filter was not a welcome insight.

I used the same exercise in a classroom setting in 2018. In this instance, the class members knew each other well and had no trouble finding mutual acquaintances to discuss. At the conclusion of the exercise, one participant said, "I was surprised to find my thought process changed in talking about our friend when I changed pronouns. When I said 'she' instead of 'he,' I found myself thinking of our friend as nurturing rather than caring, or kind instead of friendly. It's subtle, and it's gendered." The person who made this statement hadn't expected any such result; she is a women's studies professor. She went on, "Here I thought I had an inside track when it comes to understanding how gender plays out culturally and interpersonally!"

I have encouraged my MTF clients to try to relax into their transition, to see the humor in the various situations that arise, and to redefine what 'success' means. Those who are able to do so have an easier time of it and gradually come to realize they are able to blend in more easily when they are relaxed. Portland is not a tense city; people who walk around radiating the tension and anxiety of early transition will probably draw attention to themselves, whether or not passers-by actually realize they are trans.

Further, while most of my FTM clients find this sort of discussion fascinating and are able to check in with their feelings fairly easily, the majority of my older MTF clients are less able to engage in this sort of deconstruction process at first. It takes a great deal of practice for some. A few have told me that even years into their transition, they have to remind themselves that it's okay to engage with others about their emotional process and reactions. I'm not talking here about important and emotionally-charged topics, like disclosure of trans status or processing feelings related to transition, but any kind of emotional response to everyday events in people's lives. Some consistently need to remind themselves it's okay to even have an emotional process, and that they are not going to be punished in some way for showing a feeling in public.

RECONSTRUCTING SOCIALIZATION

Reconstructing socialization involves a process of making conscious one's original socialization and putting various social rules and norms on the table for examination. This is not easy, given the developmental age of the brain at the time of original socialization. The first time around we absorbed socialization as we learned to walk and talk. Behavior learned that young becomes second nature, woven into the fabric of our being and nearly inseparable from our personalities.

Perhaps the neural pathways laid down by that level of socialization can't be fully changed, despite a new hormone balance and a great deal of practice. It may be that in emergency situations the old patterns will take over. However, learning to forgive oneself for a socialization one didn't choose is a key component to finding happiness and fulfillment as a fully-functioning member of society.

My older clients, both FTM and MTF, have usually learned adaptive coping mechanisms as they age and have been able to present a fairly convincing 'front' of male or female as they move through the world. Some of my younger clients, however, never felt their birth socialization took hold. Pam (21) said, "I don't feel like I'm resocializing myself as much as I am socializing myself for the first time." She had felt so shut down and repressed during her high school years, she did not feel she was treated male or female. She avoided social contact and took refuge in books, and in playing on-line role-playing games. This withdrawal from social contact took its toll and three years into physical transition Pam had very awkward social skills. Fortunately she has a supportive family and is gradually learning the rules of living female.

Pam's story is similar to that of many who are on the autism spectrum, finding social interactions a mystery and finding it difficult to relate to those around them. In Pam's case, however, transition allowed her to blossom and begin interacting with others in a new way that felt natural to her.

In general my older clients don't express similar feelings. It's not that my older clients didn't feel awkward and repressed during their adolescent years, just as Pam did. However I have a feeling that those who could not learn the necessary coping skills, learn the persona that would allow them to have a 'front' with which to face the world, those who didn't learn to play a part – didn't survive to transition later in life.

IT'S NOT ALL BAD!

There are elements of male and female socialization that are positive, as there are elements that tend to hold people back when they transition. Joanne described cultivating relationships with people in her workplace's Human Resources department with the deliberate intention of calling on those folks in the future to help her obtain gender-confirming surgery through the company's insurance plan. (Her efforts were successful!) She began this networking process long before disclosing her trans status to anyone. This sounded like such a 'male' tactic to me, reminiscent of invoking a good old boys network, and I had difficulty envisioning most of my FTM clients having the idea to do that.

Louise felt put-upon at work, resenting that overtime was mandatory. She decided to hand in her notice, despite having received excellent workplace support for her transition, as she felt she was being taken advantage of. Her boss was dismayed at the idea of losing her skills, so offered her a different work shift, with a lighter workload, a pay raise, and a supervisory position.

Faced with this kind of response, many ciswomen would bend over backward for this boss. Louise's response was to say in session, "We'll see how it plays out. If I still feel this way in a few months, I'll begin the job search." She had a sense of self-worth that is healthy and that other women will envy in her. She is seen female in all situations and will thus be perceived as a female role model, rather than as someone who was raised male and has retained a sense of her own worth in the work world.

I pointed out to Louise that feeling self-worth within the work world is something many ciswomen strive to achieve, as it is not part of their socialization. As Louise put it when it sank in, "They are going to want to be like me." Ironically that same sense of self-worth might be seen as a straight, white male sense of entitlement by some if they found out Louise once transitioned.

On the other side of the coin, Louis (32) described asking various friends to come over and help him out after his chest surgery and told me about the schedule he'd made for his after-surgery care. Part of his female socialization had included cooperation and achieving goals within a group context, rather than the rugged individualism lone-wolf attitude instilled in my MTF clients as the epitome of self-actualization. While many of my MTF clients have been joyful when announcing their surgery date, the pronouncement is often in the context of "I'm self-actualizing and isn't that great" rather than, "I'm having major surgery and I need people to help out with my laundry."

Alicia (30) told me somewhat sadly that she realized she still had vestiges of male socialization when she visualized herself going out of town for her surgery alone, despite the fact that she has a partner who would be overjoyed to be asked to help out. Alicia knew her partner would be hurt if she *wasn't* asked to help out with the process. Alicia simply could not visualize any aspect of this particular situation in which she was not alone, despite the fact that she really does want the support and has access to it.

SETTLING INTO GENDER EXPRESSION

A few of my FTM clients went overboard in their attempts to act male and adopted the 'lone wolf' archetype more thoroughly than my MTF clients were ever able to when they were trying to be male. More of my MTF clients went overboard in their attempts to act female, dressing formal and feminine in situations that didn't call for such attire; they ended up standing out more than if they wore their old blue jeans.

The tendency to adopt the extremes of either gender role can result in a caricature and paradoxically can hinder the attempt to be seen as the intended gender. It is less critical for FTMs to have mentors when the issue involves gender expression. One of the advantages in transitioning FTM is the familiarity most have with male gender expression, though they may need to learn the subtleties of more business-like or formal styles. There may be females who have never worn pants in their lives, but I haven't met any.

My MTF clients were another story, moving as they were from a constricted range of male gender expression to a role where the range spans the extremes of sweatpants and ball gowns. Not only do transwomen need to learn the rules, they also need to track their own internal resonance with various styles, learning whether they prefer formal, feminine, casual, androgynous, masculine, or do they like aspects of all the above and choose to dress according to con-text. Early in transition, many go through a giddy stage of dressing as if their developmental age (adolescence) matched their chronological age. *"Finally* I can wear what I wanted to wear when I was 14!" wars with "I'm 46 years old and I'm dressing to go to work."

Several of my MTF clients have told me they felt like they'd reached a milestone in their transition process when they could put on their old blue jeans again and still feel that they were dressing like women. As they are! Some ciswomen buy their clothes in the men's department and have never worn other than men's jeans in casual situations. Most have never given their gender identity a second thought and would laugh at the idea that wearing men's jeans made any kind of statement about how much or little they valued their womanhood. As one cisgender partner put it, "If I put on a pair of jeans, how can they be 'men's jeans' if I'm a woman? What difference does it make which side of the aisle they came from in the store? They fit me better and have bigger pockets, so there!" *(Client session, 2008)*

There are generational (and geographical) differences at play. My younger MTF clients emerged within a milieu in which gender expression and roles are more fluid than was the case a generation ago. Many had little interest in adopting a feminine or formal mode of dress, partly because of their age but also because their attitudes were more feminist to begin with. Though they didn't have the experiential history to frame it in these terms, they epitomized one of the goals of the modern feminist movement: 'I will wear a dress when and if I want to, not because a male-determined dress code says I have to.' The influence of feminism on the larger culture stands them in good stead.

I encouraged my MTF clients to observe female gender expression in various settings: downtown weekday lunchtime, at a mall or grocery store, at the library, on the bus, etc. Many marveled at how few women they saw wearing dresses. Diana commented that she'd never noticed before how many women wear running shoes on the way to the office, then change to dress shoes once they've arrived at work. Diana is an observant person. But one of her male socialization rules was, 'Men don't stare at women.' It was difficult for her to overcome this early teaching and observe women.

My goal in helping clients resocialize themselves was to help them deconstruct the role they were raised to and construct a new role that suits their personality and world view, a role that was not in conflict with their values and ideals. Not all of their birth socialization need be rejected, nor can it be. Deciding what to keep and what to change depends first on deconstructing what the patterns and values are, and where those patterns came from. Only then can clients decide what they want to change in themselves.

TALK AMONGST YOURSELVES

Peer support groups often form along gender lines. There is value in 'cross-cultural' interaction, and I encouraged my clients to talk across the gender lines as part of their resocialization process. Just as I encouraged clients to develop cisgender mentors, I also encouraged FTM and MTF communication with each other.

Early in physical transition, or prior to beginning the process, this can be less intimidating for clients than trying to initiate such conversations with cisgender people. There is no danger of rejection at the hands of others also going through transition. In addition, discussing 'the rules' with someone who is trying to learn them can help facilitate the process of figuring out what was helpful and what wasn't in one's birth socialization. The process can help people clarify what they are motivated to change in themselves.

One thing trans people have in common is a heightened con- sciousness of gender and a greater motivation to deconstruct gender roles. Who better to discuss 'the rules' with than someone who was socialized to understand them and has spent time deconstructing them? For early-transition FTMs to discuss with each other male bathroom etiquette or for MTFs to talk with other early-transition transwomen about how formally to dress in certain situations is the blind leading the blind, though commiseration can be supportive.

Further, sharing a gender identity is no guarantee of being able to form friendship. I have played the role of matchmaker more than once (not in a romantic sense!) and offered to facilitate introductions between clients I thought would like each other and be part of each other's support systems. Not all these clients are transitioning in the same direction as each other.

Some clients were hesitant when I first broached the topic of giving and receiving socialization advice across the fence, so to speak. One FTM client said, "But I never felt female or feminine at all! How can I offer advice to an MTF who's wondering how to put on make-up!" I could say exactly the same thing; I never wore make-up. Yet one MTF friend (I'll call her Lee) a few months into transition proudly showed me a selfie she had taken of herself to send to a potential (cismale) date she'd met through an online dating site. I took one look at the picture and thought, "Oh my God, she looks like a hooker. She can't send this picture to a guy, he's going to get entirely the wrong idea. This will put her completely at risk."

Why is it I knew that immediately upon looking at the picture and she did not? Lee had shown the photo to several MTF friends, all early in their transitions, and they had thought it beautiful, encouraging her to send it. It's possible they were not being entirely honest, but if so, they weren't doing her any favors. I knew from personal experience what sexual harassment feels like and felt a familiar feeling of feminist solidarity that compelled me to say, "Lee, you can't send that picture!" My own female socialization rule, "Men are to be considered a threat until proved otherwise" came to mind and I couldn't NOT speak up.

While I would never be able to give Lee advice about make-up, I could help her understand how to move through the world safely as a woman, or as safely as a woman can. The boundaries are not the same, and learning this early-on can save a life, or at least a great deal of emotional pain. Lee would have been crushed to have gone on a date with a man only to find he assumed from her photo that she was a prostitute. This is not to denigrate those who do sex work for a living, but Lee's motivation was to find a relationship, not to be paid for sex.

I introduced an FTM (Conrad) and MTF (Frances) to each other. I felt they would be compatible as friends, which proved to be the case. A year into transition, Conrad was perceived fully male, working at a new job in a management position. He was still not used to the treatment he received from other men when he was in authority. Conrad had formerly spent years working within the non-profit sector, as a lesbian; Frances had been in the military. Their perspectives reflected their backgrounds.

Conrad commented to Frances how surprised he was that men never questioned his judgment, even when he was trying something that was a bit new. She laughed and said, "Of course they didn't. You're the boss."

He said to her, "But if I was a woman and they were women, they'd bring up various options and discuss which might work best. And if I tried to assert my authority and say, 'This is not open for discussion,' they'd consider me a bitchy boss."

Frances explained, "That's not how guys do it. If you're the boss, then you're established as the one in charge. Everyone knows the hierarchy and that's important, that you know your place in the pecking order. If you've been established as lower down than someone else, you might work to get promoted to that rank yourself but while they're in charge, you're going to follow their orders. The important thing is to know where you stand. And the guys lower down aren't going to stand around challenging orders. It's different if the boss asks for input but even then, the final decision is still going to be his and everyone understands that."

Conrad told me of this conversation and said, "It just seemed like she was talking a foreign language! I mean, I understood what she was saying, it just seemed such a weird way to approach the situation, not natural."

'Not natural' is the key phrase. 'Natural' is how our original socialization seems, lessons learned from the cradle. It takes a great deal of time before a new response or new way of viewing a situation will feel natural. Talking across the gender lines to others in transition doesn't make 'the rules' come naturally, but can provide a sounding board, a reality check, and a shortcut to under-standing what went on in a puzzling situation. For many early in their process, talking to those transitioning the other direction feels like a safe first step toward cultivating cisgender mentors.

CONTRASTING THE DIFFERENCES

My younger clients (in general) had a more fluid view of gender, were less invested in the gender binary, and were more inclined to want to be 'in your face' about gender roles and expression. Not only were they not invested in the gender binary, they wanted to challenge it. This wasn't universal, some did want to blend in and live as men or women, but activist attitudes were more prevalent among my younger clients, in keeping with their chronological age.

My older clients were more inclined to have a 'pick your battles' attitude and fighting the cultural gender binary was not a battle they were inclined to take on. With all the life they had to change, the challenge of gaining acceptance within their circle of friends, family and co-workers was all the battle they wanted. Further, many of my older clients firmly believed gender is binary and not a fluid continuum of possibility. They simply believed they should have been born the other gender.

Then there are the gender differences. More of my younger FTM clients adopted terms such as genderqueer or non-binary than my younger MTF clients. The latter were more likely than the former to want to be accepted as female. Some of this difference is based in the wide latitude given females in this day and age. Women can wear anything they want (though there are contextual differences in what is considered appropriate to wear in any given situation) while males are still limited to some variety of pants. It often took awhile before many of my MTF clients had any desire to wear other than dresses. Their socialization gave them no permission to wear a dress and to wear pants during early transition felt like a form of regression to many of them, regardless of their age.

Many more women wear pants than dresses these days (perhaps this is not true in all parts of this country but it is certainly the case in the Pacific Northwest). I had discussions with some MTF clients about being 'clocked' as trans and offered the opinion that perhaps, ironic as it seems to them, they were clocked *because* they were wearing a dress and therefore called attention to themselves.

A few of my younger MTF clients identified as butch lesbians and wanted to express gender accordingly. As a result, they were never called 'she' by those who didn't know them, as there is no difference between 'butch lesbian clothing' and 'dude clothing.' While these particular clients found this situation discouraging, they were not willing to compromise their gender expression for the sake of their gender identity. They didn't believe they should have to.

It meant a lot to these clients when I informed them that butch lesbians are often called 'sir;' it had not occurred to these clients that being misgendered is not the exclusive purview of trans individuals. They were quite happy to realize this experience gave them common ground with the butch lesbians they identified with in the first place.

The difference, however, is that butch lesbians are unlikely to engage in self-condemnation when called 'sir' by others. More likely, they'll just get angry at being mistaken for men, or laugh it off. My MTF clients often had difficulty reframing the experience to one of society's limitations regarding what 'female' looks like.

One older MTF client, usually seen female in all situations, was very discouraged upon being clocked as a transwoman four times within the space of an hour. She had dressed very formally to go to church and had gone to a local mall immediately thereafter. At the mall, she stood out to such a degree that people looked at her much more closely than they would have otherwise and thus saw her as a transwoman.

Typical for her male socialization she had taken it very hard that she was seen male that day and had come away from the experience with the idea that it was hopeless for her to ever believe she could succeed as a woman. I veered the topic into the realm of redefining 'success' and deconstructing where the message came from that she had to be perfectly attuned to her new gender role just a few months after beginning hormones, having spent the previous 60 years living the male role.

Sharon, a 50-something transwoman, has a mentor (Pam) who helps her with the nuances of female behavior. On a recent trip to the mall, Sharon took her jacket off and flung it over her shoulder. Pam signaled subtly that she should instead carry her jacket over her arm and Sharon complied. Sharon is seen as female often but is sometimes mistaken for male. The fewer 'male' cues she gives the less likely she is to be seen male. While there are certainly women who will fling a jacket over their shoulder, there are fewer men who will carry a casual jacket over their arm. This behavior is more likely to give a 'female' cue than a 'male' cue, increasing the likelihood Sharon will be perceived female, which is her goal. To date she has not encountered a situation where such a choice feels unnatural to her or as if she were compromising herself for the sake of being seen female. She and Pam have developed a special 'sign language' of their own to allow Pam to give gender cues.

One transwoman friend had a different experience of living female, saying, "I just let myself behave in all the ways I felt like I couldn't when I was still pretending to be a guy. It felt natural back then, too, so much so that I had to work to hide it."

On the other side of the spectrum, Owen got a new driver's license with his correct name and gender. He showed me the license shortly after receiving it, and I commented how serious he looked in the photo. His fiancée Andrea was with him, and she said, "I told him not to smile; it makes him look female." He protested, "Guys smile, too," to which Andrea replied, "But you smile differently, it makes you look kind and feminine, not like a guy. Besides, if you get pulled over by a cop this is what you'll look like because you *won't* be smiling."

A sense of humor and perspective is a saving grace when dealing with transition!

Renegotiating boundaries is part of what makes early transition so challenging. Coupled with the effects of a new hormone balance on information and emotional processing, early transition fulfills the ancient Chinese curse, "May you live in interesting times." While some may look on it as a curse, this stage of transition can also be viewed as a trial by fire, a rite of passage from transinfancy through transadolescence into a transadult status. Many cisgender adults look back on adolescence with the heartfelt thought, "Thank God that's over!" Many trans adults look back on their early transition process with the same heartfelt thought.

THE LAST WORD

I leave the last word to Trina, who sent me an e-mail containing a piece her family found useful in coming to understand her transition. When I read this, I knew the time would soon be coming when I would be referring to Trina as a former client.

ownership
current mood: determined
the past three years have been highly educational. moving in society from one gender to the other can be quite an experience. filled with all kinds of twists and insights.

my mother is an extraordinary woman in many regards. she is highly intelligent, analytical and trained in critical thinking. so naturally she applied her talents and skills to the announcement, "mom, i'm a girl." and the first question she asked, after the shock had diminished a little was, "what does it mean to be a woman?"

mom doesn't claim to be a feminist (my criteria for a feminist is a woman who doesn't accept limitation - and she definitely qualifies.) but she's well read and has strong opinions regarding women, culture and society.

at the time she asked, my intention was to do whatever was necessary to be accepted socially as female. this meant living up to the social expectation of "what a woman is." being stuck in the wrong box for so long, the other box still looked like a box, but a much more comfortable one. mom probably didn't like this very much ;)

during our conversation, she stripped away the social connotations of femininity. she was relentless, steadfast and determined to banish these perceptions. there was no absolute. no gauge, no meter by which to determine what a "woman is," much less what it means to be one. the only answer left was "i don't know what it means to be a woman, mom."

it was such a sensitive period, the first few months, as all the implications of being transgendered found their way to the surface. mom's interrogation seemed quite aggressive and i took it very personally. who wouldn't? there i was, telling her that i'm a girl, and she's forcing an admission that i don't know what that means.

the engines cooled down a little bit, and a full year passed while considering her question. there was no jumping immediately from one box to the other. i considered the women i admire, the girls who inspired envy and jealousy, every day people in every day activities - driving down the street, walking through parks, spending time with families, at work, at play, attending to ordinary details like groceries and shopping, etc.

and i saw jeans and faces clear of make-up. rough hands as well as manicured. dresses, skirts and t-shirts. gentleness and strength. motorcycles and minivans. rough language and irritability, consideration and nurturing.

there are a few areas where the social differences between men and women are more pronounced. men are typically less expressive in appearance and emotion. but not always. women aren't typically afraid to

241

ask for help or admit they don't know how to do something. but not always.

so what does it mean to be a woman? culture does not define a woman. expectation does not define a woman. the needs, thoughts and desires of others do not define a woman. a woman defines herself.

when people look my way, they see a woman.
what it means is mine to own.

• Chapter 13 •

PARALLEL PROCESSES: RECOVERY AND TRANSITION

EARLY IN MY TRANSITION PROCESS, I CAME OUT TO A CISFEMALE FRIEND WHO IS A LONG-TIME-CLEAN DRUG ADDICT. She remarked that it seemed to her that my transition was similar to the rein-vention of Self she'd experienced in recovering from her drug addiction. Witnessing hundreds of transitions in the ensuing years, nothing has ever caused me to doubt how right my friend was in her assessment. Those familiar with women's music may have noticed that the songs I've quoted most throughout this book are from Meg Christian's album *Turning It Over,* recorded during her early sobri-ety. It is no accident that so many of the lyrics from that album have felt applicable to the process of transition.

The similarities between transition and recovery lie in the depth of work necessary to truly embrace both processes in a manner that leads to a healthy sense of self down the road. However, parallel doesn't mean identical. The need to transition is not an addiction nor are all addicts hiding a gender issue from themselves.

Here are the twelve steps of Alcoholics Anonymous (AA):

1. We admitted we were powerless over alcohol, that our lives had become unmanageable.
2. We came to believe that a Power greater than ourselves could restore us to sanity.
3. We made a decision to turn our will and our lives over to the care of God as we understood Him.
4. We made a searching and fearless moral inventory of ourselves.
5. We admitted to God, to ourselves and to another human being the exact nature of our wrongs.

6. We were entirely ready to have God remove all these defects of character.

7. We humbly asked Him to remove our shortcomings.

8. We made a list of all persons we had harmed, and became willing to make amends to them all.

9. We made direct amends to such people wherever possible, except when to do so would injure them or others.

10. We continued to take personal inventory and when we were wrong promptly admitted it.

11. We sought through prayer and meditation to improve our conscious contact with God, as we understood Him, praying only for knowledge of His will for us and the power to carry that out.

12. Having had a spiritual awakening as the result of these steps, we tried to carry this message to alcoholics, and to practice these principles in all our affairs. (Alcoholics Anonymous, 2011)

Some don't resonate with AA as a program, however, there are certain principles underlying various AA steps that can be useful to any trans person, regardless of how they feel about AA itself.

First, the concept of powerlessness applies to growing up trans in this culture. None of us chose our identities as trans people, though others in our lives may send the message that this is a matter of choice. Such people (wrongly) interpret trans identity as a matter of behavior; the choice is not in who we are, but in what we do about it.

Differentiating between behavior and identity allows many to move forward with transition (behavior), recognizing that they are powerless to change their identity. Too many of my clients tried to accept responsibility at earlier times in their lives for the identity itself, trying in vain to cure themselves. (Or, ironically, turning to a drug to numb the pain when they realized they couldn't cure themselves.)

Many of my MTF clients developed a largely-unconscious existential checklist that could be titled "Things to Try that Might Cure Me." Some might title that list "Things to Try that Will Help Me Hide Who I Really Am." The list included: joining the military (and sometimes volunteering for dangerous assignments, hoping to be killed); marriage; having children; exerting will power (purging feminine clothing and make-up, saying firmly, 'Never again!'); pursuing a career in a male-dominated profession; and sometimes, numbing the pain with drugs or alcohol.[24]

However the result wasn't a change of identity but a growing sense of powerlessness and hopelessness. Those who faced their true selves came to realize that the real powerlessness was in the at-tempt to change their identity. This realization gave many a sense of renewed hope. Where they had been feeling low self-esteem, thinking, "If only I'd been a better husband/wife, I might have been able to be happy living as a man/woman"— their thinking gradually shifts to, "I never had a chance in trying to be a good wife/husband because I'm just not female/male inside."

The parallel with the AA model is realizing precisely what it is that one is powerless to change. In the case of the trans person, one is powerless to change identity. The Serenity Prayer, familiar to all who embrace an AA-type recovery program, translates well to the process of coming to terms with trans identity: "God grant me the serenity to accept the things I cannot change, courage to change the things I can, and the wisdom to know the difference."

Another parallel process can be found in AA's fourth step: making a fearless moral inventory. Though not based in morality, the fearless inventory of transition involves being able to face one's true self despite lifelong social pressure to the contrary. From the time we are born, enormous cultural pressure guides us (all of us, trans and

---

[24] In 2009, I heard a new addition to the list: a client said whenever the female feelings would surface, she would get another tattoo. Not only did she see tattoos as male and not female, but the pain also distracted her thoroughly from emotions she was trying to avoid. People who deliberately cut themselves accomplish the same thing, though without the tattoo to show for it.

cisgender alike) along specific gender paths. To force a path in a completely different direction, often with little support, takes incredible strength and courage, as does the honest undertaking of AA's fourth step.

Yet another analogy lies in the eighth step, making amends for past wrongs. Within the transition process, the parallel is that of disclosure. Within AA, one aspect of fully embracing the eighth step is that if making amends directly would cause further harm or damage in some way, the addict makes amends indirectly without involving the person they originally hurt. Just so, some trans people choose not to disclose their transition to elderly or terminally-ill relatives or friends, feeling the gains don't outweigh the cost.

Because transition cannot take place in a vacuum, the process entails coming out to others, facing their fears and doubts, their judgment and support. It may seem counterintuitive to list support as something difficult to face in disclosing to others. A lifetime of feeling ashamed and afraid of disclosing one's core self can make it difficult to allow the vulnerability to accept true support. For many, it feels easier to weather transition alone than to allow others in to share the journey.

It is this attitude that leads many to feel isolated and lonely within their transition process, as if their only allies will be found among other trans individuals. Yet consider the power of confiding in a cisgender friend and hearing, "I care about you for who you are, and will support you in any way I can on this journey." Problem is, this is a rare enough reaction that it can be hard for any trans person to continually come out, knowing that most reactions will be luke-warm or confused and perhaps hostile or violent.

Some trans people also find the eleventh and twelfth steps, those involving spiritual awakening, apply to their transition process. Many trans people look to science for answers when considering the meaning of their trans identity. However science can only explain observable biological processes and cannot address the underlying meaning of any form of identity. What does it mean that not everyone in a culture is heterosexual? Why is it the case that homo-sexuality has been observed in most human cultures, throughout history? (I say "most" because I don't want to say "all," though I have not heard of a culture in which there was never any observation of homosexuality at all) What purpose might it serve society that not everyone's gender identity matches what others as-sume based on their genitalia? As with any meaning of life queries these kinds of questions are the purview of philosophy and spirituality, not of science.

How these kinds of questions play out in society is the realm of sociology; how individuals make sense of these questions is the realm of psychology. *Psyche* is the Greek word for soul; *logo* is the Greek word for language. In my work with clients, I always kept these two words in the back of my mind. I tried to encourage my trans clients to view gender issues through an existential rather than scientific lens. The scientific view is the medical model and tran-sition viewed from this perspective results in terminology such as diagnosis, disorder, birth defect, etc. An existential or spiritual inquiry results in descriptive terminology such as core identity, growth opportunity, emergence, broader world view.

It is difficult to find a positive interpretation of being trans within a medical model framework, and difficult to find a negative interpretation within a spiritual model. There are certainly religious models that present trans identity in a negative light, but a spiritual inquiry is an inward journey that is not based in any particular religious belief system. The eleventh step of AA, the spiritual awakening, can result in a degree of centeredness and self-know-ledge that feels familiar to the trans person who has come to view their own trans identity as having some positive purpose.

Another parallel between transition and recovery lies not in the steps themselves, but in the process. Addiction recovery is a neces-sarily self-centered process. 'Ninety meetings in ninety days' is the mantra of the addict beginning their recovery process. It's impossible to attend that many meetings in such a short period without intense self-focus, nearly to the exclusion of all else. Early recovery assumes a place of tremendous importance in the addict's life, of necessity.

Early transition requires the same intensity of focus and self-centeredness. Centering into one's Self is the precise goal of both processes, and this can appear as selfishness to those who witness it. How else can one reinvent oneself if the Self is not the focus of complete attention? I once saw a *New Yorker* magazine cartoon that illustrates early transition perfectly. It also applies perfectly to early recovery. The cartoon depicts a large bookstore. One shelf is labeled "Self Improvement" while the one right next to it is labeled "Self Involvement." Those in transition or in recovery go through a period of self-involvement in the name of self-improvement.

RECOVERY OR TRANSITION–WHICH COMES FIRST?

Many trans people are addicted to or abusing one substance or another, attempting various forms of self-medication to numb the pain and anxiety of having the wrong hormone balance in their bodies. This leaves many of them in the unfortunate position of having to go through two parallel processes of reinvention of self – transition and recovery – in order to move on with their lives.

Neither process is a guarantee of future happiness. I never guaranteed my clients that they would be happier if they moved forward with transition. As seemed appropriate, I did tell some cli-ents that if a different hormone balance and/or gender role was in-deed right for them, transition would give them the chance for happiness that they wouldn't find otherwise.[25] The same can be said for addiction recovery. Fully embracing a recovery program, at the level of reinvention of self, is no guarantee of happiness. But remaining an addict is a sure-fire way of guaranteeing the person won't be able to attain true happiness in the future.

---

[25] It's a judgment call which clients to say this to. I would not say this to someone who wasn't emotionally prepared to transition, or to someone who would take my words to mean I was telling them they had to transition.

The self-centeredness of early transition is intensified for trans people who are also facing an addiction (or serious abuse issue). Most of the clients I helped navigate these simultaneous processes did so while single. Many were in relationships when they started along their road toward transition and recovery; only two of the clients I've seen in this situation retained those relationships along their journey. Transition and recovery processes are both very hard on relationship; to undertake both at once is so stressful, it is a rare partnership that can survive the process. To undertake both pro-cesses at once is to work two full-time jobs simultaneously.

Those of my trans clients who were addicts were in a chicken-and-egg position: should they give up their drug and go through a recovery program prior to transition, or should they alleviate the hormone imbalance first, with the knowledge that they will find it difficult to center into their true selves through recovery while they have the wrong hormone balance in their bodies? Can they get to know themselves well enough to make the best decisions about transition if they are altering their mind or mood with drugs?

Many of my parallel-process clients used a harm-reduction model[26] to lessen their addiction gradually as the hormones bol-stered their sense of self-esteem and self-efficacy. (Denning, 2004) While some felt frustrated, feeling ashamed at their occasional backslide into using drugs or alcohol again, most moved forward slowly into a healthier sense of self, eventually able to quit using their drug of choice. The transition process for such clients was typically slower than it might have been otherwise, as they moni-tored not only their resocialization process but also their recovery process.

---

[26] Harm reduction is a model of recovery that encourages small steps toward giving up a drug entirely. For instance, someone who uses other people's needles might take a step in the right direction by beginning to use a needle exchange program, to lessen the possibility of acquiring a blood-born infection, thus reducing the harm caused by their continued usage of a drug. Harm reduction is a controversial model because it seems to encourage further drug use, however many in the drug/alcohol services field believe harm reduction is a realistic method of gradually weaning people from their drug, and more effective than the "just say no" model of complete abstinence.

For these clients the recovery and transition processes were intertwined to such a degree that they didn't feel as if they were undergoing two discrete processes, but one larger process that is a combination of both. Such clients couldn't attribute their epiphanies and breakthroughs to one process or the other, as they found the processes inseparable.

Jim (24) was an alcoholic involved with a woman who did not support his transition, though her codependent nature had caused her to turn a blind eye to Jim's addiction. He broke free of the relationship when he was four months sober and six months on hormones. He found it impossible to disentangle how much of his new clarity of mind was due to his sobriety and how much to the newfound social confidence he felt finally being perceived male. He realized that his sobriety was as important a process as his transition and refused to allow any relationship to jeopardize either.

A year into his parallel process, Jim met a woman he later married. In reflecting on his previous relationship he commented, "I realize now there was no way that relationship would have survived. She was so co-dependent, she wouldn't have been right for me once I got healthier and wanted a more balanced relationship."

Jim's wife came to one session and said, "I did a lot of work on myself long before Jim and I got together, because I grew up in an alcoholic family and had my share of bad relationships, where I supported a partner at the expense of my own goals. It's so refreshing to meet a guy who not only isn't doing that, but doesn't want it! And I think part of it is because Jim was raised female, that gives him that little bit of extra awareness of what's expected of women." *(Client session, 2003)*

I used to hold the view that recovery was a pre-condition for transition. I felt that the necessary degree of self-knowledge was impossible to attain while in a mind-altered state of being. However I changed my mind over time, realizing that self-knowledge may very well be why some people turned to a drug or alcohol in the first place. Such folks know quite well how they *don't* want to live their lives –

as their birth gender – but chose a path other than transition in order to cope with the knowledge. While they are faced with a more difficult path in the long run, forcing them to retrace their steps via recovery before beginning the path of transition no longer feels appropriate or realistic to me.

Ultimately I took a case-by-case approach. Drugs differ so in their effects on information processing, getting clean prior to begin-ning hormones is advisable in some cases. Part of the early transition process involves continually checking in with oneself, to answer the question, "Does this hormone balance work for me? Am I more centered, happier with myself, with this new hormone balance?" A drug that drastically alters one's emotional baseline or thought-processing ability makes answering these questions virtually impossible.

In such cases I would suggest writing a letter so the person can get their hormones legally and take them while under a doctor's care. However I would also ask that the client commit to continuing therapy after starting hormones, not something I overtly asked of clients generally, to help ensure they have a stable support structure. Addicts have often surrounded themselves with other addicts and will probably find they can't turn to existing friends for support for their transition, making their therapist's support all the more valuable. I found putting it that way helped my clients understand that I wasn't saying they were mentally ill, more in need of therapy than non-addicted clients, etc.

None of my clients took drugs that altered their cognitive or emotional processes to that degree. In order of preference their drugs of choice were marijuana, alcohol, and heroin. Some also used various prescription tranquilizers, to check out emotionally. The drugs they gravitated toward are those that lessen emotionality.

Those who understood full well why they wanted to use a drug usually chose marijuana, believing it to be the most benign drug that would accomplish their goal of numbing emotional pain. As they proceeded with transition most of my pot-smoking clients were able to leave the pot behind fairly easily. Their levels of emotional pain decreased to the point it would not occur to them to smoke pot when they got home at the end of the day.

Colleagues who work in low-fee or free clinics are more likely to face clients with more difficult addiction issues, or those who have dual diagnoses (addiction along with another serious mental health issue). I was in private practice, which changed the nature of my clientele somewhat. The primary consideration is that no two people's processes are going to play out identically, and a case-by-case approach is always appropriate when faced with a trans client who is also an addict or drug abuser.

ACOA ISSUES AMONG TRANS CLIENTS

Many of my clients (trans and otherwise) came from families with one or more addictions forming part of the fabric of the family, alcohol being the most prevalent. Following are some of the more common patterns associated with ACOA's (adult children, or grandchildren, of alcoholics), who tend to:

1. Feel isolated and uneasy with other people, especially authority figures;
2. Become 'people pleasers,' losing their own identities in the process;
3. Mistake any personal criticism as a threat;
4. Become alcoholics, marry them, or both, or find other compulsive personalities, such as a workaholic, to fulfill a need for abandonment;
5. Live from the standpoint of victims, preferring to be concerned with others rather than themselves;
6. Feel guilty when trusting themselves, and then giving in to others;
7. Become reactors rather than actors, letting others take the initiative;

8. Willing to do almost anything to hold on to a relationship in order not to be abandoned emotionally;

9. Keep choosing insecure relationships because they matched a childhood relationship with alcoholic or dysfunctional parents.

The above are excerpts; the full text is available at:
http://www.adultchildren.org/lit/Problems.

Whether trans or not, people who are ACOA's tend to resonate with many of the above patterns. Some of the ACOA issues can be magnified by the experience of growing up trans, though not all these effects are negative. Tending to be a reactor rather than an actor can be beneficial for someone early in transition. The reactor is one who is observant, watching others cautiously to determine how to act in any given situation. While this can be detrimental in some areas of life, as it can be difficult to learn to be assertive, the habit of keen observation can help one learn a new gender role more quickly.

Trans clients have added layers to the ACOA issues. Charlene had always experienced a degree of social anxiety and introversion that felt unnatural to her. She wanted to be able to reach out to others, to be gregarious, but feared offending others. She had grown up in a household with two alcoholic parents who fought constantly. The only thing that ever caused her parents to present a united front was when one of their children did anything to draw attention away from the parental conflict. Then both parents would turn on which-ever child had drawn their attention.

In order to survive, Charlene (then Carl) learned very young to be very quiet, to move through the world without drawing attention and never to speak up or speak first. However Charlene is not an introvert by nature. At 27, finally actualizing her true gender, Char-lene chafed at the self-imposed restrictions on her public persona. Reading the first few tendencies on the above list made Charlene cry as she realized how profoundly her childhood experiences were holding her back from being her true self in the world.

Charlene began attending ACOA meetings; she did not come out in the meetings as trans. At this point in her transition she was able to be seen female all the time. She felt that her trans identity was not relevant to the ACOA issues that were holding her back socially. While she was still attempting to live as Carl, she was not bothered by her tendency to withdraw and be socially isolated as she did not feel comfortable interacting with others as male. Once she was seen female, however, Charlene found herself wanting to reach out – and terrified of doing so. At that point, the ACOA issues came to prominence on her existential priority list. She and I revisited the question, "How do I want to live my life?" and Charlene had another epiphany, realizing, "There is no reason these tendencies have to dominate my life any longer. If I could face transition successfully, I can take this on as well."

During her recovery process Charlene came to realize that her trans identity had also caused her to feel she had to hide, making her all the more grateful for her eventual transition. Had she sought out ACOA groups prior to her transition, she realized she would have been unable to reach out to others socially as she wasn't living gender in a way that felt right to her. Eventually, her ACOA recovery and transition felt like inseparable parallel processes much like addiction recovery and transition can. At that point, Charlene came out as trans in the ACOA meeting she regularly attended; she felt that coming out as trans had become part of her recovery process as an ACOA.

GRANDCHILDREN OF ALCOHOLICS AND
GROWING UP TRANS: PARALLEL EXPERIENCES

There are aspects of the alcoholic family experience that parallel the experience of growing up trans in a non-alcoholic family. This can be especially true when one considers the following scenario: growing up the grandchild of an untreated alcoholic, with parents who are not themselves addicts. This is particularly problematic if the addiction was not only untreated, but unacknowledged. (Smith, 1988)

Clients who are grandchildren of alcoholics may resonate with the list of ACOA patterns without having any idea why. In some cases I spotted the patterns in a client and asked about family history of addiction. In the situation of grandparent addiction, the parents had distanced themselves from the addiction, believing if they gave it no space to exist in the family history the patterns would not carry on through the generations. It doesn't work that way, however; the parents learned their own relational patterns at home, as we all do, and were affected by their own parents' addictive patterns. These patterns then affect their own children.

Four years into transition Mark (26) said, "I thought it was part of my personality or related to my being trans that I had so much fear of conflict. I was always so afraid that if I disagreed with a partner, they'd leave me." I showed Mark the above list of ACOA tendencies. He had no knowledge of addiction in his family but resonated with so many of the patterns on the list that he decided to make inquiries.

He did not feel his parents would be helpful so he contacted an uncle he felt might be forthcoming. From his uncle he learned his maternal grandfather had indeed been a heavy drinker, though no one talked about it. Mark's mother had never felt comfortable in her father's presence and never invited her parents over while Mark was growing up, though they did not live geographically far away. Mark's mother never allowed alcohol in the house; he recalls growing up with a sense that alcohol was poisonous, though he couldn't pinpoint actual conversations in which anyone made that statement. When Mark learned his grandfather had been an alco-holic, he cried with relief. As he said in our next session, "I felt like this weight was off me. The first thought I had was, 'It's not me after all.' And then I felt sorry for my mother and really mad at her, at the same time."

Mark began attending ACOA meetings, which further strained his relationship with his parents. His mother had never wanted to admit to herself (much less anyone else) that her father was an alco-holic.

Mark attending ACOA meetings, overtly talking about his family background, angered her. As he started deconstructing his own behavior patterns and trying to apply healthier communication techniques in his relationships, he told me, "Now, it's hard for me to have a conversation with my mother. If I try to say what I really feel about pretty much anything, that breaks the pattern of our relationship. I see now why so many people in recovery have to break old relationships and find other people.

"She never wanted to talk much about my transition, talk about something that's altogether too real for her! She's not unsupportive, it's not that, just that it's pretty well impossible to have a conversation about transition that's at the superficial level we've communicated at my whole life. I've realized that if I want my mother in my life, I have to accept where she's at and just keep my commu-nication at that level. For her, I'll try. It's not like with friends; I can't find a new mother! Who knows… maybe if I keep on, she'll start moving in that direction herself." *(Client session, 2006)*

Some of my trans clients had no history of addiction in their families yet still resonated with a number of the tendencies on the above list. They tried to be what others expected them to be, though this is very different from who they knew themselves to be. They were told who they were from a young age and found it difficult to assert anything different, or believe they have the right to assert anything different.

These are the patterns of someone living with a great and shameful secret. For grandchildren of alcoholics the great family secret is an unacknowledged addiction or a lack of recognition of addictive patterns affecting a household that does not contain an addict. (Smith, 1988) For the young trans child, whether ACOA or not, the great secret is one of unacknowledged (or unrecognized) identity. But children believe their parents know everything and don't realize their parents don't automatically know their identity. All they can recognize is that for some reason their identity is not okay. This is particularly true for young MTFs, who are usually not permitted to express gender as they would like.

A four-year-old may feel inside, "I'm not really a boy, I'm a girl," yet everyone in the child's life is telling them different, using male pronouns and treating them like a boy. At that age one's parents are the equivalent of God: all-knowing, all-powerful, omniscient, omnipresent. It's difficult to maintain a belief in oneself and one's self-knowledge in the face of 'God' saying, "You're wrong."

This experience causes many trans people to grow up not trusting their own intuition, constantly needing external validation for their beliefs and feelings, not believing in their own ability to know what's real and what isn't. Reality-testing is often challenged for trans people because of early experiences of being steered along the wrong gender vector.

So many of my trans clients, whether from alcoholic families or not, have similar stories to tell:

"I can't ever seem to hold onto a belief as my own; I have to constantly check it out with other people before I know something is real."

"It's hard for me to feel entitled to my own opinion and if others say something different I find myself going along with them, even if I was really sure how I felt before that."

"I never voice my opinion until I find out how others in the group think, even if it's a group of friends and I know intellectually they wouldn't mind if we disagreed. I'm still afraid they'll dump me."

"I'm so afraid when people around me disagree or argue. I shut down and can't take sides. Ironically this sometimes gets me in trouble, because it frustrates my friends that I won't join in the debate or voice my opinion."

I heard these kinds of statements from ACOA clients, trans or otherwise, and from trans clients, ACOA or otherwise, but rarely did such issues seriously trouble those of my clients who are neither ACOA or trans.

ACOA groups can be validating and helpful but I urge caution before automatically suggesting such a group for a trans client, particularly a client who has not yet started or is very early in physical transition. It would not be helpful were such a client to encounter social prejudice in an ACOA group or for group members to focus on the transition rather than ACOA issues. And it may be the case, as with Charlene, that the ACOA issues take a back seat to the transition process and will make their way to the top of the agenda after transition is well underway.

• Chapter 14 •

WHEN WORLDS COLLIDE: RELIGION AND TRANSITION

MANY OF MY CLIENTS WERE NOT TROUBLED BY RELIGIOUS CONFLICT. While many were raised in some religion or other, most came to terms with their trans identities in ways that made sense to them. Their religious beliefs didn't hold them back. Some turned their backs on religion altogether. Others found solace and comfort in some of the more progressive spiritual traditions or in queer-specific churches such as Metropolitan Community Church (MCC). Founded in the 1960s, MCC has long been a spiritual haven for gay men, lesbians, and bisexuals who had been rejected by more-conservative congregations. (Perry, 1992)

In addition to MCC many mainstream churches have policies of welcoming all parishioners. Some of my religiously-conservative trans clients didn't know how to find out whether a congregation would welcome them once they'd begun transition. The code words to look for are *reconciling* or *welcoming and affirming* in a church's advertising or signage. Churches use those terms to indicate they embrace gay, bisexual, and lesbian parishioners. Many (though not all) have extended the definition of welcoming and affirming or reconciling to include trans parishioners.

Spirituality can provide deep comfort but I didn't steer clients in any particular direction. Rather I modeled for them the attitude that spirituality and religion are not the same thing and that only certain denominations rigidly reject any form of queer identity. It would be just as harmful to a client's process of self-discovery were I to model the flip side of a rejecting religious stance – you must reject religion before it rejects you.

A CONSERVATIVE CLIENT'S EXPERIENCE

Some of my clients came from conservative backgrounds. Georgia was raised in a fundamentalist Christian household and married a woman with similar beliefs. Both were quite active in a fundamentalist church throughout their married life. Georgia, however, had a lifelong war going on inside her. She believed all sinners go to hell unless they can sincerely repent and make their best effort every day to live up to their Christian ideals. On the other hand... she knew from a very early age that 'Georgia' was who she was, not 'George.'

In her early 60s she realized she could not go on as George any longer. This wasn't an epiphany nor did a specific event bring about an existential crisis. A lifetime of living as George, battling each day to ignore Georgia's existence, had worn her down to the point that she no longer had the strength to deny her core identity. She'd used such emotional reserves in keeping Georgia at bay that her choices had become suicide or transition. According to her religious beliefs suicide is a mortal sin. As is transition. Georgia was caught between two mortal sins. Her beliefs were such that neither choice seemed viable.

What saved Georgia was the experience she had when she tried transition. She was so much happier and centered in her identity as a woman, it became increasingly difficult for her to believe that transition is wrong or sinful. During one session she said, "Suicide is a sin and I'd go to hell if I did it. Living as Georgia is a sin, too, and I'll probably go to hell. But I'm so much happier as Georgia that it's worth the risk of going to hell."

Ironically it was Georgia's belief in hell and the sin of suicide that kept her on the planet. Remaining George was not an option she even considered. Her depression as George was so complete she no longer had the energy (either physical or psychic) to get out of bed in the morning to face the day as a man.

Georgia's wife did not support the transition and the couple's divorce was final in 2005. Neither did anyone else in her family circle. With every day that passed Georgia was increasingly happy. She was able to be seen female in all situations, as her body type is not overly masculine or large. It was not difficult for her to speak in a female range. She had an increasingly strong sense of centered-ness and happiness with life.

Because Georgia had lived her entire life within the same religious tradition, I knew she had little knowledge about other faith traditions. I encouraged her to read other biblical interpretations of GLB and T identities and to reach out to spiritual leaders who have different views than those she had previously encountered.

She tried various churches in the Portland area; for a time she felt she had found a home in a conservative church in a nearby town. This church accepted her as a congregant, but placed restric-tions on her such as not interacting with children. Though their ac-ceptance was guarded, as Georgia put it, "That's better than my old church, which just kicked me out altogether." She had tried MCC and various other welcoming congregations, but did not find them conservative enough for her either theologically or politically.

Georgia still wondered at times if she might not go to hell and still contemplated suicide at times, when she was feeling particu-larly alone and isolated. But she could also see how much her life was a living hell prior to her transition, now that she had a happier existence to compare it to.

In 2007 Georgia gave up on Christianity altogether and has embraced a conservative non-Christian faith. Georgia has been wel-comed as a woman because she has had gender-confirming surgery. As long as she follows the woman's role as outlined in religious teachings she is welcome to remain.

Georgia now regrets her transition, feeling the loss of family has outweighed the gains. However she also recognizes that she was too depressed to go on as George. She has never said, "I made the wrong decision based on my gender." Rather, she had no way of knowing prior to undertaking the process how heavy the burden of loss would feel.

This conundrum – becoming her true self versus the loss of family and religion – weighs on her every day as she goes about her business. She now feels she was trapped by circumstance between two intolerable choices: remaining George, or losing her religion and entire family and circle of friends.

Georgia's situation is a reminder that there are no easy or right answers when it comes to transition. Like many older trans people, she believes her path would be significantly different if she were 40 years younger. She was born at a time when transition was physically possible but only barely possible socially, and the road for those who transition out of conservative religion is too often intolerably rocky.

THE CONVERSION/REPARATIVE THERAPY MODEL

Religiously-conservative clients find their trans identities collide with religious beliefs that have taught them there can be no source of ultimate truth beyond the teachings of their religion. Reparative therapy takes the position that there is no such thing as trans identity, only bad behavior. Therefore reaching out to God with heartfelt humility and asking to be cured will lead to a change of behavior. The reparative therapy model theorizes that the behavior was originally instilled via dysfunctional families.

Reparative therapy can seem like the literal answer to a prayer for a religious person who is LGBTQ. To hear someone else say, "I, too, once felt like you and the Lord cured me," would give powerful hope of change. Some reparative therapy programs are entirely secular, with no religious component, but this is increasingly rare in an era where such a therapeutic approach is condemned by profes-sional organizations and under fire legally. Secular reparative thera-py practices represent outdated interpretations of Freud's theories.

The psychological theory underlying reparative therapy is that homosexuality (and by extension being trans) is the result of inadequate parenting - absent or weak fathers, permissiveness re gender roles, dysfunctional or domineering mothers, etc. (Moberly, 2006) Because a greater burden of responsibility is placed on males over females within conservative belief systems (whether religious or secular), reparative therapy is usually aimed more directly at gay men and transwomen. The concept of the absent or weak father is seen as creating a less-than-masculine son who might be more inclined to become gay or desire to transition to female. The domineering mother doesn't allow her son to develop masculine strength.

An absent or weak father creates the potential for a lesbian daughter because the female offspring is not receiving the message that her father, the man of the family, is strong and masculine while women are not. Further, the absence of a father means someone has to take on that role in the family and a daughter may see this as a way she can help her mother, by being more masculine, thus leading her down the road of becoming a lesbian or desiring to become a man. The domineering mother provides a warped model for a daughter, not raising her to see that men are supposed to be stronger and more powerful than women. Rather, the daughter 'becomes' the man, in the form of transitioning or being a lesbian.

How these theories support the concept of a feminine lesbian daughter or masculine gay son is unclear.

According to reparative therapy proponents the removal of homosexuality from the DSM in 1973[27] was a mistake, as they believe it clearly is a disorder based in childhood experiences. However one can say that about most of the issues that bring people into the therapist's office to begin with; nearly all are rooted in family dysfunctionality. There is more to the reparative therapy model than simply a problematic family of origin. At the heart of reparative therapy programs is religion, and the belief that homosexuality is a mortal sin.

---

[27] Ego dystonic homosexuality remained in the DSM until 1987. However, this diagnosis didn't pathologize homosexuality; rather, this diagnosis was used to characterize the person who was having difficulty accepting that they were L, G or B.

And this is the crux of the matter... sin is a matter of behavior, not identity. Many people in the secular realm also misunderstand sexual orientation as a matter of behavior, not an issue of core identity. The term *sexual preference* stemmed from the belief that people chose to behave in a homosexual manner. Many secular people are also uncomfortable with homosexual or trans identities, but cannot resonate with the idea of condemning people based on a sin model. Cloaking reparative therapy in the trappings of psychology – the dysfunctional family model – allows reparative therapy proponents to reach out in a convincing manner to secular people. Yet the underlying messages of reparative therapy remain 'this is a mortal sin' and 'only God can help you toward a cure.'

I read a synopsis of a study that seemed to conclude that reparative therapy works for many people. (Spitzer, 2005) The synopsis can be found on the following website:

http://www.narth.com/docs/evidencefound.html.

What I found revealing is that according to the synopsis, well over 90% of the people seeking to be cured using this form of intervention reported that religion was extremely important to them. That seemed a suspiciously high percentage to me, beyond what I would expect from the general population, leading me to wonder:

❖ Was religion important to them prior to participating in reparative therapy, and is the religion they find extremely important of a conservative variety;

❖ How were study participants chosen;

❖ Was reparative therapy equally effective for self-identified secular individuals;

❖ How much follow-up is going to occur to check for long-term change in sexuality;

❖ How is 'successful' defined – by behavior alone, self-reported fantasies, etc.;

❖ Would the results be the same if participants were not vo-
    lunteers, but were randomly selected from the entire
    population of GLB and/or T individuals.

None of these issues were addressed in the synopsis, which led
me to question the validity of what I was reading. Further research
led me to the study's author, Dr. Robert Spitzer,[28] who had a quite
different interpretation of his results.

Dr. Spitzer felt the results of his study were being selectively
interpreted by religious conservatives to bolster their claim that reparative therapy is effective. After analyzing his own data and the
arduous process necessary to find participants who fit the study criteria, he concluded it is highly *unlikely* reparative therapy is effective
for the vast majority of those who identify as gay or lesbian. (Spitzer
CNN interview)

Dr. Spitzer felt this conclusion was logical because most of those
who responded to his call for participants were weeded out because
they had not felt cured even though they had very much wanted to
be. Participants were selected from among people who said they had
successfully switched from a homosexual to hetero-sexual lifestyle.
Those who had attempted to find a cure via reparative therapy and
felt they were still homosexual did not qualify as study participants.

The point of this distinction lies in precisely what Dr. Spitzer was
trying to analyze. This was his research question: why is re-parative
therapy effective for those who feel it's worked for them? In order to
try to answer this question, Dr. Spitzer of necessity looked for
participants who felt this form of intervention had worked and did
not include those for whom it had not. Thousands of potential
participants had responded to his call for research subjects; only a
few hundred were chosen. The rest were eliminated as par-ticipants

---

[28] Dr. Spitzer played a pivotal role in the 1973 removal of homosexuality from the DSM. The
public radio show *This American Life* aired a history of this process, titled "81 Words."

because they didn't feel reparative therapy had cured them from being gay or lesbian.

Dr. Spitzer stated, "Our sample was self-selected from people who already claimed they had made some change. We don't know how common that kind of change is.... I'm not saying that this can be done easily, or that homosexuals who want to change can make this kind of change. I suspect it's quite unusual." (Spitzer, CNN interview) His interpretation of the fact that it seemed to work for those who participated in his study? They were probably bisexual, not gay or lesbian, and thus were able to form satisfying relationships that seemed heterosexual in nature. (Additional comments by Dr. Spitzer may be found at:

http://www.religioustolerance.org/hom_spit.htm)

Any social science study is prone to researcher bias. Particularly for issues as controversial as sexual orientation or gender identity, it is impossible to find a researcher who can truthfully claim neutrality. It is impossible for any researcher to step outside their own gender or sexual identities in order to claim complete objecti-vity on the subject.

I believe reparative therapy is a potentially dangerous intervention, and that it is unethical to attempt to change any individual's core identity. The danger lies in exacerbating existing depression, despair, or anxiety, possibly to suicidal levels, by attempting to change that which can't be changed to begin with.

I am not alone in my view of reparative therapy. Most professional organizations associated with the mental health profession have issued position statements against reparative therapy. Several states have outlawed reparative therapy for minors, and there has been one successful lawsuit that found a reparative therapy group violated consumer protection laws by advertising homosexuality as a disorder. Coupled with the U.S. Supreme Court decision sup-porting marriage equality, it would seem the days of reparative therapy are numbered.

HELPING RELIGIOUSLY-CONSERVATIVE CLIENTS

I had a number of tenets I kept in mind in working with clients whose religious beliefs are very conservative:

(1) The client's religious beliefs may be as much a part of their identity as their gender or sexuality. Though I view religion as a belief system, many embrace religion as fully as they do any innate core identity. It was not up to me to try to talk them out of their religion any more than I would presume to tell them what their gender identity or sexual orientation is.

Some who hold conservative beliefs find their worldview shifts as they embrace their trans identity and they are able to find a new spiritual belief system that celebrates their trans identity. However some retain their conservative belief systems and may go through a great deal of grief if they are not welcome within their religious tradition any longer. They aren't interested in changing religions; they are trying to reconcile themselves to losing their religion and religious community against their will.

Further, if they were born within a particular religion this may also be a person for whom cultural and ethnic identity is melded with religion, making it particularly difficult for them to transition if their religious and cultural beliefs don't support trans identities. It's one thing to explore other religious traditions, but one can't switch cultural or ethnic backgrounds;

(2) While I don't promote or denigrate various forms of religion, I helped my clients begin to distinguish between spirituality and religion. Spirituality is a belief system, private to the individual. Religion is a set of codified beliefs shared by various people, giving a social context to spirituality. However, it is possible for a person to have a deeply-held spiritual belief system without ever setting foot in a church or other place of worship. It is also possible to attend worship services consistently without believing in or prac-ticing the underlying spiritual beliefs. Once a conservative trans client comes

267

to realize they don't have to retain the church to re-main spiritual, it may be easier for them to re-examine their beliefs in such a way that they are no longer conflicted about their identity, though they will still feel conflict and a great deal of grief and loss if their entire family remains within the religion. It is quite likely the client will lose most of those relationships. In many cases, trans clients remain connected to some individual family members. Yet they still grieve as they cannot participate with their family in their religion;

(3) The client suffers from not being able to actualize a core identity, and also suffers because of an ingrained belief that the identity itself is sinful. I presented to my clients for consideration a model of gender and sexuality both as core identities, emerging in their own time as the client matured, rather than as simply a matter of behavior. I helped clients pinpoint times in their lives when they realized they felt different from other children, regardless of how they behaved, so they could begin to differentiate behavior from identity. This helped them begin to distinguish between sin (beha-vior) and core identity;

(4) It is helpful to the client to model a positive interpretation of being trans. My goal was not to change their beliefs, but to introduce another possible interpretation of what it means to be trans. My religious clients had only been exposed to one belief – 'this is a sin' – and seeing another interpretation was powerful.

It can be helpful for conservative trans clients to meet other trans people, though sometimes this is counterproductive and causes the client to feel even more isolated. Many such clients come from a background of extreme conservatism on various issues. Sheryl (48) did not agree with other trans people she'd met on issues such as abortion or gay marriage, but she was also afraid of offending those she sees as her peers. She had the experience of hearing other trans people say, "Of course you left that church, why in the world would you stay?!" As Sheryl put it, "After I heard that, how could I talk about how much I missed my church?" This effectively kept Sheryl isolated from exploring her trans identity with others who shared much of her experience of gender dissonance;

(5) I tried to help clients gradually come to realize that much of what they believe about homosexual and trans identities is false – such people are inherently unhappy, miserable creatures who can never have healthy relationships, hold down jobs, or live fulfilling lives. As appropriate, I facilitated clients meeting each other, as they had often felt isolated in their experience of being trans. Isolation was particularly prevalent among my older conservative MTF clients, many of whom had not attempted to seek out others of like mind, if they even knew they were not alone in their experience.

Over time I helped clients deconstruct their own cognitive dissonance as they realized how much of their beliefs are based in mythology from present-day American culture, and not in strict biblical interpretation at all. Asking them to consider for them-selves, "How would Jesus treat me?" was powerful for such clients. Whether they were Christian or not, they tended to view Jesus as having been non-judgmental;

(6) I helped clients cope with the intense anger that often arose if their former beliefs shifted sufficiently for them to realize how thoroughly and wrongly they had been judged by the conservative or religious people in their lives. With this anger often came feelings of loss and grief, coupled with guilt and shame for having negative feelings about family members and friends of long standing. Conservative religion often results in an intense feeling of fellowship, which the client missed deeply; there is little in the secular world that can match the depth of bond members of a conservative religion may feel with each other;

(7) Those who became involved with a conservative religion as adults may have been seeking a form of spiritual practice that was

highly structured and provided them with answers to the mysteries of life. Many of my clients did not want to undertake much self-examination at earlier times in their lives, attempting instead to bury their true selves. Part of their attempt at hiding from themselves included participating in a religion that did not encourage a great deal of reflection on the nature of life, identity, etc. As their true gender identity surfaced, they also began to question the religion that had provided them with such surety about their place in the grand scheme of things. This type of questioning can bring its own feel-ings of vulnerability, and loneliness, as it may seem to them that no one else in their lives is experiencing such spiritual doubts.

MAKE NO MISTAKE!

One argument I've heard some conservative people make in their denial that LGB and T are innate identities is, "God doesn't make mistakes." I find this argument irritating, as it assumes that being trans is a mistake. I have heard too stories of people blos-soming after transition to believe this form of identity to be any kind of mistake.

Many look to science and medicine for explanations of trans identity. While I feel science may be able to eventually answer questions about brain structures and the mechanism whereby our unique identities are actualized, science cannot provide answers to existential questions of meaning. I wonder what purpose it might serve the human race that a certain percentage of the population is gender dissonant?

Our culture has no role for the shaman. However, combining the job descriptions of minister, doctor and therapist is a fair approxi-mation of the job of a shaman. My experience of living more than one gender role in the same lifetime, with more than one hormone balance, is a gift that served me well as a therapist. It is easy for me to see why being trans was considered one path toward becoming a shaman, in many indigenous cultures. (Williams, 1992; Roscoe, 2000) I find it particularly ironic that so many conservative or religious people consider any form of queer identity a perversion or disease of some sort. In rejecting trans people our culture has turned its back on an entire group of people who I believe were meant to serve in the capacity of shaman.

As any true scientist will agree, considering such existential concepts is the purview of religion or philosophy, not the purview of science. Science can only address questions that can be formulated in the precise language of the quantifiable, the verifiable, that which can be tested via the scientific method. While science can perhaps answer questions about differences in brain structure, it cannot answer (or even address) questions of the meaning of life or identity.

RECONCILING WITHIN RELIGIOUS FAMILIES

In 2011 I had a conversation with Joanna, a ciswoman familiar with fundamentalist Christianity. I asked her, "Is there any way a fundamentalist Christian can reconcile themselves to having a trans family member? Can they come to accept the identity? Is there anything the trans person can do to facilitate this process, short of giving up their identity?"

Joanna replied, "Family is of utmost importance to fundamentalist Christians. But they are more concerned with the soul of each family member than with just about anything else. Since they are probably viewing transition as a form of homosexuality, their deepest fear is that their family member is going to go to hell; their soul is in jeopardy of not being in heaven after death. To a fundamentalist Christian this is the worst outcome possible. But there is always the possibility of forgiveness by God of any sin, and that would include transition."

I then asked, "Would that mean that a trans person who wanted to reach out to a fundamentalist family member should ask them to leave it in God's hands?"

Joanna said, "Not exactly. What would probably be more effective is to ask that family member to keep praying for them. The fundamentalist family member will have a deep belief in the power of prayer to heal and bring God's blessing. If the trans person said they were praying themselves, and asked their family member to pray also, that might be a reconciling interaction."

Joanna went on to say, "This gets tricky, as the fundamentalist family member is probably going to pray for the trans person to be freed from the affliction of being trans while the trans person might be praying to be fulfilled in their identity. What they can agree on is to pray for God's understanding and forgiveness, of themselves and each other."

Joanna also felt that if the trans person is attending some form of worship service regularly this *may* appease the fundamentalists of the family that all is not lost, as God is still in the equation. Joanna felt that Unitarian or MCC churches probably wouldn't count among fundamentalists, but virtually any other form of Christian worship service would be seen as appealing to God for salvation.

Some fundamentalists have come to believe the need to transition is a birth defect and that physical intervention and tran-sition are thus medical issues, along the lines of the diabetic who needs insulin. While some trans people shy away from this interpretation of their identity, others are willing to let religious members of their families hold to this belief, recognizing it may be the only way their transition will be accepted.

Paul told me, "I was raised in a fundamentalist Christian church; my father was the minister of our congregation. I had to make a clean break, moving 1,500 miles to go to college, before I had enough distance to tell them I was going to transition. When I refused to come home or get into reparative therapy, my father contacted a minister in the city I moved to and was organizing some kind of intervention. At that point I dropped out of school. I stayed with this one transwoman friend I'd met; she was so kind to me. I had no money or income. I was terrified to get a job because then I'd have to leave the house. I thought someone would recognize me and tell my father where I was.

"This was really a paranoid reaction, because neither I or anyone in my family had ever been to this city before I started college there. They didn't know anyone there! Sure they'd sent a picture to this minister who was trying to find me, but I'd completely mascu-linized my appearance by then and there's no way he would have recognized me from any of the feminine pictures my folks had.

"It was so weird to go through those few months and then get this email out of the blue from my mom. She said she was willing to learn more. Lucky for me, this one woman in our congregation had had a nephew transition a few years before. Louise was a long-time congregant and really devout church volunteer. She told my mother all about her now-niece and what a blossoming it was to see her niece come out of lifelong depression.

"Louise said it took her awhile but now she really did realize that her niece had always been a girl inside and how unhappy it had made her to not be able to live that way. That really hit home for my mom, cuz I'd been so unhappy. My mom said Louise told her to look on it as a hormone deficiency thing that had been going on for me since I was born. I wasn't so sure that's exactly what it was, but hey, if it helped my mom come around I was all for it." *(Email correspondence, 2014)*

Paul re-established contact with his family, though he was also aware he might never feel comfortable living in the same city with them. It was one thing to reconcile within his family but quite another to know he could run into his father's parishioners whenever he was out and about.

COMPLETELY REJECTING RELIGION

Over the years I have met a few trans people who had spent their pre-transition lives within a conservative religion and turned their backs completely on any form of religion after beginning transition. They were very unhappy, ironically coming close to fulfilling the stereotype of trans people as miserable, unhappy, lonely people who can't form relationship. They were extremely angry and actualized that anger more than any other emotion. Small wonder they found it difficult to form relationship. I had sympathy for them; nothing replaced the fellowship and community they experienced as members of a conservative congregation.

By contrast I have also met conservative trans people who have found peace and comfort in other forms of spirituality, who have been able to shift their worldview sufficiently to realize their former religion is not the only interpretation possible when considering the existential meaning of life questions. These are much happier peo-ple than those who turned their backs on religion altogether; they have been able to retain a strong spiritual base in their lives and actualize their core identities at the same time.

The person whose world view is agnostic or who is raised in a progressive religion probably won't experience a spiritual crisis upon realizing their gender identity doesn't match the gender as-signed them at birth. Those participating in a conservative religion may experience a spiritual emergency that is incomprehensible to those who are not entirely convinced people even have souls, much less that the soul is in mortal danger. Unitarian trans people, for instance, are unlikely to be able to understand the spiritual turmoil of the conservative trans person. The standing joke about Unitarians is that their bedtime prayer is: "Oh God, if there is a God, save my soul, if I have a soul."

The spiritual crisis some people face when considering transition is every bit as deep and fraught with danger as the crisis of the late-stage addict who finally faces their addiction. This is yet another parallel between addiction recovery and transition – the conser-vative person who simply turns their back on religion and transi-tions anyway is similar to the 'dry drunk,' who retains the same world view and problematic behavior and relationship patterns, but without the drug. The happier person is the addict who undergoes the transformation of self inherent in fully embracing recovery.

By the same token, among religiously-conservative trans people the happier people are those who can reinvent their own spirituality in a manner that affords them a healthy, positive self-perception while at the same time allowing them to retain (or develop) a spiritual practice that is meaningful to them. The collision of worlds has shaken them up, but they have faced the ensuing spiritual crisis and emerged all the stronger.

Such folks didn't see their former belief systems as a world view, but as immutable reality on par with 'the sun rises in the east.' What has happened to them is that another immutable reality, their gender identity, has collided with that world view, shattering their reality quite effectively and permanently. The happier people are those who build a new reality from the shattered remains rather than living amidst the rubble, too angry and bitter to attempt reconstruction.

Rise up to your higher power

Free up from fear, it will devour you

Watch out for the ego of the hour

The ones who say they know it

Are the ones who will impose it on you

I ain't afraid of your Yahweh

I ain't afraid of your Allah

I ain't afraid of your Jesus

I'm afraid of what you do in the name of your God.

—Holly Near, from the song *I Ain't Afraid,* ©2000 Hereford Music (ASCAP)
Quoted by permission

• Part Three •

Relational Issues

Even after all this time,

the sun never says to the earth,

"You owe me."

Look what happens with a love like that –

it lights up the world.

– Hafiz, 15th century Persian poet

I remember my years by the people that enter and go
And I know they were good years by amounts of emotion I flow
Now I lost some and won some and gave some away to my friends
But you find that it's still you you got to be true to
to get you to some pleasant end.

Now I altered some moments—
how some moments sure altered me.
But in trying to be chained down, I constantly found myself free.
On the face of the sky shine the faces of loves long ago.
How they caught me and taught me and let me go gently,
I'm thinking they might never know.

The winds all whisper, the sky is a fly on my nose
I'm in between corners and thinking how so many go
And there's streetlight and moonlight
and leaves all aglow in the rain
and I'm thinking on bus rides and high tides and love ties
and if I'll be back here again.

—Ferron, from the song *Fly on My Nose*
©Nemesis Publishing. Recorded on *Ferron* (1976-77)
Quoted by permission

• Chapter 15 •

FOR PARTNERS ONLY

FOR PARTNERS ONLY? WELL, NO, NOT REALLY. However, partners' issues are given such short shrift that it seems appropriate to give them center stage and exclusive attention for a time. The focus of this chapter is on the experience of the partners (either cisgender or trans) of people who consider transition of some kind.

If this has not been your experience, consider for a moment how you would feel if your male-assigned partner came to you one evening and said, "I just can't stand living as a man any longer. I need to transition to female." Or if your partner is female-assigned, try to imagine hearing this statement: "I've always felt like a man inside and if I had the money I'd have an operation tomorrow."

Another difficult situation is one in which a partner hears, "I have always felt uncomfortable with my gender and need to explore it further. I don't know if this means I will transition or not." This ambiguous statement, spoken in all honesty, can propel the partner into a state of flux that is extremely uncomfortable for most people raised in a western culture. As Helen Boyd put it in *She's Not the Man I Married,* "It's like living with the sound of the other shoe not dropping." (Boyd, 2007)

We 'westerners' are not comfortable with ambiguous identities. We are most at ease with people to whom we can assign gender visually, which we are raised to do on an autopilot basis. We do not appreciate it when people change pigeonholes, particularly when it comes to personal identities such as sexual orientation and gender identity. And most especially, we do not appreciate it when some-one doesn't know which pigeonhole they belong in, or states they don't belong in the male or female category.

Some people reading this probably feel they know their partners so well, they can't even imagine their partner saying such a thing. If this is your situation consider this: many people with transitioning partners would have said exactly the same thing you're thinking – "I couldn't imagine my partner saying this." Until it happened.

WHY IS TRANSITION UNIMAGINABLE?

By the age of 3 or 4 if you ask a child, "Are you a boy or a girl?" the child knows the answer.[29] If they are being raised in an atmosphere supportive of their individuality, they will answer you honestly even if the answer is not what you expected based on how you've pigeonholed the child's gender. When a gender-dissonant child begins interacting with large numbers of peers (nursery school, kindergarten, and on through the school years), the child quickly learns that only certain roles are okay and that they have no control over which gender pigeonhole is assigned them. This is a child who will grow up with a conscious awareness of the pi-geonholes because they are put in what feels to them the wrong one.

Such children may also learn quickly that it is unsafe to express their true gender and may repress their feelings to the extent that they feel different but can't name why any longer. A gender-dissonant child of 4 may have more conscious awareness of their gender identity than that same child during adolescence. (Brill, 2007; Krieger, 2011)

A cisgender child is not gender-dissonant and does not feel uncomfortable with the pigeonhole assigned them. They are unaware of the pigeonhole. Certainly they can answer the question, "Are you a boy or a girl?" but they see the categories 'boy' and 'girl' as fixed

---

[29] One person who read the first edition of this book wrote to me and said, "I was so surprised when I read that children know this about themselves, because that wasn't my experience. I never really felt like a girl or a boy; I still don't. So I asked some cisgender friends, kind of randomly, and discovered that yes, they had always had an internal sense of being male or female. In fact they were surprised at the question! It was the social role thing that always confused me. For me that's not because of any trans thing, but because my IQ is 180 and I never fit in with either boys or girls as a result."

reality, not as pigeonholes. The person who feels like a square peg in a round hole has an awareness of the hole because it chafes. The round peg in the round hole can't feel the hole at all because there is no friction to irritate the mind into conscious awareness that it has been placed in a category.

Thus the adult trans person can imagine changing gender roles and bodily sex because they grow up with the perception of having been that square peg in the round hole. To the cisgender partner, unaware of the pigeonhole, the concept of changing genders is unimaginable in a very literal sense. The partner cannot imagine changing what they have grown up seeing as a fixed part of reality.

Cisgender people are generally content with the hormone balance that came naturally to them with puberty; it is impossible for cisgender people to understand what the imperative feels like to switch that hormone balance. Those who have an inkling what it might be like to experience a hormone imbalance are cisgender women who have been pregnant or menopausal; unwanted hor-monal fluctuations can give them empathy for what it might feel like to experience the wrong hormone balance. (Ryan, 2011)

Cisgender partners who are gay, lesbian, queer or bisexual may have memories of feeling 'different' also, growing up G, L, Q, or B but not trans. Such partners are often able to understand from personal experience the feelings of 'difference' but are unable to understand the need to transition because their feelings of 'difference' were not based in gender identity but in sexual orientation. Unfortunately this semi-intersection of experience can lead some LGBQ partners to resist the idea of transition all the more, suspecting the feelings of gender dissonance are not real or indicate difficulty adjusting to not being heterosexual.

But why is the partner often so uncomfortable with the idea of actualizing a new gender identity, if this is truly what is needed for happiness and self-fulfillment? It's not as if they are being asked to transition their gender. So why the extreme discomfort many partners feel? After all, this is the role partners play for each other, to support each other in growing through life.

One answer dovetails with why it is so unimaginable to the partner in the first place: the concept of changing gender roles, chang-ing sexes, creates a cognitive dissonance in the partner's psyche. "Wait a minute! You can't change your sex anymore than you can make the sun rise in the west instead of the east." Of course the partner is uncomfortable, if they have viewed gender as a fixed reality, determined at birth and incontrovertible.

Viewing gender in this light, the only way to conceptualize trans people is that they have a mental disorder, not that their experience of gender is valid. When faced with a partner announcing, "I may need to transition," the cisgender partner is now in the position of making a paradigm shift away from 'mental disorder' and toward 'identity emergence.' Only recently has it become more common in U.S. culture to view trans identity in this light; if the partner hasn't already made this shift in conceptualization, the upheaval to their worldview is unsettling to say the least.

SHIFTING SEXUAL ORIENTATION AND CHEMISTRY

One must also consider that relationships don't exist in a va-cuum. These people have neighbors, live in a community, with friends, possibly in a city, with family. Those who live in rural areas or small towns may have stronger bonds with those around them than those who live in more urban environments.

If a person transitions physically, the relationship also transi-tions. From being perceived as heterosexual, theirs will be per-ceived as a same-sex relationship. Whether lesbian, gay or queer prior to transition, the relationship will change to being seen as het-erosexual. Bisexual partners have it somewhat easier, or at least no more difficult than usual. They live a life of constant invisibility anyway, being seen as straight if they are involved with someone of the 'opposite' sex and being seen as gay/lesbian if they are in a 'same-

281

sex' relationship. A transitioning partner isn't going to change this invisibility, just the social perception of the relationship.

The ramifications of changing sexual orientation are profound for the partner. One obvious consideration is homophobia. How-ever, it's too easy to say of a heterosexual woman, "She's against her husband transitioning because she's afraid people will see her as a lesbian." If a heterosexual woman has qualms about being iden-tified as a lesbian, one must give credence to her experience of her sexuality. If she truly feels heterosexual and not lesbian or bisexual, why should anyone expect her to be joyful about her husband's transition to female? Given our mainstream cultural attitudes about gay, lesbian and bisexual people, homophobia is always a factor, but it would be a mistake to brush aside a heterosexual partner's resistance as based exclusively in homophobia. (Lev, 2004; Zamboni, 2006)

One issue that receives little attention is that of physical attrac-tion, what we call the 'chemistry' between two people, based in scent and pheromones. I worked with several couples who intended to stay together through transition. However, they didn't count on physical attraction waning. One partner lamented, "I used to love sex and get really turned on when Andrew would come home from a workout sweaty. Now I only get really turned on when I'm work-ing out without Ann there, because most of my workout partners are men and the male smell really does it for me. I'm finding that Ann's smell just doesn't do it for me, while Andrew's did." It would be worthwhile research to study how much pheromones and changes in scent affect whether the sexual aspect of a relationship survives physical transition.

Carla and Norma intended to remain together through transition. Norma had always been fluid in her view of her identity, and was happy when Carla emerged from Charles a happier, more well-rounded person. But Norma also found her physical attraction wan-ing, to her great distress. Further, Carla found she had unanticipated attractions to men that she needed to explore in figuring out her own sexual identity.

Carla and Norma are still together today, some ten years into transition, because they have redefined what 'family' means. They are still raising their two children together, now teenagers. They live together in the same house they've owned for twenty years. They remodeled the house, creating two master bedroom suites. They no longer sleep together and have opened up their relationship to other partners. The one hard and fast rule of their expanded relationship – any partner either gets involved with can't have an agenda of breaking up Carla and Norma's relationship. Carla and Norma are nonsexual primary partners in a poly relationship.

PERMUTATIONS OF RELATIONSHIP

One factor that greatly influences both process and outcome of transitioning within relationship is the partner's gender. Partner processes are influenced by the same kinds of factors that lead to such different resocialization and transition processes for FTMs and MTFs – generational differences, original childhood socialization, cultural influences, lifelong gender role expectations, and hormone balances. Let's break down the possible permutations of relation-ship for a moment, considering them one at a time.

"Male"-male relationships

First is the possibility of a male-assigned person saying to a cismale partner, "I've always felt more female than male inside and I think transition might be the direction I need to go." Some of my MTF clients had experimented with gay male sexuality, in their quest for self-knowledge. For most, this was a matter of sexual experimentation and not of committed relationship.

I worked with just one person transitioning out of a gay male role in the context of relationship. Sally tried to remain with her gay male partner Kevin, and he was willing to try. After Sally had been taking hormones for about six months Kevin realized he just did not feel sexually attracted any longer.

Sally's growing breasts were part of the issue, as was her electrolysis. Kevin also had done his own soul-searching and realized he wanted a partner who was happy to have a penis, which was not the case for Sally. It's also possible the hormones had shifted the pheromones sufficiently that Kevin wasn't attracted chemically, though neither mentioned that factor. The two shifted their relationship to one of close friends and no longer live together.

Somewhat more frequently, I heard stories such as Gina's. She had always known her primary attractions were to men; she had been trying to determine if it would be enough for her to live as a gay man. She was 28 when she realized transition was her path. She had been living as a gay man for about ten years at the time, but only once had she been in a committed relationship. It was that ex-perience that showed her once and for all that she could not live as a gay man. Her feeling was, "If I'm this much in love with someone who loves me and it's still not enough, nothing ever will be as long as I remain male." She realized she wanted to be with men, as a woman.

Gina told me, "I was in love with Rick but it just crushed me how stereotypical and narrow his view of women was! He'd known he was gay since he was about 14 and had never even dated a girl, much less slept with a woman. He wanted a man, not any kind of woman. I never even felt like I could talk to him about it. I felt he would be completely closed off to the idea. I tried to stay with him, as a man. I heard so many stories about transgals not having rela-tionships after transition. But I finally decided it would be better to be content with myself and alone than lonely in a relationship. It wasn't until after my transition, when I got involved with Victor, that I felt validated in my decision to give up Rick and move on with my transition." *(E-mail correspondence, 2004)*

What struck me most about Gina's story was the lack of process she experienced with her former partner Rick. Gina did not know how to broach the subject with Rick, who seemed to have no idea anything was wrong in the relationship. According to Gina, Rick was dumbfounded when she told him (still as Gene) she was ending their two-year relationship. She did not feel able to tell him the true reason, fearful of ridicule and certain of rejection. Rather, she used some of their incompatibilities as an excuse, fully aware as she did so that Rick's being a morning person was in no way responsible for her desire to end the relationship. Gina did not begin transition until about six months after ending her relationship with Rick and it was at that point that I met her. I never met Rick at all.

In other permutations of relationship, at least one of the partners is born female and is socialized to value and understand emotional processing (though some are much better at it than others!). While those socialized male can learn to process, often it does not come as easily as it does to those who are taught from the cradle that their role is to sustain and understand relationship.

Though it is an unfortunate way to put it, this is the kernel of truth in the phrase that 'women civilize men.' Estrogen seems to facilitate access to emotionality, which is the key to relational pro-cess. Testosterone tends to interfere with men's attempts to access emotionality, possibly by clouding the issue with a constant aware-ness of sex. While sex may not always be on the front burner for males, it is rarely on the back burner! Because there is no woman in the equation, it may take longer for some gay men to realize that relationship and sex, intimacy and sex, are not synonymous.

Some of the unhappiest clients I've seen were gay cismen who had come to realize they had been seeking intimacy and not just sex. These clients didn't know how to find what they were looking for but had finally realized it transcended sex. Because their sociali-zation had not prepared them to recognize or process their emotions, they didn't have words to describe what they were feeling and came into my office feeling 'connection challenged.' Unfortunately they only knew to look for connection in bath houses and adult book-stores. One cisgender gay client described an epiphany: "I realized as I drove home from the bath house that I felt worse than when I'd left home.

I'd had sex, but it left me feeling emptier than I'd felt before. That's when I realized I hadn't really been looking for sex at all. I cried as I drove home." *(Client session, 2001)*

Coupled with the lack of social permission to explore and ex-press their full range of emotionality, those raised male are hindered when it comes to processing. Gay men are somewhat freed from the social hindrance, often not buying into what society considers so-cially-acceptable male behavior. Nevertheless testosterone still causes a heightened sense of sexuality that can impede emotional processing.

The extreme difference between male and female socialization when it comes to processing (or even feeling) emotion has a drastic impact on how a couple will handle a possible transition. Gina left Rick rather than even attempt to process her gender identity with him. I was a long-time member of a peer consultation group. All of the group members worked with trans clients and not once did anyone else in our group bring to the table the scenario of a gay male couple in transition; mine was the first the group had dis-cussed. It does not seem to be a common scenario.

Only six of the MTF clients I worked with had ever identified as gay men and lived for any length of time within the gay male com-munity. Two such clients ended up not pursuing physical transition, as they both felt a strong attachment to the form of sexual expres-sion afforded them as gay men, though both recognized the strong female component of their personalities that needed expression.

As might be expected these clients embraced a drag queen iden-tity. However they also recognized the need to keep an open mind about the future. Both these clients felt more comfortable dressed female than they did putting on a male role. They saw 'drag queen' as a primarily theatrical persona, and this did not match their expe-rience of identity.

"Male"-female relationships

Many of my MTF clients tried over the years to find various ways of curing themselves of feeling female or of hiding their fe-male identities effectively. Because of the narrowly-defined para-meters of 'male' in U.S. culture, the gay male community is not a place where one could reasonably expect to hide. The only form of relationship open to those MTFs who have tried to cure themselves is the male-female partnership.

I heard a number of wives say with irony, "I thought I married a sensitive man, not a woman." Some thought their husbands had been having an affair; they had sensed a certain distance during sex. However this was because their spouse was fantasizing about *being* a woman, not being *with* another woman.

One result of this attempt at normalcy is that the women MTFs marry are usually quite traditional in their approach to gender and social roles. Yvonne (47) came into session some three months after beginning hormones, saying her wife had said jokingly, "You're not going to become a feminist, are you?" Yvonne was taken aback, as the conversation had been about a work situation in which she'd begun noticing how differently from men the women in her work-place were treated. Though she'd heard female co-workers talk about inequity and sexism over the years, Yvonne had never taken it seriously before. Now she was hearing such talk from a different perspective and realized that she and her wife might end up with opposing views on issues they used to agree on.

Also in an attempt to live up to the male gender role, many of my MTF clients had chosen male-dominated professions. I some-times felt I saw the Village People in my office: construction workers, firefighters, police officers, and a high percentage who were military veterans. Few of my MTF clients had chosen female-dominated professions, in part because those professions skirt too closely (pardon the pun!) toward the female and thus are not effect-ive places to hide a female identity.

The most common partnership I saw in my older MTF client base was the male-female marriage, usually of long duration and with children. Such clients often married young and had children shortly thereafter. Approximately half the wives in this situation were able to wrap their minds around the transition sufficiently that they did not leave the relationship immediately or deliver an ultima-tum ("move forward with this and it's all over."). They decided to attempt to make it work, sometimes successfully.

The relationship may or may not be a sexual one post-transition. If the wife does not identify as a lesbian or as bisexual, she may change her conceptualization of their marriage to one of long-time companions, best friends, or soul mates, with no sexual component. For those with 20, 30, 40 year marriages, this may be an ideal solution for both partners. The longevity of any marriage is not based on sex but on intimacy, shared memories, and the value placed on sharing one's entire life with the same person.

Despite a recognition of soul mate status, some wives are unable to live with the ambiguity and uncertainty of uncharted territory or feel unable to move beyond deep feelings of anger and betrayal. Several completely rejected the transition and immediately filed for divorce, refusing to discuss the issues.

Others were sufficiently uncomfortable with the idea of transition that their trans spouses chose one of several paths: (a) not transitioning at all (or starting to transition physically and then backing off for the sake of the relationship); (b) transitioning in a very limited way so their wives would not have to see their female gender expression; or (c) taking hormones for the internal, psycho-logical comfort they received but continuing to express a male gen-der identity in all situations.

This last option (c) is a difficult one for some MTFs as the physical changes induced by the hormones may be unacceptable to their wives. Some found creative solutions. Carla takes hormones about six months out of the year, from October through March. The clothing she wears at that time of year hides her breast growth. The other six months of the year, she does not take hormones. Her breast growth stops and the tissue sags down onto her chest, easily hidden beneath a T-shirt. She wears a nightshirt to bed, such that her wife doesn't see her breast growth.

288

A few of my MTF clients were walking a tightrope, expressing a female gender in a fairly public way but not necessarily taking hormones and not expressing a female gender while at home. Deborah transitioned at work while continuing to become Dan upon returning home every evening. Though her wife Nancy supported her as much as she could, she could not reach a point of comfort with the idea of being married to Deborah. Deborah is known by her new name at work but can't change any of her legal documentation from Daniel to Deborah; she does not want mail coming to their home in Deborah's name. Her paychecks are still made out to Daniel though her work nametag says Deborah.

Transwomen in these types of situations often feel they lead double lives, though their trans identities are no longer secret from their wives. While such a lifestyle takes its toll over time, it also points to the value these individuals place on their relationships. MTFs in this position are torn: they love their wives, place a high value on the longevity of the relationship, would be devastated to lose their soul mate – and are fully aware that if they were single they would transition without a second thought. They have been faced with the necessity of choosing priorities and have chosen to place a higher value on their relationship than on transition.

Some of my clients started on the path of physical transition and backed off when faced with the possibility of their relationship ending. Many told me they were judged harshly for their choices by other transwomen, who consider them secondary transsexuals, or just plain cowardly. Gender identity and sexual orientation are both deep, strong drives that need expression within any individual. It's a tough situation when these identities create mutually exclusive choices between transition and lifelong relationship. Both identities are an integral part of the person, and it's not fair for anyone to judge which identity should be of more importance or more valu-able to the individual.

Jan said, "I never allowed myself to realize how much I wanted to be Jan fulltime until after Alison died. I know she would want me to go for it, she told me so before her death. She knew I'd do this if I was single."

Jan had lived a double life, dressing as Jan while conducting her home-based business and putting on James again before her wife got home from work. She had managed to wrap her mind around living as a bi-gendered person while her wife was alive. About two months after her wife died, Jan asked me for a hormone referral let-ter. She would never have taken this step prior to Alison's death; their 35-year marriage was more important to her. Jan and I had done some grief work during that two-month period after her wife's death. Jan felt clean in her process, able to move forward, because she and Alison had processed through all the various feelings they had about their life together, Jan's female identity, and Alison's impending death from cancer.

"Female"-male relationships

I worked with a few FTMs who were transitioning out of female/male relationships, and some who had been married to men earlier in their lives and were now single. Alan (formerly Diana) had known his cisgender husband Paul since both were teenagers. They were married over 20 years, though both were only in their early forties when I met Alan. As Alan put it, "I lived a fairy tale marriage. I married my high school sweetheart, never looked at ano-ther man, and managed to bury my head in the sand about my gen-der issues because I had the white picket fence, happily-ever-after thing going."

Alan had never felt any sexual interest in women until he met Joan, who has identified as a lesbian most of her adult life after a brief marriage to a man. Their attraction was immediate and far stronger than any sexual connection Alan had felt with Paul.

Denial is a funny animal; though Alan had been able to be mar-ried to Paul, fairly comfortably, once Joan came into Alan's life he could not deny the attraction he felt toward her. Nor could he deny that this attraction was not lesbian, but that of a man for a woman. His identity emergence as an FTM was fairly immediate after meeting Joan. Unusual for a lesbian in her late forties, Joan had no qualms about being involved with an FTM and has never perceived Alan as female, though the person Joan initially met was Diana.

Paul did not react well, retreating from Alan and refusing to talk about his feelings. Alan wanted to remain friends with Paul, but also recognized that Paul's behavior made this impossible until such time as Paul was able to move on and form new relationships.

However, as I pointed out to Alan, just as Paul was Diana's high school sweetheart, she was also Paul's. He was going through a loss and grief process, heightened by the fact that Alan had two positive goals to move toward (transition and a new relationship) while Paul saw nothing on his side but loss. Though Paul's feelings were understandable, they were also his to deal with in his own time.

Though somewhat more common than the gay male relationship in transition, I did not work with many FTMs who were still involved with cismen at the time they sought me out. Interestingly, those of my clients who were in this situation were not expressing gender in a particularly male way, though they were certain of their male identities. They were (or had been) quite attached to their husbands, and would have preferred to remain in relationship. This is also true of Alan, who would have preferred a polyamorous situation, involved with both Paul and Joan. Paul refused to consider this option, and he and Alan are now divorced.

"Female"-female relationships

In stark contrast to Paul's rather stereotypically-male reaction to his situation with Alan, Rachel and Sara (now Steven) had a very different experience. Sara and Rachel had come out as lesbians in college. Some fifteen years later Sara (now 35) had grown increaseingly uncomfortable living a female identity and realized finally, "I can't live the rest of my life as a woman."

Rachel was torn, ultimately realizing that no, she did not want to be involved with a man. Every step of the way the two of them discussed their internal processes, sometimes in my office and sometimes at home. They tried to maintain a respectful attitude toward each other's core values and identity, though this was sometimes difficult as it became apparent their life goals were mutually exclusive. Nevertheless the heartfelt, honest process they undertook was such that they were able to shift into a close friendship once they had grieved the loss of their partner relationship.

If a lesbian partner has done her soul searching and embraced the identity 'lesbian,' how easy is it going to be for her to be seen as heterosexual? How easy is it going to be for her to see her partner as a man? Does this mean she has to see herself as a straight woman? Can she retain a queer identity over time if she is perceived to be in a straight relationship? She will have legitimate fears of losing friends, of losing the strong ties that are inherent in the lesbian community. These were some of the issues Rachel grappled with in her process of deciding for herself, "How do I want to live my life?" It is not only the trans person who needs to ask this question on a deep level, but also their partner.

Consider the situation of one couple, Kate and Tom. They were in their mid-thirties and had been in a committed relationship for eight years when Tom (then Tanya) first considered transition. They owned a house together and had adopted a child five years into their relationship.

Tom had never felt comfortable living female, which he had shared with Kate as they were getting to know each other. He had finally decided he was too unhappy and depressed to continue living 'lesbian,' that the identity was not a good enough fit. The deciding factor for him was a statement made to him by an older transwoman with whom he has an e-mail correspondence: "I just couldn't face the prospect of living the rest of my life as a man and dying without ever having fully lived my female identity." This statement hit Tom forcefully.

Kate had identified as a lesbian since she was 19. Her parents were unhappy with her lesbian identity at first, primarily because they were not sure Kate would be able to find happiness living as a lesbian.

By the time Tom began considering transition, Kate's parents had fully accepted their daughter's identity. They hosted Kate's and Tanya's commitment ceremony. They loved their granddaughter, and felt Kate and Tanya were ideal parents. Kate had many friends, most of them lesbians, and was a member of several queer organizations, one of which is completely lesbian-oriented.

Post-transition, both knew they would be seen as heterosexual, particularly by those who never knew them as lesbians. Kate felt she would be able to remain in the relationship after Tom's emer-gence. However this was uncharted territory for her. Beyond a few dates in early high school, she had never been involved with a man to any degree, on a romantic level.

Kate's attitude was: "I always knew the core essence of Tanya was more male than female, and I like that energy. I've known a number of FTMs and like them as people and think the journey they've undertaken is amazing. And yeah, the lesbian community connection is also important to me. I have to take it as it comes, see how it plays out. What makes me sad is, I know I'll lose something. I'm just not sure whether it will be the lesbian community, or this relationship." *(Client session, 2006)*

Tom began taking hormones in early 2007. He and Kate are still together as of 2018. Kate did indeed lose her place in the lesbian community. Beyond not feeling welcome, she also finds that she is no longer comfortable in all-lesbian spaces. Early in their transition she had a number of tense conversations with some of her lesbian friends, answering questions such as, "Isn't Tanya doing this in part to gain male privilege?" Kate responded, "You grew up with pa-rents who expected you to be with men as an adult. But then you realized you were a lesbian. You've done what you had to do in order to live your life being true to yourself and it didn't have any-thing to do with other people. That's what Tom is doing, it's just that his shift had to do with gender rather than sexuality." She and Tom have found new friends (lesbian or not) they've met since transition to be more accepting, as they never knew Tanya.

Kate still identifies as a lesbian, recognizing that should her relationship with Tom end for some reason the most likely outcome is that her future relationships would be with women. She has also found that her values have changed; she no longer has any time for individuals or organizations that are not trans-inclusive. Though she's willing to do the necessary education, she won't put energy into relationships (either individual or organizational) if there is no willingness to learn and grow. This shift has carried over into her own friendships, and she believes will also carry over into any new relationship she might find herself considering should she and Tom no longer be together.

As Kate put it, "My worldview is very different now. If Caitlyn Jenner had announced fifteen years ago that she was transitioning, I would have been astonished and disbelieving and not very supportive. Now, I think it's great! I'm all about people becoming fulfilled in who they are meant to be; our world would be so much better a place if everyone had the opportunity." *(E-mail correspon-dence, 2015)*

Trans relationships

I worked with a number of clients who were transitioning while involved with other trans people. And a number of my trans clients had been involved with ostensibly-cisgender people when I started working with them, only to announce at some point that their partner was transitioning also. One such client said, "I didn't realize that subconsciously I'd had an attitude like I owned the corner on the gender market, until Angie told me she was going to transition to Andy."

In general it's been my experience that my trans clients, having dealt with their own transitions already, were less frightened and insecure about a partner transition. That said, they also remembered their own experiences of shifting sexuality and the hormonal changes of early transition and didn't really look forward to experiencing these turbulent times from the partner position! Henry, 32 at the time his partner Wanda disclosed a desire to live as William instead, said laughingly, "It just seemed like kharmic payback! Here I'd felt so lucky to go through transition single, and now this!" *(Client session, 2009)* Henry got involved with Wanda six years into his own physical transition.

His experience with transition enabled Henry (and my other trans clients in similar circumstance) to weather their partner's pro-cess with their relationships intact, so far, though some experienced another round of questioning their own sexuality. The questions were familiar, however, and thus didn't cause significant distress.

POST-TRANSITION INVOLVEMENT

Quite a few of my clients became involved with new partners at later stages of their transition. One might think the partners in such relationships have no issues around the transition, since they've come on the scene after the trans person is well underway with their process. But these partners have their own unique issues.

Hannah (35) was in a quandary when she got involved with Gary, who had been taking hormones for nine years when they met. He'd had chest surgery some six years prior to their getting in-volved. Hannah had never known Gary as Rochelle.

It was a stretch for her to date Gary, as she had to struggle with the likelihood that she would lose her 'lesbian credential' if she got involved with him. Considering involvement with Gary also caused her to question her own sexuality yet again. Hannah had come out as a lesbian in her early twenties and had had an uneasily superficial relationship with her biological family ever since. In a 2010 session, Hannah said of her relationship with Gary, "It took me a good six months to admit that Gary is absolutely perfect for me. I want to spend my life with him. But he's at a point in his transition now where he really doesn't want folks to know, unless they're close friends, and my family doesn't fall in that category for either of us."

This put Hannah in the position of having to hear from her family, "Oh we're SO glad, we knew all you needed was to meet the right man!" Her mother has been puzzled by Hannah's reluc-tance to engage in family events as a straight couple.

Gary said, "It's so refreshing now to be able to just be myself, without having to constantly explain and justify my transition, be everyone's education about trans this and that. Especially with Hannah's family, because it's easy to see how unsupportive they'd be. I think eventually I'll have to have that conversation, maybe with her dad cuz he seems a little mellower, just to get her mother off her back. I can see it's driving her crazy that her mother thinks she's straight now! I sure don't see her that way, because she's not. And really, neither am I. I identify as a queer transman. I'm really comfortable being seen as a man, though, and don't want that to change." *(Client session, 2010)*

Allison (46) got involved with Anne (53), assuming at the inception of their relationship that it would be like any other lesbian relationship; Anne had been taking hormones for over twelve years at the time they met and was seven years post-vaginoplasty.

Two years into their relationship, Allison now laughs at her previous belief that Anne was no different from any other lesbian. Her take on it is, "The very qualities of character that made it possible for Anne to survive in order to transition at 40 are still with her – stubbornness, self-centeredness, a kind of 'my way or the highway' attitude that she had to develop earlier in her life. When she drives me particularly crazy that way, I just think to myself, 'If she wasn't like that, she wouldn't be yours today because she had to have those qualities in order to transition.' That helps me a lot, to think of it that way. My advice to someone getting involved with a post-transition person is to expect a certain degree of stubbornness and inflexibility, especially around identity issues. They had to develop that early in life, to survive." *(E-mail correspondence, 2010)*

HORMONAL SHIFTS

The 'teenage boy' phase of early transition can be traumatic for partners of FTMs to endure. Mary (32) tearfully, angrily, talked for twenty minutes non-stop about how badly she felt her husband Steve was acting − spending a lot of time with a mutual cisfemale friend (also married), not calling when he said he would, making and breaking plans on a whim based solely on his own feelings in the moment, and not wanting to discuss any of this, blaming Mary for being petty, emotional, and a nag.

This behavior was in stark contrast to how he'd acted toward her at earlier times in their relationship. They'd been together for some years prior to Steve's transition and married legally when he reached a point of being seen male at all times. Mary told me what drew her to Steve in the first place was his maturity, unusual compasssion and empathy.

At a pause in her account, I asked, "If a friend were telling you this story and you didn't know better, how old would you say her husband was?" Mary thought a moment and said, "Early twenties." Later in the session she amended her impression to mid-teens, saying, "It didn't seem realistic to say mid-teens, because at that age people aren't married at all."

As I explained to her, Steve's developmental age had not caught up with his chronological age. He might be 35 according to the calendar, but from a transition standpoint he *was* in his mid-teens; he had been taking testosterone for about six months. I normalized the situation for her, while at the same time supporting her expe-rience of the changes she'd observed in Steve's behavior.

Nine years later, Steve and Mary have weathered the trials of early testosterone. Though he does not process through his feelings as much as he used to, Steve is once again a thoughtful, compas-sionate person. Mary wrote to me, "I think of him as the twin bro-ther of the woman I fell in love with − all the same memories and very similar, but not precisely the same." *(E-mail correspondence, 2015)*

One 'female'-male couple had a different experience. Ed, a cis-man in his early thirties, easily recognized the male adolescent energy Ross displayed when he began transition, though he was still taken aback by what looked like a sudden fifteen-year regression in maturity. Sexual orientation wasn't an issue for Ed and Ross, as both identified as queer prior to their marriage. Paradoxically they both felt more comfortable as a male/male couple; their queer identity was now visible in a way it hadn't been when they were perceived as heterosexual.

A helpful attitude is humor, and not taking oneself too seriously. Roger (46) came into session laughing at himself. He had been taking hormones for about a month at the time. His cisgender female partner had taken him by the shoulders the preceding evening, saying with deadpan mock seriousness, "Honey, 15-year-old boys aren't attractive. Men are."

While early transition parallels adolescence as a time of self-exploration, pre-existing relationships can be at risk as a result. If the trans person can recognize and own what is going on, this can go a long way toward reconciling the partner to apparent major shifts in personality and behavior.

SEXUALITY AND TRANSITION

In addition to the social aspect of transitioning a relationship, there is the matter of sexuality. If a cisfemale partner values her trans partner's penis as a core part of their sexual life together, she is going to be less than thrilled by the idea that said penis is going to someday become a vagina. Often trans people don't have enough money for such surgeries unless insurance is footing the bill, so quite possibly that penis is going to remain intact for a long time. The transwoman is not going to view her penis with the same contentment as a cismale and may not want to use it for her partner's sexual pleasure. The enjoyment of sexual intimacy is often marred for MTFs if their penis is involved, a constant reminder of the dysphoria they live with.

Most of my trans clients, whether FTM or MTF, developed an uneasy truce with their bodies over the years. While many enjoyed and valued the ability to have an orgasm, they also recognized how uncomfortable they were with the actual apparatus and wished bodies could better match their gender identity. This often translated to self-consciousness and sometimes embarrassment when attempt-ing to be sexual prior to gender-confirming surgery.

Lana (28) viewed her penis as an overgrown clitoris prior to surgery, and her cisfemale partner (who identified as bisexual) did the same. After surgery Lana remarked that she felt she had completed transition when she felt fine strapping on a dildo for her partner's pleasure.

Six months after starting hormones, Trina became involved with a cisfemale lesbian some ten years her junior. At first her partner Paula said to her friends, "I don't care what equipment she has, I think she's hot!" Over time, Paula's attitude shifted to the point where she was unhappy with the idea that Trina would love to have surgery. Paula viewed Trina's penis as a 'built-in dildo,' and felt she had the best of both worlds: a lesbian partner with a working penis. Trina's situation turned all permutations on their head – to have a lesbian girlfriend who didn't want her to have surgery! Fortunately, after experimenting with a realistic sex toy, Paula has had a change of heart and is no longer upset about Trina's dream of eventual vaginoplasty.

A heterosexual cisfemale partner will probably have to do some mental gymnastics and the couple may have to use a great deal of creativity to reinvent their sexual life in a manner that is satisfying to both partners. If the partner desires children, this is another conversation the couple will need to have prior to transition. There may be solutions – frozen sperm, surrogate mothers – but no solution can be found without open discussion.

There are many ways to define 'relationship' and 'family' and our mainstream cultural definitions are often too limiting to accommodate transition. I encouraged clients to think outside the box, to have frank discussions with their partners about their goals, desires, and attitudes. While this can be difficult at first, many couples ultimately enjoy deeper intimacy than at any other time in their relationship; transition has propelled them into deeper modes of communication than either had ever experienced. Often the cisgender partner has concluded, much to their surprise, that the opportunity to re-examine cultural gender and sex roles has been as much a gift to them as to their trans partner. (Sanger, 2010)

Some partners have found couples counseling particularly helpful in expressing emotions they find shameful in themselves and thus difficult to admit. Sherry was in tears as she said to her 'husband,' who came to session as Kathy, "I hate it that I feel jea-lous of you! You're so happy to be dressing female, and you look really good. You look younger than I do, and I'd kill to have slim hips like you do! And at the same time I really resent that you take over Karl. I have this war going on in me because I see how much happier you are as Kathy, and I want that for you. Believe me, if you were anyone other than my husband, I'd be all on board with this transition. I'd love it that you look so good. I think. I hope!" By the end of the session, both were crying, each wanting to do what they could to help the other cope, while simultaneously recognizing that many of their needs seemed mutually exclusive.

Fortunately Sherry had her own therapist, with whom she was able to process through her feelings of inadequacy and low self-esteem, so common among women. As Sherry centered into a heal-thier, more realistic view of herself, her self-esteem improved and she was able to interact with Kathy without jealousy interfering.

Sherry and Kathy have remained married, though they are not sexual at this point (as of 2018). Kathy is resigned to this state of affairs, realizing that though she is still sexually attracted to her wife, it may be impossible for Sherry to ever feel the attraction for Kathy that she felt for Karl. For her part, Sherry is happy with the degree of emotional intimacy the two share, which is deeper than was possible for Karl to achieve. While Kathy's differing hormone balance is partly responsible for their deeper intimacy, a larger fac-tor is the depth of honesty they now enjoy and the continued appli-cation of newly-acquired communication tools.

SEXUALITY AND SELF-ESTEEM

Hormones and surgery can only take a trans person so far toward modifying their bodies to match their internal sense of gender identity. Issues of self-esteem and self-consciousness often still arise for trans people. Despite the heightened levels of conscious-ness trans people attain, knowing full well that gender does not always match genitalia, it is another matter to overcome the desire for full mind-body congruence. Those who desire a physical transformation to male must come to terms in some fashion with the knowledge that they can never have an adult-sized penis capable of a natural erection.

Many of my FTM clients were content with their body parts and only desired chest reconstruction surgery. Most derived consider-able pleasure from the 'equipment' they have, enhanced by testosterone, and have no desire to risk losing that pleasure. While some see it as a compromise, they are also able to retain (or regain, or attain, as the case may be) their self-esteem. But for all my clients, the question of body image within the context of sexuality was part of their transition journey. As might be expected these issues affected their relationships as well.

Arnie (39) transitioned out of the lesbian community. While he had had a few relationships as a female, he had been uncomfortable with his breasts and female identity to such an extent that his relationships had not been satisfying sexually to him or to his partners. At the time I met him, Arnie had been taking hormones for nine years and had had chest surgery five years previously.

Arnie had been involved with Steph, a ciswoman, for six years and said in session that he had no idea sex could be so good. Steph (who identifies as straight) came to one session and said she had never been with a man who understood her body as well as Arnie and that she felt very lucky to have fallen in love with a transman. Arnie remarked that he would never have imagined that he could allow anyone to perform oral sex on him, however he now gets tremensdous pleasure from this form of sex, despite the fact he has had no lower surgery. Knowing Steph never sees him as a woman has made all the difference in his ability to accept his body as it is.

Nevertheless Arnie said in an individual session that until a few years before he still looked at cismen with longing and some bitterness, thinking to himself, "You guys take your dicks for granted! You have no idea how lucky you are to have one!" What helped Arnie move past this attitude was developing close friendships with some cismen and talking to them frankly about their experiences as people whose sexual pleasure is derived from their penises.

In his conversations with cismen of various sexual orientations, Arnie slowly came to realize that anxiety over sexual performance and body image is not confined to trans people. While Arnie still wishes he could have a penis, he is more at peace with his body than he used to be and less envious of cismen. He said, "At least mine works all the time. I don't ever have problems sustaining erections with a strap-on!"

He also realized after these conversations how lucky he and his partner were to be able to shop in a sex-positive store and find just the right size penis for his partner's satisfaction. His feelings of inadequacy gradually dissipated, to Steph's relief. As she put it in one session, "He kept on asking me if he's man enough for me, and I would get so angry when he wouldn't believe me when I told him if he was any MORE man I'd probably leave him!" *(Client session, 2005)*

Some of my transmen clients have come back into therapy some years into transition to talk about the disappointment they feel in their bodies. As the years have gone by the only aspect of transition that still feels incomplete to them is their lack of a penis. For these clients this has become an increasing weight as the years go by; they are far removed from their early days of transition and the only thing left to consider now is lower surgery.

Matt (52), said in exasperation, "I just don't know how to become content with what I have. I'm scared to contemplate phallo-plasty or metoidioplasty, partly because it's so expensive I don't know if I could ever afford it. Even if insurance covers it someday, the time off work would be a problem. But also what I have now gives me a lot of pleasure sexually. But it's not the equipment I want to be experiencing that pleasure *with*. But I'm scared to tamper with it surgically, what if I couldn't have an orgasm after surgery, or if it wasn't as explosive as it is now. I get so tired of the 'buts'!" *(Client e-mail, 2010)*

Dwayne is a 42-year-old transman who had been taking hormones for ten years when he decided on a phalloplasty, now co-vered by his insurance plan. He told me, "For a long time, I resisted the need to have a phallo. But eventually I realized this was because of other voices in my head – 'Being a man is more than having a penis' and 'You're participating in the gender binary fully if you have a phallo and don't keep your equipment as it was born.' Problem is, those weren't *my* voice.

"When I found out my work would cover any form of transition I needed, I took my own voice more seriously. And what THAT voice said was, 'You'll never be able to be the man you truly are if you don't have a phallo.' Now it's been two years since I listened to that voice and I've never looked back. It was absolutely the right thing for me. And it's made me realize that listening to other peo-ple's experience and supporting their decisions isn't the same as letting their experience dictate my decisions about my life and body. I saw a great cartoon not long ago, and I put it on my fridge. It said 'You don't have to set yourself on fire to keep other people warm.' And I've realized it's okay to let people go if they don't support my decisions the way I'd support theirs." *(Email correspondence, 2017)*

Many of my MTF clients spoke of their genitalia more in terms related to social safety than sexual satisfaction. When they did speak of sex, it was usually with relief: without the heightened sex drive associated with testosterone, sex was not a pressing issue in their lives any longer.

After eight months of suppressing testosterone, Marilyn (39) said, "I never fully realized before what an unwelcome distraction my sex drive was until it pretty much disappeared." Marilyn has been married for fifteen years, and she and her wife Lara are plan-ning to remain together through the transition. They have been experimenting sexually, finding new methods of sexual intimacy that don't require an erect penis. One welcome byproduct of this experimentation has been a newfound emotional intimacy. As Lara put it, "It's been like a second honeymoon!" *(Client session, 2004)*

The common element among those who come to terms with their bodies is communication. Arnie and his partner communicated about what they each enjoyed, and specifically how they could have sex in ways that satisfied both. Arnie also made himself vulnerable to some of his cismale friends; though the content of their issues differed, his friends had their own feelings of inadequacy that paradoxically reassured Arnie in his male identity. Marilyn and Lara had frank conversations about sex, discussing the issue more deeply than they ever had before, in preparation for Marilyn's transition from Marve.

RELAXING AFTER SURGERY

Eileen and Nora met shortly after Eileen began taking hormones in 2008. Nora, a 41-year-old ciswoman, had been a lesbian for many years and her relationship with Eileen (39) was her first with a transwoman. Both eagerly awaited Eileen's gender-confirming surgery date, which had been booked some months prior to their meeting. Nora went with Eileen to Thailand to support her post-surgery. Some months after surgery their relationship was on the rocks and they broke up about a year after the surgery.

Nora sought therapy with me at that point, confused about her motivations and wanting help clarifying what had gone wrong for her. She said in session, "I just felt like she acted more like the woman I expected *before* her surgery. Afterward it's as if she had the attitude, 'OK, I'm done with that now, I don't have to act so much anymore, I can just be myself.' And that 'self' she acted like seemed to me an awful lot like a guy, way more than I want in my relationships."

A few weeks later I heard Eileen speak on a panel, though we never had a one-on-one interaction. I heard her say, "Once I had surgery I felt like I could just relax. I didn't have to worry anymore that people wouldn't see me as a woman."

Ironically, Nora *didn't* see her as a woman once Eileen had had surgery, though this had not been an issue for her pre-surgery. The relaxation both mentioned seemed to be a return to living on autopilot, without the hypervigilance that had been part of Eileen's 'safety net.' That autopilot seemingly included reactions that came from Eileen's male socialization and that irritated Nora as a result. Nora described various kinds of incidents that amounted to feeling Eileen wasn't taking her feelings into account, that Eileen wanted to just get on with things rather than talk them through, and that she wasn't listening to Nora. [30] Such complaints are fairly commonplace in male-female relationships.

Joanna (43), on the other hand, is quite content with her relationship with Phyllis (48), an MTF over ten years on hormones and four years post-surgery. Joanna had little sympathy for Nora (they know each other socially), commenting, "Well, what did she ex-pect? She's involved with someone who was socialized male and lived that role most of her adult life. I don't expect Phyllis to be 'just a woman' and I just laugh sometimes when she does some of the things she does. I don't expect her to change all that much, not at her age. I love her for who she is, which is a transwoman, not for some image of a woman that I expect her to act like." Joanna and Phyllis met nine years ago and had a commitment ceremony three years after they met. They married legally a year ago, celebrated by their church community.

---

[30] It is possible that Nora didn't see Eileen as fully female prior to surgery, but thought the surgery would somehow complete the process so Eileen would seem fully female to her afterward. Nora herself brought up this possibility, realizing it was impossible for her to put herself back in time to know how she had felt at the time. Nevertheless while she might have had some unconscious expectation that the surgery would make Eileen more female in some way, she was clear that what actually happened was a complete surprise to her.

WHAT HELPS RELATIONSHIPS SURVIVE?

There are a number of factors that can help sustain a relationship through the traumatic upheaval of transition.

First, the partner has to be able to sustain the relationship without a whole lot of help from their transitioning partner. Transi-tion is a necessarily self-centered process. The trans person has to put themselves first for a time, going through a personal process of self-knowledge that borders on wallowing in oneself. ("Navel-gazing," some describe it)

Eventually, the transitioning partner will become less self-involved and able to be a full partner in the relationship again, but this is an indefinite process that varies in length from individual to individual. There is no predicting how long it might take or whether the relationship will survive on the other side of transition. Partners may find they are no longer compatible for various reasons and may break up anyway. It's a leap of faith to take the chance.

Sometimes the partner feels the transitioning partner remains self-involved for too long and the transition never seems to end, leaving the partner feeling they are bearing too much responsibility for sustaining the relationship. This is a difficult position for the partner, not knowing whether things will change in the future, whe-ther they are being selfish for wanting more of their partner's emotional attention, or whether they are being co-dependent.

Being able to talk with other partners, either in person or on the Internet, can be a good reality check,[31] as well as feeling able to bring up their concerns and insecurities to the transitioning partner. If the partner 'stuffs' these feelings in the name of being supportive, this repression can poison the relationship and lead to extreme resentment, unacknowledged anger, and passive-aggressive beha-

---

[31] Some of the partners one may encounter are too impatient with the transition process or are resistant to the whole idea of their own partner transitioning. Such people may be too quick to judge other people's relational process, and are not necessarily helpful to a partner seeking support for trying to stay in the relationship.

vior. Good communication skills and boundaries, then, are factors that can help sustain a relationship through transition.

Humor can be invaluable in helping couples retain a sense of perspective and a feeling of pulling a cosmic joke on the world. Trina and Paula (mentioned previously) were walking down the street together, and a man in a pickup truck whistled out the window at them. He then pulled his truck over and said to them sug-gestively, "I've got the biggest cock you girls have ever seen." They were completely taken aback and stared at him in shock, which must have puzzled the man mightily.

Trina said in session, "I was absolutely speechless; he obviously had NO IDEA who he was talking to." At the time Trina was several years away from having enough money to afford gender-confirming surgery. She and Paula still tell this story, years after the fact, they found it so amusing.

Yet another factor is adaptability and flexibility. Partners who have a very rigid worldview, who do not incorporate new ideas or allow their beliefs to be challenged, are likely to have great diffi-culty with the concept of transition. They are likely to cling to the view of gender as a fixed reality. These partners will also have difficulty changing their perception of their own sexual orientation, or even entertaining the possibility. While it is not a given that such relationships will automatically end, it is more difficult for this type of partner to adjust because adjustment does not come easily or wil-lingly to them.

The transitioning partner can help here by bearing in mind that a rigid worldview is often a fear-based attitude, a fear that change means chaos or loss of control. A good therapist may be able to help an overly-rigid partner come to understand where their fears are based, allowing them to relax a little about the concept of facing big changes. Still, there is no doubt that transition will be a big chal-lenge, possibly insurmountable, for a very rigid partner.

Being willing to examine deeply-held beliefs about the nature of gender, gender roles, gender expression, social acceptance, etc. is a key component for both partners. Each will discover, from their own perspective of the transition, that nothing is really fixed reality when it comes to issues of gender. (Sanger, 2010)

In all cases, support is a key aspect of success. If you are a partner seeking support, check to see if there is a trans support group in your area. If so, encourage the moderator to consider facilitating such a group for partners. If there is neither, it might be helpful if you can organize partners to meet once in awhile. Knowing that one is not alone in one's experience can be a huge benefit, and another factor in helping sustain a relationship through transition.

Seeking support from peers is crucial, as partners often find little support elsewhere in their effort to stay with their partners through transition. Their friends and especially family members may actively encourage them to leave the relationship, providing all kinds of support for breaking up and not understanding why anyone would want to work through the issues to stay together.

Further, support group members are more likely to respect confidentiality, understanding from their own experience that transition is not light gossip to be spread far and wide. It will not help the trans person in their process if the partner talks to people who then spread the word. It's a tricky balance. Yes, the trans person has the right to own their own identity and come out as they are ready. And yes, the partner has the right to find others to talk to as part of their own process. These may seem to be mutually-exclusive needs, but negotiation between the partners can resolve the situation.

Partners often find it useful to form groups along generational lines and based on the gender of the transitioning partner. A 50-year-old ciswoman who is married to a transwoman may feel she has little in common with a 22-year-old non-binary person whose partner is transitioning to some version of not-male. Though they can listen to each other's stories and provide support, they may not feel a sense of commiseration over issues they don't share.

I salute partners who try to stick it out. They are too often un-sung heroes. It's one thing to go through a transition because one must, because it is one's personal destiny in life. It's quite another to marry into it. My hat's off to you.

THE INTERSECTION GENDER AND SEXUALITY

I have met many trans people who found their sexuality morphed after beginning physical transition. Some of my older MTF clients would have sworn they had no attractions to men yet after beginning physical transition found they were attracted to men (trans or cisgender), sometimes instead of women and sometimes in addition to. Other trans clients found their attractions didn't change at all. Some have discovered their attractions lie with other trans people, preferring intimate relationships with others who hold an expanded view of gender.

I met one FTM who had given up trying to pigeonhole his sexuality. He used to be a lesbian separatist (to hold at bay the man inside, he told me) and assumed he'd be a straight man post-transition as he'd only ever been attracted to women. But after he started taking testosterone he gradually realized he was more at-tracted to men (either cismen or other FTMs) than to women.

He finally decided what attracted him was the dynamic of a same-sex relationship. As a lesbian that meant being involved with women. After transition that meant being involved with men. He now embraces the term pansexual, which he defines to mean 'any-thing that moves.' I don't want to imply that this man is promiscu-ous. Rather, he has adopted non-binary language that supports his non-binary sexual identity.

This transman's process is a striking example of what can hap-pen when one allows the emergence of a core aspect of identity – other aspects of core identity can then emerge in their fullness as well. Denial can't be applied selectively to one emotion or aspect of identity. In repressing gender identity, sexuality is often stunted or at the least misinterpreted.

Another factor in shifting sexuality is the resocialization process inherent in transition. Transition induces a second puberty that offers the opportunity to grow up again, this time in one's true gender. This process allows for a deeper maturation, a centering into one-self, that leads to the opportunity for more intimate and mature relationships than were possible prior to transition.

Social gender roles can come into play also. One client (Adam) transitioned out of the lesbian community. Earlier in his life Adam had taken refuge in that community because the gender expression available to him as a lesbian fit him very well. But he'd always been dimly aware of being more attracted sexually to men than to wo-men. He could not allow such attractions to surface to conscious-ness, as there was no part of him that resonated with the identity 'straight woman.' He realized that prior to his transition men would have related to him as a woman and that was so unacceptable to him that he dampened down the attractions altogether. Six years into his physical transition, Adam is involved with a cisman in a mono-gamous life partnership, living (privately) within gay community rather than lesbian community.

While they are not the same aspect of identity, it isn't possible to consider sexual orientation separate from gender identity; our society persists in linking them. As a culture we draw harsh distinct-ions between a woman-to-woman or man-to-man relationship and a man-to-woman relationship. (And we don't talk about polyamory at all in discussions of mainstream relationships. Polyamory is respon-sible non-monogamy, as opposed to having secretive affairs or one-night stands.)

As a society we have created a link between the gender of two partners and the degree to which a relationship between them is so-cially sanctioned. While neither the fact of having a gender or sexual identity is socially constructed, the pigeonholes known as sexual orientation *are* a matter of social construction. The gender identity of the two partners determines the sexual orientation of each, by our culture's standards. In order to be seen as a lesbian or gay couple, both partners must be seen and pigeonholed 'female' or 'male' by others. To be seen as straight, the partners must be pi-geonholed 'female' and 'male.' The gender assignment precedes the sexual orientation label, and this is the intersection of gender identity and sexuality.

• Chapter 16 •

THE SPECTRUM OF SUPPORT

MY PHYSICALLY-TRANSITIONING CLIENTS experienced a wide range of reactions to the news of their impending transformation, from outright rejection and hostility through varying degrees of tolerance and acceptance to the rare and admirable response, "That's wonderful, congratulations! Go you! What do you need me to do to support you?" Core identities such as gender and sexuality represent the most fundamental uniqueness of each individual. Allowing others to bear witness to one's true self by coming out to them is a coura-geous act.

What makes physical transition so difficult is that it usually involves initiating a process of redefining all of one's relationships – from casual to professional to familial – at about the same time, while the individual is simultaneously learning who they are with a new hormone balance in their bodies and brains.

Because we live in a culture which has so misinterpreted trans identity, there is no protocol or chapter in any etiquette book titled *How to React when a Friend or Family Member Tells You They are Going to Transition.* Likewise there is no protocol outlining how to make the disclosure in the first place. Often it is impossible to predict how the news will be received and this vulnerability leaves the individual open to a great deal of psychic pain if the news is perceived as negative. The closer the relationship, the more vul-nerable the individual is to being hurt by the way in which the news is received. And the more likely it is the person receiving the news will have a deeply emotional reaction, often not initially positive.

THE NEGATIVE END OF THE SPECTRUM

"How can you do this to me/us?" and "Where did I/we go wrong?" are two of the more-common negative reactions parents or other family members may have. "What will the neighbors think?" is a variation my clients sometimes heard. Since family members (partners and spouses are in this category) have to let go of the old to embrace the new, their initial feelings are probably not going to be positive. They don't *want* to let go and may resent the trans fami-ly member for putting them in the position of having to. Sometimes partners are supportive, particularly if they knew about a possible transition from the start of the relationship. Nevertheless many fa-mily reactions are not initially positive; that does not predict what those reactions may become over time.

"How can you do this to me/us?" and "What will the neighbors think?" are self-centered reactions, taking into account how transition may affect the family and not taking into account what it means to the person undertaking the transition.

"Where did I/we go wrong?" is based in the erroneous view that transition is a matter of chosen behavior and not identity actuali-zation. This attitude harkens back to the idea that gender is strictly a matter of socialization and not innate identity. This deep-seated cultural belief is only now slowly changing. Hence many parents will react as if they are responsible for their children's identities. If this were indeed the case parents would be able to successfully steer their children toward (or away from) particular identities.[32] From this viewpoint, a person announcing, "I'm transitioning" can be seen as parental failure to provide a good example of how to be a man or woman.

If one views gender as an innate identity that is not malleable, then parents are absolved from blame regarding their children's identities. Note that this is different from being absolved from re-sponsibility regarding learned behavior. While a child's innate gen-

---

[32] As gay and lesbian activists have long pointed out, if this were true all children would grow up to be straight and cisgender, as these identities reflect our socialization.

der and sexual identities are not determined by parental example, parents influence other aspects of development: healthy boundaries in relationship, respect for themselves and others, honesty and integrity, etc. Healthy (or unhealthy) parenting will not lead to a change of identity on the part of the offspring, but will affect how well the offspring can accept who they are, have a sense of self-worth and self-efficacy, etc. Healthy parenting leads to a child's healthy ego development and to the internal strength to weather the trials of transition.

Healthy parenting implies healthy parents, who also have healthy boundaries in relationship, respect for others, are honest, etc. Parents with these characteristics are much more likely to react positively to the news of transition, over time. Parents have years of history with their child in a certain gender role and need time to adjust. Parents who are themselves healthy individuals are usually able to make this adjustment and come to value their 'new child' just as fully as they did the 'original model.'

No parent can forget that particular people are their offspring, or vice versa. However healthy parenting does allow a transformation of the parent-child relationship into a more adult-adult interaction between parent and offspring. This is a transition in its own right, involving parent and offspring seeing each other in a new light.

The relationships between parent-child and parent-adult-offspring differ from culture to culture. Within mainstream Euro-American culture, independence and self-sufficiency are seen as hallmarks of mature adults. This is not true of all cultures. For example, Asian cultures revere family connection such that a desire for independence is seen as a selfish, immature attitude. 'Healthy adult' will look different depending on cultural context. Never-theless every culture differentiates in some way between the status of children and adults, thus involving a change in the relationship between parents and children as the child becomes an adult.

Parents who cling to their children to an unhealthy degree often have a difficult time accepting transition no matter what their child's age when the announcement is made or what their cultural

314

background. Such parents have never seen their children as individuals in their own right and are more likely to react in a self-centered manner, along the lines of "How could you do this to me/us?"

Ed remarked, "My mother has never seen me as a person in my own right. She defines her identity as a person by the fact that she had three daughters. So it's been impossible for her to accept having two daughters and a son." *(Personal conversation, 2007)* Ed was 29 and had been taking hormones for five years at the time we met. Such stories remind me of a poem by Kahlil Gibran:

> "Your children are not your children.
> They are the sons and daughters of
> Life's longing for itself.
> They come through you, but not from you.
> And though they are with you, they belong not to you.
> You can give them your love, but not your thoughts
> For they have their own thoughts.
> You may house their bodies, but not their souls,
> for their souls dwell in the house of tomorrow,
> which you cannot visit, not even in your dreams.
> You may strive to be like them,
> but seek not to make them just like you."
> (K. Gibran, 1923, from *The Prophet)*

Both reactions "How could you do this to me/us?" and "Where did I/we go wrong?" are examples from the negative end of the support spectrum. Family members having such reactions often have a change of heart as they go through their letting-go process. All the transitioning person can do is wait, and provide information as needed. It's very difficult to watch a family member or close friend grieving the loss of a persona the transitioning person is moving away from with alacrity. Nevertheless the family transition process is not avoidable, despite how hard it can be to witness. (Nult, 2015)

Some family members never shift from their original rejection of the transition. Amanda (57) has a cisgender brother (Joe) who refused to meet with her or to allow his wife or children to have any communication with her. He refused to set foot in their parents' house unless Amanda's photos were hidden away. Amanda's mo-ther was in a difficult position; she fully supported Amanda's transi-tion but also wanted to know her grandchildren as they grew up. Joe made it clear his children could not visit their grandmother unless she hid Amanda's photographs and never mentioned her.

Amanda exchanged e-mails with Joe for nearly a year after dis-closing her transition to him and methodically printed out their entire correspondence as she received his emails, storing them in a binder. At one point she sat down and read the entire correspond-ence, start to finish, and had a sad epiphany. She realized she had to let her brother go because his first e-mail to her was almost identical to the most recent in her binder, nearly a year later. Joe had not 'heard' one word she had said in her attempts to help him know and understand her. This situation caused her great grief; she and Joe had been close at earlier times in their lives, and she had enjoyed getting to know her nieces and nephews prior to her transition.

Had Amanda continued to try to reach out to her brother after realizing she was having no impact on him, her self-esteem would have eroded from the attempt. Once she'd concluded he was not going to change through any effort of hers, remaining open to his negative attitude would have been detrimental to her own desire to maintain healthy boundaries in her relationships with others. She sent him a final e-mail, telling him she would be open to talking with him again if he ever had a change of heart, but that she could not have communication with him otherwise.

Amanda sent her final email in 2003. In 2013 Joe contacted her. He and his wife were divorcing. In reflecting on the meaning of family and the shortness of life, he realized he had been wrong to allow the estrangement to grow between himself and Amanda. Though he freely admitted he still didn't understand why she had to transition, Joe believed his mother when she told him how much happier and joyful Amanda was post-transition. They have rebuilt their relationship and Amanda has once again been able to enjoy her nephews and nieces, though she regrets missing ten years of their childhood.

I worked with a number of clients (fortunately a small number) whose entire family permanently rejected their transition. While family of choice can become a source of comfort, support, and 'home' over time, for the newly-transitioned person the amount of time involved has not been sufficient for these new relationships to feel like 'home' and 'family.' And no matter how much time passes, no one else can replace 'mom' or 'brother' or any other family of origin relationship.

Georgia (mentioned in the chapter *When Worlds Collide*) became severely depressed by the rigidity and finality of her family's rejection of her identity as a woman. Not one would speak to her about it and the few who retained contact with her would only interact with her if she put on her male persona again. She felt as if she was hanging on by a thread, as if no one would ever love her. In addition to her work with me she called upon the services of suicide hotlines and emergency room psychiatric services more than once early in her transition.

Georgia's need for such services diminished considerably when she adopted a dog. More than once clients told me that the one source of unconditional support they received early in their transi-tion came from a pet. I have experienced this myself – my cat didn't care about gender. Early in my transition process it was a relief to come home at the end of the day and be greeted by someone who loved me for who I was, without regard to gender. I didn't have to wonder how she was seeing me or whether she accepted me or not; she always had and I could count on the fact that she always would. I did not lose friends or family members during my transition, yet still felt overwhelming gratitude for the unconditional love of my cat. I didn't have to watch her go through any loss or grief process over my transition.

The sense of complete isolation some clients experienced was due to the fact that no one in their family would accept their transi-tion. In general if even one family member is supportive, this is enough to prevent a sense of total isolation and hopelessness. On occasion I found it worthwhile to remind such clients of the family members who did offer them good support, to help counter the ne-gativity they experienced from those who were rejecting them.

TOLERANCE AND ACCEPTANCE

Though better than overt negativity, tolerance and acceptance can be more insidious. They may still carry a negative message, but can come across as positive. Amanda had no difficulty recognizing Joe's attitude toward her as negative. His views were so out of step with what she knew to be the truth of her identity and process, she had no difficulty seeing it as his problem and not taking it on as her fault in any way.

But consider what happened with Jared, 24 at the time he began physical transition. His sister Sara is a year older than he and the two had always been close as sisters. After he told her in person of his impending transition to male, Sara thought about it and then wrote him an e-mail that said, "I can accept that, it's not going to affect my love for you. You'll always be my sister."

At first Jared was delighted to hear this. Over time he found himself angry with Sara and not wanting to talk to her about his transition. She was hurt and confused by his attitude, accusing him of being unreasonably self-centered. He wondered if she might not be right and brought a printout of the e-mail into session, asking if I thought he was being selfish.

I read the e-mail, and rather than responding to his question I asked him one of my own, "How would you have felt if she'd just said, 'You'll always be my sister'?" Jared didn't even have to think about that, replying immediately, "Terrible!" Then he had a mini-epiphany, realizing he'd been seduced by her prefacing words, "I can accept that." He'd been so relieved to read that, the tag line didn't really register, "You'll always be my sister." Unconsciously those words angered him.

I encouraged Jared to talk with Sara openly about how he felt to read, "You'll always be my sister." Sara was taken aback and re-alized she had some work to do: she had to wrap her mind around seeing Jared as her brother and not her sister. The essence of what she'd originally said to him was, "I'm going to love you the same way I've always loved you, which means not altering my view of you – you'll always be my sister."

About six months after her initial reaction Jared told me Sara had given him a 'brother' birthday card for the first time rather than a 'sister' birthday card. In it, she told him she felt she'd made it when she found herself getting angry at a mutual friend who com-plained to her about how hard it was to use male pronouns for Jared, expecting Sara to fully agree and sympathize with her for having to make this shift in attitude.

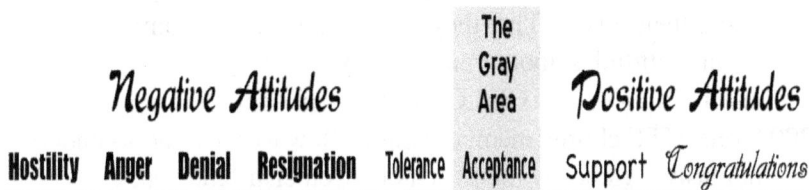

Negative Attitudes				The Gray Area		*Positive Attitudes*	
Hostility	Anger	Denial	Resignation	Tolerance	Acceptance	Support	*Congratulations*

'Tolerance' carries the subtext: 'I am tolerating who you are.' How positive is that, to feel someone is remaining part of your life in spite of who you are rather than because of who you are? 'Ac-ceptance' may carry the subtext: 'I accept this new identity of yours; isn't that magnanimous and big of me and aren't you proud of me!' Often there is an undercurrent of condescension in accept-ance, as there is an undercurrent of distaste in tolerance. It may seem counterintuitive, but acceptance falls in the middle region of the spectrum of support, forming the bridge between positive and negative attitudes.

Whether an accepting attitude is positive or negative depends on its emotional impact on the trans person. Sara's original attitude was negative in its impact on Jared. But consider Connie's situation. Her brother Hank said to her, "I accept you whether you're Connor or Connie." Connie didn't feel residual anger toward her brother, as Jared had toward Sara. Connie was happy with Hank's statement and this causes her to see his reaction as a positive form of acceptance.

CONGRATULATORY SUPPORT

Though supportive of his emerging sister Connie, Hank also did not say, "Way to go! Good for you! Congratulations!" This reaction is uncommon among family members. Occasionally, a client came in beaming, having told a cisgender friend of their transition and received this level of congratulatory support. What I find sad is that such clients were ecstatic, overwhelmed with gratitude, and exceedingly surprised when they experienced such reactions. Trans people should not have to feel grateful for being congratulated on becoming themselves. That they usually do is a sad commentary on our cultural attitudes about trans identity.

I used to sing in a mixed LGBT chorus of about 50 singers. In late 2004, one MTF chorus member (Carla) flew to Thailand to undergo vaginoplasty. A chorus member put together a 'care pack-age' for her, with presents and cards from others in the chorus. The idea was that Carla would be able to open one present and/or card for each day of her stay in Thailand. She was there 21 days and never ran out of gifts to open.

During the winter holidays of 2004, another MTF chorus member (Sharon) flew to southern California with her (cisgender) girlfriend Patti, also a member of the chorus, to meet the in-laws. Various chorus members knew of this trip before it happened and kept in touch during the visit, in case support was needed. When Sharon flew to Thailand in early 2006 for her own surgery, Patti sent periodic email updates to the chorus, knowing everyone in the group would want to know all was well.

Over time I noticed a pattern among the trans members of the chorus. As they received unconditional support from their 'chorus family,' they gained self-esteem and a new perspective on their life as trans people. They began assessing the degree of support they received from others in their lives, and to question the value of relationships with those who were not supportive: "Why is it okay that you treat me this way? Don't I have the right to expect better?"

Carla was married for years, as Chuck, but the relationship had grown distant; the relationship survived largely because of inertia. Carla's transition shifted them out of their inertia long enough to divorce. Before joining the chorus, Carla was unhappy and as private as possible, not wishing to disclose her trans status unless absolutely necessary.

Carla now has a philosophical attitude about being private. On the one hand it's nice to just move through life as herself without having to explain anything; on the other hand she enjoys educating people about what it does and doesn't mean to be trans, recognizing that such openness is what effects social change. If she is private now in any particular situation, it is not out of fear or shame but because she hasn't been recognized as trans and there is no edu-cational opportunity in the interaction.

Sharon also was married for years, as Rob. She and her wife Jean separated over Sharon's transition but got back together a year later, feeling they were soul mates. Jean tried as hard as she could to shift her own cultural upbringing and sense of her sexual orientation to embrace Sharon's identity, but just could not wrap her mind around being involved with Sharon. An outspoken, articulate wo-man, Jean couldn't realize how much her process, her word choice, felt like a knife in the heart to Sharon, from the male pronouns to the obvious grief she felt (and could not move past) over the emergence of Sharon.

When Sharon joined the chorus and experienced unconditional support from a group of (largely) cisgender people, she began reevaluating her relationship with Jean and realized she could not continue their marriage without seriously eroding her self-esteem. Since she began seeing Patti, Sharon has blossomed. She is now experiencing a positive relationship with someone who is not trying to tolerate her female identity, but embraces it as the core of who she is.

INTO THE LIGHT OF DAY

In considering family support, there are new possibilities as trans identities emerge into the light of day – is there a chance a family member might figure it out on their own? How will they feel about it if this is the case? Might this cause more problems in the long run than coming out to them proactively? New issues are on the table for discussion as the client contemplates disclosure.

Alice was 43 when she began physical transition in 2007. Now living in the San Francisco Bay Area, she never told anyone in her rural Mississippi family about her transition; her parents were aging and her mother was the key support person for her father, who had been coping with a degenerative disease for some years. After much thought, Alice decided not to add her transition to the complication of their lives. Her biggest worry concerned negative community reactions affecting her family and her father's health.

Though she talked to her mother on the phone every few weeks, Alice only saw her family in person for a week every year at Christmas time. She dressed in guy mode to visit them, and didn't bring her partner Judy; she didn't want to put Judy in such a position. All her documentation had been changed to reflect her identity Alice, so she would fly into the area, rent a car, and change into what she called 'Bobby clothes' on a back road before reaching her parents' neck of the woods.

At one point she told me, "I'm seen as a woman everywhere I go in my daily life. Most of my friends think I'm crazy for not just coming out to my family and getting it over with, but I've come to look on it as a game. It is so affirming to me that it's difficult to dress convincingly as a man! I'm sure my mother thinks I'm gay, though we've never talked about it." *(Email correspondence, 2012)*

This was Alice's situation for eight years. Her intention was to wait until her parents had died to come out to the rest of her family. Then fate took control. In the summer of 2015 Alice's 75-year-old mother called her and said, "I just saw a TV show about that Caitlyn Jenner... And suddenly I understood you, I think..."

Alice's breath was taken away, so unexpected was this recognition on her mother's part. Heretofore trans people have been able to take comfort from the double-edged sword of marginalization: yes, this meant having no voice in the public discourse, but it also provided a certain peace through obscurity. Alice had always thought her coming out to her family was completely in her control.

With a great deal of trepidation Alice confirmed her mother's guess. She had never intended to lie to her family, other than by omission. But it also had never occurred to her that anyone in her family would figure it out. Fortunately her mother went on to say, "I do see why you never said. There's plenty of folks around here who just wouldn't understand. I just wanted you to know that *I know* and I love you and I'm proud of you. When I heard Caitlyn's story and I looked at that picture of Bruce Jenner again, it just made me see how *hard* this must be."

Her mother then asked Alice about her life and they had a marvelous two-hour conversation. Alice and her mother made new sense of their history together. Alice told her mother in no uncertain terms that her worry had been for her father's health, knowing how their small community might react to the news and fearing their support system might be affected. She wasn't surprised her mother had accepted her identity, and made sure her mother knew that. Alice emailed her mother a current photo of herself, and one of her partner Judy. Her mother cried when she learned Alice had chosen to take her mother's first name as her own. She and her mother talked it through and decided it would be easiest if Alice continued to visit in guy mode. Her father was declining fast, and they felt if an opportunity arose he should meet Alice. And when Alice visited in the future, her mother suggested they treat themselves to at least one "gal's afternoon out" in Jackson, the nearest city – with Judy.

Shortly after this conversation, Alice wrote me, "My mother always did see me for who I am, but now she was able to understand exactly what it was she was seeing all those years." *(E-mail correspondence, 2015)*

Alice's father died in early 2016. During her visit the preceding Christmas, Alice introduced herself to him as it was clear he would soon die. This visit, she also brought Judy for the first time. Though confused initially, her father eventually realized who Alice was. She told me, "My mom was with us, and his biggest reaction was relief that I was with her and she was okay with me. He was living in the moment by that time, so didn't have historical baggage attached to transition like you so often hear with parents. I'm so glad he met me and Judy before he died."

SUPPORT WITHIN THE FAMILY

Many trans people experience varying degrees of discomfort on the part of friends, acquaintances and co-workers upon hearing of an impending transition, but usually not overt hostility or complete rejection of the idea. The more hostile and rejecting reactions tend to come from those who already have an emotional relationship with the person in transition. These are the folks who have the most to lose, from their perspective, as they have an investment of one sort or another in the client's current gender presentation and role (and in the case of partners or spouses, the physical body).

Family relationships are primarily gendered in both their labels and conceptualization. Brother, sister, wife, husband, mother, fa-ther, aunt, uncle, grandmother, grandfather – all family labels are gendered in English, with the exception of cousin[33]. As a result, the gendered images and archetypal-level roles associated with those labels are

---

[33] In some languages, 'cousin' is also a gendered term.

deep-seated and resistant to change, much more so than the label 'friend.'

What is most difficult for cisgender people to understand is that the person who transitions has never fully owned the gender identity they have expressed in the past. The person in transition is not changing their gender, they are changing their gender role, expression and perhaps their physical body to better match what is present inside them. (Lev, 2004; Herman, 2009)

The person may have been labeled 'brother' without fully owning the role associated with brother. The façade may have been quite convincing and never been more than skin-deep. The gen-dering inherent in the family labels often makes it difficult for trans people to be able to consider their own family members good sources of support as they move forward with transition; family members need support themselves as they move forward with their own transition, letting go of 'sister' to embrace 'brother,' for instance. (Nult, 2015)

Some clients told me ecstatic stories of finding that a close family member was in their cheering section unreservedly, but that was not the norm among my clients. And it may be that some in the cheering section had their own private process of letting go without their trans family member being aware of it.

More often than not the trans person hears more than they would like about how hard it is for everyone else to make this shift in relationship. The experience Sharon had with her then-wife Jean is more common than I'd like to see. Sharon has no regrets over losing 'Rob,' and it was hard for her to listen to her wife talk of resenting 'Sharon' having taken over 'Rob.'

Sharon tried for a year to be patient while Jean went through her process. But once Sharon had the experience of being amongst cisgender people who liked and appreciated her for who she is, she found it difficult to sustain support for Jean, particularly since there did not seem to be any change of heart coming her way.

Growing up in a trans-hostile culture makes it difficult for trans individuals to believe that they do deserve support for who they are, and that support is not too much to ask. While each transitioning individual needs to allow their family members to undergo a loss and grief process, that doesn't mean the trans person can't even-tually say, "Enough is enough. Contact me when you're done with this. I can't support you through this at the expense of my self-es-teem." This is precisely what Amanda did with her brother Joe.

This is another parallel between addiction recovery and transi-tion: just as the alcoholic is responsible for their own recovery pro-cess, so the non-alcoholic partner or family member is responsible for working through their own enabling patterns. The co-dependent has the responsibility not for supporting the alcoholic through reco-very, but for changing their own patterns to those of mutual respect and personal responsibility within the context of relationship. (Beattie, 2001)

Just so, the transitioning individual is not responsible for sup-porting the partner through their loss and grief process. Both partners have their own transition to undertake and neither should expect the other to provide support if that support is co-dependent in nature. Both processes are valid, both individuals need support, and neither is more entitled to support than the other.

Just as the alcoholic seeks support outside the relationship, so must the co-dependent partner. Just as the trans person seeks sup-port outside the relationship, so must the non-transitioning partner. Where the boundary lies between support and co-dependency is up to the individuals to determine, but both must start from the premise that the other's life-transforming process is worthy of support. Each is on a journey of transition, though the paths are different.

Peer support groups provide support from people who have no learning curve about the issues. However peer support can only take the trans person so far. At some point during transition, one has to reintegrate back into the larger culture. It's a stretch, as it involves disclosure and vulnerability, sharing one's core identity with people who probably won't understand without some degree of explanation and education. Finding support among cisgender people helps the trans person gain a sense of self-esteem and self-efficacy. "I can do this! I will be accepted as my true self!" is a powerfully positive experience that comes from finding community among cisgender people who are not sending negative messages.

It was a stretch for both Sharon and Carla to join a chorus. To their surprise, the visibility of performing before an audience turned out to be the least of the stretch; allowing the 50 other people in the chorus to support them while they actualized a core identity was the true stretch. At the end of one rehearsal Sharon raised her hand to announce that her birthday was approaching, three weeks since she'd begun living full-time as Sharon. The accompanist immedi-ately hit a chord and the chorus joyfully sang "Happy birthday."

LIMITATIONS OF SUPPORT

Unfortunately this type of support is not available to all trans people, especially MTFs trying to fit into the baby-boomer gene-ration lesbian feminist community. Much of the opposition is rooted in the ingrained belief female-assigned people grow up with in this culture (myself included): 'Men you don't know should be consi-dered a threat until proved otherwise.'[34] Women are not socialized to believe other women to be a threat. The mainstream cultural belief that an MTF is a man in a dress dovetails with this socialization lesson, creating a situation where an MTF is considered a threat until proved otherwise and therefore can't be viewed in the same light as a ciswoman.

Many feminists also hold the belief that male socialization con-fers male privilege and a sense of entitlement that cannot be un-learned. Prevalent particularly among Euro-American, middle-class feminists, this attitude gives more credence to gender as an instru-ment of oppression than to race, sexual orientation, or class. Though these attitudes are not universal, they are prevalent enough that membership in many all-women organizations is closed to MTFs.

---

[34] The actual lesson was, "Don't talk to strangers," but somehow I always knew that meant men, not women.

Even if membership is not overtly denied, a chilly or hostile reception can make it feel closed.

For Euro-American, middle-class, heterosexual, able-bodied cis-women living in the United States, gender *is* the main source of oppresssion in their lives, particularly if their gender expression is not especially masculine. From their subjective reality, this places gender at the head of the list in importance. It is difficult to move beyond one's subjective experience to stand in another's shoes long enough to recognize their experience of oppression may feel com-pletely different. It is also difficult for many people who live as lesbians to understand that they do indeed hold some power of op-pression over others in the arena of trans identity. They benefit from cisgender privilege. (Scott-Dixon, 2006; Vanderburgh, 2016)

Often issues of this sort only make it onto the agenda when a specific person's membership is under consideration. Such person-alization can cloud the general discussion, which should instead fo-cus on: "How does gender play out in this organization? How do we define 'man' and 'woman'? Do we need to make those dis-tinctions? If we are a 'lesbian' group, what does that mean? If we are a 'women's' organization, what does that mean? What does it mean to be 'feminist'?"

This last question – what does it mean to be feminist – strikes at the heart of the discriminatory policies of those organizations that exclude MTF individuals. The modern feminist movement was a backlash against biological determinism, an affirmation of freedom of choice. Women wanted the power of self-determination, to be free to choose whatever career path suited them, to be free to have children (or not) in their own time, to be free to expand the female gender role beyond the narrow confines of the 1950s. (Friedan, 1964) The irony is the right of self-determination is the central point for trans people as much as it is for those who embrace a feminist philosophy of life.

Part of self-determination is the right to determine one's own identity and to adopt whatever self-descriptive terminology feels true to that identity. Trans people grapple with this identity issue on the level of gender, coming to terms with the limitations of English, finding (or creating) language with which to describe themselves. It is inappropriate for others to lay claim to specific identifying language as if there can be a linguistic copyright on 'man' or 'woman.'

However with that self-determination comes a certain social responsibility. While I disagree with blanket discrimination against an entire group of people based on a label or shared characteristic, I am also well aware of the long history of oppression that led to the modern feminist movement in the first place. I have witnessed the results of unconscious feelings of entitlement playing out among a few MTFs I've encountered. It's unpleasant. The scenes I've witnessed,[35] along with my 20+ years in the lesbian community, give me a certain compassion for those who desire to exclude MTFs.

Yet I've met many other MTFs who do not trample others, who are respectful of others' viewpoints, etc. And I have met a number of ciswomen who DO trample others, and who are NOT respectful of others' viewpoints. Male socialization is not the only road lead-ing to disrespect and a sense of entitlement, nor is female sociali-zation a guarantee that an individual is safe to be around, physically or psychically.

The question arises, "Can someone raised male really embrace feminism in the same way as one who has lived a female experience lifelong?" While the route is different, the result can be a deep appreciation for what it means to live as a woman in American culture. Not many younger ciswomen stop to consider that they themselves can't know what it was like to live as an adult woman in the 1960s or 70s, at the beginning of the modern feminist movement. They can only have a historical appreciation for what it was like to live at a time when girls would be sent home from public school if

---

[35] The most egregious incident I witnessed took place at a largely-FTM conference. The keynote speaker was a renowned transwoman activist with years of experience working for trans civil rights. At one point in her speech, she quoted several statistics, counting numbers of trans people. From the back of the room, another transwoman activist called out, "Love ya, _____, but I gotta challenge your statistics." The two had what amounted to a pissing contest with an audience of some 400 transmen. I was sitting next to a transman friend of mine, and at one point I whispered to him, "Can you envision two transmen acting like this?"

they wore pants, for example. Why should there be a higher standard for transwomen? The learning curve is different, but no more or less insurmountable.

For those transwomen who identify as lesbians, there will be some unlearning required in order to shift from 'heterosexual male' to 'lesbian woman' in relationship. There is no equivalent of lesbian community available for heterosexual men and it can take some time to even recognize the significance of that community to those who embrace it.

Harriet (46) and her cisgender partner Sue (44) had some difficulties early in their relationship. Sue had been a lesbian for over twenty years and had strong ties to the lesbian community. Harriet had been physically transitioning for about two years when they got involved; Sue represented her first attempt at relationship after beginning transition.

Transitioning out of a heterosexual male role, Harriet had no conception of the power and importance the lesbian community held for Sue and found it difficult to understand Sue's position. Sue came of age at a time when the modern feminist movement had al-ready strongly affected the lesbian community and thus did not re-member a pre-feminist time. Sue suggested some books for Harriet to read, literature that had informed her own worldview as she was coming of age. They also had deep conversations about relationship, gender roles, and their previous experiences of the world.

In addition to these intellectual approaches, Harriet now moved through the world female; her visceral experience of living as a woman also helped shift her out of 'heterosexual male' toward 'lesbian feminist' in her perspective on life and relationship. These experiences were central to Harriet's resocialization process and led her to value lesbian community as Sue did.

Sue came to value the opportunity presented her to question her own assumptions about feminism. She said in session, "Once I got Harriet to understand that I wasn't just talking about wanting to go to a movie with a friend once in awhile, that the lesbian community meant more to me than social activities, it was great to talk about all this stuff with someone who had never even thought about it before. Knowing Harriet has really expanded my view of people."

She laughed as she said, "I even have a more well-rounded view of men these days." One thing Sue came to appreciate is the differing agendas of gay male community and lesbian community. She now jokes, "Gay men want to be accepted into and participate in mainstream society; lesbians want to *change* society, believing our way to be innately superior. And neither gay or lesbian commu-nity as a whole respects or understands the other, from what I've seen. But I can laugh about it all now and not take everything quite so seriously, because I feel like I have a little more objective dis-tance. Transwomen are outside both communities, so now I feel like I have one foot in and one foot outside lesbian community. In a weird way, though, that doesn't make me feel like I've lost any part of lesbian community, but like I've gained a part of something else. I don't know quite what to call it. Knowing Harriet has given me that." *(Client session, 2007)*

One of the paradoxical gifts trans individuals have to offer cis-gender people is the opportunity to face (and perhaps alter) funda-mental socialization questions and cultural assumptions about the meaning of gender identity, sex and gender roles, and the role of feminism. Those organizations (and individual members) that em-brace the opportunity are able to attain a more holistic, well-rounded view of people, leading to an ability to greet and learn about each new member rather than making assumptions about the individual based on birth gender assignment.

IT'S NOT MONOLITHIC

It's been my experience that gay/lesbian organizations of long-standing often have difficulty embracing the 'T' component of 'LGBT.' Too many organizations, wanting to be supportive, don't do their homework sufficiently to determine, "What do we need to do in terms of examining our mission, or the services we provide, to make sure we're trans-inclusive?" The organizational attitude main-tains a 'we're all gay here' flavor, whether conscious or not. When trans people encounter this 'lack of homework,' they often become discouraged, believing this will be the case in every gay/lesbian organization. (Vanderburgh, 2017)

A few years ago I discovered an LGB organization that is trans-inclusive by its nature. Rosetown Ramblers is Portland's gay and lesbian square dance group; founded over twenty years ago, the Ramblers are part of a national association of gay and lesbian square dance groups. The way the group approaches gender roles makes it a perfect fit for trans members. In square dancing each set of dancers is divided along gender lines, half the dancers in the male role, the other half in the female role. However, in Rosetown Ram-blers, as in other gay and lesbian square dance groups, the actual gender of the dancers has no bearing on whether they're dancing the male or female part.

Two gay friends introduced me to Rosetown Ramblers, and at my first dance I saw femme lesbians dancing the male role, mascu-line gay men dancing the female role, and various people trading off to dance the other role later in the evening. It occurred to me that what I was witnessing was a group activity where gender roles didn't matter and could be mixed and matched without a second thought. This freedom to switch roles can make such a group a breath of fresh air for anyone who is grappling with the stresses of transition.

I had a conversation with Tom, a long-time Rosetown Rambler member, about trans presence in gay and lesbian square dance clubs. Tom pointed out that it is a form of cisgender privilege that the cisgender dancers give little thought to whether they are dancing the male or female role; it is a matter of preference, not a challenge to core identity. To a trans person, choosing one role or the other will be a hot-button issue for a long time into transition. The fact remains that gay and lesbian square dance clubs represent the only arena I am aware of in gay and lesbian community in which cisgen-der males and females mix and match gender roles, making it an excellent place for trans people to make forays into gay and lesbian space.

CARICATURES

Twenty years into my own transition, after living within the lesbian community for over twenty years, I now realize my previous view of men was a caricature of the actual experience of living male. Those who transition physically are given the gift of being able to experience more than one life in the same lifetime. In des-cribing her experience of shifting gender roles Sharon said, "When I was still a guy I never used to understand why women I'd be out with at night would hesitate to walk certain places. I'd say, 'Come on, there's nothing to be afraid of.' Now I get it, because I've felt it." No description or intellectual analysis can replace somatic experience.

But just as cismen can't understand what it is to live female in the world, neither can ciswomen understand what it is to live male. Norah Vincent tried, as told in her 2005 book *Self-Made Man,* but Vincent could only go so far in the experience. Not only did she not take testosterone, she moved back and forth between gender roles, unable to fully experience what it would mean to live male in every aspect of her life. The experience of going back and forth led to a breakdown of her identity, stripping away her surety of what was real and what was a social construct. Writing *Self-Made Man* was part of her journey back to her sense of self.

Feminism has afforded women an excellent forum for airing the female side of the equation. Nothing has afforded men the same opportunity. If a man tries to speak honestly to his experience of the world, all too often his opinion is discounted or invalidated by women, as if it's just not possible that men might have difficulties with the male gender role just as women do with theirs. The difficulties are not the same, but are there nonetheless. Until both sides of the equation are fully aired and taken seriously, society will not change in a manner that is healthy and helpful for all. While feminism expanded the female gender role considerably, no counterpart movement has expanded the male role, which remains nearly as constricted as it was in the 1950s.

Those men who have tried to participate in feminism may find themselves derided for their efforts. While I don't recall the details, I remember hearing in the late 1970s that Alan Alda was partici-pating in an event to raise money for a feminist cause. One of my lesbian feminist roommates rolled her eyes and said scathingly, "Save us from the Alan Alda's of the world!"

A few years ago, I told this story to a gay cismale colleague and he was completely confused, not understanding her point. My lesbi-an feminist friend was articulating a position common among lesbi-ans of that era and which I still encounter today at times: men don't get it, men can't get it, men are incapable of true compassion and empathy, and are therefore not trustworthy allies. Or they are con-sidered so much work to educate that it's not worth the effort.

This attitude seems somewhat less prevalent these days. In the late 1970s I helped break the gender barrier in the organization of Portland's Gay Pride Day. Until that time it had been organized exclusively by Euro-American gay cismen; the men we approached were resistant to the idea of incorporating lesbians into the planning.

Those of us trying to change the planning process held the attitude: "The gay men just want a beer wagon and the loudest sound system possible so they can have one big disco party. There are no politics here!" The gay men held the attitude: "If we let the lesbians in on this, they're going to want to turn it into one big long political speech and the whole event will be completely boring!"

In 2018 it would be unthinkable that a monogendered group would even consider planning Pride Day. If the planning committee happened to find itself monogendered, the group would im-mediately realize it was not diverse enough and would seek addi-tional committee members. The same now holds true for diversity in general, around issues of race, gender, ethnicity, etc. In the mid-2000's the Pride committee chair was an open transman; this would have been impossible in the late 1970s.

What does this have to do with transition? Those who transition often feel outside the American gender system looking in, with a clearer view of the dynamics than was available to them while they were unconscious of the cultural power of gender. Being on the out-side looking in means not only transitioning away from one's birth gender assignment, but also not being able adopt a different gender role unconsciously. I have come to realize that the power of the American gender role system is largely based in its invisibility, leading most cisgender people to operate on a form of gender autopilot in their interactions with others.

The heightened consciousness available to those who transition in some way can lead to a greater ability to analyze and discuss gen-der roles. While no one can claim complete objectivity about gender roles, trans people (even those who are invisibly trans) view gender from a place of consciousness of the power of gender, leading to an opportunity for greater objectivity than is available to those who never consider transition.

My long experience living within the lesbian community gives me a degree of credibility among my long-time lesbian friends as I talk about gender roles. They cannot so easily dismiss me, "Save us from the Reid Vanderburgh's of the world." I speak from a place of personal experience with more than one gender role, and people who understand this can usually hear what I'm saying without feeling attacked. Clients made similar observations as they inter-acted with long-time friends, from a different gender perspective.

This is the gift trans people have to offer our culture and I look forward to the day when our insights are brought to the table on the many issues that continue to divide cismen and ciswomen. Trans people view our culture's gender roles from the holistic perspective of lived experience.

I have also noticed generational differences that inspire hope. In 2010, I led a training at a local mental health agency. I mentioned that I often feel 'dumbed down' if I find myself in a group of women who don't know I once transitioned. Their tone is one of condescension, as if I, a mere male, can't understand processing or nuances of relational experience. In the training, I said, "If I come out to the group as a transman, I witness the dynamic change, as I am 'grandmothered' in and given the benefit of the doubt. 'Perhaps he gets it after all,' I can almost hear them thinking."

When I said this I could see the older women in the group laughing and nodding their heads, aware that this is exactly how they would feel. But one woman (I later learned she was 26) wrinkled her brow and said, "I don't get it." In her circle, that's not what would happen. She had never had the experience of being in a group of women her age that automatically assumed men incapable of deep thought and emotion.

THE EVOLUTION OF SUPPORT

Many men have behaved badly toward many women (and continue to do so) and our society has been slow to take domestic violence and institutionalized sexism seriously. While this remains the case it is all too easy for many feminists to view MTF presence as an encroachment in women-only space, such as at the Michigan Womyn's Music Festival (MWMF, or Michfest).[36] With an almost atavistic, knee-jerk response, a deeply-held resentment and hostility toward men emerges. Simplistic generalizations such as 'once a man, always a man' emerge from women who hold a fairly complex worldview when discussing other issues, such as racism.

There is a generational divide here: some who have attended Camp Trans have noticed much more acceptance for trans identity among younger attendees of MWMF. Camp Trans began in 1992, a sit-in protest across the road from the main festival, protesting the exclusion of transwomen from the main festival.

In 2004, Jon (a transman, formerly trying to be a lesbian) related to me a conversation he had with a cisfemale lesbian friend (Lois) who had returned from the MWMF angry at the existence of Camp Trans, which had begun loudly broadcasting its own performances, disrupting the MWMF performers across the road.

Prior to transition Jon had attended the Festival five times over the years and told Lois that he understood the attitudes of those who

---

[36] 2015, its 40ᵗʰ year, marked the last Michigan Womyn's Music Festival.

wanted to exclude MTFs altogether. He remembered well the feeling of total safety he'd felt while on 'the land.' But he also told her he now understood the viewpoint of those MTFs who want to attend, who never felt male in the first place and feel more at home among women than among men.

Jon now understood that transwomen were no more a threat to the other festival attendees than any other woman in attendance. He also expressed to Lois dismay at what he saw as divisive tactics at Camp Trans, recognizing they were going to alienate many po-tential allies by disrupting the performances at the Festival.

He told Lois, "I do get it, I've seen bad behavior by MTFs and some by FTMs, but to generalize from that isn't right. And it wasn't *dangerous* behavior. Besides, there have always been transwomen at the Festival, so it's hypocritical to say that somehow it's different if you know they are trans than if you met them in the food line, struck up a conversation, and never realized they were trans-women."

Lois grew increasingly angry at his assertion that there is more than one point of view to consider in this situation, finally saying to him, "Why can't they just understand 'No' means 'No'?"

Jon told me, "This reaction took my breath away and my first thought was, I'll bet that's exactly what the Daughters of the American Revolution said in exasperation when Marian Anderson tried to do a concert in Constitution Hall, because the DAR wouldn't allow an African-American to perform on their stage.

"My second thought was, 'Who is 'they' and who is 'us'?' I'm not so sure that I am 'they' to Lois, even though I identify as a man now and she's a lesbian. The people she was referring to as 'they' identify as women, and so does she. It's like she thought she had nothing left to learn because she went through my transition with me, and because lesbians somehow are automatically better on these issues than anyone else."

While Lois was able to transition their relationship in her mind, offering Jon very good support early in his process, she had not taken it to the next level by examining her own assumptions about the nature of gender. She did not generalize her experience with Jon to her worldview of others who might also transition. Jon had a conflicted reaction to Lois' attitude. He had viewed her as a supportive ally during his transition process. He now wondered where to place her on the spectrum of support if she could be there for him while having such exclusionary attitudes about MTFs.

Jon eventually realized he had to set a boundary, as Amanda did with her brother Joe; the work was Lois' to undertake, in her own time. She approached Jon very early in his process, before he knew her well, and offered proactive support. Their friendship had be-come very close as a result of her offer of support. This caused Jon to hold the hope that someday her view of transition and gender would evolve to a deeper understanding of the issues.

What it means to be an ally is to move beyond the level of specific friendship and into the realm of supporting the larger social issues that people face because of particular labels they own. It is a matter of self-education, and transcending the 'us and them' kind of thinking behind exclusionary policies or attitudes.

Another point this brings up is that support can be contingent on birth socialization. Jon was socialized female and believes Lois was able to trust him because she has a deeper innate trust of those socialized female than those socialized male. This left him wondering, however, whether her support for him would waver over time as his female history receded further into the background of their lives.

Jon and Lois have very little contact now. Jon's trust in Lois wavered after the interaction described above and he stopped contacting her to do regular kinds of tasks together, such as shopping, or going to movies or other events. Lois still participates in lesbian community events, which the two used to attend together, and Jon has moved beyond seeing the lesbian community as his tribe. As he stopped calling her, Lois' calls to him also became infrequent.

When I initially asked Jon if I could relate the story of his argument with Lois over Camp Trans, I asked him if I should change details so she would not recognize herself in the story. He replied at the time, "She won't read your book. She thinks she already knows it all." In 2018, I asked if that turned out to have been true, and he replied, "I think so, because if she'd recognized herself, or even if she thought it was someone similar to her, she would have wanted to talk to me about it. She never did."

OFFERING SUPPORT: HOW TO BE AN EFFECTIVE ALLY

Many trans people have experiences similar to Jon's, with friends able to accept their transition while not able to translate that to the level of being a cisgender ally. Allies develop an understand-ing of trans issues as applied to people who are not personal friends. It is this last hurdle, coming to understand trans issues apart from how they affect friends or family members, that must be overcome in order to effect societal-level change, one heart at a time.

Allies take it upon themselves to try to turn off their own gender autopilot. One way to do this is to walk around with a button that says *Trans and Proud* and track the reactions. Allies can also cross-dress, trying to achieve invisibility, and then note the differences in how they are treated by others. The social and cultural nature of gender is made visible by these kinds of exercises.

Another level of education is intellectual, coming to understand what issues are important to trans people. This level of work is par-ticularly important for cisgender people who own other letters of the LGBTQQIAA acronym; they have familiarity with their own issues and may not understand initially that the T of the acronym has its own unique issues that they don't share. For example, insurance co-verage for transition processes is an important goal of trans people.

As outlined in the chapter *The Therapist's Own Work,* allies can strive to achieve the same goals I recommend for therapists desiring to work with trans people:

- ❖ To stop automatically assigning gender;
- ❖ If an ally does assign a gender category, they do so after conscious thought and observation, or after asking;

❖ To be able to switch names and pronouns upon request, and to notice when they slip;

❖ To notice other people's automatic assumptions, and unconscious slips.

At first, many allies become crusaders, challenging gender stereotypes and autopilot processes wherever they crop up (which is everywhere). As allies become more comfortable with dismantling their own unconscious 'gendering' process, they often become more compassionate over time, as they also notice that trans people themselves have a gender autopilot to grapple with. Anyone raised in U.S. culture will have a gender autopilot process of some sort, and the true ally will have compassion for others' processes while at the same time helping others achieve the above goals.

Ally work doesn't have to be overtly political, or militant. A cisgender friend of mine (I'll call her Roberta) told me of an expe-rience she had at a suburban DMV (Department of Motor Vehicles) office. Roberta was waiting in line, filling out a form and distracted by all the errands she had to run on her lunch hour. Gradually, she became aware of an unusually tense atmosphere in the room. Glancing around, she saw the room was populated primarily by cis-women, and that they were gossiping amongst themselves. This might not have seemed unusual to Roberta at church or in some other setting where everyone knew each other, but it did seem unusual at a bureaucratic office.

It took awhile for her to notice that the person in front of her in line was a transwoman and that this MTF was the focus of the gossip Roberta had observed. Several thoughts went through her mind: "If I don't do something, everyone here is going to assume we all agree that she should be an object of gossip. Should I say anything that shows I saw her as transgender, or is she trying to be invisible?" Then Roberta was inspired to say something that MTF may always remember. She tapped the transwoman on the shoulder and said, loudly so all the other women could hear as well, "That's a really pretty dress you have on." That is the response of an ally.

340

Some trans people retain a negative view of transition and trans identity, believing there is something fundamentally wrong with being trans. This translates to a negative view not only of themselves, but of other trans people as well. Trans people in this position can't be seen as allies to themselves, much less to other trans people. It can be a challenge for cisgender trans allies when they encounter a trans person who is less of an ally than they are.

As is the case with LGB communities, ownership of a particular label does not confer automatic ally status. Many a lesbian can attest to the fact that many gay men are not particularly good allies to L community issues; many a gay man would laugh at the idea that all lesbians are good allies to G community issues. And bi-sexuals would laugh at the idea that either G or L people are their automatic allies, on any issue.

Ally status is individual, not based on any particular community affiliation. I know allies who are gay, lesbian, straight, bisexual, religious, non-religious, married, single, partnered − the list runs the gamut. All they have in common is they have attempted to dismantle their gender autopilot, doing their own work to develop a conscious relationship to their own gender identity and how it plays out in the world. They have also educated themselves about the community, its political goals and history. From this position, their actions support trans people, as Roberta did at the DMV.

I helped clients understand that just as they held no one else responsible for their transition process, they were not themselves responsible for anyone else's process. All the trans person can do is remain open and available, trusting their own feelings and judgment about how much is too much. Some will have experiences such as Amanda's with her brother Joe, and will have to let go. More will experience reactions such as Connie's brother Hank, "I can accept you whether you're Connor or Connie." And many will have experiences such as Jon's, painfully realizing that personal friendship does not make an ally.

And many will also have the experience of feeling they've let go permanently, only to find as Amanda did that there may be an unexpected reconciliation down the road. Some may find it difficult to forgive the original rejection. It may help to look on the relationship as completely new, and not a recreation of what used to be. As indeed it is new – a relationship built from the place of a new identity and social role, with someone of long familiarity, all family to each other.

Though not an easy or quick process, helping a friend or family member reach ally status is both rewarding and inspiring, and can help a trans person view their personal process as one of contri-buting to eventual social change.

Little girls in their dresses, and boys and their guns,
and me in some center just sitting.
I'm neither the other, nor neither this one,
and I feel like a poem half written.

Go inward, go inward, go deep where you lie
You find you a kingdom with acres to fly
Where you won't feel losses
and you can't measure gains.
You find yourself humming a freeing refrain.

Freedom, come to me now,
I feel like a feather pinned under a plow.
The mask I could wear seems to choke me somehow,
and I can't find the courage to cry right out loud.

—©Ferron, from the song *Freedom*
Nemesis Publishing
Recorded on *Ferron* (1976-77)
Quoted by permission

• Chapter 17 •

HOW YOUNG IS TOO YOUNG?

I DO DOZENS OF PRESENTATIONS each academic quarter, and often the question arises, "I saw on Oprah that a twelve-year-old was allowed to begin hormones. How can a child that age be making that kind of irreversible decision? Their sexuality is just emerging, how can they possibly know transition is right for them?"

Not only does this question reflect a fundamental misunderstanding of the difference between gender and sexual identities, the premise itself is suspect. Despite being pre-pubescent, many children already have a sense of who they find attractive, who they have crushes on. In recent years, the Portland PFLAG chapter has been accessed by two different families with young children (5 and 7 years old) announcing to their parents, "I'm a lesbian."

Unheard of in previous generations, this phenomenon might seem new. However, many older gay men and lesbians have told me stories of having crushes on other boys or girls when they were 6 or 7 years old, never developing strong feelings for anyone other than those of their same sex. They didn't have language to describe their identity to others, and might not have felt safe enough to talk about it even if they'd understood their identity. Nor were their identities reflected back to them in popular media, a change that is now allowing non-heterosexual children to recognize their sexual ori-entations at younger ages.

In the realm of gender identity...If a child has been consistently saying throughout their short life, "I am not a boy, I'm a girl," (or vice versa), across all situations, I would support this person in beginning a social transition as soon as is practical and a physical transition at the onset of puberty.[37] It may be they are asserting a non-binary identity, not requiring medical intervention but a social process of adopting gender neutral pronouns. Regardless of the specific situation, identity stability is the key to supporting social transition.

What does this sort of identity stability look like? One four-year-old crawled into mom's lap and stated matter-of-factly, "Mommy, I know you think I'm a tomboy, but I'm really a boy." A year later, Jerry enrolled (as a boy) in kindergarten. His parents and teachers closely monitored his assertions of identity, both in language and behavior. Now 16, he takes his male identity for granted. He began taking puberty-blocking medication at 12, and started taking testosterone at 14. No one at his current school knows of his transition, other than any necessary school administrators. Jerry's identity has been stable since he was a small child, and his transition has given him a normal childhood and adolescence.

A TRANS-MITZVAH

In 2005 I worked with the parents of 11-year-old Sam. His parents fully supported his transition; they were primarily con-cerned with: (a) how to approach his school, and (b) how to prevent his sister (two years younger) from outing him during his transition, perhaps through sibling rivalry. His parents carefully considered which middle school would be most appropriate to send their new son, allowing him input based on his own transition process. I wrote a letter to the school, outlining the steps they could take to smooth Sam's path and offering to do a staff training, if necessary (it wasn't – the school was completely on-board). When he was about to turn 12, Sam began taking estrogen-blockers, to prevent the onset of female puberty and any further breast development (he was unfortunately an early-bloomer).

---

[37] Physical transition for adolescents usually does not mean administering cross-sex hormones at the beginning of puberty; rather it entails blocking the birth hormones to prevent puberty in the "wrong" direction.

The Hansens looked at various spiritual traditions, seeking some form of ritual that would allow them to celebrate Sam's transition. They found it in the Jewish Bar Mitzvah, to celebrate their son's rite of passage. In the spring of 2006 I received the following invitation:

Carly & Tom Hansen

invite you to join them in celebration

and support of their son

Samuel David Hansen's Trans Mitzvah

We have been so blessed with the love and support

of our family, friends, and wonderful community.

Please share in our joy as Samantha's

life-changing transition to Samuel begins...

Sam entered high school in 2009. Though he had not started taking testosterone yet, he had been living and going to school as a boy. His father Tom contacted me to talk about Sam's depression. In keeping with most adolescents, Sam didn't talk to his parents about his feelings and his parents were worried about him.

I talked with Tom about chest surgery and offered to put him in touch with the parents of a trans son Sam's age, who had had chest surgery not long before. I also helped Tom see that living with the wrong hormone balance could cause depression despite Sam's so-cial transition to male.

Tom told me he had not given as much credence as he felt he should have to the importance that chest surgery or testosterone might hold for Sam. Tom and Carly had believed that the social transition would be enough until after high school graduation. Sam had received unqualified social support from old friends, and new friends weren't aware he was female-assigned at birth. Tom and Carly had believed this was the most important consideration, but now realized the physical aspects of transition might be looming large for Sam.

I suggested to Tom that Sam might be more forthcoming about his feelings if he felt there was a chance such a conversation might result in an outcome such as chest surgery, rather than merely being an opportunity to vent. Tom and Carly did some research about chest surgery, and contacted the family I'd referred them to.

Within a week they contacted me about obtaining a hormone referral letter. Sam began taking hormones a few months before he turned 15. Over winter break that year Sam had chest reconstruction surgery. Tom called me a few weeks later to say the surgery result was excellent and that Sam was back in school. Tom said, "I knew intellectually, it just made sense, about what a difference hormones make in terms of brain function. But *seeing* what a difference it's made to Sam – he's a different kid! Happy, alert, participating in his own life."

Sam's sister Julie was thrilled to have a big brother, a role Sam was happy to fill. She never outed him, perhaps understanding with the clarity of childhood that some things aren't fodder for teasing.

THE CHEERLEADER

Another case involved 14-year-old Dana, who began her social transition in 2005. Her parents were completely supportive, having recognized their child's 'difference' from the time it emerged. As Dana's mother Mona put it, "She was just such a girl from about 18 months on, it's almost difficult to recall any moment of emergence. In her toddler years we assumed we were raising a gay male. It would be several more years before we recognized and acted on the reality of having quite a different scenario." *(E-mail correspon-dence, 2006)*

It took Dana's parents more years still to find any social service or medical professionals who knew how to help them.

Dana received support from both classmates and teachers. Her cheerleading coach told the squad they were going to wear less-revealing uniforms than had been the norm. Dana had not had breast implants, which would have been apparent in the original uniforms the cheerleaders wore. The coach made her statement in a matter-of-fact way, without going into detail, and all the cheerleaders were in complete agreement with the decision.

Dana was very popular in high school. Her mother told me that Dana never lacked for dates to dances and the like, and that most of the young men of her school were very protective of her. Like many adolescents, Dana and her friends went on group dates. She and her parents both shied away from the idea of individual dates, partly for safety reasons and also because Dana wasn't interested in that level of relationship at that point in her transition.

Dana graduated from high school in June of 2008. She and her parents talked about the timing of gender-confirming surgery and decided that she would take a year off after high school, specifically for that purpose, prior to starting college. Dana spent her gap year having and recovering from gender-confirming surgery.

I saw Dana socially six months post-surgery; she looked radiant, feeling she was now on her way with no further barriers to living her life. She asked me to include in this book the fact that it was four months after surgery before she finally felt like her body was her own to command again. She had a slow recovery, despite her youth and excellent physical health. She had no particular complica-tions from the surgery. She asked me to pass along the idea that it is important to build into surgery plans sufficient time for recovery, easy to overlook when one is so young.

Her mother felt it important to add that friends and family members need to make room in their lives and schedules for time to help out with the first few weeks post-lower-surgery. As Mona put it, "I had no idea just how much help she'd need. She moved back in with us for a time, and it's a good thing she did. She needed help with every little thing. She became the center of our household rhythm for about two months."

Dana is now 26, well on her way. Her boyfriend Martin is fully aware of her transition. He was certainly thrown when she told him, about a month after they started dating, but adjusted well to the news. Dana told me, "I told him over Skype, that way he could have his reaction in private and if it was bad, I was still safe. He hung up on me and I was devastated. But he called me the next day; he'd realized I was the same girl he loved, he just knew me better now."

The next evening he brought flowers over to her house, though he knew Dana was out to dinner with her father. Mona answered the door and started to tell Martin that Dana wasn't there, but he handed her the flowers, saying, "These are for you, for being such a great mom." Mona later told me, "At that point I knew he was a keeper! I sure hope it works out!" (Still together, three years later)

NO CHOICE ABOUT TRANSITION

All the parents I've worked with adamantly state that they would do whatever it took to protect their children, to help smooth their path through school and into adulthood While recognizing how dif-ficult transition is, these parents also understand how miserable their children would be if they did not transition and how likely it is they would attempt or commit suicide if forced to remain their birth gender through adolescence and into adulthood. Dana told her mother, at about age 7, "Mom, I no longer wish to live in this world." She had realized through peer interactions at school that she was expected to be a boy and wanted no part of it.

Sam had always been one of the guys and his mother Carly told me that prior to finding resources to help Sam transition, she deeply feared he would become an addict as a teenager, so depressed would he be at having his body develop along female lines. Both Carly and her husband Tom have been in recovery for many years, and were aware this puts their children at risk for addiction. Carly worried less about this possibility when Sam was able to transition socially in middle school and then take hormones and have chest reconstruction surgery. Once he reached high school few of his classmates were aware of his trans identity, which is precisely how Sam preferred it.

RESISTANCE TO NAMING

While these parents shared a common goal of wanting to help their children actualize their gender identity, the mothers also shared an interesting reaction: both had a deep-seated resistance to the idea of their children choosing their own names.

By happenstance Dana's real name is gender-neutral; she is not planning on choosing a new name. Sam, however, had a very feminine name given him at birth. Tony had no particular attachment to the renaming process, but Carly wanted to be able to rename her son. On hearing this, Dana's mother said she completely understood that reaction, as she would want the privilege of renaming her daughter had it been necessary.

In my case 'Reid' is not a family name and when I told my mother I was changing my name, she surprised me by asking if I was changing my last name as well. I told her I had no reason to change anything other than my highly-feminine first name. Curious, I asked why that had occurred to her as a possibility and she replied, "I wondered if you wanted to retain connection to the family." She was, on some level, viewing my transition as a form of becoming someone else rather than becoming more fully myself and thought that might include changing my last name. As I proceeded with transition and didn't change into someone she didn't recognize, she relaxed into acceptance of my identity as Reid.

Parents wanting a part in the renaming process may have similar fears to my mother's: 'Are you still my child? Can I still claim you as my child?'

IT MAKES ALL THE DIFFERENCE

I have met hundreds of trans people as clients, colleagues, or friends. I have yet to meet any who had what they consider a normal, healthy, or happy adolescent experience. Wait. I take that back. The exceptions are the young trans people I've met whose trans identity was supported by their families. While not as normal as they would like, their childhood and adolescence is made more bearable by their social presentation, family support, and sometimes by hormonal and/or surgical interventions.

The more common transadolescent experience goes something like this. Throughout childhood, gender is somewhat easily ignored (especially for those who can adopt the tomboy role). At puberty, however, there is a 'gender divide.' The girls go one way, boys go another, and the trans-adolescent is left at the starting gate. "Can't go this way, 'they' won't let me, can't go this way, it's just not me... Nowhere else to go." So the transperson simply stops developing emotionally and shuts down. Many trans people go through adolescence in a state of quiet depression, perhaps unconscious that their gender identity is not matching their body's maturation process, perhaps having no idea why they feel so wrong or different. (Krieger, 2011)

Sometimes the transadolescent experience is one of doing everything possible to blend in, rather than withdrawing and sitting on the sidelines. One 2003 client said, "I was captain of the wrestling team and could bench press more than any of the football players, but it was all a façade. I was hiding from myself, not just from them. I had sex with lots of girls, but I wouldn't call it having relationships; I never learned how to do that because I wasn't really being me when I was male with my girlfriends. I didn't want to just be with them, I wanted to *be* them."

If they survive to adulthood (too many commit suicide, or die from one type of drug abuse or another, trying to numb away the pain), those who couldn't transition learn to cope and adapt to society, but never being true to themselves. If a person is capable of developing truly intimate, honest, fulfilling adult relationships in the gender assigned them at birth – they're probably cisgender. Part of what it means to be trans is an inability to truly mature into adulthood in one's birth gender assignment. It's just not the right gender vector for the journey through life. (Note: The reverse is not true, that a person who can't develop intimate, honest adult rela-tionships must be trans! There are many reasons why adults may have difficulty forming and maintaining relationships.)

THE SEX WORKER

Marla, a friend of a friend, contacted me in early 2016 and invi-ted me to her home for lunch; she didn't want to meet at a restaurant as the situation she had to discuss wasn't for public consumption. A few days earlier, she had come home from work unexpectedly early and found her 22-year-old trans daughter Ashley engaging in sex work in the living room. Her daughter had been living with her during her early transition, a process Marla supported.

Marla was very emotional, as one might expect. "I just don't un-derstand it. I'm supporting her financially; it's not like she needs the money. She's not doing well in school, either, and I'm afraid she's going to drop out of college." Ashley had been studying accounting prior to beginning physical transition six months earlier; now Marla feared for the future.

"I can't support doing sex work! It's so risky, not just for Ashley personally but also for me – bringing it home like that! Please ex-plain to me why she doesn't just DATE. Why sex work???"

Ashley was 21 when she began taking hormones. Adding tran-sition to that late adolescent stage, changing the hormone balance and going right back to a 14-year-old state of mind, is part of the issue. Like many transwoman, Ashley was experiencing the gid-diness of finally being able to 'act like a girl.' And like many ado-lescents, her decision-making was questionable.

However, all transwomen who take hormones go through a si-milar giddy experience of revisiting early adolescence; many do not engage in sex work. I helped Marla figure out where this behavior might originate. It turned out that several family members had badly hurt Ashley with statements such as, 'No one is ever going to want you, this will just turn you into a freak' or 'You had such promise, now you're throwing it all away. You'll never amount to anything now.'

Marla had been angered by such statements, and had defended Ashley to the point of drawing a line in the sand with several family members: continue with this attitude and you won't be part of our lives. It hadn't occurred to Marla, however, that such statements would more than anger Ashley. Much of her sex work was rooted in deep hurt, as Marla confirmed when she had a deeply emotional conversation with Ashley after our lunch. Ashley cried in Marla's arms; she loved her grandfather deeply and hearing his judgmental and harsh statements had driven her over the edge.

Bound up with her hurt was an 'I'll show them' attitude about men in general; she didn't feel the men who paid her were ex-ploiting her – she felt she was "leading them around by the cock they're slaves to," as she put it to me when we met later. She was making them vulnerable to her by arousing them. In her mind, there was no difference between these men fetishizing her and the guys who used to bully and harass her in high school. She felt she was getting back at them in some way by taking their money. She felt empowered, and some part of her believed this was the only way she would ever have any power. Further, she believed that in satisfying men sexually, she was defying her grandfather's state-ment, "No one will ever want you." Had she remained a sex worker longer, that belief might eventually have eroded; being fetishized isn't the same as being wanted for herself in a relationship.

Ashley and I had some long talks as I mentored her; she then felt able to call a therapist I recommended. A year later, she has ceased doing sex work and is doing well in school again. I talked with her to get an update, and she said, "I was such a mess of hurt and fear. When I was doing sex work was the only time I felt something else, like I was in charge. But now, I really AM in charge. I don't want to date yet. I still have a sour feeling about men in general and want to just be friends with some guys for awhile so I can get over that. My therapist gave me a great way to look at it – I'm dating myself now. I take myself out to a movie."

FUTURE DISCLOSURE

One issue that arose with Sam's parents was that of disclosure. Sam's mother had become quite used to asserting her son's identity in a variety of settings, from school to his soccer team. His mother is a forthright woman who actively defended her son's right to be himself regardless of the circumstances. He could not ask for a better ally.

I gently pointed out to her early in our work together that the time was coming when disclosure decisions would rest with Sam, not with her. She was taken aback, not having considered the time when Sam would be seen as male without any intervention on her part. At that point she would have to take her cue from Sam: how open would he want to be? My guess was – not very, especially dur-ing adolescence. And later in his life, how likely is it that he will tell many people that until the age of 11 he was living as a girl? The jury is out on that one, but it's Sam's call.

Jason began transition in middle school, starting testosterone at 14 and having chest surgery at 17. (He was able to have a keyhole procedure; his breast growth was fairly minimal because of the age at which he started hormones) Recently turned 21, he has already graduated from college and has his sights on grad school. But he has a transition goal to accomplish first. His father's workplace insur-ance now covers transition processes and Jason is accessing it to pay for a phalloplasty while he is still covered by his father's insur-ance. Jason's girlfriend, mother and sister are planning to come with him when he has his surgery.

Jason has found his disclosure boundary. A few close friends know of his transition, but that's about it. As he put it to me, "How can I be really good friends with someone and hold this information back? That just doesn't make sense to me. The thing is, going through something this big as a kid, I find myself gravitating toward people who have also gone through something big that made them grow up faster. My best friend was in a bad car accident when he was 9. He had to go through a lot of physical therapy and he's still living with pain. I don't think it's a coincidence that my best friend went through something that big. He's got a really big heart and I think his experiences have just made it bigger. I look for that in people, because I learned so young how important it is to have that. I'm so lucky I had parents with big hearts. I've heard so many stories of trans kids kicked out." *(Email correspondence, 2015)*

Jason volunteers as a tutor at a local agency that works with homeless youth. He said, "When I find out someone I'm tutoring is trans I always come out to them. I want them to know they can make it. I think that's especially important since I'm mixed race; I want QTPOC (queer or trans people of color, pronounced 'cutey-pock') to understand they can do this, too."

A NORMAL ADOLESCENCE

Other parents reading these stories may look at their own children in a new light. Some who had thought their children gay or lesbian may seek out more information, wondering if perhaps they have a trans child instead. I would only recommend early transition for those who are asserting a cross-gender identity very clearly, across all situations, from an early age. I recommend watching the film *Ma Vie en Rose* for a wonderful depiction of the experience of a gender-dissonant child. When I try to visualize the child in that film experiencing a male adolescence, I am horrified by the thought.

Many trans people, myself included, didn't have such a clear childhood experience of their gender as these particular children have had. However with the advent of the Internet and a growing public awareness of the true nature of trans identity, more people will have the opportunity to put a name to their feelings of dif-ference at earlier ages than has been the case in the past. And just as importantly their parents will be able to find accurate, non-judgmental information about gender identity and transition pro-cesses. Parents are more amenable to the concept of having a trans child when they have accurate information.

The Portland-area families I worked with received support from the Portland PFLAG chapter. The national PFLAG organization has adopted a stand of only supporting other organizations if they are inclusive of trans issues. PFLAG chapters are autonomous, and not all will contain members with existing knowledge of trans issues. (The Portland chapter does have the necessary knowledge) How-ever all chapters adhere to the same code, and that code includes providing support for families with trans members as well as gay, lesbian, or bisexual members. Just as Sam and Dana could not ask for better allies than their parents, their parents couldn't find better support for their own issues than PFLAG. Dana's mother has been involved in her local PFLAG chapter since Dana came out to her over ten years ago.

A companion organization, Trans Youth Family Allies (TYFA), provides support specifically for families with trans children. TYFA provides resources to help parents advocate for their trans children in school settings. TYFA started as a PFLAG program, then branched out to specifically support families with trans children. TYFA is aware of what local and regional resources are available, and can point parents in the right direction, as well as providing services themselves (at no cost to the family) for those who live in areas without such local support available.

Those who transition later in life are forced to revisit ado-lescence, to grow up in their proper gender after having tried to grow up in a more inappropriate role. In addition to the difficulty of changing all that life, it costs a lot of money to undo the physical effects of their first experience of puberty. While the psychic pain undeniably builds character, most trans people would gladly have given up the opportunity for personal growth in favor of a gender-appropriate adolescent experience.

UNUSUAL? YES. UNFORTUNATELY.

Some may feel I have presented an unrealistically rosy picture of adolescent transition. However I did not want to reinforce the norm, which remains that of parents misinterpreting or not recognizing their child's identity, placing too much emphasis on what others will think, or rejecting trans identity as 'unacceptable behavior.' I wanted to present life as it should – and could – be for children who so clearly need to transition. Early transition is not the right path for many. But for those called in that direction, to deny the call is a matter of life or death, as these parents can attest.

This is not a rural vs. urban issue, with the former unable to transition at all while still living at home. In 2005 I met a mother from a small town in Wyoming; she was attending a conference hundreds of miles from home, seeking resources to help her young FTM son transition. Another mother traveled from small-town Arizona to a conference to present a workshop on helping youth transition. Her FTM son is transitioning in middle school, quite successfully. In 1999 I met a mother and her FTM son; he had begun transition at 12 and was attending middle school as a boy, in rural northern California.

The factors common to these families are:

❖ Every parent recognized their child's 'difference' early-on, and rather than trying to change the child in a punitive or judgmental fashion, allowed the difference to emerge over time;

❖ Every parent assumed initially that their child was gay or lesbian, which would have been fine with their parents, though not what they would have chosen for their children given the difficulties lesbians and gay men face;

❖ Every parent gradually came to realize the 'difference' in their child was not about sexuality. Some talked with gay or lesbian

friends about their childhood experiences and came to
understand that suicidal ideation is not the norm for gay or
lesbian children who are accepted for who they are;

❖ Every parent tried to find answers by talking to pediatricians,
   psychologists, or psychiatrists, none of whom had any idea what
   was going on;

❖ Every parent continued seeking answers, not blaming their child
   for what was happening, though many went through a grief
   process in letting go of who they had thought their child to be;

❖ Every parent eventually realized the nature of the problem,
   whether through reading an article, finding something on-line,
   or meeting someone who was able to explain it to them;

❖ Every parent subsequently advocated for their child every step
   of the way, to enable them to live as their true selves in all
   arenas of life;

❖ Every parent drew a line in the sand amongst family and
   friends: if you do not support us in this you will not be part of
   our lives. The parents placed the life and well-being of their
   child before all other relationships, and before their own
   comfort level. (I don't know what would have happened if the
   relationship in question had been a trans child's sibling, but as
   long as the parents are sensitive to the fact that their other
   children have their own paths and needs, and set a tone of
   respect, love and acceptance, siblings will probably become
   allies. Such has been the case in all the families mentioned in
   this chapter.)

School disclosure processes are similar to workplace disclo-sures.
I advise adult clients to read the materials presented on the Human
Rights Campaign (HRC) website about workplace tran-sitions.
Similarly, I advise parents to contact PFLAG and TYFA. If there is
no local PFLAG chapter, contact the national organization. Consider
starting a PFLAG chapter locally. PFLAG National helps parents
start local chapters if there is none near them.

Those parents who have become advocates for their children find that if the school administration is called to task with the charge of protecting all the children in their care, they have risen to the occasion. Given sufficient accurate information, knowing other schools have handled such situations successfully, schools respond in a manner similar to workplaces: "Oh. Others have done this before and it has not been too disruptive. Perhaps this can work."

Often to their surprise, school administrators find the majority of students responding, "Yeah, what's the big deal? We can see Joey is a boy. We get that." The pushback is more likely to come from a few parents and a few bullies, who will torment other students for any number of reasons other than gender identity. If the admini-stration stands firm, the tone is set for all in the school that intolerance will not be tolerated. Over time, as there are no negative consequences to any student in the school, the transition slowly becomes history.

Dana, Jason and Sam all had a loyal circle of friends who were protective of them. Dana said, "I was hardly ever alone at school. There were a few bullies that lots of kids had problems with for one reason or another. But I never did because my friends took care of me. We were a pack, and I felt so supported. I was given a key to a teacher's bathroom to use when I was in high school. One time I was hanging back in the hall when my friends all trooped into the girls' bathroom. None of our guy friends were with us at the time. The last girl into the bathroom looked back at me and said, 'Oh come *on*," and literally dragged me into the bathroom. That was the last time I used that teacher's bathroom."

A NEW PHENOMENON?

During my career as a therapist I worked with over 450 adults, most of them trans in one way or another. However I've only had about a dozen families approach me, either knowing they have a trans child or wondering if that might be the case. Coupled with recent mainstream coverage of the concept of childhood transition, this makes it appear as if childhood trans identity is a new phenomenon.

However an examination of my clinical records showed me that about 40% of my clients (MTF and FTM alike) knew from a very early age, usually pre-school, that they were boys and not girls or vice versa. Most of the others knew they were somehow different, but did not understand what it meant. Many of my older clients lament that childhood transition wasn't available to them while simultaneously feeling happy for those who can transition in elementary school now. I believe that a few generations from now the concept of a 40-year-old transitioning will be relatively rare – they will have already done it long since.

To many, the idea that people have gender identities set in stone at early ages is not new; however the phenomenon of children being allowed to transition socially in elementary school *is* new, and uncharted territory in many parts of this country. Thus it is all the more important for parents to contact organizations such as TYFA and PFLAG as they consider how to best support their children and themselves.

As is true for adult trans people coming to terms with their identity, families have various stages of coming to terms with having a trans child. Often the child is clear about who they are and can't understand (a) what the big deal is, or (b) why everyone else can't see it, too. (Bartlett et al, 2000; Lev, 2004; Dykstra, 2005; Brill, 2008; Krieger, 2011) This is particularly true for those child-ren who aren't yet in school, exposed to other children who are growing up with quite different views of gender and gender roles than their family might have.

Families have issues that diverge from those of trans adults. Unlike a trans adult, it is not the trans child who is calling the therapist for an appointment on their own behalf – their parents are making the phone call. And unlike a trans adult, it is the parent who is put in the position of making decisions on behalf of their child, based on their child's identity. It is the parent who will have to be proactive with doctors, mental health professionals, and school administra-tors, on behalf of their child. This can be a scary proposition for parents, given how few role models exist to point the way.

Because I am trans myself and publicly denounce reparative therapy, no parent approached me if their goal was to change their child's identity or if they were viewing the issue as one of bad behavior. The families who came to see me accepted the idea their child might be trans, though they were uncertain what it might mean or whether they could support a public transition at an early age.

A knowledgeable therapist can be an invaluable resource as the family proceeds with transition. But this can be as scary for a therapist as it is for the parents! Given how few families have undergone this journey, it follows that few therapists have the requisite experience to consider themselves adequate as a guide along the way. Let's examine more closely what the therapist's role might be in supporting a family with a trans child, as the journey is a bit dif-ferent than that of the adult trans client.

THE THERAPIST'S FIRST TASK: FAMILY ASSESSMENT

The first step in working with families seeking services on behalf of a trans child is to assess the family structure for dysfunc-tionality. There may be various dysfunctional patterns on the part of the parents that could cause a child to behave in a manner that appears to be trans (Zucker, 2000; Hill et al, 2005). Narcissistic desires on the part of the parents for a boy and not a girl, or vice versa, could cause the child to behave in a manner consistent with the parents' desired gender, in a desperate attempt to win the parents' approval. Or a child who has been sexually abused over a period of time may actualize a different gender identity, in a vain attempt to become someone else in order to escape the abuse.

Assessment of the family structure is thus an essential initial focus for the therapist. Because it is the parents who are seeking help, one of the therapist's first tasks is to determine if a family dynamic is driving the identity issue. Or are the parents hurrying a social transition along to get it over with, when the child may not be so sure?

This might reflect parental discomfort with the idea of middle-ground gender identities, or a desire to get out of the limelight as quickly as possible by hurrying the transition.

In cases of extreme family dysfunctionality the family may have come to the attention of Child Protective Services (CPS) through a mandated reporter such as a teacher or guidance counselor. It may be a CPS caseworker seeking help on the child's behalf, having noted what appears to be a gender identity issue and desiring an expert opinion. In such cases the therapist mustn't conclude too quickly that family dysfunctionality has caused gender-related behavior in the child and dismiss the possibility of trans identity. It is possible the child is trans and the parents or other family members have reacted abusively toward the child as a result.

Such cases are made more difficult by the fact that within a dysfunctional family system, the parents' assessment of the child cannot be trusted to reflect the child's reality; it would be in the child's best interest that the therapist talk to others who are prominent in the child's life (teachers, perhaps other relatives). This allows the therapist to gain a more holistic view of the child's sense of self in real-world settings removed from the somewhat-rarified atmosphere of the therapist's office.

If the therapist concludes that the family has some form of dys-functionality that may be affecting interpretation of the child's identity, it would be in the best interest of the child to involve a child therapist to help the child find their own sense of self. The therapist can then work with the parents separately to help decon-struct and dismantle the dysfunctionality, to the degree possible.

In addition to assessing the family structure, a therapist should also assess the child for various conditions that may appear similar to a gender identity issue, such as autism. As Atwood points out, "Some children with Asperger's syndrome dislike who they are and would like to be someone other than themselves, someone who would be socially able and have friends. A boy with Asperger's syndrome may... recognize that girls and women... are naturally socially

362

intuitive; so to acquire social abilities he starts to imitate girls."
(Atwood, 2007)

Current estimates of the prevalence of the autism spectrum
conclude that 1 in 250 children fall somewhere on the spectrum
(Atwood, 2007). Accurate statistics are difficult to come by, but
estimates of numbers of trans people fall far short of 1 in 250, no
matter which statistics one examines. Estimates of the prevalence of
trans identity range from 1 in 9,000 to 1 in 100,000, several orders of
magnitude removed from 1 in 250 (Lev, 2004). Thus it is im-portant
to eliminate the possibility of a more-prevalent condition.

It is also possible a person may be autistic *and* be trans. A number of my clients were in this situation, some not discovering they
were on the autism spectrum until they began transition. Ned (28) had
always thought his extreme social anxiety and difficulty relating to
people was solely due to his need to transition. When his feelings of
being a 'social misfit' (his words) intensified post-transition, he was
mystified until he read several accounts written by people who are on
the autism spectrum. He found Dawn Prince-Hughes' book *Songs of
the Gorilla Nation* particularly helpful.

Ned had an "Aha!" moment and has since read all he could find
about autism. He is now much more forgiving of himself for what he
calls his social awkwardness. He also views his family in a new light,
recognizing probable undiagnosed autism in his long-de-ceased
father.

WORKING WITH FUNCTIONAL FAMILIES

If the family assessment doesn't lead to any conclusion of dysfunctionality or abuse, and an assessment of the child doesn't lead to
alternate possibilities such as autism, the next step is to focus on both
the child's self-assessment and the parents' anecdotal history of their
experience of their child. The therapist can only view the child in
session, a snapshot in time, outside the child's everyday milieu. The
parents are in a much better position to observe the child's behavior,
and self-descriptive language, over time. One of the hallmarks of

gender identity is its stability over time and across situation, thus the parents' input is crucial. This is one reason families must be assessed first for any form of dysfunctionality that might affect the parents' interpretation of reality.

Families are more the expert on their child's experience of identity than the therapist can hope to be. A therapeutic approach consistent with this clinical philosophy will be most helpful to the parents, and least harmful to the child in question (Anderson, 1992). Absent serious family dysfunctionality, what is the therapist's role in helping families with trans children if their desire is for identity actualization? If there is no family issue requiring therapy, and if the issue is indeed one of emerging identity, is there a role for a therapist? Families in this situation need the following:

❖ *Information about trans identities of various kinds, the distinction between sexuality and gender identity, etc.* This is not an issue that is private to the therapist/client relationship, as is the case with issues such as adults dealing with residual effects of abuse at the hands of a now-deceased perpetrator, for example. Trans identity is a real-world, whole-life issue that the therapist can only glimpse during a session. Thus it is incumbent on the therapist to seek out trans people in their community, and read the existing literature (both professional literature and the personal accounts of trans people).

In addition to accurate information about terminology the parents may have heard, such as transsexual, the therapist should also introduce the parents to terms and definitions unfamiliar to them, such as the concept of genderqueer or non-binary identities. While there is space for such identities in some cultures, mainstream American culture is not one of them and the parents may be completely at sea when confronted with such a declaration from their child (Nanda, 1990, 2000; Williams, 1992; Herdt, 1994; Kuklin, 2015; Nult, 2015).

❖ *Information about the physical realities of transition.* In conjunction with learning about living a trans identity, the therapist will face questions from the family such as, "Should we start hormones at the beginning of puberty?" or "Does our child have to have surgery?" It is a good idea for the therapist to consult with a knowledgeable physician (this can be done via the Internet if there is no local doctor with expertise) in order to understand the intricacies of childhood or teenage transition. Though it is outside the scope of the therapist's expertise to offer medical advice, it is helpful to the client that the therapist has a good working know-ledge of the effects of cross-gender hormones as well as those medi-cations available to block the onset of puberty.

❖ *Psychoeducation about the cultural nature of gender.* Looking at other cultures' perspectives can help parents understand that their own attitudes about gender roles, norms, etc. are cultural in origin and are not fixed reality. There are other situations therapists may be more familiar with that provide useful analogies when concept-ualizing how to work with trans families. A child born into a multi-racial, multi-ethnic, or multi-religious family will mature in a man-ner that incorporates elements of the various backgrounds of other family members (Newman, 2002). Children meld these various backgrounds into a cohesive worldview that makes sense to them, but that is unlike the individual backgrounds of their parents. Just so, a trans child will develop a gender lens that does not match either 'male' or 'female' as other family members experience those gender identities. A trans child will experience a cultural identity similar to their siblings, but their experience of gender will not match that of their siblings.

❖ *Psychoeducation about the ramifications of disclosure.* Those families who do not have experience being in a minority position culturally may need help navigating the emotions that arise when they experience discrimination or other negative reactions to trans identity. Discussions should focus on safety, privacy, and how to maintain the child's self-esteem in the face of hostility or teasing from peers. Discussions can also focus on the nature of gender identity, gender roles, and gender expression. If a parent is challenged by others about their child's identity, it is helpful if they have already thought deeply about the various issues involved, developing their own language and cognitive understanding of trans identity with which to defend their position.

Discussions can also focus on how much gender expression is appropriate or safe for a trans child in various common life situations, especially if their gender identity or expression challenges the gender norms prevalent in their community. Does the family live in an area where the child would be at risk if they dress as their true selves outside the home? Does the family belong to a church or other social institution such that the entire family will be ostracized completely if the child actualizes their identity outside the home? Are certain common situations safe while others are not? Individual family circumstances vary widely, such that there is no right or wrong answer to any such question, but in all cases such circumstances should be addressed.

❖ *Introductions to other families.* These families may feel they are alone in their experience. While they may find other families on the Internet, living in other parts of the country, it is in the best interest of the parents that they meet other families in their region who are experiencing similar issues (Zamboni, 2006; Nult, 2015). If the therapist is working with more than one such family, it is a good idea to introduce them to each other unless there is an underlying clinical reason why such introductions would be counterproductive.

With mutual permission I facilitated introductions between the families I worked with. In some cases this resulted in close friendships between the parents. In other cases, while friendships have not resulted the families have nonetheless been comforted with the knowledge they are not alone.

In no case did a family refuse the opportunity for introduction to other families. Quite the contrary, they were eager for the opportunity. Among my clients the parents benefitted greatly from such introductions, though the trans children did not. In these particular cases the children were not the same age or gender, had little in common beyond their gender dissonance, and thus did not form close friendships with each other.

❖ *Possible advocacy within the child's school setting.* Pre-pubescent children don't need hormone therapy but can benefit greatly from being allowed to actualize their gender identity (Dykstra, 2005; Brill, 2008). For those trans children whose gender is clearly male or female, at odds with how their bodies appear, this advocacy can result in allowing the child to attend school as their true gender. To date the schools I've worked with (or heard about via e-mail ac-counts) have allowed such social transitions successfully with little pushback from other students, though initially some administrators or parents were resistant to the idea.

Some children, however, are gender-independent in some way, not feeling their gender is reflected by the binary choices of male or female. As some adults do, they may adopt language such as genderqueer or non-binary. Such children can best be aided by allowing them as full gender expression as possible, though this can be difficult for school administrators to accept if a child's chosen gender expression is not clearly male or female as the admini-strators define those roles. It may be that the family, with input from the child, will be forced to choose male or female. In this situation part of the therapist's job will be to help the family sustain the child's self-esteem in the face of not being able to actualize their true gender at school.

Acknowledging the unfairness of the situation, reinforcing for the child that the most important people in their lives do understand who they really are, will help the child retain a positive sense of self that will stand them in good stead as they mature. In addition, providing school administrators with accurate information about trans identities can go a long way toward helping the child by making allies of those in positions of power within the school.

Acceptance is a top-down attitude and if the school administration sets a tone of not tolerating intolerance, the child's experience at school can retain the focus it should – on learning and social development. Too often the trans child is blamed for others' hostility and the child is then perceived as having difficulty with peer relationships (Brill, 2008; Kuklin, 2015; Nult, 2015). School administrators who approach the issue as one of safety for all concerned, with a zero-tolerance policy toward bullying or discrimination for any reason, will find social transition all the smoother at their schools.

It is important to note that children who are perceived to be gender-dissonant (particularly those who are male-assigned at birth) are at higher risk for verbal or physical abuse by peers, thus necessitating support from administrators to send a zero-tolerance message regarding abusive or bullying behavior (Pilkington, 1995; Remafedi, 1987; Bartlett et al, 2000). The professional literature in this realm has primarily studied the experiences of gay or lesbian adolescents. However it can be inferred logically that the adolescent who is most at risk for abuse has an appearance that causes others to perceive them as lesbian or gay, when in fact the adolescent may be trans and expressing their gender accordingly. Most often it is gender expression that leads to bullying, rather than actual knowledge of sexual orientation; the masculine gay or feminine lesbian ad-olescent may experience less bullying than the gay boy who doesn't 'do male right,' or the lesbian who is masculine in appearance or mannerisms.

Unfortunately the current lack of support within educational or social welfare institutions for trans identities does not allow parents much leverage with which to pressure administrators to accept their children for who they are (Chen-Hayes, 2001; Mallon, 2006). This is particularly true in areas of the country with many supporters of President Trump. Thus accessing organizations such as TYFA and

368

PFLAG is all the more crucial for such parents, as such groups have information about successful social transitions that have taken place in various parts of the country.

Bringing in any available local resources can also have a powerful impact on school administrators in conservative school districts, who may feel social transitions are possible in progressive areas but not in a conservative region. Of the families I worked with, roughly half lived in urban areas; the rest lived in conservative towns or suburbs. The non-urban families I worked with were able to negotiate a successful social transition and didn't feel they had to move to a large city in order to facilitate a transition for one of their children, though they also felt they needed to maintain strong vigilence.

❖ *Helping families develop appropriate support structures.* The GSA/QSA model (Gay/Straight or Queer/Straight Alliance) is useful for high school or college students, whose developmental needs include social groups that allow them to form alliances and friendships beyond the bounds of their families of origin (Bilodeau, 2005). Younger children transitioning socially are more tied to their families of origin; consideration of support structures must take into account this developmental difference. As an example, one mother took it upon herself to organize a periodic Skate Night at a local roller skating rink her husband manages. Families with trans child-ren were invited to a private event on a night when the rink was ordinarily closed. This kind of all-family event is appropriate for the developmental level of a pre-pubescent child.

❖ *Rethinking confidentiality.* When working with families with trans children, therapists must reconsider the ramifications of confidentiality. Maintaining the strict confidentiality normally inherent within the therapy profession helps reinforce a model of secrecy that may be detrimental to the family. Secrecy about identity may be a precursor of shame and the legacy of the 'family secret' (Kaufman and Raphael, 1996). Introducing families to each other may seem a violation of confidentiality but it can also be a powerful clinical intervention, allowing families to get used to discussing the issues openly with others who already understand what they are going through. This practice will give family members an oppor-tunity to develop more fully their own cognitive understanding of trans identity, which will be helpful when they later encounter less-supportive reactions.

❖ *Information about support groups and organizations.* In all cases the families I work with have benefitted from being intro-duced to the local PFLAG chapter and various other peer support groups as available (Griffiths, 2002). On a national level TYFA provides resources to help families transition within their com-munity, providing advocacy within schools. If there are other local or regional resources available, it is a good idea for therapists to keep abreast of such resources in order to make them available to families. Having a resource table in the office and a list of available resources on a website are invaluable tools for helping families.

❖ *Names of other service providers.* Parents need other providers as well and it is helpful that the therapist have business cards or a resource list of some kind available: pediatricians or pediatric endocrinologists, attorneys knowledgeable about trans issues, child therapists and/or psychologists, and other therapists for family members to consult. In more-conservative areas, the therapist might feel entirely alone. However it's worth considering: "If I'm sup-portive, maybe there are others around here who would be also." The therapist may need to do some outreach and help cultivate the support network.

❖ *A forum in which to process the various emotional reactions family members will have to shifting their gendered perceptions of the child.* This is the most traditionally-therapeutic role the therapist will find themselves undertaking in supporting a basically-healthy family with a trans child. While a mother may be able to recognize that her daughter feels like a boy and may support her male-affirmed child, she will also grieve the loss of her daughter. She will probably not feel it appropriate to show such feelings to her child, not wanting to cause any feelings of guilt or shame, but she needs a place to process her own quite-valid emotional responses. While fathers and mothers may process such emotions differently, it is important that the therapist make space for both to express whatever feelings are arising in them around having a trans child (Zamboni, 2006).

Other children in the family system need a place to talk about their feelings. Do they feel ignored or that their problems are unimportant in comparison with transition? Are they being bullied or teased at school because of their sibling's trans identity? How do they feel about losing a brother, or sister? The older the sibling at the time of transition, the more this last question might be an issue for them.

As is true with adults who transition, letting go of the old gendered conception is the key to being able to embrace the new. For some parents this involved a slow process of self-examination and questioning social norms and beliefs. One parent expressed feeling guilty after discovering prejudicial feelings she had not known were present in herself; she had thought of herself as an open and affirming person, easily able to accept her children just as they were, and found that having a trans child challenged her self-concept as a non-judgmental parent (Boenke, 1999).

WORKING WITH NON-SUPPORTIVE FAMILIES

If you are a therapist, counselor, or social worker, one of the most heartbreaking situations you may face is that of a probable trans child in the midst of a family that does not support their identity. In some cases you may find psychoeducation helps over-come parental resistance to identity exploration. I worked with a number of families in which one parent was initially opposed to considering the possibility of trans identity among their children. In some cases the oppositional parent changed their mind, sometimes to the point of active acceptance, upon meeting other families with trans children. The opposition had been rooted in misperceptions of what 'trans' meant. However the parent had also observed how unhappy their child was; after hearing stories of night-and-day transformations of other children from suicidal depression to delight with life, some of the oppositional parents I worked with softened their positions.

Several parents, however, did not move from their original opposition. In some cases conservative religion was a major factor; the parent gave no credence to advice or counseling from anyone other than the minister of their church. In other cases the opposition was rooted in the self-centered reaction, "What will the neighbors think?" In several cases this divergence of acceptance on the part of the parents ended in divorce. The supportive parent drew that same line in the sand I mentioned earlier, "If you don't support us in this, you won't be part of our lives." In this case, the 'us' in question was the trans child and the supportive parent.

If you are a therapist in such a situation, your interventions and treatment plan will depend on who your client is: is your client the trans child, the supportive parent, the unsupportive parent, the parents as a couple, or the entire family system? Your job is to be part of a support system for your client and how you provide that support will depend in large part on who your client is.

If you personally favor youth transition on an as-needed basis, you may have a strong negative reaction to working with a parent who automatically opposes any idea of transition for their child. However, if you can view your role as one of helping your client – the oppositional parent – clarify and work through their feelings about the situation (pain, distress, anger, frustration), you will have done your job regardless of the differences between your viewpoints. In some cases you may feel so strongly about the issue that you feel it would be in the client's best interest that they work with a different therapist.

In all cases, your job is to facilitate process and provide support and psychoeducation as feels appropriate. If your client is the trans child, the support you provide will be similar to what you would provide in various other unsupportive family situations: supporting a child who is a genius in a family that would prefer conformity; supporting a child growing up in a family of addicts. The commonality in all such situations is to support the child in who they know themselves to be and help them develop the inner strength and tools to cope with living in an unsupportive family environment.

You may find yourself working with trans children in situations that seem hopeless; it may be that they won't be able to transition within their family. But you can help them survive to an age at which they can then transition on their own, looking back on you as the counselor that gave them the strength to hope for the future while surviving the present.

NON-BINARY IDENTITIES

In some cases the child may not identify as male or female, but as some form of non-binary identity the child may not have lan-guage to describe. Such identities will probably challenge the parents' view of reality. One parent remarked in session, "If you'd told me a year ago that there were gender identities beyond 'male' and 'female,' I would have said, 'That's like saying the sun rises in the west.'" *(Client session, 2006)* Some of these children may identify as male or female later, some may not. I helped parents develop patience with ambiguity and fluidity, allowing their child-ren to 'be' and unfold in their own time.

What I have observed is that when they are accepted and al-lowed to behave in accordance with their internal gender identity, the children themselves may not need therapy at all. They are usual-ly content and mystified as to why everyone else is having trouble with their identity (Bartlett et al, 2000; Lev, 2004; Dykstra, 2005; Brill, 2008; Kuklin, 2015).

One of the reasons these children are content is because they are receiving support for their identity from their parents. A consistent theme among many of my adult clients is that those who tried to tell a parent or teacher who they really were, learned young that this was not acceptable 'behavior.' This message, usually delivered quite consistently, led many of my clients to internalize a great deal of shame and guilt over their core identities, feelings that are difficult to dismantle as adults.

• Chapter 18 •

In the Best Interest of the Children

MANY OF MY TRANS CLIENTS WERE PARENTS. They tried to cure themselves via marriage and having children at earlier times in their lives. Upon realizing the cure didn't work, my clients eventually realized some form of transition was in their future. There are a number of variables to consider in disclosing transition to a child, but the short answer is that children are not harmed if the disclosure is handled appropriately and with the specific child in mind. Such information certainly will not change the child's innate identity.

As with any major life transformative event it is not a good idea to lie to the child. When the issue under consideration is controversial one has to imagine the impact on the child if this is treated as a family secret. The message the child will internalize is some form of, "This is a bad and shameful thing." While some people in the family probably believe exactly this, it is not in the child's best interest to believe their parent to be bad or shameful.

Regardless of other adults' beliefs, it is better for the child to be told some variation of the truth without moralizing on the part of the adults in the child's life. This is particularly true in the case of pre-adolescent children, who have probably not attained the capability of critical, abstract logic. (Davies, 2004) Pre-adolescent children may not be able to discern for themselves that adults have their own agendas that may be colored by their own pain or feelings of betrayal. As in the case of divorce, using the child as a pawn to play out anger at the trans person is not in the child's best interest.

The most important consideration is the child's developmental age. A child who is a baby at the time of parental transition is not going to remember their parent's previous gender role, but will need to be told at some point about the transition as a historical fact. Otherwise it is probable the child will find out at a later time, perhaps accidentally, through transmission of family history. If the child finds out about a parental transition through secondary sour-ces, this is likely to lead to feelings of betrayal, anger, shattered trust, confusion, etc. This scenario is unlikely to have any positive component to it.

COLAGE is an organization providing support for children with GLB and/or T parents. Their mission is: "COLAGE unites people with lesbian, gay, bisexual, transgender, and/or queer parents into a network of peers and supports them as they nurture and empower each other to be skills, self-confident, and just leaders in our collective communities." COLAGE provides support to the children of LGBTQ parents, while PFLAG provides support to parents and other family members of those who are LGBTQ.

DISCLOSURE TO PRE-ADOLESCENT CHILDREN

Pre-adolescent children are not yet conscious of sex as a driving force. They are curious about bodies and already have a sense of their own gender identity, but it is not until puberty that sex assumes an urgency out of proportion to its place in everyday life. Because their gender identity has long-since emerged and sex differences are still in the realm of curiosity, it is not going to impact a pre-pubescent child's own sense of identity to find out daddy is becom-ing a woman, or that mommy has always felt like a man inside and is going to become male on the outside. If they do ask whether this means they will grow up to be a different gender themselves, most will be reassured by the explanation that if they already know themselves to be a boy or girl, that's not going to change.

The exception to this is the gender-dissonant child. Since one can't rule out gender dissonance as a possibility, it may be a good idea to explore the child's gender identity with them in a matter-of-fact way. Children can understand an explanation along the lines of, "Some people when they're born are told they are boys, or girls, but it might not be how they feel inside. They might feel like they were supposed to be boys instead of girls, or girls instead of boys. There is nothing wrong with this; this is what mommy (or daddy) has felt like." This type of explanation does not force the child to disclose anything they aren't ready to, but does let them know that their own identities will be accepted when the time comes.

What will impact any child most are questions such as, "Are you going away? Can I still call you 'mommy' (or 'daddy')? Are you getting a divorce? Where are you going to live? Where am I going to live?" Loss of consistency, loss of continuity, loss of love – these are the primary concerns of younger children. (Emery, 2004)

As in a divorce situation (even if the transitioning couple is not divorcing), children need to know: (a) this is not about them, (b) they are still loved and cherished, and (c) they are still going to be part of both parents' lives. If the child sees 'daddy' disappearing and turning into a woman, the child needs reassurance that the per-son they knew as 'daddy' is still there for them, the love is no less than it's always been, and the child can count on this new person to be there in the same capacity – as a loving parent.

Over time, if this message of constancy and love is consistently reinforced the child will probably relax into acceptance as their fears of loss and abandonment are alleviated. (If this does not hap-pen, it may be time for some family therapy, to help the child express whatever feelings they're experiencing about the transition that are preventing them from fully accepting the situation.)

KEEP THE DOOR OPEN

Another important aspect to disclosure is keeping the door open for questions and discussion. Once word gets out that a parent has transitioned the child may hear gossip and unkind remarks about the parent. It is helpful if the parent overtly says to the child, "People might say things you don't understand, or that seem wrong or hurt-ful. There's nothing wrong with me, or with you, but a lot of people just don't know what they're talking about and might say things.

Let's talk about those things because I want to help you if you're hurt by what they say." It may help to reiterate this sentiment in various ways as time passes; the child may be reluctant to repeat the most hurtful remarks they hear, for fear of hurting or angering the parent.

Children often experience varying degrees of anger at the transitioning parent for the considerable upheaval transition inevitably causes. Allowing this anger space to exist, normalizing it, can go a long way toward keeping the communication lines open. As is true for any other family member children will experience a range of emotions related to transition and need the overt support of their parents or caregivers to express such feelings.

Olivia's 8-year-old son Owen was angry when told his father was going to become a woman. He would not talk about his feel-ings, though Olivia and her wife Anne tried to explain they were not divorcing, not moving, and nothing else about their life as a family was going to change. Baffled, Olivia finally decided to allow Owen the space to express his feelings when he was ready.

All became clear one Saturday when Olivia asked Owen if he'd like to go to a baseball game. Owen's face lit up and he said, "You mean we can still do that?" He had thought Olivia would no longer do 'boy things' with him, and this was the source of his anger. His mother Anne had no interest in sports, and Owen had internalized the belief that it just wasn't a 'girl thing.' Once Olivia reassured Owen that they could still play catch, go to games, and fish toge-ther, Owen was fine with the idea of having two moms. He came up with the idea of calling Olivia "Momtoo," to differentiate between his two mothers.

Many children grow up experiencing discrimination of one sort or another. Race, religion, class background, ethnicity, sexual orientation – if the child's experience (either personally or vicariously, through a family member) places them in any minority position, they are likely to be teased or bullied to varying degrees throughout their childhood.

At younger ages children don't have a large enough worldview to understand history and the transmission of misinformation and prejudice through generations. They will take things personally that are in no way personal to them, or their family. All parents can do at younger developmental ages is reassure the child, "It's not you, it's not me. Some people just don't understand. As long as we love each other, we'll get through."

As the child matures the parent can provide more historical education, placing discrimination in a cultural context. It is impossible to specify chronological ages at which particular forms of informa-tion are appropriate or not. Children develop at different rates and even in the same family, one child may be ready for the larger-culture perspective at 9 while a sibling may not be ready for that level of discourse at 11.

DISCLOSURE TO ADOLESCENTS

Adolescence, bridging childhood and adulthood, is a maëlstrom of shifting hormone balances and abrupt physical changes that can wreak havoc with self-esteem, self-in-relation, and social poise. Some adolescents weather the storm more easily than others, particularly if their home life is relatively stable and they are living with boundaries appropriate to their developmental age. (Rice, 2001) Regardless of how appropriately parents behave, there is no doubt adolescence is a time period usually remembered in later life with relief that it is over.

The adolescent is often self-conscious and may feel others have more awareness of them and their behavior than is the case. Some adults speak of adolescents in a disparaging manner, saying, "They think everything is about them, and the world exists for their pleasure and convenience." I think this attitude attributes too much agency and deliberateness to the adolescent. I believe adolescent self-consciousness makes it difficult for an adolescent to know that not everyone *is* paying as much attention to them as they are themselves.

The adolescent world isn't as large as the world of the adults around them; as far as the adolescent is concerned their school and family life *is* as big as the world gets. One client described the difference: "I was away at college and then in the military, and when I did visit I was busy with family things. I was about 30 when I came home for one visit and took a walk, revisiting old hangouts. I was shocked when I went to a part of town I associated with going to church with my grandparents, and realized my high school was just over a hill. It wasn't geographically far away, but somehow I never made that connection when I was a kid or even when I was in high school. The city seemed bigger to me than when I was a kid and yet it was all connected in a way it never had been before." *(Client session, 2007)*

There are many parallels to be drawn between adolescence and early physical transition, beyond the obvious physical effects of hormones bringing about a feeling of second puberty for the transitioning individual. As with early stages of transition, adolescence is an unavoidably self-centered process of self-knowledge. As puberty brings about major hormonal upheaval in the individual's system, sexuality emerges and with it new possibilities of relationship that were not present at earlier times in life. The same questions posed by the transitioning individual are at the forefront for the adolescent: "What are the boundaries now in relationship? What kind of man (or woman) am I becoming? What are the options open to me re gender roles?"

Imagine the effect on the adolescent, in the midst of this sort of existential process, to learn one of their parents is going through a similar process. The self-centeredness of transition and the degree to which others focus on the trans person can leave adolescents feeling affronted and as if they are unimportant. They also are going through a transition, from childhood to adulthood. They also are undertaking a self-centered process. However the self-centered nature of adolescence isn't apparent to the adolescent themselves, while the transitioning parent *can* recognize that their transition process is self-centered in nature. The parental figures can help by not allowing the self-centered nature of transition to take over and become the entire family focus.

There is a fine line here (or perhaps not so fine, but a broad gray area) between supporting the adolescent and giving up one's identity in order to try to keep the adolescent happy. Each family finds this balance in its own way. The most important component is the need for communication and mutual respect. Adolescence is a maturation process, often in a milieu of harsh judgmentalism by peers. Transition is a revisitation of core identity after a lifetime of invisibility and inappropriate socialization. Neither is an easy pro-cess to navigate, and all involved need to understand it isn't easy for any of them.

Adolescents value straightforward honesty. They are not children any longer, and have developed the capacity for abstract thinking and considering the feelings of others as separate beings from themselves. (Rice, 2001) The primary concern in disclosing to adolescents is to explain the nature of the process, as the transitioning parent understands it, and to be sure to reinforce that the parent's identity does not reflect on the adolescent's emerging sexual identity. Psychoeducational work about trans identity will also be necessary, as the adolescent is not going to understand on their own precisely what it means to be trans. Information shared amongst their friends and on the Internet may be somewhat vague and lacking in accuracy.

While the adolescent brain is fully capable of abstract logic and understanding the concepts of emerging identity, the familial relationship and homeostasis is still deeply affected by a possible transition. As with younger children, reassurance of stability and continuity can go a long way toward reconciling the adolescent to-ward the idea of a parent transitioning. The adolescent may be able to understand the nature of transition as an adult would, but they still need reassurance in the midst of an existential upheaval to the family system when the transition involves a parent. They need the explanation given adults *and* the reassurance given children, as they are in a bridge period in their own lives, not yet independent adults but not fully-dependent children.

DEVELOPING A WORLDVIEW

Adolescence is also a time of coming to understand social issues on a broader scale than is possible for younger children. Adole-scents begin to form a worldview at this point in their lives, adopting political opinions and taking stances on various issues. These views are often polarized, with black and white, right or wrong judgments the norm. (Rice, 2001) Some adolescents may see the social discrimination against trans individuals as a civil rights issue and be appalled at the pariah status of trans people in U.S. cul-ture. Others may continue to see gender as polarized; the black and white thinking that characterizes adolescence dovetails unfor-tunately well with the gender binary concept. I have known several families in which adolescents withdrew from a transitioning parent on this basis, only to come around later in their lives, when their worldviews had evolved beyond the black and white of ado-lescence.

Adolescence is also a time of life when the need for peer acceptance and approval is at its highest. It is important the parent reassure the adolescent that as much as possible, it is the adole-scent's choice whether or not to tell their friends and teachers about the parent's transition and that the parent will do what they can to ease the adolescent's way among their peers. The school milieu belongs to the adolescent, and the transitioning parent can help their adolescent children weather transition by keeping their distance from the school setting.

Patrice began transition in 2003 as her daughter Angela entered adolescence; she was about to start middle school. Patrice made it clear to Angela that middle school was her territory and that it was up to Angela whether she disclosed having a trans parent. Patrice's wife Charlene attended school functions alone, though the family decided this might change once Patrice was confident of being seen female in all situations. Angela had no qualms about having lesbian parents, as this would give her status among her peers, given where the family lived. She wasn't so sure having a trans parent would do the same.

Angela told her classmates about Patrice's transition midway through her second year in middle school, at age 14. She had learned that one of her classmates was transitioning socially. She reached out to her classmate and told him that one of her two mothers used to be her dad and that it would all be okay. Patrice wrote: "I was so proud of her! She didn't tell us beforehand, she just did it! She even told Jason that she would go with him to the princi-pal if he wanted her to. Of course his parents were handling all that already, but I thought it was a brave thing for her to do." *(E-mail correspondence, 2005)*

As I prepared this third edition, Patrice told me that Angela, now 24 and in graduate school, wanted to send me an e-mail of her own. Angela wrote me: "The main thing I want kids to know is, it really can be okay. It helps if you get to see some other transgender people. One thing that helped me a lot, I went to the *Rocky Horror Picture Show* with a group of friends and seeing all the different people who showed up for that, how they were all dressed, made it all seem kind of cool. I remember thinking, 'My dad is this cool, too!' My friends and I thought we were cool, but some of those outfits, my mom would have killed me if I dressed like that even in my room! OMG!

"I don't think I even told my parents about this part of the evening, one of them thought they could shock us and said something about what was it like for us to be around trannies. I loved being able to say, 'My dad is a tranny, too!' That got us a LOT of points! Some of my friends didn't know yet, but they were cool with it. If they weren't, they wouldn't have been at *Rocky Horror!* So then when Jason told us all a couple of days later that he was tran-sitioning, it was easy for me to step up and be there for him." *(E-mail correspondence, 2016)*

DISCLOSURE TO ADULT CHILDREN

Many of my clients transitioned midlife, having waited until their children were grown. They had waited not only to transition but to disclose their gender dissonance. More of my older MTF clients are parents than my older FTM clients, who often took refuge in the lesbian community. In addition to this difference, bodily sex differences play a role here as well – the male-bodied individual who fathers a child has a very different relationship to the developing fetus and baby than the female-bodied individual who moves through the world pregnant for nine months. Many of my FTM clients would cringe at the thought of having undergone that experience, at any time of their lives.[38] Those who are parents are glad now that they have their children but have also said that with the consciousness they now have of their gender identity, they would never be able to repeat the experience of being pregnant.

Unfortunately a number of my MTF clients' adult children had a backlog of resentment toward their father, who was not emotionally present during their childhood and in some cases, self-medicated with a drug to numb their own pain. Their children had no idea (usually) what was going on and internalized the belief, "If I were a better son/daughter, daddy would pay more attention to me, love me, play with me, not feel the need to drink" etc. Once adult, having lived through their entire childhood with a miserable parent, it can be difficult for the adult child to forgive the parent. (Howey, 2004)

It's a tough decision: "Do I wait to transition until my children are fully grown and living independently?" Many people (trans or otherwise) may judge the trans person harshly for transitioning while their children are still underage, feeling, "You had children, now you

---

[38] While there have been a few transmen who bore children after having started physical transition, this is rare. When such cases were publicized, most of my FTM clients shook their heads in bewilderment, not understanding how any transman could undergo pregnancy. I gently pointed out to them that these FTMs must really want a child and that there probably wasn't any other way to accomplish that goal.

have to do what's best for them and put your own needs and desires on hold until they're on their own. It's your duty."

The problem with that logic is that it's a false assumption that remaining one's birth gender is automatically best for the children. What's better for the family in this kind of situation is probably disclosure, not 'toughing it out,' which is a male-kind of solution that just doesn't work. To try to live a false identity does not serve the individual well at all or the people they are emotionally involved with. When an individual is living a false identity, the result is a person who is emotionally dampened down such that they are not fully present in the family system. This emotional unavailability does not serve children well.

If they have never disclosed their trans identity, those who do transition after their children are fully grown may find themselves making amends for quite some time, particularly in establishing a new relationship with their adult children. They may find them-selves faced with a great deal of anger and bitterness. Making amends does not mean apologizing for being trans. It means apo-logizing for not having the means to face owning a trans identity earlier in life. The trans person was doing what they thought was best, given the information available to them at the time. They were not deliberately hurting anyone, but were acting in a manner that seemed the best course of action.

As I outlined in the chapter *The Spectrum of Support,* all the transitioning person can do is provide information and remain open as their family members work through their own issues in order to embrace this new identity. It is difficult to watch an adult child go through this, with no certainty that the child will want a relationship with their parent in a new gender role. As with partners or parents, all the trans person can do is hope for the best while remaining open and available.

COMPROMISE AND HONESTY

Here's an example of a healthy way to handle a tough situation. In 2005 Rhonda told her 14-year-old daughter Connie that she planned to transition MTF at some point in the future. Living in a town of 3,000, Rhonda had no intention of transitioning physically until Connie graduated from high school. Rhonda realized how difficult Connie's high school experience might be were she to transition immediately.

Rhonda had been very unhappy and had realized through her work with me that her unhappiness was directly caused by her need to transition and her frustration at feeling she couldn't. Her bitterness at her situation was negatively affecting her relationship with Connie. The only other person in the household, Connie bore the brunt of Rhonda's moods. They lived on their own, Rhonda's wife having deserted the family many years before.

After much reflection and processing with me, Rhonda disclosed her identity and eventual transition to Connie and they developed a system that worked for them. Connie always called before bringing friends home from school, to give Rhonda time to put on 'Kevin' again. They made mother-daughter forays into neighboring towns. With the directness of adolescence Connie had no qualms about telling Rhonda when she dressed or behaved in a way a 45-year-old woman would not. Rhonda was easily able to be seen female, so being in public with her did not draw undue attention, which might have given Connie pause.

Connie's experience of being in her parent's confidence improved their relationship tremendously. As Rhonda said in one 2006 session, "I was depressed and angry a lot of the time while I was still trying to deny that I was really female. I'm so much more open and emotionally available now." Rhonda was in an ideal situation, as she was able to behave in some fairly feminine ways without drawing much attention in her small town, forced as she was to be mother as well as father to Connie. No one commented when Rhonda showed up (dressed as Kevin, of course) to events typically only attended by mothers.

A parent courageously actualizing an unpopular identity presents a fine example to their children of being true to oneself and standing up for one's beliefs. A parent remaining a stunted, repressed individual does not serve their children well or provide a good example of self-actualization and healthy development. For these reasons, though it seems it would be harder on the children, it is healthier for all concerned if trans parents face their identities honestly and address the question, "How do I want to live my life?" The trans person who owns their own identity, facing it honestly and in an aboveboard manner, has a better chance of maintaining genuine, deeply intimate relationships with family members than if they keep their identity secret.

As is true in Rhonda's case this does not necessarily mean full physical transition right away – there are often valid social or work-related reasons for not transitioning immediately – but honesty about identity can go a long way toward alleviating the stress, guilt, and shame of owning a trans identity. Being honest, showing one's true self to one's family, can also help family members realize (with relief) the reason for the previous emotional unavailability and unhappiness.

I could have rewritten the above section in providing updated information about Rhonda, but I have instead chosen to keep the above paragraphs intact as an example of how transition can progress. About six months after I wrote this section, Rhonda e-mailed me and said the double life of switching back and forth had blurred the lines so that she was having difficulty putting on 'Kevin' again in a convincing manner. She had decided to take the plunge and fully transition in all aspects of her life. She consulted her daughter, who said, "If any of my friends have a problem with it, that's tough. I think you should go for it." I wrote Rhonda a hormone referral letter and gave her some advice about coming out at work.

Rhonda did not experience much resistance at work. Not one to take anything for granted, Rhonda applied for other jobs out of the area, fully disclosing her trans status. With the knowledge that she would be welcomed with open arms at two other workplaces, she approached her Human Resources department. Given how far her gender presentation had shifted, her fellow employees had guessed her to be gay and no one was overly surprised by the news. Because everyone wore the same uniform on the job and single-stall bathrooms were readily available, Rhonda did not have difficulty with her on-the-job transition.

In 2006, a year into her physical transition, Rhonda accepted a job in a town about 300 miles from where she transitioned. Connie was about to start high school, and she and Rhonda both felt it would be easier if they lived in an area where no one knew about Rhonda's transition. The two moved shortly after school let out for the summer. Though they had not experienced much overt discrimination in their previous situation, both had felt the pressure of the 'fish bowl' of early transition, having no control over this intensely personal information.

In 2010 Rhonda came to see me for a letter to get an orchiec-tomy. She was very happy in her transition, completely invisible as a transwoman and loving having control over her information. She brought Connie (now 18) to the session with her; the two continued to have an excellent relationship, based in mutual trust, humor, and respect.

RELOCATE, OR STAY HOME?

I worked with quite a few families that had relocated to Portland specifically because a parent was transitioning, recognizing transition would be much more difficult in a small town. One client said, "We finally moved to Portland. Months into my transition, when I was living full-time as Stephanie, I'd be walking down the street and guys who'd known me for 30 years would say, 'Hi, Steve' as if nothing was any different." *(Client session, 2005)*

Stephanie's mother was fairly accepting of her new identity, her father somewhat less so. Stephanie had been his only son. She had been doing chores around their farm for years and did not want to move to Portland. She felt obliged to support her parents as they aged and became more dependent on others to help out. She also wanted her children to have the small-town upbringing she and her wife Grace had enjoyed.

But Stephanie gradually realized she could not remain in her small town and expect to find work or acceptance among people who referred to her as Steve, ignoring her stunning transformation. She also feared the experience her children might have in school, among the children of those who still referred to her as Steve.

Stephanie and her family have now lived in Portland for seven years. Their children are seen at school as having lesbian parents, which is fine with them; they have not experienced any discrimination on that basis. The family as a whole rarely visits their hometown any longer, preferring that supportive family mem-bers visit them in Portland. Stephanie returns once a month, to help her parents. She is still referred to as Steve by others in the com-munity. She typically goes alone, not wanting her family subjected to such treatment.

Her mother has a philosophical attitude, wishing she saw more of Stephanie and at the same time not wanting Stephanie to expe-rience being called Steve. Her mother's circle of friends has changed somewhat, as she won't have anything to do with anyone who won't accept Stephanie. Her father is a stoic farmer and has never talked much but when he does refer to Stephanie, he uses cor-rect language. Stephanie terms this "remarkable support" and more than she'd expected from her father.

Though finding it difficult to transition in smaller communities, many of my clients didn't want to move to a big city, preferring a less urban lifestyle. Some transitioned and then moved to a different small community, preserving their privacy while allowing them to live as they wanted to. A few transitioned in smaller communities and found they could remain without difficulty, in large part be-cause the towns in which they lived were college towns. The populace was more used to various kinds of identities than is typical in small towns.

LESSONS LEARNED

As with keeping partner relationships together, similar factors can help families stay together through transition:

❖ Mutual respect and good communication;
❖ Giving accurate, age-appropriate information to children;
❖ Flexibility and adaptability;
❖ Seeking support outside the relationship and family.

Whether a family is able to stay in the same community or not, the factors that can help keep them together remain the same, and are based in remembering that at the end of the day, it's all about love, compassion and respect for individual identity.

• Chapter 19 •

TRANS IN THE NEW MILLENNIUM

THE MID 2010'S WERE A REMARKABLE FEW YEARS. Chaz Bono. Caitlyn Jenner. A favorable vote for marriage equality by the U.S. Supreme Court. The military announced it would lift its ban on trans service members serving openly. And we have witnessed events that did not make major headlines but nevertheless signified big social changes ahead. The Girl Scouts of America returned a $100,000 donation because it came with an unacceptable string attached: the money could not be used for anything related to trans girls participating.[39] And an event occurred that received no mainstream media coverage but also signified big changes afoot – 2015, its fortieth year, was the last for the Michigan Womyn's Music Festival. Times are changing, and new generations are seeking community in ways that are different from what worked for previous generations.

And in the midst of all this momentum of change toward trans inclusivity – Donald Trump was elected president of the United States. If the course of change seemed unpredictable prior to his election, the uncertainty is ever higher now.

The catalyst for the modern gay and lesbian civil rights movement was a 1969 uprising in Greenwich Village of a people sick and tired of police harassment; though not the first such incident in the United States to provoke a reaction on the part of those being harassed, a police raid on the Stonewall Inn was the last straw. As the years went by after the Stonewall uprising, increasing numbers of gay men and lesbians came out to their friends and families. As people coming out

---

[39] When the returned $100,000 donation was announced, within a few days the Girl Scouts had received over $200,000 in donations specifically meant to replace the lost money.

put a realistic face to the identities 'gay' and 'lesbian,' mainstream media depictions of gay and lesbian characters went through a series of successive approximations toward realism, in part because those gay men and lesbians who worked in the television and movie industries are now open about their identities, enabling them to weigh in on how their communities are depicted.

I felt gay and lesbian identities had reached a point of some legitimacy in popular media when I saw an episode of the television police procedural show *Bones* ("Beautiful Day in the Neighborhood") in which three suburbanites, two straight and one gay, killed an obnoxious neighbor in the heat of the moment and then covered up their deed. The gay identity of one of the killers was neither gratuitous nor relevant to the killing, but was reflective of the fabric of U.S. culture. And when the killers' respective partners found out the truth about the killing they were equally horrified, whether straight or gay.

It has taken nearly fifty years for the gay and lesbian civil rights movement to reach the point it has. And the work is nowhere near done. Shortly after the Supreme Court announced its decision to support marriage equality, several states promptly announced they would not support the decision. One state said it would no longer issue marriage licenses to *anyone,* effectively ducking the issue. Several counties saw their entire court clerk staff resign in protest at having to issue same-sex marriage licenses. One county clerk in Kentucky became something of a martyr to the cause when she forced the issue all the way to the U.S. Supreme Court. (She lost.) Though the momentum toward equality is strong, so is the backlash, reflected most strongly by Donald Trump's election.

The Stonewall Inn was primarily patronized by drag queens and some transwomen; it was they who first fought back in the early hours of June 28, 1969. But the subsequent civil rights movement has largely benefited gay men and lesbians, not trans people. The different trajectory of trans identity development has led – nowhere much, slowly, when compared to the progress made on behalf of gay men and lesbians.

Gay men and lesbians began coming out in order to live in integrity with their core identity, giving them an opportunity to be self-respectful. Those who chose a full physical transition, however, have found that the transition process and resulting invisibility in their true gender has given them the opportunity to live in integrity with their core identity; most have not felt they needed to come out in order to live with self-respect. Undergoing transition gave them self-respect.

For many years the paradigm of transition has been to blend into the mainstream post-transition. If they were gay or lesbian post-transition, trans people blended into their particular community without coming out. If they were straight, they were living mainstream lives, also not coming out. Few remained in the limelight, working on trans issues, once they were well underway with their own transition. It's hard to form a civil rights movement if your people aren't lining up behind you. Though a few cities adopted anti-discrimination policies, other forms of broad-based support remained elusive. Support has been most successful in helping indi-viduals transition at their specific jobs or fight against discri-mination specific to them. Progress at the sociological level has been slow, because of a lack of visibility.

AN INVISIBLE IDENTITY

The nature of living a trans identity is such that visibility is difficult for most who transition physically. I've known Walt, a gay cisman, for years. He and his partner Ned are good friends of mine. Not long ago I had a conversation with Walt about the nature of transition and he surprised me by remarking, "When I met you, I thought you were a rather odd gay man. You met Ned first and he didn't tell me you were trans. I didn't find out for quite awhile, and only because you mentioned it in passing as if I already knew."

Another friend (Barry) said to me recently, "I didn't know you before your transition, so I don't think of you as trans even though I know you are. But it was really hard for me when our mutual friend L. transitioned. I still call him 'her' a lot. I feel bad about it, but it just slips out." Barry is a 60-something cisgender gay man. He has known a number of post-transition individuals and never slips on pronouns for any of us; he did not go through transition with us, and nothing in our gender presentation leads him to slip.

I write about trans issues extensively, teach classes and give lectures on trans identity – even still, no one knows I'm trans unless I tell them. More often, I am seen as a 'rather odd gay man.' My partner happens to be female-assigned and appears cisgender, which many find confusing as it seems to contradict the 'odd gay man' image.

There are two categories of trans people who are visibly identifiable as trans: those who are transitioning in the direction of female and have a hard time being seen as women, and those who are non-binary and make a point of trying to be seen as owning a non-binary gender identity.[40] The former usually wish they could be seen as women. The latter are trying to broaden cultural perceptions beyond the binary of 'male' and 'female' in order that their identities be seen as legitimate. The problem isn't which specific identity anyone claims; the problem is only having room for two gender identities, making unconscious assumptions about various gender identities, and then not believing or respecting people who challenge those assumptions.

Rather than a broad spectrum of trans people coming out and staying out, as happened to gradually propel the gay and lesbian civil rights movement, broader public awareness of trans people has resulted from a few prominent individuals transitioning. Chaz Bono and Caitlyn Jenner embraced the spotlight in their individual ways, realizing that providing carefully-selected interviews would give

---

[40] I did not mention those who are planning to transition physically but haven't started yet, or those who are transitioning physically to male and are early in the process; they are not seen as trans, but rather are misgendered as men or women.

them some control over how their identity was presented to the public.

Though a few prominent people transitioned before Bono and Jenner, most notably Jan Morris in the 1960s and Renée Richards in the 1970s,[41] such transitions happened before Internet-driven information sharing. At that time, access to the media was controlled by a handful of television networks and major newspapers; it was not possible for individuals or groups to disseminate information instantly and widely, as happens routinely today.

After the Stonewall uprising, gay and lesbian communities in major cities began publishing their own newspapers, providing information for and about their communities in ways mainstream media outlets did not. The complete marginalization of any form of acronym-based identity (lesbian, gay, trans, etc.) resulted in mini-mal mainstream coverage of events such as the Stonewall uprising. Or transitions such as that of Jan Morris or Renée Richards. Both published memoirs after they had transitioned, the only means they had of telling their stories in order to accurately convey their journey or inspire others coming along after them.

When a close friend or family member discloses an acronym-based identity, the person hearing the disclosure has the opportunity to rearrange their beliefs about identity, reality, and the meaning of relationship. They have been given the gift of a deeper understanding of someone they are already close to. Hearing of a celebrity transitioning does not have the same effect; it is possible to hear of Chaz Bono or Caitlyn Jenner without the resulting thought, "I know this person well and I *know* they're not crazy, sick, or evil, so maybe what I always thought about this identity is wrong." Only friends and family members of Bono or Jenner have the opportunity for that thought process around their respective transitions.

---

[41] Christine Jorgensen was the first trans person whose transition was widely publicized. Unlike Jan Morris and Renée Richards, however, Jorgensen wasn't a public figure prior to her transition.

People have been transitioning physically since the late 1940s, with the availability of hormones and the development of surgical techniques. The most common goal of transition has been to live as a man or woman, never coming out except to intimate partners. Only in recent years has it become more common to transition and then own a trans identity well into physical transition. Coupled with the very public coming out of Bono and Jenner, trans identity is now more accurately on the mainstream radar than at any other time in history. As happened with gay and lesbian identities, this is gradually leading to successive approximations toward realism in media depictions of trans identity. *Trans America, Normal, Sens8, Transparent*, and *Orange is the New Black* provide a few examples of moving toward realism.

Rather than a gradual process of change, as happened with acceptance of gay and lesbian identities, change is happening rapidly, driven by the instantaneous process of Internet information sharing. Incremental policy and legal changes supporting trans people have led to a snowball of momentum, leaving many with their heads spinning at how fast change is happening now. Every day a new policy supporting trans identity is announced, or another insurance company announces coverage for transition processes.

As with any other civil rights issue, policy and legal and social change happen at their own varying pace. Trans people will continue to be the butt of jokes and violence (both verbal and physical) as laws and policies continue to change in support of trans identity. The pace of social change is the slowest, and it will be a long time before this form of change catches up with the rapid legal and policy changes currently underway. The pace will be even slower if the Trump administration succeeds in all its goals of limiting or reversing LGBT civil rights.

Those who transitioned years ago, accustomed to having no mainstream support for their identity, are now in the position of readjusting their view of how their identity fits into the fabric of the larger culture. I had a conversation recently with a 60-something transman (I'll call him Chuck) who transitioned in the 1970s. He continues to live as privately as possible. We were talking of security clearances and he said, "This one job I had, they didn't have background checks at that time like they do today. I could never get that job today; they'd find out I transitioned." Knowing something of the field he'd been in and where he'd worked, I said to him, "But Chuck – today it wouldn't matter."

As therapists work with trans clients these days, there is a new component to the therapeutic process: how does the client feel about their personal and private journey being more in the public eye than ever before? How do they feel about the possibility of family members understanding their trans identity in advance of being told? How safe do they feel under the Trump administration? It has never been possible to transition in the closet. But now, with increasing awareness of trans issues, many who have no desire to be activists may find eager cisgender allies trying to put them in an activist position without asking first. Therapists will find such issues increasingly on the table for discussion as trans identities emerge further into the light of day.

AGENT VERSUS TARGET

The nomenclature of identity politics is useful in discussing trans in the new millennium. Target: a person whose birth identity or status places them in a subordinate position within their main-stream culture's sociopolitical hierarchy. Agent: a person whose birth identity or status places them in a position of privilege within their mainstream culture's sociopolitical hierarchy. A rule of thumb is that agents have difficulty seeing their privilege or the benefits that accrue to them as a result of their agent identity or status. Targets, on the other hand, are usually quite aware of the privilege they *don't* have.

A few examples that fall in the agent category in U.S. culture: straight, Euro-American, male, able-bodied. A few examples of the target category: queer, African-American, female, disabled. Only a minority of people are in the agent category in *all* arenas of life in the

U.S.: straight, Euro-American, at least average intelligence, able-bodied, cisgender, male, Christian, born in the U.S., and at least middle class. (And even these folks will eventually end up in a target category, if they live to old age) Most people's identities and status place them in both agent *and* target categories, depending on which form of identity or status is under consideration.

The combination of target and agent status within the same person can make it confusing to be told, "You have privilege." A Euro-American transwoman may be very aware of her target status everywhere she goes; it may be difficult for her to see that she would be more at risk if she was a transwoman of color. She still holds the privilege of being Euro-American.

Those who transition physically in the direction of male often grapple with the idea of switching from the target status 'female' to the agent status 'male.' It is confusing, as 'male privilege' is too broad a brush to apply to cismen and transmen alike. The transman who is living privately has male privilege conferred on him; 'male' is not the status assigned him at birth. The male identity he has acquired makes him simultaneously a target; if anyone finds out he is a transman, his privilege disappears, possibly turning into high risk. There is little privilege to be found in having to keep one's identity a secret in order to live. 'Male privilege' is a cisgender concept. Conditional privilege is a more accurate descriptor. Race must also be taken into account; several African-American transmen have told me they feel more in danger and marginalized than prior to their transitions; male privilege is not only a cisgender concept, but also a Euro-American concept.

THE TRUE ALLY: OWNING AGENT STATUS

The path toward being an ally to a target group means first exploring one's agent status. It can be all too easy to develop a strong feeling of guilt. I once worked with a cisgender gay client who was German. He had moved to the U.S. in 1970, at the age of 20. He said to me, "I didn't learn about the Holocaust when I was growing up. I learned that Hitler was a leader attempting to expand German ideals, but we lost the war. It wasn't until I was living in Berkeley that I met some Jewish friends who enlightened me. Such guilt I felt! My God! My people had done this? I tried to talk to my parents about all this, and I found out my father had been part of Hitler Youth. I was so ashamed. I've found out since that younger Germans are learning about the Holocaust in school now. One young man told me *The Diary of Anne Frank* was one of his required books. I'm glad, because maybe they can work through the guilt together. It helped me a lot when this young man told me vir-tually all young men my father's age were part of Hitler Youth. It was like being a Boy Scout. It didn't mean they knew any more about the Holocaust than I did growing up." *(Client session, 2000)*

That feeling 'my people have done this' can lead to a strong desire to dissociate oneself from any connection to what is per-ceived as an oppressive heritage. For instance: far from being an un-populated land settled by a westward expansion, the North Ameri-can continent was home to many cultures that had thrived for thou-sands of years – until Europeans came along, leading to genocide. Only in recent years has the word 'genocide' been applied in a mainstream context to the gradual formation of the United States; U.S. history books have historically used terms such as 'westward expansion' and 'homesteading,' as if the land was previously empty of civilization. Indigenous peoples were presented as savages who popped up unexpectedly and wreaked random havoc on those at-tempting to bring order to wilderness.

Those Euro-Americans who internalize the guilt of ancestral and current misdeeds are not allowing themselves to finish the process of becoming allies. Some attempt to claim a target identity as their own, trying to make clear they are not oppressors. But the very idea that one can change identities and claim another is an appropriation of identity that comes from the top-down position, that of the agent.

More powerful is to continue the process of personal growth, perhaps becoming a Euro-American member of the NAACP

(National Association for the Advancement of Colored People), a cisgender male member of NOW (National Organization for Women), a straight singer in a gay men's chorus, or an HIV- person participating in the AIDS walk. The true ally feels no need to explain to others, "Oh, I'm participating in the AIDS walk on behalf of a friend, but I'm HIV-" or "I'm in the lesbian chorus because I like to sing, but I'm straight."

ABNORMAL NO LONGER

Trans in the new millennium includes an awareness of trans issues that places 'cisgender' officially in the category of agent and 'trans' officially in the target category. Though these identities have existed in these categories for decades, it is only recently that public awareness has been raised sufficiently to recognize the target/agent dynamic at play.

In previous years the mainstream conceptualization was normal/abnormal rather than agent/target. This conceptualization had the effect of legitimizing discrimination. It was okay to fire someone for being trans. It was reasonable to deny housing to someone who appeared trans. Though I put these scenarios in the past tense, one of our current culture wars is that the discrimination remains okay in many people's minds. A gradual shift is underway, making the discrimination no longer socially acceptable.

This shift in perception is leading to a mainstream push for trans civil rights. The backlash has been inevitable, and is coming from the same kinds people who resisted the Supreme Court marriage equality decision. We are witnessing attempts to legislate and moni-tor public bathroom usage in an attempt to force people to use the bathroom consistent with their birth gender assignment. Gender has been brought into focus once again, leading to debate among feminists about just what makes a woman a woman, for instance. These are not new questions. However, the focus of the questions is now from a deeper level and in a more mainstream context than ever before. Allies have never been more important to trans people.

And now Donald Trump has been elected president, causing many who had been considering transition to reconsider the whole idea for the time being; they don't feel safe, physically or emotionally. Some who had been taking their time making documentation changes are now hastening the process, particularly at the federal le-vel; they no longer take for granted that they will be able to change their name or gender through the Social Security Administration, or get a passport reflecting their true identity. The backlash has taken a more serious turn, and there is no knowing how long it might be before the pendulum swings once again in the direction of civil rights and identity affirmation. Taking the long view, it may bolster our spirits to keep Ghandi's words in mind:

First they ignore you

Then they ridicule you

Then they fight you

Then you win.

• Chapter 21 •

ANSWERS FOR A SKEPTIC

IN CHAPTER 3 *(QUESTIONS OF A SKEPTIC)*, I said I would respond to Kenneth's skepticism later in this book. I lied, sort of. I am not going to write a detailed answer to his objections (mental illness, self-diagnosis, his distrust of emotional process). It would be repetitious. I've responded to Kenneth, in great detail, through the course of this book.

For the therapists in the audience: Your trans clients will be best served if you have a well-thought-out therapeutic approach to gender identity issues that matches your general clinical philosophy of therapy and worldview. If you can also come to recognize the degree to which gender permeates our cultural interactions, you will be in a good position to work with trans clients.

Keeping abreast of policy and legal changes that may affect your clients will help you be of good service to them. Many have been so focused on their own internal turmoil they may not have kept up with the rapid changes that have been happening around them. The slow pace of social change is reflected in the fear and low levels of self-esteem you will see in many clients contemplating transition.

The political appointees of Donald Trump may lead to significant changes in policy and laws related to trans identity at the federal level, with possible trickle-down effects at state and local levels; you can best serve your trans clients by keeping a close watch on policy changes at various levels of government. In this time of uncertainty, clients need more than ever to feel the know-ledgable support of their therapist.

In addition to attaining this sociopolitical knowledge, doing your own work to determine your comfort level with the gender assigned you at birth will enable you to be useful to clients questioning their gender identity, or pursuing transition (whether physical or not).

For friends and family members: Your trans family members and friends are at their most vulnerable right after disclosing to you that they are trans. They are no different inside than they have always been, but they have gifted you with the opportunity to know them far better than you could if they had never told you, "I'm trans." While you may not be able to recognize the knowledge as a gift at first, take courage from the strength of bond you have always had with your trans family member or friend. That bond can grow stronger as we trust each other with our true selves.

Learn what you can about trans issues in your particular social milieu; your trans friends and family members need allies now more than ever, to prevent the hard-won changes we're seeing today from being dismantled in the future as those in opposition take power. Tell your trans friends and family members that you support them; it may seem obvious to you that you do, but these days, they need to hear it overtly stated. More than once.

For those who are trans: Trans identity is among the last frontiers of civil rights in this culture. You may not welcome the opportunity of living a civil rights issue. Nevertheless your identity does pave the way for you to experience incredible personal growth. Not many have the opportunity to live more than one life in the same lifetime. Let your cisgender allies support you, and take courage as you move forward into your future. Congratulations!

It's in every one of us to be wise,

Find your heart, open up both your eyes.

We can all know everything,

without ever knowing why.

It's in every one of us, by and by.

—Heather Alexander (now Alexander James Adams)
from the CD *Wintertide* (2007)
Quoted by permission

Terminology

Assigned birth gender: The gender that was put on a person's original birth certificate.

Biofemale: A person who was assigned a female gender at birth and is content with that gender assignment (as opposed to a person who had to transition in order to become female). Largely replaced by the term cisgender.

Biomale: A person who was assigned a male gender at birth and is content with that gender assignment (as opposed to a man who had to transition in order to become male). Largely replaced by the term cisgender.

Bodily sex: The chromosomal/physical attributes of a person's body that cause them to be assigned "male" or "female" at birth, usually based on visual examination of external genitalia. These attributes can be altered to a degree as an adult, during the process known as physical transition.

Chest reconstruction: The preferred terminology among FTMs, referring to removal of the breasts. This term is used instead of "double mastectomy."

Cisfemale or cismale, ciswoman or cisman: These are the cisgender companion terms to transwoman or transman.

Cisgender: "Cis" is a prefix that means the opposite of "trans." "Trans" is to move across, and in the realm of transgender means to change something related to gender/bodily sex. "Cisgender," then, refers to those people who don't transition. This term creates a level playing field, rather than some variation of "transgender" and "normal."

Crossdresser: An individual (usually male-bodied) who enjoys wearing "opposite gendered" clothing at times. There is sometimes a sexual/erotic component to the desire, though this may fade over time.

Demi followed by boy, girl, man, woman, etc.: Someone who identifies partially, but not entirely as boy, girl, etc. This identifier reflects a non-binary identity.

Female-affirmed: A person who was assigned a male gender at birth, but who identifies as female. I usually use this term in referring to those who transition in childhood/adolescence.

Female-assigned: A person assumed to be female at birth.

FTM: Female-to-male transperson. Other terminology you might hear: transman, transguy, MTM (man-to-male, meaning the person never identified as female at all), trannyboy, and many others. People are constantly coming up with new self-descriptors. I use FTM throughout this book for those who transition physically, meaning "female-assigned and transitioning to living as a man."

Gender: A relational process inherent in all relationships between people, based on the assumptions people make about one another re the culturally-defined roles, dress, and behaviors deemed "male" and "female."

Gender-confirming surgery: The various surgeries trans people undertake to change their bodies to more fully match their internal sense of gender identity. An older term for this is sex-reassignment surgery.

Gender dissonance: A term I prefer to gender identity disorder, gender variant, or gender dysphoria. Gender dissonance refers to a feeling of one's body and mind being at odds with each other in terms of gender identity. The sex of the body does not match the brain's expectation, or vice versa. Etiology completely unclear.

Gender dysphoria: A feeling of discomfort with one's bodily sex. For a transman, for instance, it is not the size or shape of his breasts that bother him as much as their presence on his body. I prefer the term gender dissonance, as some trans people don't feel dysphoric, but still desire transition. It's about hormone balance and gender role, as well as body issues.

Gender expression: How does a person like to dress and "perform" gender? This may be different in private than in public.

Gender identity: A person's internal sense of being male, female or some other gender which they probably have to make up words for because English limits us to two choices.

Gender queer or *genderqueer:* A catch-all term, most often used by those who wish to challenge the gender binary paradigm and replace it with a model of gender fluidity. Some who transition (particularly among teens and 20-somethings) will use this term to describe themselves, wanting more fluid labels than "male" or "female," much as some younger people will use "queer" rather than "lesbian" or "gay" as a self-descriptor, despite exclusive attractions to people of just one sex.

Gender role: A social construction that consists of a proscribed set of relational boundaries determining how "men" and "women" behave; there are nuances to these roles depending on age, race, ethnicity, class, and the gender of the person one is dealing with.

406

Gender variant: A term for those whose identities don't match the gender assigned them at birth. I don't like this term, as it implies there is a gender norm that people are deviating from. "Variant" is a statistical term used to describe data as it relates to a norm. I prefer thinking of gender as existing along a continuum of possibility, and doubt that there is a norm.

Intersexed: A condition, present at birth, of having (a) indeterminate genitalia, such that physicians can't clearly determine a baby's bodily sex, and/or (b) having anomalous sex organs internally, which make the person sterile or unable to bear children. Newer terms: disorders of sex differentiation, and divergence of sex development (preferred by many who claim this identity).

Male-affirmed: A person who was assigned a female gender at birth, but who identifies as male. I usually use this term in referring to those who transition in childhood/adolescence.

Male-assigned: A person assumed to be male at birth.

Man v. male: "Man" is the cultural construct expected of the adult person who has a "male" body. "Man" is a social construct; "male" is biology. That said, it is misleading to believe "male" and "female" are mutually-exclusive and binary; if this were so, physical transition would not be possible. A more useful conceptualization might be that there are all different kinds of bodies, some with more testosterone or estrogen than others.

MTF: Male-to-female transperson. Other common terminology: transwoman, transgal, grrls, tranny, and many others. People are constantly coming up with new self-descriptors. As with FTM, I use this term because it's short and descriptive. When I use this term, I mean "male-assigned and transitioning to living as a woman."

Metoidioplasty: A lower surgery for FTMs. The clitoris is released from the folds of the labia, which are used (with saline implants) to create testicles. Given typical degrees of clitoral enlargement due to the introduction of testosterone, the result is a small penis, with full orgasmic capacity retained.

Misgender: Use of the wrong pronoun and gender conceptualization, whether deliberate or not. For instance: *Her cousin continues to misgender her.*

Non-binary: An umbrella term used to describe those who don't resonate with the gender assigned them at birth but feel 'male' and 'female' don't describe the totality of their experience of gender.

Orchiectomy: Removal of the testicles.

Phalloplasty: A lower surgery for FTMs. Using skin from the forearm or abdomen of the patient, a penis is sculpted from the flesh and grafted in the appropriate position. Clitoral tissue is incorporated into the new penis to preserve sexual sensation and orgasmic ability.

Private: Some who transition prefer living their lives invisibly, as their intended gender, without disclosing they had to transition to do so. This is known as living privately. This does not require surgery or hormones, for those fortunate enough to be seen as their intended gender without body modification of any kind. Another widely used term for this process is stealth, though I prefer the word private. Stealth implies hiding or skulking around, neither of which is a nice way to describe living one's life privately.

Queer: A largely-reclaimed word, encompassing the entire spectrum of sexual/gender identity possibilities within the GLB and/or T communities. Not as widely used by older GLB and/or T people, who remember it being used as an insult and seldom as a self-descriptor by anyone with good self-esteem.

Sex-reassignment surgery: Also termed gender-confirming surgery, this term refers to the various surgeries trans people undertake to change their bodies to more fully match their internal sense of gender identity.

Sexual orientation: A person's psychoemotional-physical affiliations – who does the person fall in love with, feel most comfortable in relationship with, feel sexually attracted to.

Sexual preference: How does a person like to have sex? Do they enjoy S/M, for instance? Or bondage?

SRS: Short-hand terminology for sex reassignment surgery. Also sometimes called GCS for gender confirming surgery.

Standards of Care: Developed by the World Professional Association for Transgender Health (WPATH), the Standards provide guidelines for mental health care providers, physicians and surgeons in helping transgender people transition.

Stealth: See *private*.

Trans: An umbrella term encompassing all transgender and transsexual persons.

Transgender: A person who does not resonate to some degree with the gender assigned to them at birth. This is a continuum of possibility.

Transition: A combination of processes that often includes some or all of the following: Body modification, resocialization, education, and disclosure leading to a person changing their social gender role/physical body from their birth gender assignment to one more in tune with their actual identity. The very act of bringing gender into consciousness as a social process is itself a transition.

Transman: One of the more common terms used as a self-descriptor by female-to-male persons. This term is not appropriate in referring to those who were born male-bodied and now live female.

Transsexual: A person who does not resonate with the gender assigned to them at birth, to such an extent that they would like to alter their bodies to bring their gender expression/bodily sex more in line with their internal gender identity.

Transwoman: One of the more common terms used as a self-descriptor by male-to-female persons. This term is not appropriate in referring to those who were born female-bodied and now live male.

Vaginoplasty: Creation of a vagina/labia from the tissue of the penis/scrotum. Retains sexual functioning and is cosmetically nearly identical to an actual vagina.

Woman v. female: "Woman" is a social construct; "female" is biology. That said, it is misleading to believe "male" and "female" as mutually-exclusive and binary; if this were so, physical transition would not be possible. A more useful conceptualization might be that there are all different kinds of bodies, some with more testosterone or estrogen than others.

Frequently-Asked Questions

Following are some of the most common questions I am asked when I do educational presentations. Disclaimer: These are my answers. Others may disagree, or use slightly different language. One of the first things I say to audiences before opening up a presentation for questions is that there is no consensus among trans people on definitions, answers to questions, etc. Cisgender people may feel they don't understand the issues when trans people seem to give very different answers to similar questions. We probably are!

How do I know what pronoun to use for a trans person?
The short answer is, ask. If this is not practical or appropriate to the situation, go by the gender presentation cues you see before you, though this may not work in the case of someone whose gender presentation appears to you to be a butch lesbian; they may identify as male. The only way to be certain is to ask. Those who identify as non-binary may be deliberately presenting gender ambiguously. Such folk are often hoping you will ask what pronoun they prefer, as this is the only way they can answer something like, "I don't use female or male pronouns, I prefer hir," or some such. They are also hoping you won't just take your best guess and assume "he" or "she" to be correct.

What's the difference between transgender and transsexual?
There is no consensus among trans individuals about definitions and categories. Some transsexuals will say, "I am not transgender, that's for people who have no intention of physically transitioning." Others will say, "Transsexual is a subset, and transgender is the umbrella term that embraces us all." Semantics and the subtleties of identity politics create a situation that is most confusing for cisgender people (and for some trans people!). Personally, I use the term "trans" as the umbrella term.

Can people change all their documentation to their new gender or do they always have a driver's license that has their original gender?
Every state has different laws about name changes and changing gender on driver's licenses. Some states require proof of physical alterations such as surgery in order to change the gender designation on one's driver's license. I wrote "carry letters" for some clients, explaining that the person in question was in transition and was entitled to be treated as their intended gender. Such letters also explained why a person's documentation may not be entirely congruent in terms of name and gender designation. A carry letter is useful if not all documentation has been changed by the time of a trip requiring use of legal identification.

410

When should a trans person switch bathrooms?

A person who is transitioning physically and wishes to live full-time in a new gender role will eventually switch bathrooms. There is no right or wrong time to make this switch, as there are many variables to take into account. Safety, feelings of self-consciousness or discomfort (in either bathroom!), local laws and attitudes all combine to make the process uncomfortable for most people who transition. Many avoid gendered bathrooms when possible until they are well into their transition and fairly certain they are being seen as their intended gender, or until they reach a point of not minding what others say or think. Gender-neutral bathrooms are a haven for many trans people.

How does male privilege play out for transmen?

I have noticed that I am given more credibility in some situations than I would be if I were still perceived as female. Very few people have questioned the validity of my statements when I make educational presentations, for example. In all-female settings, on the other hand, I am given less credibility as I am assumed to have no clue about emotional processing. Further, FTM male privilege is conditional – if we come out as trans, we may feel at risk for violence or discrimination. A better way to put it is that we have conditional privilege rather than male privilege.

In terms of personal safety moving through the world... I know intellectually that I'm safer walking around male, but that doesn't mean I *feel* safer. I am still hypervigilant, just as aware of who is in my physical proximity as I used to be. The socialization lessons I learned as a small female-assigned child are with me still, though I know everyone sees me as a man.

When do you tell someone you're trans?

It depends on how close I want to be to them, and I'm not talking about sex. If I want any degree of intimacy with someone, I can't leave out the first 40 years of my life. I generally wait until I know the person well enough to determine whether I want to pursue a friendship of some sort with them. If I sense immediately that I like someone, I'll tell them at the time. I don't want to wait too long, as this can become a barrier to intimacy.

I told clients I'm trans if the knowledge would be helpful to their therapeutic process in some way. My trans clients generally already knew; that's why they sought me out in the first place. I have had the experience, however, of having a trans client who had no idea why they were referred to me in particular. It came as a shock to them when I mentioned something about my own transition and it became clear to me they had not known I was trans. However I also noticed they immediately relaxed and became much more forthcoming about their feelings and process. For this reason, I made a point of coming out to all trans clients.

If you are a cisgender therapist, you have an advantage a trans therapist doesn't; you may be in the position of being able to offer unconditional and unqualified congratulatory support to a trans person who is verbalizing for the first time, "I've always felt like a girl (or boy) inside and I think I need to transition." You then become the first cisgender person to hear this news, allowing the trans client to see that it can be okay to tell this news to someone who is cisgender. Trans clients expect a trans therapist to support them; you have the opportunity for your cisgender identity to be an intervention.

I think a guy friend of mine might be transgender, but he hasn't said anything to me. How can I let him know it's okay with me?

It's not always easy to bring trans issues into a general conversation! However, you can find some way of bringing up the issue to make it clear you are supportive. For example, you could say something like, "I saw that movie *Trans America* the other evening, and I was really cheering Bree on when she reconnected with her son. I thought it was a great movie." General statements like that are cues to your friend; whether your friend follows up on the statement and comes out to you becomes part of their disclosure process. And it's also possible that your friend is gender balanced, with no intention of transitioning. I have met some cismen who had great respect for the feminine energy in themselves and did not give in to the societal pressure to act 100% male. Such men can appear to be gay or transgender, when they may be quite happily heterosexual and cisgender.

Do people ever change their minds after they've gone through the whole procedure?

In 1999 I met someone who had transitioned FTM in the 1980s and 'detransitioned' some years later. She had tried living as a man and realized it wasn't the right thing for her. However she is the only person I've met who reached that conclusion long in transition. I don't know how far she had gone surgically, but she had been on hormones long enough for her voice to have deepened. When I met her I thought she was an MTF, because of her voice.

I stressed self-knowledge with my clients and facilitated their meeting others who had gone through the process to help prevent someone getting that far along the path of physical transition before realizing it's not for them. On the other hand one can't really know hormones are the right course of action without trying them out. I encouraged clients to closely monitor their emotional reactions and state of mind once they'd started hormones.

Several clients (all MTF) ended up deciding transition was too hard and backed away from the process. Some did so because they felt unemployable or in danger, based on where they were living. One did not feel entitled to ask others to switch names and pronouns for her; she would probably resume transition if she reached a point of self-esteem that allowed her to feel it was okay to be herself.

How can you tell if a child is really transgender?

Listen to the child's self-descriptive language rather than just watching behavior. A male child who says, "I like playing with dresses" is not necessarily saying the same thing as a child who states emphatically, "I'm not a boy, I'm a girl." A female child who likes playing with the guys may be a tomboy, or may be a budding FTM. "I like playing with boys" isn't the same statement as "I am a boy."

The distinction to be made is between behavior and assertion of identity. (Watch the film *Ma Vie en Rose* for a clear depiction of a child who will transition as soon as possible.) I advise parents to just let their child be who they are; it's not possible to change identity anyway and making a big deal of it will only teach the child there is something wrong with them. If a child is asserting a gender identity at odds with their physical body, in all situations and across time, early adolescence is the time to address the issue in terms of physical transition or suppressing puberty through medication. Social transition is enough for a young child whose gender is emerging differently from what's on their birth certificate.

What's the weirdest question you've ever been asked?

"Are you single?" This question was asked in the context of an audience member trying to find a tactful way of asking what dating was like for me as a post-transition transman. The poor woman who asked the question nearly died of embarrassment as she realized (a split-second too late, as the room erupted in laughter) how her question might be interpreted. The best question I've been asked was, "Why do you come out?" Writing and teaching are my avocations. Coming out is a natural extension in each case. For every trans person like me, who is in a position to come out and put a face to the word "trans," there are 1,000 others who are off living their lives, quite contentedly. I come out so they don't have to.

Range of Client Occupations

The following represent the occupations of my transitioning clients, as of October, 2011. Some occupations were shared by a number of my clients. Unless otherwise noted, all were able to transition on the job.

acupuncturist	advertising sales
architect	art student
attorney	auto mechanic
barista	bicycle messenger
bicycle repair	boat repair
bookstore employee	brewpub manager
call center employee	car salesman
car warranty rep (fired for transitioning)	carpentry/handyman work
City of Portland (various careers)	college professor
college or trade-school student	community newspaper employee
computer engineer/programmer	computer repair technician
construction work (various aspects)	customer service representative
craft fair worker	dept. store sales
ER security guard (felt unsafe; quit)	executive asst. in a bank
filling station employee	graphic design/web design
grocery store checker	hair stylist
iron worker (didn't feel physically strong enough to continue, switched positions in the company)	IT manager
kite shop employee	legal secretary (felt forced to resign)
loan officer in a bank	maintenance person
massage therapist	medical student
middle school student	military, various branches
Multnomah County (various careers)	newspaper reporter
Oregon National Guard soldier	park ranger
parking attendant	photographer
physician	pilot
pizza parlor	police officer
Port of Portland	printer
professional musician	retail sales
retired military	security guard
short-order cook	sign-painting shop employee
small engine repair	State of Oregon (various careers)

social worker or therapist	student (various disciplines)
teacher	telephone solicitor
waiter	writer

Standards of Care

The following is not the full text of the SOC (2011). I have excerpted sections that pertain to mental healthcare. You can find the full text of the current SOC at: http://www.wpath.org/publications_standards.cfm

"Health professionals throughout the world – even in areas with limited resources and training opportunities – can apply the many core principles that undergird the SOC. These principles include the following: Exhibit respect for patients with nonconforming gender identities (do not pathologize differences in gender identity or expression); provide care (or refer to knowledgeable colleagues) that affirms patients' gender identities and reduces the distress of gender dysphoria, when present; become knowledgeable about the health care needs of transsexual, transgender, and gender nonconforming people, including the benefits and risks of treatment options for gender dysphoria; match the treatment approach to the specific needs of patients, particularly their goals for gender expression and need for relief from gender dysphoria; facilitate access to appropriate care; seek patients' informed consent before providing treatment; offer continuity of care; and be prepared to support and advocate for patients within their families and communities (schools, workplaces, and other settings)."

"Transsexual, transgender, and gender nonconforming individuals are not inherently disordered. Rather, the distress of gender dysphoria, when present, is the concern that might be diagnosable and for which various treatment options are available.... [W]hile many individuals need both hormone therapy and surgery to alleviate their gender dysphoria, others need only one of these treatment options and some need neither.....Some individuals describe themselves not as gender nonconforming but as unambiguously cross-sexed.... Other individuals affirm their unique gender identity and no longer consider themselves either male or female.... Instead, they may describe their gender identity in specific terms such as transgender, bigender, or genderqueer, affirming their unique experience that may transcend a male/female binary understanding of gender."

There is a long section in the 2011 SOC outlining working with trans children and adolescents. I have not reprinted it here as it closely resembles the contents of the chapter *How Young is Too Young?* The current SOC support the concept of social transition for young trans children and physical intervention for adolescents. The other reason I did not reprint the child/adolescent section, as pertains to mental health, is that much of it is repeated in the section pertaining to adults, as follows.

"The following are recommended minimum credentials for mental health professionals who work with adults presenting with gender dysphoria:
1.   A master's degree or its equivalent in a clinical behavioral science field. This degree or a more advanced one should be granted by an institution accredited by the appropriate national or regional accrediting board. The mental health professional should have documented credentials from a relevant licensing board or equivalent for that country.
2.   Competence in using the Diagnostic Statistical Manual of Mental Disorders and/or the International Classification of Diseases for diagnostic purposes.
3.   Ability to recognize and diagnose co-existing mental health concerns and to distinguish these from gender dysphoria.
4.   Documented supervised training and competence in psychotherapy or counseling.
5.   Knowledgeable about gender nonconforming identities and expressions, and the assessment and treatment of gender dysphoria.
6.   Continuing education in the assessment and treatment of gender dysphoria. This may include attending relevant professional meetings, workshops, or seminars; obtaining supervision from a mental health professional with relevant experience; or participating in research related to gender nonconformity and gender dysphoria.

In addition to the minimum credentials above, it is recommended that mental health professionals develop and maintain cultural competence to facilitate their work with transsexual, transgender, and gender nonconforming clients. This may involve, for example, becoming knowledgeable about current community, advocacy, and public policy issues relevant to these clients and their families. Additionally, knowledge about sexuality, sexual health concerns, and the assessment and treatment of sexual disorders is preferred. Mental health professionals who are new to the field (irrespective of their level of training and other experience) should work under the supervision of a mental health professional with established competence in the assessment and treatment of gender dysphoria."

"Tasks Related to Assessment and Referral

1. Assess gender dysphoria. Mental health professionals assess clients' gender dysphoria in the context of an evaluation of their psychosocial adjustment
2. Provide information regarding options for gender identity and expression and possible medical interventions
3. Assess, diagnose, and discuss treatment options for co-existing mental health concerns..... Addressing these concerns can greatly facilitate the resolution of gender dysphoria, possible changes in gender role, the making of informed decisions about medical interventions, and improvements in quality of life.... The presence of co-existing mental health concerns does not necessarily preclude possible changes in gender role or access to feminizing/masculinizing hormones or surgery; rather, these concerns need to be optimally managed prior to or concurrent with treatment of gender dysphoria.
4. If applicable, assess eligibility, prepare, and refer for hormone therapy..... It is important for mental health professionals to recognize that decisions about hormones are first and foremost the client's decisions – as are all decisions regarding healthcare. However, mental health professionals have a responsibility to encourage, guide, and assist clients with making fully informed decisions and becoming adequately prepared.

The recommended content of the referral letter for feminizing/masculinizing hormone therapy is as follows:
1. The client's general identifying characteristics;
2. Results of the client's psychosocial assessment, including any diagnoses;
3. The duration of the referring health professional's relationship with the client, including the type of evaluation and therapy or counseling to date;
4. An explanation that the criteria for hormone therapy have been met, and a brief description of the clinical rationale for supporting the client's request for hormone therapy;
5. A statement about the fact that informed consent has been obtained from the patient;
6. A statement that the referring health professional is available for coordination of care and welcomes a phone call to establish this. "

The section pertaining to surgery referral letters is much the same as the section pertaining to hormones. There is one important difference in this iteration of the SOC from previous versions. While lower surgery still requires two letters of referral, *it is no longer a requirement that one of those letters be written by a practitioner with a doctoral-level degree.* The requirement now is that both referrals come from mental health practitioners who have experience working with trans clients.

417

Sample Genogram

Genogram date: June, 2008
Ages are shown relative to genogram date.

This is a sample, not reflecting any specific person's actual family experience.

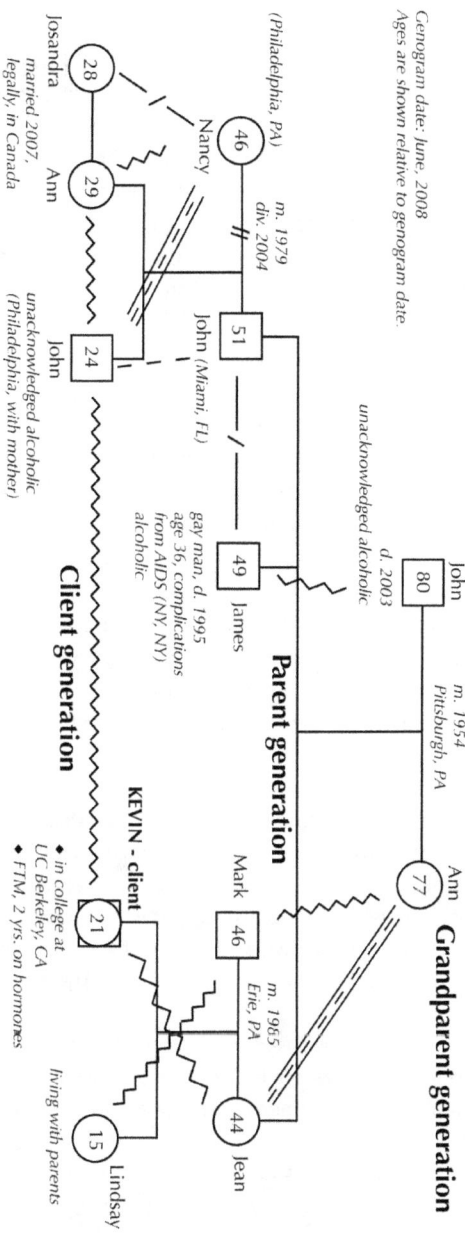

Grandparent generation

m. 1954
Pittsburgh, PA

John | 80

d. 2003
unacknowledged alcoholic

Ann | 77

m. 1979
div. 2004

(Philadelphia, PA)

Nancy | 46

Josandra | 28

Ann | 29

married 2007,
legally, in Canada

John | 51

John *(Miami, FL)*
unacknowledged alcoholic
(Philadelphia, with mother)

John | 24

Parent generation

James | 49

gay man, d. 1995
age 36, complications
from AIDS (NY, NY)
alcoholic

Mark | 46

m. 1985
Erie, PA

Jean | 44

Client generation

KEVIN - client

21

- *in college at*
  UC Berkeley, CA
- *FtM, 2 yrs. on hormones*

Lindsay | 15

living with parents

Genogram symbols

~~~~ Conflicted relationship
==== Too close/enmeshed relationship
-#- Divorced
- - - Estranged/little contact
-/- No contact at all

☐ Male   ○ Female   ◯ Transgendered

Genograms are useful snapshots of families, showing how various dynamics play out through generations, especially around issues such as addiction. Note: If there is no line drawn between various family members, this signifies a neutral or positive relationship. The close/enmeshed relationship indicates an unhealthy degree of closeness.

419

Sample Referral Letter

In writing a hormone or surgery referral letter, I focused on issues such as: how many people had the person told thus far; how was their workplace or school disclosure going; did they understand what to expect from the hormones. My underlying approach was to address the questions, "Did they believe this can be done without ever telling anyone?" and "Did they have realistic expectations of what is going to happen physically?" Following is a sample referral letter. Note that this letter is not addressed to a specific doctor. I sent referral letters to the client; it's their letter to use when they're ready. Sometimes I added a line, "Jane meets many of the criteria for a diagnosis of Gender Dysphoria as defined in the current DSM," if the client was accessing a doctor or surgeon who followed a diagnostic model. The 2011 Standards of Care don't require a DSM diagnosis, but some doctors or insurance providers may require it. My surgery referral letters weren't much longer or different; most of my clients were accessing surgery after starting hormones, so I would state how long they had been taking hormones and how life was going for them in their new role with a new hormone balance. In the case of non-binary clients, I would use their own words in a referral letter, describing their sense of self and how surgery or hormones was going to be beneficial to them moving forward.

To whom it may concern:

Jane Doe is a 26-year-old transwoman seeking hormones. Jane has never felt comfortable as a male, and has reached a point in her life where she feels compelled to correct her birth gender assignment and live as a woman. Jane has a good understanding of what hormones will and won't accomplish in her transition process and is well prepared psychoemotionally for the stresses of transition. She has realistic expectations concerning what hormones will (and won't) accomplish in helping further her transition process.

Jane has already disclosed to some of the key people in her life, and has good social support around her transition process, including a supportive partner. She has disclosed her intentions to her supervisor at work; she and her supervisor are in the process of developing a transition plan for her workplace.

If you have further questions or would like clarification of any of the points herein, feel free to contact me either by phone or e-mail.

Suggested Reading

Boenke, Mary (ed.). ***Trans Forming Families: Real Stories About Transgendered Loved Ones.*** One of the only books that includes pieces written by trans and cisgender people, and family members. The editor is the founder of the Roanoke, Virginia PFLAG chapter.

Bornstein, Kate. ***Gender Outlaw*** and ***My Gender Workbook. Gender Outlaw*** deconstructs gender as a social phenomenon, in an often lighthearted and gentle way. ***My Gender Workbook*** allows readers to explore their own relationship to gender.

Boyd, Helen. ***My Husband Betty: Love, Sex and Life with a Crossdresser*** and ***She's Not the Man I Married.*** Highly recommended for those desiring insight into a partner's experience.

Boylan, Jennifer. ***She's Not There: A Life in Two Genders***. Memoir of an MTF, especially focusing on the changes wrought in her marriage by her transition.

Califia, Pat (now Patrick). ***Sex Changes: The Politics of Transgenderism.*** As a female, Pat Califia rose to prominence in the early 1980s, writing for and about lesbians who participated in the bondage/discipline, sado/masochism, or leather community. ***Coming to Power*** was Califia's most widely-read book at that time. ***Sex Changes*** was written shortly before Pat began transitioning to become Patrick.

Colapinto, John. ***As Nature Made Him: The Boy who was Raised as a Girl.*** Well-written book that tells the true story of David Reimer. This book is very important, as it exposes the truth of the "twin study" that was the basis for John Money's claims that an infant could be raised as either gender successfully as long as the decision was made by age 22 months. As the leading sexologist of his day, Money's claims determined the treatment protocols for transsexuals and intersexed people, protocols that are only now changing.

Feinberg, Leslie. ***Transgender Warriors.*** Paying homage to those trans people who have paved the way for others.

Green, Jamison. *Becoming a Visible Man.* A memoir of transition blended with history, theory, analysis, and useful information. James' book also won the award for "Best book in Transgender Studies" for 2004 from the Center for Lesbian and Gay Studies at CUNY, and was a Lambda Literary Award finalist. Highly recommended.

Herman, Joanne. *Transgender Explained for Those Who Are Not.* Several clients told me their parents were able to read a book written by someone who was cisgender; it would have been a harder sell in those cases to have their parents read my book, or any other book written by a trans person. This useful book can help bring loved ones along in their understanding of what is (and isn't) going on when someone transitions.

Howey, Noelle. *Dress Codes: Of Three Girlhoods – My Mother's, My Father's and Mine.* Excellent account of an adult daughter coming to forgive her 'father' for his emotional absence during her childhood. Great psychological insight.

Kailey, Matt. *Just Add Hormones.* The first FTM autobiography I've read written by someone who did not transition out of queer community. Matt identified as a straight woman for years and post-transition identified as a queer transman. Written with great humor.

Kotula, Dean. *Phallus Palace.* Photos and stories of transmen. Some of the surgery photos are very graphic, making it unsuitable for use in educating many people's families.

Krieger, Irwin. *Helping Your Transgender Teen: A Guide for Parents.* It's exciting to me that professionals are writing books helpful to trans people and their families. This is one such book! Highly recommended for parents and families of trans children/adolescents.

Lev, Arlene. *Transgender Emergence.* This book is a great therapist's reference book, presenting gender as an identity that emerges, rather than as automatically matching biological sex. Good historical treatment of how we got to where we are in terms of the standards of care, the medical model currently in use in the U.S., etc. Somewhat dated as of 2017.

McCloskey, Deirdre N. *Crossing: A Memoir.* Very well-written and thoughtful autobiography of an MTF who transitioned on the job at the

University of Illinois, Chicago. McCloskey is an economist and professor of Human Sciences.

Morris, Jan. *Conundrum*. This is the autobiography of Jan Morris, a British travel writer who transitioned MTF in the 1960s. Morris has some very thought-provoking ideas about gender, sex, and being born trans.

Pepper, Rachel ed. *Transitions of the heart: stories of love, struggle and acceptance by mothers of transgender and gender variant children*. For many years, Mary Boenke's book *Transforming Families* was the only book written from the family's perspective of transition. For parents coming to terms with having a trans child, these two books are must-reading. And for trans people who would like more insight into what their parents may be feeling, or might go through once they're told, both books can be helpful.

Richards, Renee. *Second Serve* (1983) and *No Way Renee: The Second Half of My Notorious Life* (2008). Richards was a professional tennis player prior to transition and was barred from playing on the women's circuit post-transition; the various organizations that govern professional tennis required her to undergo a chromosome test, which she refused. She won a lawsuit challenging this requirement, and played several more years before retiring from professional tennis.

Rudacille, Deborah. *The Riddle of Gender.* This is a great book, analyzing the nature of gender. Well-researched, easy to read.

Vincent, Norah. *A Self-Made Man.* Vincent made herself over into "Ned" Vincent and over an 18 month period made forays out into society to experience what it's like to live male.

Walworth, Janis. *Transsexual Workers: An Employer's Guide.* Recommended by a client who found it useful during her transition at work.

References

Alcoholics Anonymous Services Inc. (2011)

American Psychiatric Association. (1973). "Position Statement on Homosexuality and Civil Rights." American Journal of Psychiatry, 131 (4), 497.

American Psychological Association. (2008) *Just the Facts* http://www.apa.org/pi/lgbc/publications/justthefacts.html

Anderson, H., & Goolishan, H. (1992). "The client is the expert: A not-knowing approach to therapy." In S. McNamee & K. J. Gergen (Eds.), *Therapy as social construction* (pp. 7–24). Thousand Oaks, CA: Sage.

Andrews, A. (2014). *Some assembly required: the not-so-secret life of a transgender teen.* New York, NY: Simon & Schuster, Children's Publishing Division.

Bartlett, N., Vasey, P., & Bukowski, W. (2000). "Is gender identity disorder in children a mental disorder?" Sex Roles, 43, 753–785.

Beattie, M. (2001). *Codependent no more: Beyond codependency.* New York NY: Mjf Books

Bieschke, K., Perez, R., DeBord, K. (2006). *Handbook of counseling and psychotherapy with lesbian, gay, bisexual and transgender clients.* Washington, D.C.: American Psychological Association

Bilodeau, B., & Renn, K. (2005). "Analysis of LGBT identity development models and implications for practice." New Directions for Student Services, 111, 25–39.

Boenke, M. (Ed.). (1999). *Transforming families: Real stories about transgendered loved ones.* Imperial Beach, CA: Walter Trook Publishing.

Boyd, H. (2007). *She's not the man I married.* Emeryville, CA: Seal Press.

Bray Haddock, D. (2001). *The Dissociative Identity Disorder sourcebook..* New York, NY: McGraw-Hill Cos.

Brill, S., & Pepper, R. (2008). *The transgender child: A handbook for families and professionals.* San Francisco, CA: Cleis Press.

Chen-Hayes, S. (2001). "Counseling and advocacy with transgendered and gender variant persons in schools and families." Journal of Humanistic Counseling, Education & Development, 40, 34–49.

Conrad, F. (2015). *Transgender: fact or fetish – reality or delusion?* Independently published, The Transcend Movement, Barcelona.

Cromwell, J. (1999). *Transmen and FTMs: identities, bodies, genders, and sexualities.* Champaign, IL: University of Illinois Press.

Davies, E. (2004). *Child development, second edition: A practitioner's guide (social work practice with children and families).* New York, NY: The Guilford Press.

Denning, P. (2004). *Practicing Harm Reduction Psychotherapy.* New York, NY: The Guilford Press.

Dolan, Z. (2015). *Transgender no more.* Independently published, Kindle platform.

Dykstra, L. (2005). "Trans-friendly preschool." Journal of Gay & Lesbian Issues in Education, 3, 7–13.

Emery, R. (2004). *The truth about children and divorce: Dealing with the emotions so you and your children can thrive.* New York, NY: Viking Penguin.

Ehrensaft, D. (2011). *Gender born, gender made: raising healthy gender-nonconforming children.* New York, NY: The Experiment LLC.

Erickson, L. ed (2014). *Trans bodies, trans selves: a resource for the transgender community.* New York, NY: Oxford University Press.

Erikson, E. (1980). *Identity and the life cycle.* New York, NY: Norton Inc.

Friedan, B. (1964). *The feminine mystique.* New York, NY: WW Norton and Co.

Griffiths, M. (2002). "Invisibility: The major obstacle in understanding and diagnosing transsexualism." Clinical Child Psychology and Psychiatry, 7, 493–496.

Herdt, G. (Ed.). (1994). *Third sex, third gender: Beyond sexual dimorphism in culture and history.* New York: Zone Books.

Herman, J. (2009). *Transgender explained for those who are not.* Bloomington, IN: Author House.

Hill, D., Rozanski, C., Carfagnini, J., & Willoughby, B. (2005). "Gender identity disorders in childhood and adolescence: A critical inquiry." Co-published simultaneously: Journal of Psychology & Human Sexuality, 17, 7–34.

Hoare, C. (2002). *Erikson on development in adulthood: New insights from unpublished papers.* Oxford, England: Oxford University Press (p. 103)

Hoffman, L. (1981). *Foundations of family therapy: A conceptual framework for systems change.* New York, NY: Basic Books, Inc.

Holmes, T.H. & Rahe, R.H. (1967). "The social readjustment rating scale." Journal of Psychosomatic Research, 11, 213-218.

Howey, N. (2002). *Dress codes: of three girlhoods—my mother's, my father's and mine.* New York, NY: Picador Inc.

Jennings, J. (2016). *Being Jazz: my life as a transgender teen.* New York, NY: Crown Books for Young Readers.

Kaufman, G., & Raphael, L. (1996). *Coming out of shame: Transforming gay and lesbian lives.* New York, NY: Doubleday Books.

Kassin, S., Fein, S., Markus, H.S. (2010). *Social psychology* (8th edition). Belmont, CA: Wadsworth Cengage Learning.

Kepner, J. (1999) *Body process: A gestalt approach to working with the body in psycho-therapy.* Cambridge, MA: Gestalt Institute of Cleveland Press.

Kluft, Richard P. Michelson, Larry K. (Ed); Ray, William J. (Ed), (1996). *Handbook of dissociation: Theoretical, empirical, and clinical perspectives.* New York, NY: Plenum Press

Krieger, I. (2011). *Helping your transgender teen: A guide for parents.* New Haven, CT: Genderwise Press.

Kuklin, S. (2015). *Beyond magenta: transgender teens speak out.* Somerville, MA: Candlewick Press.

Leahy, R. (2003). *Cognitive therapy techniques: A practitioner's guide.* New York, NY: The Guilford Press.

Lev, A. (2004). *Transgender emergence.* New York, NY: Haworth Press.

Levay, S., Valente, S. (2002). *Human sexuality.* Sunderland, MA: Sinauer Associates.

Mallon, G., & DeCrescenzo, T. (2006). "Transgender children and youth: A child welfare practice perspective." Child Welfare, 85, 215–241.

McGoldrick, M., Gerson, R., Shellenberger, S. (2008). *Genograms: Assessment and intervention (third edition).* New York, NY: W.W. Norton & Company, Inc.

Moberly, E. (2006). *Homosexuality: A new Christian ethic.* Cambridge, England: The Lutterworth Press.

Nanda, S. (1990). *Neither man nor woman: The hijaras of India.* Belmont, CA: Wadsworth.

Nanda, S. (2000). *Gender diversity: Cross-cultural variations.* Prospect Heights, IL: Waveland.

Newman, L. K. (2002). "Sex, gender and culture: Issues in the definition, assessment and treatment of gender identity disorder." Clinical Child Psychology and Psychiatry, 7, 352–359.

Nult, A. E. (2015). *Becoming Nicole: the transformation of an American family.* New York, NY: Random House.

Pepper, R. ed. (2012). *Transitions of the heart: stories of love, struggle and acceptance by mothers of transgender and gender variant children.* Berkeley, CA: Cleis Press.

Perry, T., Swicegood, T. (1992). *Don't be afraid anymore: The story of Reverend Troy Perry and the Metropolitan Community Churches.* New York, NY: St. Martins Press.

Pilkington, N. W., & D'Augelli, A. R. (1995). "Victimization of lesbian, gay, and bisexual youth in community settings." Journal of Community Psychology, 23, 34–56.

Remafedi, G. (1987). "Male homosexuality: The adolescent's perspective." Pediatrics, 79, 326–337.

Rice, F., Dolgin, K. (2001). *The adolescent: Development, relationships and culture (10th ed).* New York, NY: Allyn & Bacon

Roberts, V. (2016). *Talking points: transgender.* Centralia, WA: The Good Book Company.

Roscoe, W. (2000). *Changing ones: Third and fourth genders in native North America.* New York, NY: Palgrave Mcmillan.

Ryan, P. (2011). *First aid for your menopause emotions.* Amazon Digital Services, Kindle edition.

Sanger, T. (2010). *Trans people's partnerships: Towards an ethics of intimacy.* New York, NY: Palgrave Mcmillan Studies in Family and Intimate Life.

Schilt, K. (2011). *Just one of the guys: transgender men and the persistence of gender inequality.* Chicago, IL: University of Chicago Press.

Scott-Dixon, K. (Ed.) (2006). *Trans/forming feminisms: Transfeminists voices speak out.* Toronto, ON, Canada: Sumach Press.

Smith, A. (1988). *Grandchildren of Alcoholics: Another Generation of Co-Dependency.* Deerfield Beach, FL: Health Communications Inc.

Spitzer, R. (2003). "Can Some Gay Men and Lesbians Change Their Sexual Orientation? 200 Participants Reporting a Change from Homosexual to Heterosexual Orientation." Archives of Sexual Behavior, Vol. 32, No. 5, 403-417.

Spitzer, R. Interview, CNN, 5-9-2001

Teich, N. (2012). *Transgender 101: a simple guide to a complex issue.* Cichester, NY: Columbia University Press.

Vanderburgh, R. (2009). "Appropriate Therapeutic Care for Families with Pre-Pubescent Transgender/Gender-Dissonant Children." Child and Adolescent Social Work Journal, Vol. 26, No. 2, 135.

Vanderburgh, R. (2016). *Journeys of transformation: stories from across the acronym.* Portland, OR: Odin Ink.

Vincent, N. (2005). *Self-made man: One woman's journey into manhood and back.* New York, NY: Viking Adult.

Weiss, J. (2007). *Transgender workplace diversity: policy tools, training issues and communication strategies for HR and legal professionals.* North Charleston, SC: BookSurge Publishing.

Williams, W. L. (1992). *The spirit and the flesh: Sexuality diversity in American Indian culture.* Boston: Beacon Press.

World Professional Association for Transgender Health (2011). "Standards of Care for the Health of Transsexual, Transgender, and Gender Nonconforming People, Seventh Version."

Zamboni, B. (2006). "Therapeutic considerations in working with the family, friends and partners of transgendered individuals." The Family Journal, 14, 174–179.

Zucker, K. J. (2000). "Gender identity disorder." In A. J. Sameroff, M. Lewis, & S. M. Miller (Eds.), *Handbook of developmental psychopathology* (2nd ed., pp. 671–686). New York, NY: Kluwer Academic/Plenum.

Index

ABOUT THE AUTHOR

Reid Vanderburgh received his BA in Psychology from Portland State University in 1998, and his MA in Counseling Psychology from John F. Kennedy University's Graduate School for Holistic Studies in 2001. During his career as a therapist, he worked with over 450 people asking the question, "How do I want to live my life?" in the context of gender identity.

Reid is the author of two peer-reviewed journal articles: "Appropriate Therapeutic Care for Families with Pre-Pubescent Transgender/Gender-Dissonant Children," *Child and Adolescent Social Work Journal*, (2009) and "The Story of Mary, Diana and Daniel," *International Journal of Childbirth Education* (2012). He is the author of the book *Journeys of Transformation: Stories from Across the Acronym*, now in its second edition. He has also written numerous book chapters and several blog entries for the Oxford Dictionaries Press. He is a member emeritus of the World Professional Association for Transgender Health (WPATH).

Reid sings baritone in the Portland Gay Men's Chorus, and holds the distinction of being the only person to have sung in every adult GALA chorus that has existed in northern Oregon. In 2016, he was chosen as a recipient of a GALA Choruses Legacy Award for Distinguished Service. Reid also sits on the board of the Portland PFLAG chapter and is a member of the Advisory Board of Bridging Voices: Portland GSA Youth Chorus. Visit his website: www.reidvanderburgh.com

www.ingramcontent.com/pod-product-compliance
Lightning Source LLC
Chambersburg PA
CBHW060019030426
42334CB00019B/2097